ENGAGING SCHOOLS

Fostering High School Students' Motivation to Learn

Committee on Increasing High School Students'
Engagement and Motivation to Learn

Board on Children, Youth, and Families
Division of Behavioral and Social Sciences and Education

NATIONAL RESEARCH COUNCIL
INSTITUTE OF MEDICINE
OF THE NATIONAL ACADEMIES

THE NATIONAL ACADEMIES PRESS
Washington, D.C.
www.nap.edu

THE NATIONAL ACADEMIES PRESS **500 Fifth Street, N.W.** **Washington, DC 20001**

NOTICE: The project that is the subject of this report was approved by the Governing Board of the National Research Council, whose members are drawn from the councils of the National Academy of Sciences, the National Academy of Engineering, and the Institute of Medicine. The members of the committee responsible for the report were chosen for their special competences and with regard for appropriate balance.

This study was supported by Contract/Grant No. B 7128 between the National Academy of Sciences and Carnegie Corporation of New York. Any opinions, findings, conclusions, or recommendations expressed in this publication are those of the author(s) and do not necessarily reflect the views of the organizations or agencies that provided support for the project.

Library of Congress Cataloging-in-Publication Data

National Research Council (U.S.). Committee on Increasing High School Students' Engagement and Motivation to Learn.
Engaging schools : fostering high school students' motivation to learn / Committee on Increasing High School Students' Engagement and Motivation to Learn, Board on Children, Youth, and Families, Division of Behavioral and Social Sciences and Education.
p. cm.
Includes bibliographical references and index.
ISBN 0-309-08435-0 (hardcover) — ISBN 0-309-52690-6 (PDF)
1. High school teaching—United States. 2. School management and organization—United States. 3. Motivation in education. I. Title.
LB1607.5.N39 2003
373.12′0073--dc22

2003017626

Additional copies of this report are available from the National Academies Press, 500 Fifth Street, N.W., Lockbox 285, Washington, DC 20055; (800) 624-6242 or (202) 334-3313 (in the Washington metropolitan area); Internet, http://www.nap.edu

Printed in the United States of America.

Suggested citation: National Research Council and the Institute of Medicine. (2004). *Engaging Schools: Fostering High School Students' Motivation to Learn.* Committee on Increasing High School Students' Engagement and Motivation to Learn. Board on Children, Youth, and Families, Division of Behavioral and Social Sciences and Education. Washington, DC: The National Academies Press.

THE NATIONAL ACADEMIES

Advisers to the Nation on Science, Engineering, and Medicine

The **National Academy of Sciences** is a private, nonprofit, self-perpetuating society of distinguished scholars engaged in scientific and engineering research, dedicated to the furtherance of science and technology and to their use for the general welfare. Upon the authority of the charter granted to it by the Congress in 1863, the Academy has a mandate that requires it to advise the federal government on scientific and technical matters. Dr. Bruce M. Alberts is president of the National Academy of Sciences.

The **National Academy of Engineering** was established in 1964, under the charter of the National Academy of Sciences, as a parallel organization of outstanding engineers. It is autonomous in its administration and in the selection of its members, sharing with the National Academy of Sciences the responsibility for advising the federal government. The National Academy of Engineering also sponsors engineering programs aimed at meeting national needs, encourages education and research, and recognizes the superior achievements of engineers. Dr. Wm. A. Wulf is president of the National Academy of Engineering.

The **Institute of Medicine** was established in 1970 by the National Academy of Sciences to secure the services of eminent members of appropriate professions in the examination of policy matters pertaining to the health of the public. The Institute acts under the responsibility given to the National Academy of Sciences by its congressional charter to be an adviser to the federal government and, upon its own initiative, to identify issues of medical care, research, and education. Dr. Harvey V. Fineberg is president of the Institute of Medicine.

The **National Research Council** was organized by the National Academy of Sciences in 1916 to associate the broad community of science and technology with the Academy's purposes of furthering knowledge and advising the federal government. Functioning in accordance with general policies determined by the Academy, the Council has become the principal operating agency of both the National Academy of Sciences and the National Academy of Engineering in providing services to the government, the public, and the scientific and engineering communities. The Council is administered jointly by both Academies and the Institute of Medicine. Dr. Bruce M. Alberts and Dr. Wm. A. Wulf are chair and vice chair, respectively, of the National Research Council.

www.national-academies.org

COMMITTEE ON INCREASING HIGH SCHOOL STUDENTS' ENGAGEMENT AND MOTIVATION TO LEARN

DEBORAH STIPEK (*Chair*), School of Education, Stanford University
CAROLE AMES, College of Education, Michigan State University
THOMAS J. BERNDT, Department of Psychological Sciences, Purdue University
EMILY COLE, Principal Emeritus, Jefferson Davis High School, Houston Independent School District
JAMES COMER, Yale University School of Medicine Child Study Center
JAMES CONNELL, Institute for Research and Reform in Education, Toms River, New Jersey
MICHELLE FINE, Department of Psychology, City University of New York
RUTH T. GROSS, Professor Emeritus, Department of Pediatrics, Stanford University School of Medicine
W. NORTON GRUBB, Graduate School of Education, University of California, Berkeley
ROCHELLE GUTIERREZ, Department of Curriculum and Instruction, University of Illinois at Urbana-Champaign
CAROL LEE, School of Education and Social Policy, Northwestern University
EDWARD L. MCDILL, Department of Sociology and Center for the Social Organization of Schools, The Johns Hopkins University
RUSSELL RUMBERGER, School of Education, University of California at Santa Barbara
CARMEN VARELA RUSSO, Baltimore Public School System, Baltimore City Public Schools
LISBETH B. SCHORR, Project on Effective Interventions, Harvard University

TIMOTHY READY, *Study Director* (until September 2002)
ELIZABETH TOWNSEND, *Senior Project Assistant* (from July 2002)
MEREDITH MADDEN, *Senior Project Assistant* (until June 2002)

BOARD ON CHILDREN, YOUTH, AND FAMILIES

Foreword

The National Academies have long worked on issues related to education, focusing primarily on the scientific foundations of teaching and learning. With this report we look at a different ingredient in education—motivation—and the important role it plays in fostering academic achievement.

We all know that our interest in or desire to learn is critical to the amount of effort we are willing to put into a task, particularly if it means mastering difficult or unfamiliar material. Children often come to school eager to learn but, as this report suggests, many lose their academic motivation as they move through elementary school into high school. In fact, by the time many students enter high school, disengagement from course work and serious study is common. The consequences of becoming disengaged from school are extremely serious, particularly for adolescents from urban and poor high schools who may not get the "second chances" afforded those who are more economically privileged. Even the best teachers, curricula, standards, and tests cannot be effective if the students to whom they are addressed are not engaged in learning. What can policy makers, school administrators, guidance counselors, teachers, parents, or others do to influence that motivation, so as to enable our youth to remain engaged in learning throughout high school? This important report provides evidence that high schools can be designed to provide a challenging and rigorous program to all students, and it makes a compelling case for the real possibility of improving the quality of urban high schools throughout our nation.

This volume, like most products of the National Research Council, was prepared by a committee of volunteer scholars and other experts. We are indebted to them for their willingness to tackle an important and difficult question in service to the nation. For this particular study, we are especially indebted to the committee chair, Deborah Stipek, for her extraordinary leadership and commitment.

Deborah agreed to chair this important activity even though she had just become the dean of the Stanford School of Education. Then, when unforeseen circumstances left the committee with reduced staff, she expanded her role in drafting and redrafting the text through the final stages of committee consultation and the intensive review process. It is the devotion of leaders like her to the common good that makes it possible for the National Research Council to be such an effective instrument for guiding the nation.

On behalf of the National Academies, I thank Deborah and the committee for this report. They have made an important contribution to an ongoing dialogue in the United States that focuses on improving the education of our next generation of citizens. Nothing that we do is more important.

Bruce Alberts, *Chair*
National Research Council

Acknowledgments

The committee could not have completed its work without the help of our sponsor and able consultants and staff. This report was supported by a grant from the Carnegie Corporation of New York to the Board on Children, Youth, and Families of the National Research Council and the Institute of Medicine as part of an initiative on Adolescent Education and Urban School Reform. A study committee was formed to address the particular topic of adolescent motivation and school engagement. We are indebted to consultants who provided important background information, assisted in data collection, and prepared written summaries. Amy Ryken, University of Puget Sound, did a thorough review of the motivational effects of high schools that use occupations as themes for instruction. Brenda Arellano, University of California, Santa Barbara, contributed to the literature review on high school dropouts. April Burns, City University of New York, examined evidence on the economic and educational disparities in suburban and urban schools. Adena Klem, Institute for Research and Reform in Education, reviewed comprehensive reform models in urban high schools. Nettie Legters, Johns Hopkins University, reviewed the recent movement toward career academies in high schools. Karen Strobel, Stanford University, summarized evidence on the developmental outcomes associated with adolescents' participation in organized nonschool activities. Lonna Murphy, Purdue University, contributed to the literature review on peer influences. Andy Furco, University of California, Berkeley, reviewed literature on issues of motivation and engagement in service-learning.

Special thanks are owed to Cary Watson for her multiple and critical roles in completing this report. Ms. Watson, a graduate student at the Stanford University School of Education, did much of the research on students' nonacademic needs and assisted in revisions of the entire volume.

Our study director, Timothy Ready, was invaluable in launching our work. He ably organized all of our meetings and helped structure our task. Although he left the National Research Council before our study was completed, his broad searches for relevant evidence and early drafting were critical to our progress. We are also grateful to Patricia Morison, deputy director of the Center for Education, for her guidance and advice during the late stages of report revision. Laura Penny, a freelance writer and editor, was our invaluable critical eye in shaping the text. Elizabeth Townsend served as an extraordinarily capable project assistant, maintaining all our email contacts, keeping track of innumerable drafts, and otherwise keeping the project humming, all with good cheer.

This report has been reviewed in draft form by individuals chosen for their diverse perspectives and technical expertise, in accordance with procedures approved by the Report Review Committee of the National Research Council. The purpose of this independent review is to provide candid and critical comments that will assist the institution in making its published report as sound as possible and to ensure that the report meets institutional standards for objectivity, evidence, and responsiveness to the study charge. The review comments and draft manuscript remain confidential to protect the integrity of the deliberative process.

We thank the following individuals for their review of this report: Joshua Aronson, Department of Applied Psychology, New York University; Joyce L. Epstein, Center on School, Family, and Community Partnerships and the National Network of Partnership Schools, Johns Hopkins University; David A. Goslin, Former President and CEO, American Institutes for Research; Pedro A. Noguera, Graduate School of Education, Harvard University; Richard M. Ryan, Department of Psychology and Psychiatry, University of Rochester; Richard S. Stein, Conte Polymer Center, University of Massachusetts; Joan E. Talbert, School of Education, Stanford University; and John Tyler, Departments of Education and Economics and The Taubman Center for Public Policy, Brown University.

Although the reviewers listed above have provided many constructive comments and suggestions, they were not asked to endorse the conclusions or recommendations nor did they see the final draft of the report before its release. The review of this report was overseen by Catherine Snow, Graduate School of Education, Harvard University, and Elsa M. Garmire, Thayer School of Engineering, Dartmouth College. Appointed by the National Research Council, they were responsible for making certain that an independent examination of this report was carried out in accordance with institutional procedures and that all review comments were carefully considered. Responsibility for the final content of this report rests entirely with the authoring committee and the institution.

Deborah J. Stipek, *Committee Chair*

Contents

ENGAGING SCHOOLS

Executive Summary

Learning and succeeding in school requires active engagement—whether students are rich or poor, black, brown, or white. The core principles that underlie engagement are applicable to all schools—whether they are in urban, suburban, or rural communities. Yet although engagement is important for all students and all schools, the consequences of disengagement vary substantially. When students from advantaged backgrounds become disengaged, they may learn less than they could, but they usually get by or they get second chances; most eventually graduate and move on to other opportunities. In contrast, when students from disadvantaged backgrounds in high-poverty, urban high schools become disengaged, they are less likely to graduate and consequently face severely limited opportunities. Failure to earn even the most basic educational credential or acquire the basic skills needed to function in adult society increases dramatically their risk of unemployment, poverty, poor health, and involvement in the criminal justice system.

Schools do not control all of the factors that influence students' academic engagement. Particularly in disadvantaged urban communities, academic engagement and achievement are adversely influenced by the economic and social marginalization of the students' families and communities. These disadvantages can be lessened, however, by participation in an engaging school community with high academic standards, skillful instruction, and the support students need to pursue their educational and career goals.

Engaging adolescents, including those who have become disengaged and alienated from school, is not an easy task. Academic motivation decreases steadily from the early grades of elementary school into high school. Furthermore, adolescents are too old and too independent to follow teachers' demands out of obedience, and many are too young, inexperienced, or uninformed to fully appreciate the value of succeeding in school.

Although there are important exceptions, as a group urban high schools fail to meet the needs of too many of their students. In many urban high schools with large concentrations of students living in poverty, it is common for fewer than half of the ninth graders who enter to leave with a high school diploma. Dropping out of school is but the most visible indication of pervasive disengagement from the academic purposes and programs of these schools. Many of the students who do not drop out altogether attend irregularly, exert modest effort on schoolwork, and learn little.

To address these problems, the committee was charged to "review, synthesize, and analyze research on academic engagement and motivation that might apply to urban high schools." The committee examined how curriculum, instruction, and the organization of schools can promote involvement of urban youth in the academic program and the broader school community, also taking into account influences such as peer culture, family, and community resources.

A system of schools that has fully implemented the core principles needed to provide engaging, rigorous education for all students is yet to be seen. Nevertheless, the evidence reviewed in this volume demonstrates that much has been learned about the conditions in schools that enhance student engagement, and that there are many examples of schools in which students deemed at risk of disengagement and failure are productively engaged and achieving at high levels. Although far too rare, these success stories prove that schools can engage the enthusiasm for learning of economically disadvantaged students.

The committee drew on psychological research on motivation, studies of the effects of various educational policies and practices on student engagement and learning, and students' own voices. This research base is mostly qualitative, correlational, or quasi-experimental, thus falling short of the random-assignment design that is believed by some researchers to be necessary for causal conclusions. Nevertheless, the evidence is consistent enough to give credibility to the committee's recommendations.

A common theme among effective practices is that they address underlying psychological variables related to motivation, such as competence and control, beliefs about the value of education, and a sense of belonging. In brief, engaging schools and teachers promote students' confidence in their ability to learn and succeed in school by providing challenging instruction and support for meeting high standards, and they clearly convey their own high expectations for their students' success. They provide choices for students and they make the curriculum and instruction relevant to adolescents' experiences, cultures, and long-term goals, so that students see some value in the high school curriculum.

Although learning involves cognitive processes that take place within each individual, motivation to learn also depends on the student's involvement in a web of social relationships that supports learning. The likelihood that students will be motivated and engaged is increased to the extent that their teachers, family, and friends effectively support their purposeful involvement in learning and in school. Thus a focus on engagement calls attention to the connection between a learner and the social context in which learning takes place. Engaging schools promote a sense of belonging by personalizing instruction, showing an interest in students' lives, and creating a supportive, caring social environment.

This description of engaging schools applies to few urban high schools. Instead, the picture that emerges is of schools that engender low expectations, alienation, and low achievement. Resources are lacking and services are fragmented. The teachers are the least qualified, and the buildings are the most dilapidated. The curriculum and teaching often are unresponsive to the needs and interests of students—especially students of color, English-language learners, students from high-poverty neighborhoods, or those who entered high school with weak skills in reading and mathematics. Students often do not get to know or to be known by their teachers. As a result, many experience schools as impersonal and uncaring. Because few urban schools are well connected to the communities they serve or to the educational and career opportunities potentially available to their students, many students fail to see how working hard in school will enable them to attain the educational and career goals to which they aspire.

Improving the quality of urban high schools in the United States is critically important, not only to the futures of the students who attend them, but also for the future prosperity and quality of life of cities and for the nation as a whole. Fortunately, knowledge derived from research and practice provides more than a sufficient basis to proceed with urgently needed reforms.

CONCLUSIONS AND RECOMMENDATIONS

The evidence reviewed by the committee leads to a number of conclusions and recommendations as a means to achieve the goals of meaningful engagement and genuine improvements in achievement. Because our deliberations revealed significant limits in the available evidence, the committee also outlines in its full report some recommendations and directions for future research.

Recommendation 1: The committee recommends that high school courses and instructional methods be redesigned in ways that will increase adolescent engagement and learning.

The evidence is clear that high school courses *can* be designed to engage urban high school students and enhance their learning. The instruction typical of most urban high schools nevertheless fails to engage students cognitively, emotionally, or behaviorally.

Evidence indicates that when instruction draws on students' preexisting understandings, interests, culture, and real-world experiences, the curriculum becomes more meaningful to them. Students stay engaged when instruction is varied and appropriately challenging for all students, when students are active participants, and when teachers allow students to use their native language abilities and other resources to master the material and complete tasks.

Recommendation 2: The committee recommends ongoing classroom-based assessment of students' understanding and skills.

Instruction that is appropriately challenging for all students in a class requires that teachers have information about each student's current knowledge and skills. Teachers' instructional decisions about tasks and next steps will be more effective when they are informed by daily or weekly data about student progress. Standardized testing done annually does not provide enough useful information for teachers to make instructional decisions in their classrooms.

Teachers should monitor continually the effectiveness of curriculum and instructional practices, not only for progress in learning, but also to see whether students are staying engaged behaviorally (e.g., attendance, completion of work), cognitively (e.g., efforts to understand and apply new concepts), and emotionally (e.g., enthusiasm for learning activities).

Recommendation 3: The committee recommends that preservice teacher preparation programs provide high school teachers deep content knowledge and a range of pedagogical strategies and understandings about adolescents and how they learn, and that schools and districts provide practicing teachers with opportunities to work with colleagues and to continue to develop their skills.

Teaching in a way that engages students requires a complex set of skills and knowledge. High school teachers need to know about different methods of teaching and about adolescent learning, and they must have a deep understanding of the discipline they teach. High-quality teachers need to have a range of available strategies to use with their students and skill at adapting instruction to the needs of individual students.

Teacher education programs should provide beginning teachers with an understanding of student-centered pedagogy that is focused on understanding, and teach them strategies for involving students in active learning. New teachers need explicit preparation in order to be effective with diverse, heterogeneous groups of high school students as well as those who have special needs, including English-language learners, students with special disabilities, and students who are substantially behind in their basic skills.

Teachers already working in high schools cannot meet the needs of their students unless they also have opportunities to learn and develop new skills. District- and state-level administrators need to provide resources—time and experts—for teachers to continue to develop their teaching skills. These opportunities for professional development have to translate into new practices and their effects on student learning need to be discussed among colleagues who can hold each other accountable.

Recommendation 4: The committee recommends that schools provide the support and resources necessary to help *all* high school students to meet challenging standards.

Standards and high expectations are critical, but they must be genuinely achievable if they are to motivate student engagement. Students are most likely to be academically engaged when they are challenged with demanding learning goals and when they have opportunities to experience a sense of competence and accomplishment about their learning. Setting high standards and holding students accountable for reaching them can serve as an incentive to exert effort, but only if students know what to do to meet the standards and believe that they can succeed and that the standard is achievable. Simply asking students—especially low achievers—to attain higher standards without providing the assistance and support they need is more likely to discourage than to motivate them.

Thus, for example, we urge districts and school administrators to provide individualized instruction, tutoring, and summer programs for students who are behind to help them progress in their skills. Teachers need to help students develop short-term goals that are calibrated to their preexisting knowledge and skills, while students work toward meeting the high standards.

Recommendation 5: The committee recommends that tests used to evaluate schools, teachers, and students assess high-level, critical thinking and that they incorporate broad and multidimensional conceptions of subject matter that includes fluency, conceptual understanding, analysis, and application.

The tests that are used for accountability have substantial impact on what gets taught and how, and these in turn affect student engagement. It is unrealistic to expect teachers to exert effort to provide a coherent and integrated curriculum and focus on understanding and critical thinking and writing if the tests used to evaluate them and their students measure only fragmented, decontextualized, basic skills.

Recommendation 6: Districts should restructure comprehensive urban high schools to create smaller learning communities that foster personalized, and continuous relationships between teachers and students.

Supportive personal relationships are critical in promoting and maintaining student engagement. Although learning involves cognitive processes that take place within each individual, motivation to learn also depends on the student's involvement in a web of social relationships that support learning. Most urban high schools are too large and fail to promote close personal relationships and a sense of community between adults and students.

Restructuring can be achieved by starting new schools, by breaking up large schools into new and completely autonomous schools, or by creating smaller connected but somewhat autonomous units in large schools. Block scheduling and looping (teachers staying with the same group of students for multiple years) are promising strategies for promoting longstanding, respectful, and mutually accountable relationships.

Creating small learning communities may be necessary, but it is not sufficient to improve student engagement. The social climate of the school and the quality of interactions are critical. Principals and teachers need to promote an environment of trust and respect—of each other and of students. They need to model these behaviors and refuse to tolerate disrespectful behavior among students.

A social context centered on learning—in which all administrative decisions are made with student learning in mind and teachers leverage their closer relationships with students to "press"[1] students to challenge themselves and develop deep understanding—is also critical. This focus can be conveyed by implementing school policies that recognize students who respond to academic challenges quickly and that provide preemptive interventions when problems of poor attendance, failure to complete homework, and poor performance arise.

Recommendation 7: The committee recommends that both formal and informal tracking by ability be eliminated. Alternative strategies should be used to ensure appropriately challenging instruction for students who vary widely in their skill levels.

---

[1]"Academic press" has been defined as offering demanding curricula and having high expectations for learning, without pressuring performance or undermining autonomy (Phillips, 1997 and Shouse 1996a, 1996b, 1997).

Currently, students who are most at risk of disengaging from school have too little contact with peers who have high expectations for academic success. Groups of students with similar achievement levels are often tracked, formally or informally, into different courses, thus isolating and grouping the relatively low-performing and disengaged students with one another. In addition to preventing interaction among low and high achievers, tracking precludes for some students access to the curriculum needed to prepare for postsecondary education. Tracked courses, especially at the low achievement levels, can also reinforce lower standards and engender in students the belief that they lack academic competence.

Classes that do not prepare but prevent students getting on to rigorous grade-level work should be eliminated, and challenging courses, including Advanced Placement courses, should be as available to students in urban schools serving low-income students as they are in schools serving more affluent students.

A more challenging curriculum with heterogeneous grouping can only be successful if teachers are well trained to address individual student needs. Teachers need support to develop instructional approaches that will meet the needs of a class of students who vary dramatically in their skill levels. We suggest, in particular, training in individualized and peer group learning strategies that have been shown to be effective in promoting learning in a heterogeneous class. Another strategy, used previously only at the college level but which merits experimentation in high schools, is connecting help from a reading or English-as-a-second-language specialist directly to substantive courses. Thus, rather than isolating students with special needs, the additional assistance that some students need is provided in the context of a regular course with more skilled peers.

The committee also recommends that school administrators create opportunities for low-achieving students to interact with and develop friendships with more academically successful peers. Because students tend to choose to interact with students with the same ethnicity and similar achievement levels, concerted efforts must be made to create activities that will attract diverse students, and to promote a climate in which students feel comfortable venturing beyond familiar peer and instructional contexts.

Recommendation 8: The committee recommends that school guidance and counseling responsibilities be diffused among school staff, including teachers, who are supported by professionals.

Serious social or psychological problems can interfere with adolescents' own academic engagement as well as undermine a positive learning climate. Currently many problems go unnoticed or untreated. Professionals who have relevant expertise are responsible for far too many students and they have too little time to provide the support and intervention students need.

The problem is especially serious in urban high schools serving low-income students, where social and psychological problems are more prevalent.

A climate of learning is also undermined when students do not understand the consequences of disengaging from school. Many urban high school students are poorly informed about postsecondary educational and career options. In particular, they have only a vague understanding of what they need to learn during high school to have a realistic chance of achieving the ambitious educational and career goals to which many aspire. Because they don't see the connections, students are not motivated to engage in purposeful and challenging academic activities. In most schools, helping students make these connections is the responsibility of guidance counselors who oversee large numbers of students and have little opportunity to know their individual interests and needs.

A promising new strategy is to provide every student and family with a member of the school staff who can act as an adult advocate and who in turn has a trained expert (like a counselor) to consult and to whom students or families with serious problems can be referred. To help students achieve a realistic understanding of how what they are learning in high school is related to their educational and career options after high school, we suggest also providing students with experiences in work settings, teachers with curriculum materials and instructional supports to integrate rigor and relevance into the core curriculum, as well as close coordination with postsecondary educational institutions.

Recommendation 9: The committee recommends that efforts be made to improve communication, coordination, and trust among the adults in the various settings where adolescents spend their time. These settings include homes, religious institutions, and the various organized extracurricular activities sponsored by schools and community groups.

High schools cannot, by themselves, achieve high levels of engagement and academic standards for all students. Most urban high schools function quite independently of the other adults in adolescents' lives, such as parents, health care providers, and those involved in extracurricular or religious activities. Many efforts to improve schools are too "school-centric" in the sense that they focus exclusively on school resources and programs and fail to take advantage of the resources in the larger community.

School administrators and teachers should also expand and enrich the high school curriculum and help students see the real-world meaningfulness of school learning by taking advantage of resources in the community. For example, artists, civic leaders, and community members and parents with cultural or historical knowledge and experiences can be invited to schools to share their knowledge and interact with students. Teachers and administrators should also provide students with opportunities to engage in service learning and internships that take them into community contexts.

Recommendation 10: The committee recommends that schools make greater efforts to identify and coordinate with social and health services in the community, and that policy makers revise policies to facilitate students' access to the services they need.

The committee finds that most urban schools are unable to deal with the many problems (e.g., poor physical and mental health, instability in parenting, substance abuse, homelessness) that some low-income adolescents face and which interfere with their engagement in academic work. Schools cannot be expected to compensate fully for problems associated with factors such as economic and social inequalities and the lack of effective policies to address them. However, such problems cannot be ignored in urban communities with high concentrations of poverty. Although personalized, supportive high school communities can help protect adolescents from environments that place them at risk for negative academic outcomes, some high school students need additional services. Policy makers can and should do more to help students whose personal circumstances interfere with their ability to learn, and school administrators can make better use of the resources that are available.

School administrators often encounter barriers to partnerships and collaborations with community service providers. Federal, state, and local policy makers should remove barriers to coordination. Schools and social service and health agencies should seek ways to improve communication among school personnel and service providers who see the same adolescent.

CHALLENGES OF IMPLEMENTATION

The urgency of reform must not lead us to seize upon quick fixes or silver bullets. The research reviewed in this volume illustrates repeatedly that student engagement and learning are directly affected by a confluence of organizational factors and instructional practices in particular schools, by family and community influences, and by a wide range of national, state, and local policies. No single educational policy or practice, no matter how well grounded in research, can be expected to increase students' academic engagement if the policies and practices in which they are embedded are ignored. For example, small, personalized schools may not enhance meaningful cognitive engagement and learning if they do not also provide effective teaching and a strong press for achieving high academic standards; the most engaging teaching practices may have little effect on a student who is homeless, has serious untreated health problems, or faces the chronic threat of violence. Allowing students to choose among different small, thematic learning communities can recreate tracking based on social class, ethnicity, and achievement levels without policies and special efforts to avoid this. Teachers cannot be expected to provide meaningful and engaging instruction if they do not have deep knowledge of their subject matter and principles of effective pedagogy.

Student engagement and learning are affected by a complicated set of nested variables. Some factors affect the motivation of individual students in specific classrooms of specific high schools, while others stem from broad federal or state policies that may affect a large number of very diverse high schools. The array of policies and practices that affect student motivation and learning must be aligned so that efforts in one area (e.g., the classroom) are supported rather than undermined by policies at another (e.g., broader educational and social policies). Although it is neither necessary nor realistic to expect that all potential policy conflicts can be resolved before students can engage productively in learning, educators and policy makers should, at the very least, consider how their policies and practices interact to affect student engagement.

A fundamental transformation of American high schools and the policy contexts in which high school education is embedded is needed to engage all students in learning and to ensure high standards of achievement. There are no panaceas, and some of the simple solutions that have been proposed, such as raising standards, can alone do more harm than good. Realistically, the reforms that are needed will require greater resources than are currently provided. At the very least, the inequities in resource allocation, with schools serving students with the greatest needs having the fewest resources, will need to be redressed. In addition to increased funding of high schools, we suggest investigation of ways to use current resources more effectively. The committee did not address ways to acquire resources because it was beyond its charge.

Although the focus is primarily on what can be done *in* high schools, the policies and practices described in this volume have important implications for many issues beyond its scope—including, for example, policies that affect who is attracted into the field of teaching, preservice teacher and leadership training and credentialing policies, state and federal testing policies, graduation requirements, and school funding and resource allocation.

Policy makers and educators must not become discouraged or give up when they encounter difficulties. Difficulties are inevitable, and overcoming them will require persistence, continuous evaluation, and using what is learned to fine-tune, and possibly to alter the course of, but not to cast aside, their efforts.

As a society, we should not fail our youth by failing to provide them with the kind of educational program they need to achieve high standards of learning. Much is known about what needs to be done, and we are learning more every day about how to do it. What is needed now is the will to use this knowledge where it is most needed—in our urban high schools.

1

Student Engagement and Disengagement in Urban High Schools

We can require adolescents to attend school, but learning requires conscious and purposeful effort, which cannot be legislated. This volume is about motivating adolescents to be engaged—cognitively, behaviorally, and emotionally—in their coursework and in the broader array of school-based activities. Motivation is essential to learning at all ages (Finn and Rock, 1997; Jessor, Turbin, and Costa, 1998; National Research Council, 2000), but it becomes pivotal during adolescence as youth approach the threshold to adulthood. Younger children who become mentally and emotionally disengaged generally are compliant enough to attend school, or they do not have the means to avoid it. But adolescents who are bored, distracted, emotionally troubled, or do not see the value of schooling have the means to drop out of school altogether.

Even if they do not drop out of school, adolescents have many alternative activities to occupy their time and attention, including working for pay, sports, video games, social activities, and for some, less socially sanctioned activities. A national survey of more than 2,000 youth in grades 7 through 12 found that about 40 percent of the students worked a median of 3 hours on an average school day, and spent 2 hours "hanging out with friends." The median number of hours worked by Black students was 4 hours. The average adolescent watches nearly 3 hours of television a day, and adolescents of color watch more on average (The Kaiser Family Foundation, 1999). Schools, therefore, have considerable competition for the attention of their clients. It is not surprising that homework does not necessarily have a high priority, despite its apparent contribution to learning (Cooper, Lindsay, Nye, and Greathouse, 1998).

Research on motivation and engagement is essential to understanding some of the most fundamental and vexing challenges of school reform. Improving meaningful learning depends on the ability of educators to engage the imaginations of students—to involve them in new realms of knowledge, building on what they already know and believe, what they care about now, and what they hope for in the future (National Research Council, 2000). At the very least, increasing students' academic achievement requires improvements in attendance, attention, and completion of schoolwork.

Increasing motivation and engagement is unlikely to be accomplished by simple policy prescriptions, such as raising standards, promoting accountability, or increasing school funding—although these may be helpful in the right set of circumstances. The fundamental challenge is to create a set of circumstances in which students take pleasure in learning and come to believe that the information and skills they are being asked to learn are important or meaningful for them and worth their effort, and that they can reasonably expect to be able to learn the material.

As this volume makes clear, there are no silver bullets. Some students are motivated even under adverse circumstances, but for many students their engagement and motivation to learn depend on a confluence of supports, none of which is sufficient on its own. These supports include

- a challenging but individualized curriculum that is focused on understanding;
- knowledgeable, skilled, and caring teachers;
- a school culture that is centered on learning;
- a school community that engenders a sense of support and belonging, with opportunities to interact with academically engaged peers;
- strong ties linking the school with students' families and communities;
- an organizational structure and services that address students' nonacademic needs; and
- opportunities to learn the value of schoolwork for future educational and career prospects.

Motivation to be actively engaged is essential to learning, whether students are in schools that are located in urban, suburban, or rural communities. The focus of this volume, however, is on what urban high schools can do to more effectively engage students—especially low-income students and students of color who are disproportionately concentrated in these schools. Although the core principles involved in making schools more engaging apply to all schools, we chose to focus on high-poverty urban high schools because students there are more likely than others to become disaffected and drop out, and the social and economic consequences of disengagement for them are severe.

A great deal is known about the needs of adolescents and about the conditions that motivate them to learn and stay in school. We know how to do a better job of engaging high school students in learning activities that will help them achieve the kinds of postsecondary educational and career opportunities they desire. We also know of urban schools serving low-income students and students of color that have substantially decreased dropout rates, increased attendance, and improved achievement and the educational and career prospects of their graduates.

We have seen youth considered at risk of school failure fighting to be heard in an English class discussion on Shakespeare and insisting on finishing a science experiment long after the bell has rung—students who experience the joy of learning and take great pride in their accomplishments. Although far too rare, such success stories undermine the credibility of pessimists and naysayers.

We focus on what schools can do, recognizing that many of the reasons for a young person's disengagement from school lie far beyond school. We are also mindful of the difficulty of increasing adolescents' motivation and engagement in schoolwork in urban neighborhoods where joblessness and poverty are endemic, violence and homelessness are common, and access to resources and opportunities are scarce. The effects of poverty on child and adolescent outcomes, regardless of the schools they attend, have been well documented (see, for example, Duncan and Brooks-Gunn, 1997). Urban schools, however, do not usually take advantage of the resources their communities offer. Paradoxically, although many of the most troubled neighborhoods are located in metropolitan centers of great wealth and resources, access to the alluring educational and career resources of the city has been all but blocked for most students in high-poverty, urban high schools.

Poverty conditions affect children's opportunities to learn in elementary and middle school as well, and many urban high schools are challenged by a large proportion of students who have very poor skills, have experienced failure for many years in school, and as a result have become seriously alienated from academic work. It is not easy to promote enthusiasm in students who enter with low motivation and have a long way to go to master a high school curriculum.

The obstacles created by poverty and the legacy of racism are profound and need to be addressed in any truly comprehensive approach to improving urban adolescents' engagement and motivation to learn. As a society, we should not tolerate the ways in which children's opportunities are limited by the circumstances of their birth, and as we work to improve schools, we must also work for better conditions in our communities and a fairer and more equitable society.

Despite limitations in what can be accomplished in high schools alone, we believe we have a responsibility to use what we know to better engage adolescents in learning and prepare them for future opportunities and the adult roles and responsibilities they are about to assume. With sufficient societal will and the knowledge that now exists, we can make a measurable difference.

HIGH STANDARDS AND DEMOCRATIC VALUES

Nearly half a century ago, educational philosopher John Dewey and others claimed that if schools were to succeed in preparing the great majority of young people, not just a select few, to be responsible and productive citizens, they would have to do a much better job of motivating and engaging the broad spectrum of students in learning (Cremin, 1961; Dewey, 1956; Hall, 1969). The history of high schools in the United States nevertheless shows alternating emphases on academic rigor associated with the need to prepare some students for college, and the democratizing function of schools—having schools address the needs and engage the interests of all students, including those who traditionally have not been college bound (Powell, Farrar, and Cohen, 1985).

In the past half-century, the emphasis on academic standards of the 1950s gave way to a concern for equity in the 1960s, and then back to high standards and basic academic skills in the early and mid-1980s. Since then, there has been some wavering, but the dominant policy emphasis that has emerged at the start of the 21st century has been to hold all students accountable for achieving high educational standards (National Research Council, 2002a; U.S. Department of Education, 2002), focusing especially on reading and math. For this to occur, a much broader range of students must become engaged in learning the kinds of curricula that, until recently, only students bound for 4-year colleges were expected to master.

Some education analysts have expressed concern that raising standards for students who are performing poorly will increase their alienation or disengagement from school rather than motivate them to exert more effort (e.g., Futrell and Rotberg, 2002; Sheldon and Biddle, 1998), or that the concentration on English and math only will impoverish the curriculum. If imposing higher standards is the only intervention, these are likely outcomes. But the research discussed in Chapters 2 and 4 of this volume indicates that under the right circumstances, challenging students to learn more demanding curricula increases their motivation and engagement. Unfortunately, few high schools to date have provided the context or supports that enable most students to achieve high standards. Significant reforms will be needed to motivate all students to be sufficiently engaged in their schoolwork to meet more demanding expectations.[1]

IMPORTANCE OF SOCIAL RELATIONSHIPS

Although learning involves cognitive processes that take place within and between the individuals, motivation to learn depends on a student's involvement in a web of social relationships. The likelihood that students will be motivated and engaged in learning is increased to the extent that their teachers, family, and friends, as well as others who shape the instructional process, effectively support their purposeful involvement in learning (Cohen and Ball, 1999). Thus the focus on motivation and engagement calls attention to the interface between the learner and the social context in which learning takes place.

The notion that the personal value of our lives is determined largely by the social relations that take place in the communities to which we belong reflects a classic Aristotelian perspective on human nature (Lee, Bryk, and Smith, 1993; see also MacIntyre, 1981; Newmann and Oliver, 1967). It is also a perspective that is very much consistent with the views of John Dewey. For Dewey, building an engaging school community is not just a strategy to improve academic outcomes; it is essential to education itself (see Lee et al., 1993, p. 226).

It is not coincidental that many of the qualities associated with engaging schools also have been found to foster healthy youth development (Eccles et al., 1993; Institute of Medicine, 1997; McNeely, Nonnemaker, and Blum, 2002; National Research Council, 2002a; Rosenfeld, Richman, and Bowen, 2000) and to confer resilience to individuals who otherwise might be at risk for adverse psychological and social outcomes (Berand, 1992; Connell, Spencer, and Aber, 1994; Finn and Rock, 1997; Jessor et al., 1998; Rutter, 1985). High schools, like other programs for youth, promote positive development in adolescents by addressing their needs for safety, love and belonging, respect, power, and accomplishment. They do this by establishing caring relationships with adults, maintaining positive

[1] "High standards" is not defined in this volume as being able to pass a high-stakes test, such as an exam required for a high school diploma, although that might be one indicator of the standards of achievement that students are achieving. By "high standards" we mean that high school graduates should have mastered the skills they need to succeed in a postsecondary academic education program. Expectations for students on the path to meeting this ultimate standard need to be individualized, so that all students are challenged by their instructional program.

and high expectations, and providing students with opportunities to participate and contribute (Berand, 1992, 1997).

THE STATUS QUO

Unfortunately, various studies have found that high schools are failing to engage their students, thereby providing them with neither the kind of social environment that fosters healthy psychosocial development (McNeely et al., 2002; National Research Council and Institute of Medicine, 2002) nor one that is conducive to learning (Finn and Rock, 1997; Jessor et al., 1998; National Research Council, 2000).

In 1974, Urie Bronfenbrenner described high schools as potent breeding grounds of alienation, and recent studies provide some empirical support for this proposition. Some studies have found that 40 to 60 percent of high school students are chronically disengaged; they are inattentive, exert little effort, do not complete tasks, and claim to be bored. This figure does not include those who already have dropped out (Marks, 2000; Sedlak, Wheeler, Pullin, and Cusick, 1986; Steinberg, Brown, and Dornbush, 1996).

Low motivation is not unique to urban schools. In a 3-year study of students from nine high schools, Steinberg et al. (1996) found that fewer than half of the students reported taking school or their studies seriously; this was equally true of students in affluent suburban schools and those in poor urban communities. Half of the students they surveyed considered their classes to be boring. A national study of a representative sample of high school seniors found that only 27 percent indicated that "knowing a lot about intellectual matters" was of great importance for having "high status" at their school (National Center for Education Statistics, 2001b, p. 141).

When students do exert effort, it is primarily to earn grades. A survey of more than 100,000 7th through 11th graders in 15 ethnically mixed school districts serving students at all economic levels asked students, "When you work really hard in school, which of the following reasons are most important to you?" The most frequently checked option, chosen by about three-quarters of the students from all ethnic and socioeconomic groups, was, "I need the grades to get into college." An ethnographic study of students in a high school in an affluent community also revealed that students considered their efforts to obtain good grades as the price of admission to a competitive college. Students were strategic, even conniving, focusing on "doing school" rather than on learning or mastering academic material (Pope, 2000).

Poor motivation to learn is more serious at the high school level than in earlier grades. Many studies show that as students progress from elementary to middle school and on to high school, motivation and academic engagement steadily decline (Eccles and Wigfield, 1992; Eccles, Wigfield, and Schiefele, 1998; Epstein and McPartland, 1976; Marks, 2000; McDermott, Mordell, and Stolzful, 2001; National Center for Education Statistics, 2000b; Stipek, 2002). Recent national data show that student absenteeism (measured as cutting classes or skipping school for reasons other than illness) increases substantially with grade level—11 percent of 8th graders, 17 percent of 10th graders, and 33 percent of 12th graders reported skipping at least 1 day of school during a 4-week period (National Center for Education Statistics, 2002).

Corresponding to the gradual decline in student engagement, international comparisons reveal that the academic performance of U.S. students in mathematics and science slips from near the top of the list of 48 countries at the elementary level to near the bottom during the high school years (National Center for Education Statistics, 1999a). The poor performance of U.S. high school students is explained partly by the increasing disparities in performance associated with race/ethnicity and socioeconomic status found as students progress through school. But the academic achievement even of the top-performing high school students from the United States compares unfavorably with that of their counterparts in other nations (National Center for Education Statistics, 1998b).

Explanations for the poor showing of American high school students abound, but themes do emerge. Darling-Hammond (1997, p. 15) notes that several analyses of American education (cf. Boyer, 1983; Goodlad, 1984; Sizer, 1984) have been remarkably similar in their critiques of a system that has sought to "manage schooling simply and efficiently by setting up impersonal relationships, superficial curricula, and routinized teaching." High schools that are large, bureaucratized, and fragmented compound the problem of uninspired pedagogy. Unless students in these schools come with their own intrinsic motivation to learn (or at least to get good grades), they are likely to feel alienated from their teachers and coursework (Boston Plan for Excellence in the Public Schools, 2001; Halperin, 1998; William T. Grant Foundation, 1988).

The typically large, comprehensive high school offers a wide range of courses intended to match students' diverse interests and skill levels. Although the specialized topical courses of the "shopping mall high school" (Powell et al., 1985) provide students with choices, such schools lack a sense of community and the kind of unifying sense of purpose that the research reviewed in this volume indicates is needed to effectively engage students in what Hill, Foster, and Gendler (1990) call "high schools with character," with distinctive purposes and identities. The "shopping mall high school" is also not sharply focused on ensuring that all students acquire the intellectual skills they need to be well prepared for adulthood.

The large, comprehensive high school, the predominant model in the

United States, is in serious need of reform. Too many students are falling through the cracks—physically dropping out and psychologically tuning out. The steady decrease in school engagement and motivation to learn that occurs as students progress from the early grades, through middle school, and into high school, and corresponding drop in the ranking of U.S. students relative to their international counterparts in standardized measures of learning, strongly suggest that something is seriously wrong with American high schools. The current situation is aptly described in a summary of a focus group conducted with Boston high school students:

> In Boston's non-exam high schools, the profound alienation from school of the majority of the students and their intense need for belonging cannot be exaggerated. Though Boston has well-developed career pathways, the bottom half of students is largely invisible and left out, leaving the majority of students with no trajectory or sense of where school might get them. Many of these students drop out before they enter grade ten (Boston Plan for Excellence in the Public Schools, 2001).

URBAN HIGH SCHOOLS

Some urban high schools have excellent records of equipping their students with the skills they need to succeed in postsecondary education and in the workplace. But as a group, they are failing to meet the needs of too many of their students (Hill, Campbell, and Harvey, 2000; Lippman, Burns, and McArthur, 1996). Improving the quality of urban high schools is critically important not only for the students who attend them, but also for the future prosperity and quality of life of cities and the nation as a whole (Hill et al., 2000).

High schools do not exist in a vacuum. The environments students live in before high school and those in which the school and its students are enmeshed greatly shape what goes on in a school (Brooks-Gunn and Duncan, 1997). Although the growing complexity of life for children and families across the socioeconomic spectrum has made school engagement a challenge for all, the problem is greatest for schools in marginalized urban communities with high concentrations of poverty (Balfanz, 2000; Neild and Balfanz, 2001; Orland, 1990).

Despite facing greater challenges, resources are relatively poor in urban schools (Augenblick, Myers, and Anderson, 1997; Parrish, Hikido, and Fowler, 1998; Schwartz, 1999), which explains in part why urban schools serving low-income children also have the least qualified teachers (Darling-Hammond, 2002; Ferguson, 1998; Oakes, 1990) and the highest teacher absenteeism and turnover (Lippman et al., 1996, pp. 88-97). Inequities exist even within urban districts, with the schools serving relatively more affluent students spending more per student than schools serving very low-income students (Roza and Miles, 2002). Conditions in some urban schools are deplorable, with students neither expected nor given much opportunity to learn (see Fine, 1994; Kozol, 1992; Meier, 2002; Valenzuela, 1999). It is commonplace for the weakest and least experienced teachers to be assigned to the neediest students and for course offerings to preclude most students from meeting college entry requirements. School buildings are frequently dilapidated and nonfunctioning, and provide no opportunities for recreation.

These conditions make it difficult to establish trust, respect for authority, and the kinds of relationships in the school community among students, teachers, staff, and parents that are needed for students to develop and achieve their potential (Comer, 1980; Comer, Haynes, and Joyner, 1996). It is not surprising that students in urban high schools claim to feel less socially connected to their schools than do students attending suburban high schools (Anderman, 2002). Thus, students with the greatest needs currently receive the least adequate resources.

Urban Students

The exact statistical profile of urban students depends on how "urban" is defined. More than 28 percent of all students are enrolled in urban schools when urban is defined to include all cities with a population of at least 50,000 that are the core of a metropolitan statistical area (MSA) or consolidated metropolitan statistical area (CMSA). Slightly more than 15 percent of all students attend urban schools using a more restrictive definition that includes only cities of at least 250,000 (National Center for Education Statistics, 1998a). However "urban" is defined, urban students disproportionately come from families with incomes below the poverty line, attend schools where a high percentage of students are poor, live in socially and economically distressed neighborhoods, and are from a racial or ethnic minority group.

Nearly a third (30.5 percent) of children ages 5 to 17 living in the 100 largest cities are living in poverty, compared to 22 percent in midsize cities, 13.3 percent in suburbs, and 19.3 percent in towns and rural areas (Council of Great City Schools, 2000). The concentration of poverty in urban areas is growing. Between 1970 and 1990, the percent of U.S. children who resided in distressed neighborhoods in the 50 largest cities rose from 3 to 17 percent (Annie E. Casey Foundation, 1997).

Given the large proportion of urban children who live in poverty, it is not surprising that children living in large urban areas are most likely to attend schools with substantial concentrations of economically disadvantaged students. One national sample of elementary, middle, and high school students showed that 40 percent of urban students attend high-poverty

TABLE 1-1 Percentage of Urban Elementary and Secondary Students by Race/Ethnicity

	White	Asian/ Pacific Islander	Black	Hispanic	Total
Big city	24.8	7.3	35.5	31.7	99.3
Medium city	53.7	3.6	24.3	16.6	98.2
All schools	61.4	4.0	16.9	16.0	98.3

NOTE: Nationally, Native Americans are 1.4 percent of all students. Data are unavailable for urban locations.
SOURCE: National Center for Education Statistics (2000a).

schools (defined as schools where the poverty concentration is at least 40 percent), compared to only 10 percent of suburban students and 26 percent of rural students (Lippman et al., 1996).

Black and Hispanic students are far more likely than Asian and white students to attend urban schools in general, and high-poverty urban schools in particular (Lippman et al., 1996, p. 10).[2] Furthermore, urban schools have a disproportionate number of students of color (see Table 1-1). In a report documenting a trend toward the growing segregation of low-income students of color in poorly performing urban schools, Orfield (2002) has found that in schools where 50 to 60 percent of the students are Black or Hispanic, on average at least 60 percent of the students are poor. In schools where at least 80 percent of the students are Black or Hispanic, an average of 80 to 90 percent of the students are poor.

All of the demographic characteristics of urban school students are statistically associated with poorer educational outcomes (Halpern-Felsher et al., 1997; Jencks and Phillips, 1998; National Research Council, 2002c), although the causal mechanisms that produce these outcomes are not well understood (Connell, Halpern-Felsher, and Brooks-Gunn, 1997). Concentrated poverty in the neighborhoods where students live is also associated with lower school achievement (Abt Associates, 1993; Catsambis and Beveridge, 2001; National Research Council, 1990; Orfield, 1999; U.S. Department of Education, 2000). Furthermore, an analysis of data from the National Longitudinal Survey of Youth (Guo, 1998) found that poverty in adolescence, or concurrent poverty, has a greater influence on adolescent achievement in school than poverty earlier in life. Schellenberg (1999, p.130) concludes from his review of four interlocking studies he conducted in the St. Paul, MN, public schools " . . . the degree to which poor children are

[2]Information on Native Americans was not given in most of the demographic data found.

surrounded by other poor children—both in their neighborhood and at school—has as strong an effect on their achievement as their own poverty. Concentration of poverty in the neighborhood and the school affects all children, poor and non-poor." Lippman et al. (1996) examined whether differences in measures of engagement and achievement persisted after controlling for the effects of school poverty concentration. They found that after the greater concentration of poverty in urban schools was statistically controlled, differences between groups of students on virtually all indicators of engagement and achievement either disappeared or were greatly diminished.

Variables associated with neighborhood poverty (e.g., violence, instability in living arrangements) can have an effect on academic achievement as well. For example, McLanahan (1985) found that among white single-parent households, poverty and the stress associated with family disruption accounted for nearly all of the negative effects of family structure on children's educational attainment (i.e., dropping out from high school); for Black households, the results were more mixed. In households of all ethnic groups, young adolescents living in poverty received fewer opportunities for learning stimulation and spent less time with their parents, especially their fathers (Bradley, Corwyn, McAdoo, and Coll, 2001).

Research by Brooks-Gunn and Duncan (1997) explores the ways in which neighborhood conditions create "pathways" or mechanisms through which family income operates to affect indicators of children's well-being. These indicators include school achievement (e.g., grade repetition, expulsion or suspension, dropping out of school), cognitive outcomes (e.g., difficulty in learning to read), emotional outcomes (e.g., being treated for an emotional problem), and physical health outcomes (e.g., lead poisoning, chronic asthma). The mechanisms are complex, and there is still much to learn. What is clear is that the deck is stacked against children who live in large urban communities with a high concentration of families living in poverty.

Making matters worse, as the percentage of students at a school who are living in poverty rises, the school conditions needed to enable those students to succeed (e.g., sufficient resources, teacher quality, educator stability, small school size) decline (see Darling-Hammond, 1990; Lippman et al., 1996; National Research Council, 2002d; Rebell, 2002; Wasley et al., 2000). Hochschild (in press) calls these conditions "nested inequalities." The very students who need the most resources receive the fewest, and in the end, pay the biggest price in terms of school performance and nonschool outcomes (Darling-Hammond, 1990, 2002).

This demographic profile of urban students and communities highlights the challenges faced by urban high schools. Equally important, but less studied, are the cultural richness and strengths for teaching and learning of many urban communities (Delpit, 1995; Irvine, 1990). What is usually conceived of as a problem, such as a large population of English-language learners or new immigrants, is also an asset and a resource. Immigrants bring a wealth of opportunities for all students to be exposed directly to political issues, social and cultural issues, art, music, language, customs, religions, and trades that they might otherwise have to read about in textbooks. The harsh realities and challenges cannot be ignored, but greater attention to the opportunities that urban centers provide for education is essential to improving the schools in those communities. Engaging students who are growing up in areas of concentrated poverty will require exploiting the many strengths and opportunities available in most culturally diverse urban communities as well as addressing the challenges.

DROPPING OUT: THE ULTIMATE IN DISENGAGEMENT

Dropping out of high school is for many students the last step in a long process through which students become disengaged from school. Indeed, many urban schools plan on substantial attrition in the number of courses they offer at the 11th and 12th grade levels (Fine, 1994). Graduation rates vary by ethnicity. Green (2001) calculated graduation rates[3] nationwide and for major school districts. At the national level, the graduation rate in 1998 was 74 percent. Differences were found among ethnic groups, with white students substantially more likely to graduate than Black and Latino students. Students in big city high schools were found to be substantially less likely to graduate from high school than their counterparts in suburban and rural schools. Both the overall dropout rate and the degree of disparity among ethnic groups varied across cities (see Table 1-2).

Although some cities have only a few problem high schools, in other cities they are the norm (Balfanz, 2001). Balfanz and Legters (2001) identified approximately 250 urban U.S. high schools in which fewer than half of the entering freshmen advance to the 12th grade with their classmates. These failing schools enroll approximately 60 percent of all students of color in the 35 large urban school districts that were examined.

High dropout rates are not inevitable in urban schools, however. Even

[3]The graduation rate was calculated by dividing the number of regular diplomas awarded in 1998 by the number of 8th-grade students enrolled in 1993, multiplied by 100. Calculations of graduation rates for school districts were adjusted for changes in total and racial/ethnic subgroup enrollment in those districts in the 5-year period between 1993 and 1998. Green's calculations yield graduation rates that are much lower than NCES High School Completion Rates. This difference is largely explained by the inclusion of GED recipients in the NCES calculations. Other technical differences are discussed by Green (2001: pp. 8-9).

TABLE 1-2 Graduation Rates (percent) for Selected Urban School Districts, 1998

District	General Graduation Rate	Black Graduation Rate	Latino Graduation Rate	White Graduation Rate
New York City	54	42	45	80
Los Angeles USD	56	56	48	81
Chicago District 299	47	45	43	59
Philadelphia	70	65	53	91
Houston ISD	52	55	42	84
Baltimore City	54	55	NA	48
Cleveland	28	29	26	23
Detroit	57	57	49	43
Memphis	42	39	NA	50
Milwaukee	43	34	42	74
San Diego USD	62	54	43	79
Dallas ISD	52	60	39	72
U.S. Total	74	56	54	78

NOTE: Selected cities correspond to "Big city" classification in Table 1-1. NA means not available.
SOURCE: Green (2001).

controlling for a student's family background, the school a student attends has a strong effect on whether that student persists or drops out. Rumberger and Thomas (2000) estimated 10th-grade dropout rates from 1990 to 1992 for a sample of 247 urban and suburban high schools in 1990. Only about half of the variation in school dropout rates could be attributed to the background characteristics of the students who attended them. Another study found that only 20 percent of the variability in mean school attendance rates could be explained by the background characteristics of students (Bryk and Thum, 1989). Some of the remaining variance presumably was explained by qualities of the schools, such as school size, quality of the teachers, and the social and academic climate. The variation in dropout rates among high schools that serve predominantly low-income students of color suggests that reforms could increase schools' holding power.

OUTCOMES AFTER HIGH SCHOOL

Dropping out has serious consequences for students. The manufacturing jobs with good wages that used to be available to unskilled workers are rapidly disappearing (Drucker, 1996). National Youth Employment Coalition (1999) estimates show that only about 15 percent of jobs available in 1999 could be filled by unskilled workers, compared to approximately 60 percent in 1950. Furthermore, the Coalition's estimates show that nearly half of all young people ages 17 to 24 who have not completed high school are unemployed or hold jobs paying less than $300 per week. The median annual earnings of men ages 25 to 34 who dropped out of high school plummeted from $30,346 in 1970 to $18,582 in 1999.[4] Although the average income of women ages 25 to 34 who dropped out of high school increased slightly between 1970 and 1999, the average annual income of female dropouts in 1999 was only $10,174—far lower than that of male dropouts and not a living wage (National Center for Education Statistics, 2001b, p. 137).

During the same period, the average earnings for high school graduates without postsecondary education decreased by 27 percent for men, and rose only slightly for women. For both men and women, obtaining the kind of solid educational foundation during high school that would prepare one for postsecondary education has become indispensable for access to adequately remunerated employment.

Although finishing high school is indeed an asset for job security after graduation, even students who complete urban high schools in disadvantaged communities do not necessarily leave with the skills they need to be gainfully employed. In the 35 largest central cities in the country, more than half of entering high school students read at the sixth-grade level or below (Grosso de León, 2002), and many of these students make little progress while they are in high school (Campbell, Hombo, and Mazzeo, 2000; Dreeben and Gamoran, 1986; Education Trust, 1999; Guiton and Oakes, 1995). The problem is acute for low-income students of color. On average, African-American and Latino 17-year-olds taking the National Assessment of Educational Progress (NAEP) read about as well as white 13-year-olds. The findings in math are equally distressing. In 2000, 40 percent of 12th graders in central cities scored "below basic" on the NAEP (National Center for Education Statistics, 2001a), compared to 32 percent in urban fringe (suburban) and large towns, and 35 percent in rural and small towns. An important point to remember is that although the differences between urban and suburban 12th graders are not great, the picture is actually worse than these data suggest. Because the proportion of students who have dropped out by the 12th grade is much higher in urban than suburban schools, the urban 12th graders assessed in these data can be considered the high achievers in their class—"survivors" of the central city schools.

Attending a failing high school, and thereby being placed "at risk" of dropping out or being undereducated, also places youth at risk of involvement with the criminal justice system (Fine et al., 2001; Poe-Yamagata and

[4]In constant 2000 dollars.

Jones, 2000). A full 54 percent of inmates in New York State facilities enter the system as dropouts, with neither a GED nor a high school diploma (Gangi, Schiraldi, and Ziedenberg, 1998; New York State Senate Democratic Task Force on Criminal Justice Reform, 2000). Using data from the National Longitudinal Survey of Youth and U.S. census microlevel data on state prisoners and local jail inmates, a recent study found evidence that high school students attending high school in a state in which educational resources are relatively low have a much higher probability of ending up in jails and prisons as adults (Arum and LaFree, submitted). High student/teacher ratios in high school also have been linked to higher adult incarceration rates (Arum and Beattie, 1999). Attending a poorly resourced high school or leaving high school without graduating does not necessarily lead youth to the prison door, but it is a well-worn path, particularly for low-income students of color.

This sad litany of statistics highlights the importance of the topic of this volume. For the sake of the youth involved and for the sake of society, we cannot ignore a pervasive problem with such serious consequences. The data we have just summarized should strengthen our resolve to do what is necessary to make high schools more inviting and engaging for their students.

THE POTENTIAL OF SCHOOL REFORM

Nearly all cities have at least some high-performing high schools that serve economically disadvantaged students (Jerald, 2001). In 2001, The Education Trust (Jerald, 2001) published a list of more than 4,000 high-performing schools that serve primarily low-income students or students from historically disadvantaged racial/ethnic minority groups.[5] Although the great majority of these schools were at the elementary level, the presence of even a smattering of urban high schools on the list gives reason to hope that outcomes can be improved in critically underperforming urban high schools.

School reform efforts to date, however, have not improved outcomes for urban high school students on a large scale (National Research Council, 2002a; Puma et al., 1997). Evaluations of whole-school reform efforts over the past decade have been mixed at best (e.g., Berends, Chun, Schuyler,

[5] "High-performing" schools were those serving students with reading and/or math performance in the top third among all schools in the state at the same grade level; schools "serving disadvantaged students" were those with at least 50 percent low-income students and at least 50 percent African-American and Hispanic students.

Stockly, and Briggs, 2002; Berends, Heilbrunn, McKelvey, and Sullivan, 1999).

Admittedly, a few success stories—often involving a highly select group of teachers and administrators and more resources than are available to most schools—do not give us total confidence that large-scale improvement is within our grasp. But now we also have promising models for high school reform (American Federation of Teachers, 1998; American Youth Policy Forum, 2000; George and McEwin, 1999; see Chapters 7 and 8, this volume) and a fair amount of knowledge about educational policies and practices that produce high levels of engagement and learning for even the most disadvantaged students (National Research Council, 2002a; Stringfield et al., 1997; see also Chapter 5). Although the powerful effects of students' demographic and social circumstances on their educational attainment and achievement should not be underestimated (Coleman et al., 1966; National Research Council, 2002c; National Center for Education Statistics, 2000a, 2001a), educational policies and support services can mitigate the effects of such circumstances (see Chapter 6, this volume). It is too soon to know whether these reform approaches can be successful on a large scale, but it is also too soon to become discouraged.

What would be required to increase students' motivation to succeed and their engagement in learning? After a thorough review of the evidence, the committee finds merit in the succinct answer provided by Newmann, Wehlage, and Lamborn (1992, p. 19): "If students are to invest themselves in the forms of mastery required by schools, they must perceive the general enterprise of schooling as legitimate, deserving of their committed effort, and honoring them as respected members." High schools must make students believe and feel that they are respected and that they belong, that they can learn what they are being required to learn, and that the lessons of school "make sense" within the context of their own lives. All this, of course, is much easier to prescribe than to do—especially in high-poverty, urban school communities.

We do not believe that a universal formula to accomplish these goals exists, or that one is likely to be discovered. But we do believe that the general principles that we have learned about motivation and engagement can be applied and adapted to improve the way that schools carry out their core activities, and thus the engagement and investment of their students in learning.

This volume summarizes evidence that can be used to guide efforts to improve adolescents' engagement in school. Because research at the high school level is sparse compared to that at the elementary and middle school levels, the committee was broad and flexible in its search. We examined tightly controlled experiments, program evaluations, surveys, and case studies. We refer occasionally to well-informed but still untested theories and conjectures. But we make recommendations only when the accumulated evidence points us clearly in a particular direction, and we are careful to be clear about the source and nature of the evidence described to allow readers to draw their own conclusions.

Again and again the evidence reveals the complexity and interconnections among practices. Most of the reforms we suggest are necessary; none is sufficient. Furthermore, all of them need to be adapted to the particular circumstances of individual communities and schools.

ORGANIZATION OF THE REPORT

In Chapter 2, we discuss general principles of achievement motivation and summarize research on the effects of educational practices on student motivation and engagement. The research reviewed in this chapter includes many experimental as well as classroom-based studies. Chapter 3 discusses how these principles of engagement can inform classroom teaching, focusing on literacy and mathematics. It also discusses the importance of supporting teacher learning and provides examples of strategies for promoting teacher collaboration and development. Moving from the classroom to the school, Chapter 4 focuses on the larger school context, especially the importance of an intense focus on learning within a supportive school community. Research on organizational features of schools, such as tracking, and on the student population and size of schools is also reviewed.

Chapter 5 moves beyond the school by discussing strategies for connecting schools better to their communities and to students' families. It also summarizes research on peer effects on high school student engagement, and suggests strategies for maximizing positive and minimizing negative peer effects. Creating connections with the community is discussed in Chapter 6 as one among several strategies for addressing nonacademic needs (e.g., health, mental health, family problems, pregnancy, and neighborhood violence) that can interfere with students' ability to engage in academic work. This chapter discusses what high schools can do to meet students' nonacademic needs without becoming overly distracted from their core academic mission.

The next two chapters move to the issue of scaling up the development of intellectually engaging high schools by reviewing current approaches to high school reform. Chapter 7 discusses theme-based schools, especially those that emphasize education for occupations as a strategy for engaging students' interest and giving them instruction and experiences in the community that strengthen their commitment to school. Chapter 8 reviews recent efforts at designing and implementing comprehensive reform approaches in urban high schools, and the challenges of scaling up.

The volume ends with Chapter 9, which presents conclusions and recommendations for aspects of high school policies and practices and for future research.

For each of the topics addressed in this volume, the discussion focuses on what the evidence suggests intellectually engaging high schools should look like and the factors that appear to support and undermine engaging educational policies and practices. Less is said about the *process* of school reform—how these practices get implemented on a large scale—although a chapter is devoted to the qualities of some of the major current reform models. In brief, this volume focuses more on where we want to go than on how we get there.

Although the focus is primarily on what can be done *in* high schools, the policies and practices described in this volume have important implications for many issues beyond its scope—including, for example, policies that affect who is attracted into the field of teaching, preservice teacher and leadership training and credentialing policies, state and federal testing policies, graduation requirements, and school funding and resource allocation. References are occasionally made to these policies, but they are not discussed in detail.

2

The Nature and Conditions of Engagement

WHAT IS ENGAGEMENT?[1]

Engagement in schoolwork involves both behaviors (e.g., persistence, effort, attention) and emotions (e.g., enthusiasm, interest, pride in success; Connell and Wellborn, 1991; Johnson, Crosnoe, and Elder, 2001; Newmann, 1992; Skinner and Belmont, 1993; Smerdon, 1999; Turner, Thorpe, and Meyer, 1998). It is important to consider mental or cognitive behaviors (attention, problem solving, using meta-cognitive strategies) as well as observable behaviors (active participation in class, completing work, seeking assistance when having difficulty, taking challenging classes) because relying only on observable behaviors as evidence of engagement can be deceiving. (Who hasn't had the experience of appearing engrossed in a lecture while writing a letter, making a grocery list, or daydreaming?) Attention to mental behavior is important because only genuine cognitive engagement will result in learning.

Students also can be socially engaged in school by participating in extracurricular activities, having friends at school, feeling a sense of loyalty

[1]One might distinguish between "engagement" and "motivation"—with motivation as the precursor (the reason for being engaged) and engagement as the psychological experience or behavior. But in everyday contexts, people tend to use these terms interchangeably, presumably because motivation is inferred from observed emotions or behavior. Thus, the word "motivated" is just as likely as the word "engaged" to be used to describe someone who appears to be concentrating intently or to be actively involved in a learning activity.

to the school, and more generally by believing in the legitimacy of school. Promoting social engagement may have considerable value because it appears to motivate youth to attend and to stay in school (Johnson et al., 2001; Newmann, Wehlage, and Lamborn, 1992; Tinto, 1993; Wehlage, Rutter, Smith, Lesko, and Fernandez, 1989). This is why dropout prevention efforts often focus on keeping at-risk students socially attached to school (Finn and Rock, 1997).

Motivation to attend school is not sufficient, however, because students can participate actively and enjoy the social affairs of school without making meaningful academic progress. Although assessing proximal goals such as increasing attendance and reducing dropout rates can mark progress that reassures us that we are moving in the right direction, ultimately we need to achieve the more ambitious goal of promoting deep cognitive engagement that results in learning. Our focus is aptly captured in Newmann's (1992, p. 12) definition of engagement: " . . . the student's psychological investment in and effort directed toward learning, understanding, or mastering the knowledge, skills, or crafts that academic work is intended to promote."

The levels of both behavioral and emotional engagement can vary—from paying minimal attention (as in the lecture example) to actively processing information (e.g., making connections to previously learned material, critically analyzing new information); from being minimally interested to feeling excited and enthusiastic. Csikszentmihalyi (1975, 1988) describes the ultimate cognitive engagement as a state of "flow," in which people are so intensely attentive to the task at hand that they lose awareness of time and space. We are not proposing that all high school students be in a constant state of flow, but we have seen youth deeply and enthusiastically engaged in schoolwork and we believe this high standard should be our goal. The nature of the work may vary—from puzzling over a mathematical problem or reading a novel to trying to design an eye-catching Web page. Whatever the task, the goal is attentiveness and active problem solving that will promote learning, understanding, and the development of new skills.

Both the form and consequences of engagement are influenced by students' reasons for engagement (Ames, 1992; Linnenbrink and Pintrich, 2000; Meece, 1991; Nicholls, 1983). For example, students who attend class and complete assignments to avoid punishment or bad grades are less likely to become engaged beyond a superficial (just get it done) level, whereas students who complete assignments because the material captures their interest or because they experience a sense of pride in accomplishment are more likely to go beyond the minimal requirements and become actively and deeply engaged. This distinction between coerced and voluntary engagement is important, and we return to it later.

Just as there are many forms of engagement, there are many forms and reasons for disengagement—from not paying attention and not completing homework to cutting classes and school. Behavioral problems are also evidence of disengagement and often a precursor to leaving school (or being asked to leave; Finn, 1989). The ultimate disengagement is to drop out of school. But because dropping out is usually preceded by less dramatic forms of disengagement (e.g., absenteeism, poor attitudes toward school), it is viewed as the final stage in a dynamic and cumulative process (Fine, 1991; Finn, 1989; Newmann et al., 1992; Wehlage et al., 1989).

THE CONTEXT MATTERS

People often refer to motivation as a personal quality and describe some students as motivated and others as unmotivated. Teachers usually prefer to teach students who they perceive to be "self-motivated." Indeed, students enter high school with well-developed beliefs, dispositions, and behavioral patterns. But these personal beliefs and dispositions developed partly as a consequence of the educational environments they experienced. There is considerable evidence for the power of the educational context, even as late as high school. If teachers could observe one of their own students in other classes or learning contexts, they would see substantial variation, making it difficult to characterize any one student as uniformly high or low on motivation. The same adolescent who is unable to pay attention in one classroom for more than a few minutes may persevere on demanding cognitive tasks in another class or in an after-school program. Within-student variation in engagement also is seen in class attendance rates, with students skipping some classes substantially more than others (Davidson, 1999).

The committee believes that all youth, even the most alienated, deserve a chance to regain the enthusiasm for learning that they most likely had as young children. We recognize that students vary in their abilities, disposition toward learning, and level of engagement when they enter high school, and that many students living in poverty endure serious hardships and have family responsibilities, such as providing income and sibling care, which make it difficult to actively participate in high school. School contexts, however, make a difference, and can diminish, if not eliminate, negative effects of poverty on student engagement. Our focus, therefore, is on what schools can do to engage (or reengage) adolescents in learning.

PSYCHOLOGICAL MEDIATORS OF ENGAGEMENT

There is substantial empirical evidence on the educational conditions that promote intellectual engagement. The evidence suggests that the effect of the educational context on engagement is partially mediated by three sets

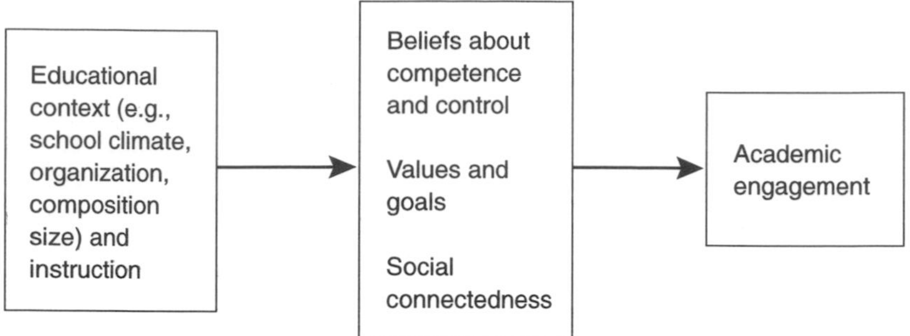

FIGURE 2-1 A theory on educational conditions that promote intellectual engagement.

of psychological variables—beliefs about competence and control, values and goals, and a sense of social connectedness. This theory is represented in Figure 2-1.

For example, in schools that meet teachers' needs for resources, professional development, and collegiality, teachers are more likely to be caring and effective. Such teachers are much more likely to give students a feeling of being cared about, and to promote students' confidence in their ability to succeed and the belief that academic success is important for future goals. These positive beliefs and feelings, in turn, should lead to high levels of effort and persistence. In contrast, teachers in large, impersonal schools with a climate of low standards are likely to give up on students and teach a watered-down curriculum that engenders in students doubts about their ability to succeed, the belief that academic work has little personal value, and generally negative feelings toward the teacher and school. These beliefs and feelings lead to low effort or ultimately to dropping out of school altogether.

The importance of these psychological variables in affecting student behavior is supported by studies of out-of-school programs that engage youth effectively. Successful programs address adolescents' needs for competence, control, and a sense of belonging (Catalano, Berglund, Ryan, Lonczak, and Hawkins, 1999; Eccles and Barber, 1999; Eccles and Templeton, 2001; Hawkins, Catalano, Kosterman, Abbott, and Hill, 1999; Kahne, Nagoaka et al., 2001; McLaughlin, 2000). We elaborate on these three sets of psychological mediators next, and later summarize what is known about how educational contexts affect them.

Perceptions of Competence and Control (I Can)

Students will not exert effort in academic work if they are convinced they lack the capacity to succeed or have no control over outcomes

(Atkinson, 1964; Eccles et al., 1983; Skinner, Wellborn, and Connell, 1990; Skinner, Zimmer-Gembeck, and Connell, 1998).[2] They need to know what it takes to succeed and to believe they can succeed. Thus, the student who doesn't believe she can do the homework assigned will not attempt it; the student who believes he is incapable of passing the courses he needs to graduate will not exert much effort in class and may stop coming to school altogether.

The effects of feeling incompetent on the decision to leave school were demonstrated in a national longitudinal study that tracked the educational careers of more than 13,000 eighth graders. About 32 percent claimed they dropped out because they could not keep up with schoolwork (Berktold, Geis, and Kaufman, 1998, Table 6). Perceptions of incompetence may also contribute to the disproportionate number of low-income students and students of color who drop out of high school. In Ferguson's (2002) survey of more than 100,000 7th through 11th graders in 15 school districts, students from families with low socioeconomic status and students of color reported less understanding of teachers' lessons and comprehension of the material they read for school. Although they spent nearly as much time on homework as the other students in the same classes, they were much less likely to complete their homework.

One high school student interviewed by Davidson and Phelan (1999, p. 259), in their ethnographic study of urban high schools, succinctly describes the typical helpless reaction to feeling incompetent: "Mr. Yana, when he talks I just can't follow what he's saying. So I just give up."[3]

Students' beliefs about their academic competence may affect behavior in the United States more than in some other countries because Americans tend to have a concept of intelligence that is inherited rather than developed

[2]Self-determination theory posits that feelings of competence and control are basic human needs and that people will not be engaged or otherwise function effectively in environments that do not meet these needs (Connell and Wellborn, 1991; Ryan and Deci, 2000a; Ryan and La Guardia, 2000). Perceptions of competence and control are also central in social psychology theories of learned helplessness (Diener and Dweck, 1978; see Dweck, 2000). Substantial bodies of research, both experimental and embedded in real classrooms, provide support for the importance of perceptions of competence and control for promoting academic engagement (reviewed in Stipek, 2002).

[3]This study of students' experiences of high school (Davidson and Phelan, 1999) followed 48 students in four urban high schools in two large California school districts over a 2-year period. Students were selected to represent the diversity of race/ethnicity and academic performance of ninth graders. Research methods included repeated interviews, surveys, class observations, and shadowing of a subsample of students. The study focused on conditions in classes and schools that affected students' engagement and success.

through effort (Dweck, 1999). Although Americans are not alone in embracing a notion of ability that is stable and that limits the effects of effort on performance, they do so more than people in the Asian countries that have been studied (Chen and Stevenson, 1995; Stevenson and Stigler, 1992). A student who believes that academic ability is fixed *and* that she is low in ability has little hope for success and therefore little reason to try.

The notion of fixed intelligence may be particularly problematic for students of color. Steele and his colleagues have shown repeatedly that high-achieving African-American students, as well as Latino students and women (in math) perform relatively poorly on tests when the tests are introduced as measures of their intellectual ability (e.g., Cokley, 2002; Gonzales, Blanton, and Williams, 2002; Steele and Aronson, 1995, 1998). Steele coined the term "stereotype threat" to explain the effect, suggesting that anxiety about not being able to contradict a stereotype (e.g., that African-Americans have relatively low intelligence or females are not good in math) undermines students' performance.

Students' judgments about their ability can be global or specific. The years of failure in school that many urban high school students have experienced can lead to general judgments of incompetence that bring about low expectations for success in any academic subject, and consequently pervasive low effort. Perceptions of ability usually vary from subject to subject (I'm good at math, but not in foreign languages), and they can certainly vary from one context to another, depending on factors discussed later.

Students' perceptions of their competencies can be difficult to change because they interpret feedback and their own performance outcomes through this lens. A student who believes she is smart and expects to succeed is likely to attribute success on a test or assignment in part to her ability, and poor performance, when it occurs, to low effort or a poor strategy. This pattern of attribution reinforces an optimistic view of the future, even after a setback, because it implies that spending more time studying or changing the strategy will lead to improved performance. In contrast, a student who believes he is not smart is likely to attribute failure on a test to his low ability and success to luck or an easy test. Such attributions reinforce his expectation for continued failure. Because students make attributions that are consistent with existing beliefs, it is difficult to raise expectations in students who have had years of failure experiences in school and have come to believe they lack the capacity to succeed.

Even for students who have confidence in their academic ability, if they believe their achievements will not be recognized because the teachers are racist or prejudiced against them, or that rewards are dispensed on the basis of behavior they aren't willing to engage in (e.g., ingratiating themselves with the teacher), they are not likely to put much effort into trying to do well in school. Studies have shown that low effort for some students also can be traced to a failure to understand what it takes to succeed (Skinner et al., 1998). The rules of the game are not always made clear, or they are not consistently applied. Even when the rules are clear and consistent, some students need help to understand them.

Students' beliefs about their competencies and expectations for success have a direct effect on their intellectual engagement; they also lead to emotions that promote or interfere with engagement in schoolwork. Students who have negative views of their competence and low expectations for success are more anxious in learning contexts and fearful of revealing their ignorance (Abu-Hilal, 2000; Bandalos, Yates, and Thorndike-Christ, 1995; Harter, 1992; see Hembree, 1988). They anticipate embarrassment and humiliation, and are thus reluctant to ask questions even when they are confused (Newman and Goldin, 1990; Ryan and Pintrich, 1997). Sometimes they exert less effort on tasks to provide an alternative explanation to low ability if they fail ("I could have done it if I tried, but I didn't feel like doing it"; Covington, Spratt, and Omelich, 1980).

Self-confidence and expectations for success also affect academic interests and values. In one study of a diverse group of middle school students, changes in students' perceptions of their competence in a class over the course of a semester was a powerful predictor of changes in their interest in the course topic (whereas changes in interest did not predict changes in perceptions of competence; MacIver, Stipek, and Daniels, 1991). Similarly, Jacobs, Lanza, Osgood, Eccles, and Wigfield (2002) found, in a longitudinal study of children from grades 1 though 12 that declines in competence beliefs accounted for much of the age-related decline in valuing academic work. Students enjoy academic tasks more and learn more when they feel competent (Gottfried, 1990; Harter, 1992) and when they expect success (Bandura, 1993, 1997; Pajares, 1996; Schunk, 1995). Feelings of competence give them a feeling of personal control, which has been shown to be critical for enjoyment, effort, and actual learning (deCharms, 1976, 1984; Deci and Ryan, 1985; Ryan and Deci, 2000a).

Values and Goals (I Want to)

Even if students believe they can succeed in school, they won't exert effort unless they see some reason to do so. Adolescents can have many reasons for engaging in academic work, and typically there is a complex set of reasons for engaging in any one task. For example, a student may take real pleasure in learning, or she may have internalized the values of learning and getting a good education. Some reasons for doing academic work are weakly, if at all, connected to learning and academic achievement. For example, a student may not enjoy schoolwork or value education, but may see high school graduation as a means to achieving a long-term goal, such as getting a good job. Another student may desire an extrinsic reward (e.g., being able to play football) that has been made contingent on some form of engagement or academic outcome, or he may want to avoid punishment or disapproval for poor performance.

Reasons for being engaged vary in the degree to which they come from within the self (giving students a feeling of self-determination—that they are working because they *want* to) in comparison to being imposed externally (giving them a feeling of being coerced—that they are working because they *have* to). The nature of students' reasons, especially the degree to which they feel self-determining and autonomous versus coerced and controlled, has important implications for the quality of their effort and their learning. We will elaborate below on the implications of various reasons high school students might have to be engaged in academic work.

Intrinsic Interest

Ideally, students take pleasure in learning. They engage in academic work because they are interested in the topic and take pride in their achievements. The advantages of intrinsic motivation have been shown in many studies, although not specifically involving urban high school youth. For example, researchers have found that students who are intrinsically interested in an activity are more likely than students who are not intrinsically interested to seek challenging tasks (Pittman, Emery, and Boggiano, 1982), think more creatively (Amabile and Hennessey, 1992), exert effort (Downey and Ainsworth-Darnell, 2002; Miserandino, 1996), and learn at a conceptual level (Ryan, Connell, and Plant, 1990).

Internalized Values

Some students are diligent whether or not they enjoy a particular course or activity because they have adopted values related to schooling. They believe it is important to work hard in school and get an education—not to achieve a particular outcome or reward, but because it's the right thing to do. The internalization of academic values has not been well studied, but there is evidence that students who believe in the importance of school are more productively engaged (e.g., attend more regularly, complete homework, pay better attention) than students who do not value education (Taylor, Casten, Flickinger, Roberts, and Fulmore, 1994).

Academic values are assumed to develop just like any other values. When children observe significant others expressing and modeling particular values, such as trying hard in school, and when they are recognized and supported for behavior consistent with those values, they adopt the values as their own and behave in ways consistent with them (Connell and Wellborn, 1991; Downey and Ainsworth-Darnell, 2002; Ryan, Connell, and Grolnick, 1992; Ryan and Deci, 2000a; Ryan and La Guardia, 1999). The more students have internalized positive education values, the more autonomous they feel, and the more they voluntarily persist in the face of challenge and in the absence of immediate rewards.

Negative values presumably are internalized through the same process. Students who spend their time with adults and peers who devalue school and who are not encouraged and reinforced for their efforts on schoolwork may develop antiachievement values. To them, it is just as reasonable not to exert effort (or at least appear not to be exerting effort) as it is for other students to be diligent (see Chapter 3, this volume).

A few theorists have argued that students of color, especially African-American youth, often develop antiacademic values because they do not see any tangible return to schooling (Fordham, 1988; Ogbu, 1992, 1997; Osborne, 1995, 1997). Ogbu and others propose that African-American youth do not expect their own success in school to be rewarded with jobs and higher incomes. According to the theory, the youth buffer themselves psychologically from the failure they believe is inevitable in an unfair society that is biased against them by disidentifying with academic achievement values and by developing a strong identity with their own race that is "oppositional" to the dominant culture. Although there are case studies that are consistent with Ogbu's notion of disidentification, large-scale surveys, summarized in Chapter 5 in this volume, do not support these claims. Antiachievement subcultures may exist, but the evidence does not suggest they are pervasive among students of color.

However, there is evidence that connects beliefs about the potential returns to education directly to academic engagement. Students' perceptions of social injustice and discrimination have been associated with low engagement and persistence in school, and perceptions of opportunities and connections between effort in school and success in the workplace have been associated with high engagement and persistence (Fine, 1991; Mickelson, 1990; Taylor et al., 1994).

Extrinsic Goals and Incentives

Students also may become engaged in schoolwork because they see courses and activities in school as having some utility value. Succeeding in them is a means to achieve goals that might not be related to the course or activity itself. The most prominent extrinsic rewards in school are good grades and social recognition. Ideally, such forms of extrinsic motivators would not be the only or even the most salient reasons for students to exert effort in school. Realistically, however, external incentives are powerful motivators if they are believed to be genuinely available. Because a substantial proportion of students in urban high schools serving economically disadvantaged youth have never received high grades or recognition for the academic accomplishments, the challenge is to convince them that these rewards are within their reach and have value.

Long-term goals can also be important. For example, understanding chemistry and biology would have considerable utility value for a student aspiring to be a doctor, but may be seen as having little value to a student who has no expectation for any higher education. Analyses of the National Education Longitudinal Study (NELS) data conducted by Downey and Ainsworth-Darnell (2002) provide correlational evidence for the importance of believing that school is a means to long-term goals. Tenth-grade students of all ethnic groups who agreed with the statement "Education is important to getting a job later on" were rated by teachers as less disruptive and exerting more effort, and reported that they spent relatively more time on homework. Educational and occupational aspirations also predict mobility and dropping out, even controlling for the effects of achievement.

Utility value related to academic work usually requires some future time perspective, and an understanding of the links between immediate tasks and long-term goals (Husman and Lens, 1999). It also requires a belief that the goals are linked to school, and that they are genuinely obtainable.

Research on urban high school youth suggests that they are often poorly informed about the utility value of particular high school courses and activities for college entry (Davidson, 1996; Yowell, 1999). For many students, the problem is not a lack of aspiration or even expectation, but a lack of knowledge about what is required to achieve their educational and professional goals (see Chapter 7, this volume).

Sometimes students will work if something they desire is made contingent on being productively engaged, or if some undesirable outcome will occur if they do not do the work. Policies such as making scholarships and a driver's license contingent on staying in school, making participation in team sports contingent on maintaining a C average, or giving gift certificates to fast food restaurants for every book read are based on the assumption that behavior can be influenced by extrinsic incentives.

In the past decade, many programs have been created that offer college scholarships to motivate students to work hard and complete high school. For example, the state of Georgia's HOPE program offers scholarships for students who complete high school with at least a B average and enroll at an eligible Georgia public college. Students must also maintain a B average while in college to retain the scholarship. Florida similarly offers "Bright Futures" scholarships. "I Have a Dream," "Gear-Up," and "Project GRAD" offer scholarships as well as additional supports, such as mentoring, tutoring, enrichment programs, and college visits. The effects of the scholarship incentive on student engagement are usually difficult to determine from available evidence because records are often poor, there is no control group to which students in the program can be compared, or the effect of the scholarship cannot be untangled from the effects of other aspects of the program. One well-regarded evaluation of Georgia's HOPE Scholarship program (Dynarski, 2000) cautions that modeling a national scholarship program on the Georgia incentive will likely widen the already large racial and socioeconomic-level gaps in college attendance. Dynarski's study suggests that the HOPE Scholarship program has successfully increased the college attendance rates in Georgia, but at the expense of widening the gap between Blacks and whites as well as between low- and high-income families (Dynarski, 2000, also see Cornwell and Mustard, 2002). The danger of higher income families taking advantage of a system without income restrictions, as well as the observed pattern of students reducing course loads in order to maintain the necessary B average, is an important caveat to consider (Glenn, 2003).

Extrinsic rewards for intellectual engagement may be effective, and for some students, they may be the only effective strategy, at least initially. But there is considerable evidence to suggest that extrinsic rewards should be used cautiously and no more than necessary. The effects are often superficial—they promote compliance (showing up, getting the work done), but not deep cognitive engagement. For example, researchers have found that students who are motivated primarily by the anticipation of rewards do not exert effort when tasks are difficult, and they do not take on challenging new work or put forth effort when they do not expect a reward (see Lepper and Henderlong, 2000; Ryan and Deci, 2000b; Stipek, 2002, for reviews). The short-term positive effects of extrinsic rewards also can be undone by negative long-term consequences on attitudes toward school and toward learning (it's just to achieve the reward). Furthermore, when students are motivated by a desire to achieve extrinsic rewards, they do not feel autonomous, as though they are doing work because they want to; the feeling of being controlled undermines deep engagement on challenging tasks (deCharms, 1976, 1984; Deci and Ryan, 1985; Ryan and Deci, 2000a).

Reliance on "carrot and stick" approaches can be particularly problematic for secondary students, who, for many reasons, do not value the rewards typically available in schools, and may want to appear independent rather than compliant. The promise of good grades and the threat of bad grades will have no impact at all on the behavior of students who don't care about grades. A student who is a member of a peer group that devalues or ridicules high academic performance may consider a good grade or public recognition to be a punishment, not a reward. Students who have experienced years of failure are likely to conclude that no amount of effort will lead to such a reward. In brief, extrinsic incentives that are genuinely achievable are often necessary. However, they should not be the only strategy for motivating students.

Social Connectedness (I Belong)

Sociologists have long promoted the value of "communality" and collective identity in the workplace (Blauner, 1964). This notion also applies to schools. Students who feel disrespected or socially isolated are not likely to function effectively at school, and they may simply leave to seek more psychologically comfortable environments. Although feeling psychologically connected to school is not sufficient for meaningful engagement in academic work, it is probably necessary for many students. Bryk, Lee, and Smith (1990) speculate that the importance of positive interpersonal relationships is amplified by modern life, in which traditional sources of personal support, such as community, religious institutions, and extended family, are often unavailable.

When asked about factors that affected their ability to connect with school and learning, the urban high school students interviewed by Davidson and Phelan (1999) focused on caring adults. Half of the students referred to the importance of meaningful relationships with adults and teachers who showed an interest in them as individuals (see also Davidson, 1996, 1999). In the Public Agenda (1997) phone survey, 64 percent of students claimed that they would learn a lot more if their teachers "personally cared about his students as people." (Only 30 percent claimed that most of their teachers did care.)

Students who quit school before graduation frequently report that they dropped out in part because "nobody cared." In the national longitudinal study that tracked the educational careers of students who were 8th graders in 1988, 23 percent of the students who dropped out cited feeling that they did not belong as a reason (Berktold et al., 1998, Table 6).

The research on belonging in educational contexts is relatively new, and the direction of causality has not been definitively established. Nevertheless, many correlational studies have shown that students who report caring and supportive interpersonal relationships in school have more positive academic attitudes and values and are more satisfied with school (Baker, 1999; Battistich, Solomon, Kim, Watson, and Schaps, 1995; Ryan and Deci, 2000a; Shouse, 1996a; Skinner and Belmont, 1993; Wasley et al., 2000; Yowell, 1999). They are also more engaged in academic work (Connell and Wellborn, 1991) and they attend school more and learn more (Bryk and Driscoll, 1988; Bryk, Lee, and Holland, 1993).

Some experimental studies with college students by Baumeister and colleagues (Baumeister, Twenge, and Nuss, 2002; Twenge, Catanese, and Baumeister, 2002) support the hypothesis that feeling a sense of belonging is crucial to cognitive engagement. Their work shows strong negative effects of social exclusion on cognitive performance (Baumeister et al., 2002) and self-regulation (Twenge et al., 2002). Study participants who were made to feel socially excluded or rejected showed a decline in cognitive test performance (on IQ tests and the GRE), as well as an increase in self-defeating behavior like taking irrational risks and procrastinating. Such findings are powerful because of the studies' experimental designs, and may well apply to individuals in educational settings as well as in controlled conditions.

Ferguson (2002) found in his large survey of high school students that African-Americans were particularly responsive to teachers who showed that they cared about their learning. When asked why they worked hard when they did, 47 percent checked the option, "my teachers encourage me to work hard." The proportion of African-American students who referred to teacher encouragement was notably higher than for other ethnic groups and higher than the proportion of African-American students who claimed that when they worked hard, it was because the teacher demanded it (15 percent).

In adolescence feeling connected and accepted by peers in school may be as important as feeling connected to teachers. Research consistently shows the critical role that positive, supportive peer relationships play in adolescents' mental health and well-being (e.g., Berndt, 1996; Parker, Rubin, Price, and DeRosier, 1995). Although studies have not specifically connected peer relationships to engagement in school, inasmuch as they promote positive mental health, they might be expected to support students' ability to be constructively engaged in learning. Close relationships to other students is also likely to promote attachment to school.

A sense of belonging involves an identification with the values and goals of schooling as well as a feeling of connectedness to others in the school, both students and teachers. Thus students whose values and culture conflict with those of the institution, or who see schoolwork as meaningless, may also feel that they don't belong. Case studies suggest that a sense of belonging might be affected by the combination of a student's own ethnic identity and the ethnicity of the students in the school and their classes. Davidson's (1996) intensive study of 55 students in urban schools provides many examples of the ways in which students of color silenced themselves and limited their participation because they didn't feel like they belonged. As one African-American student explained:

> I can never ask a question [in advanced math] cause everyone is so smart in that class. . . . In biology, I could just ask questions with no pressure. I feel better when there's more diversity because there's different people around you. You're not alone, you know. Only one who's not the same as all the rest (p. 39).

Summary

To summarize, the effects of high school contexts on student engagement are partly mediated through their effects on psychological variables—especially beliefs about competencies and control, values and goals, and social connectedness. Efforts to enhance student engagement, therefore, need to consider the effects of policies and practices on these psychological variables. The next section summarizes research that examines the conditions that promote positive beliefs, values, and a feeling of belonging.

ENGAGING LEARNING CONTEXTS

Research on both school and out-of-school contexts provides substantial empirical evidence that can be used to guide efforts to improve adolescents' academic engagement. We describe here what can be gleaned from the achievement motivation literature about the qualities of engaging learning contexts. We limit our summary to principles of motivation that have strong empirical support and broad applicability, although many of the studies cited do not include urban youth. The research evidence that we summarize briefly is reviewed extensively in Brophy (1998), Pintrich and Schunk (1996), and Stipek (2002).

Promoting Perceptions of Competence and Control

A fair amount is known about practices that promote perceptions of competence and control over achievement outcomes. Tasks that are challenging but achievable are essential. Students do not develop a sense of competence when they are given easy work, and they certainly do not develop confidence in their abilities by doing work that is too difficult for them. Adjusting tasks to students' skill levels is also important because learning is an active process, and learners' preexisting knowledge, skills, beliefs, and concepts influence how they make sense of new information (National Research Council, 1999). If preexisting levels of skills and understanding are not considered, students will transform and distort new information according to what they already understand.

This principle of "optimal challenge" may be the most important—as well as the most commonly violated. It is violated because it requires considerable skill and is difficult to implement in a classroom of students with varying skill levels. Teaching that produces meaningful gains in skills and understandings requires assessing students' understanding frequently and in different ways, and building on students' incomplete or naïve understandings and false beliefs.

Related to optimally challenging tasks is the second essential ingredient of a context that supports students' self-confidence and the belief that their efforts will lead to success—high expectations (Eccles et al., 1983; Wigfield and Harold, 1992; see Chapter 5, this volume). Many studies show that schools in which students achieve high levels of performance have high expectations for student learning and hold students to high standards (Baker, Terry, Bridger, and Winsor, 1997; Evans, 1997; Lambert and McCombs, 1998; Lee et al., 1993; Lee and Smith, 1999; Marks, Doane, and Secada, in press; Phillips, 1997). Phillips (1997) found that the level of "academic press" (offering demanding curricula and having high expectations for learning, without pressuring performance or undermining autonomy) was a more powerful predictor of student learning than was the degree to which there was a positive, democratic social environment. Researchers have concluded that a focus on learning partly explains why students attending Catholic schools perform better academically, even when adjustments are made for population differences (Bryk et al., 1993). A student in the Davidson and Phelan (1999, p. 249) study of urban youth referred to academic press in his description of a teacher who made him feel connected: "he pushes you to think about college math, as a freshman, like last year he used to push me into taking math." He continues, "like he'll call [on the telephone] . . . 'Have you done your work?' "

Expectations can be conveyed directly (e.g., "I know you can do it"). But studies suggest that subtle and even counterintuitive responses to students' achievement efforts can affect their achievement-related beliefs. There is evidence, for example, that under some conditions students interpret pity or sympathy following poor performance as an indication that the teacher believes they did the best they could do and are not capable of doing better (Graham, 1984). They reason that the teacher would be angry if he thought they hadn't tried and were capable of a better performance.

In a study by Wentzel (2002), students' perceptions of their teachers' expectations for their learning was a strong predictor of how responsibly they engaged in their academic work, how helpful they were to classmates, how interested they were in class, and how much they desired to learn. Rutter, Maughan, Mortimore, Ouston, and Smith (1979) also provide correlational evidence for the importance of clarity in expectations. They found that schools with a high degree of consensus on goals and enforcement of rules—where there was little ambiguity about expectations—had the best attendance and student participation and the lowest levels of delinquency.

Most high school students do not feel particularly pressured to do well in school. A recent national representative survey of more than 2,000 students asked them: "Overall how much do teachers encourage you to do your best?" (MetLife, 2001). Students' choice of "very much" fell from 50 percent in the 7th and 8th grades to 36 percent in the 11th and 12th grades. Pressure was especially lacking at all grades for students from low-income families. Whereas 47 percent of the more affluent students claimed that their teachers really encouraged them to do their best, only 30 percent of students from low-income families made this claim. Low-income students were also more likely to claim that their teachers expected their schoolwork to be "just OK" (18 percent) than were high-income students (0.8 percent).

Surveys also show that high school students want to be challenged. In a telephone survey of 1,000 randomly selected public high school students, 66 percent claimed that they would learn a lot more if their teachers would "challenge students to constantly do better and learn more." Only 33 percent reported that their teachers did this (Public Agenda, 1997). An especially high proportion of African-American students (79 percent compared to 63 percent of white students) claimed they would learn more if their teachers challenged them more.

In case studies, low-income students of color report a disproportionate number of negative comments about their ability, which, as one African-American student explains, take a toll: "If somebody keeps telling you you're gonna be nobody, you're going to take that in and you're going to say 'Well damn, I'm going to be nobody. Look at my grades, they're right' " (Davidson, 1999, p. 351). Another urban student interviewed by Davidson (1999, p. 351) gives an example of a comment made by a teacher passing out paper for students to do a collage: "I don't think you'll do it, but I'll give it to you anyway."

Many researchers have documented low expectations and standards in schools serving low-income children (Hallinger, Bickman, and Davis, 1996; Hallinger and Murphy, 1986; Leithwood, Begley, and Cousins, 1990), and low expectations prevail for students placed in lower tracks (Oakes, 1985, 1990). Yet when these students are asked about teachers who are motivating, they often describe teachers who hold them to high standards and provide the support to achieve those standards ("he just sticks with you all the way till you get something right"; Davidson and Phelan, 1999, p. 249), and they complain about teachers who don't seem to care whether they learn. One urban high school student laments: "I give up on my test or homework because I don't understand it. When the teacher comes around to collect it, I put it in my book bag and no one notices that I didn't hand it in. They don't notice" (Cushman, 2002, p. 8).

Students of color may be at particular risk of experiencing low expectations. More than a third of the students of color interviewed by Davidson (1996) perceived differential expectations from teachers that were based on students' race. A Filipino-American student gives the following example: "If she's talking about a bad neighborhood, she'll say the Black kids. The whites are all in the good neighborhoods and stuff" (p. 41). A Mexican-American student describes the behavior of another teacher: "When he talks about people that will end up on the streets . . . and then he turns and looks at all the Mexicans. I want to get up and tell him off or just walk out" (p. 41).

McLaughlin and Talbert (2001) documented teachers' behavior in schools in which the population of students had shifted from relatively high-achieving, middle-class students to less skilled, low-income students. They found that many teachers lowered their expectations and watered down instruction to the extent that the students had no hope of ever catching up. Equally destructive was the response of a second group of teachers, who continued to teach the regular curriculum without any adjustment, making it inaccessible to students with low skills, but then complaining about their low skills and motivation. A third group of teachers showed an effective response; they built on students' current skills and level of understanding while pushing them hard to master the high school curriculum.

Many students who enter high school with very low skills need extra educational resources such as tutoring and summer- or after-school programs to develop their skills and confidence. Although all students should be able to master the basic high school curriculum, some require substantially more assistance and time. Without additional support, they will have difficulty making progress. Consequently, they will develop (or maintain) feelings of incompetence, and they will not want to engage in intellectual work. The challenge is to provide these extra supports in a way that does not feel punitive and interfere with opportunities to engage in other activities, such as sports and jobs.

A third critical area related to students' perceptions of competence and control is evaluation. Evaluation is pervasive in high school and affects each student every day. The potential impact of evaluation on perceptions of competence and future expectations is enormous. The research evidence indicates that evaluation should be based on clearly defined criteria, improvement, and achieving goals or standards, and it should provide specific and useful feedback that can guide future efforts (see Stipek, 2002, for a review). In addition, evaluation practices should be varied to give students opportunities to demonstrate their competencies in different ways.

Promoting Academic Values and Goals

Research has not examined the qualities of educational context that promote a commitment to education, although studies of the development of other values provide clues. The factors that appear most likely to contribute to student beliefs about the value of education are (1) being reinforced for behaviors reflecting educational values, (2) having role models who express their own commitment to education, and (3) being encouraged by others, including teachers, counselors, and peers, to seek and take advantage of educational opportunities.

In contrast to general values related to education, both experimental and classroom studies tell us a great deal about the specific practices that enhance students' desire to be engaged in intellectual work. Choice is a critical ingredient. Students are more likely to want to do schoolwork when they have some choice in the courses they take, in the material they study, and in the strategies they use to complete tasks (Cordova and Lepper, 1996; Deci, Nezlek, and Sheinman, 1981; Eccles, Early, Fraser, Belansky, and McCarthy, 1997; Guthrie, Wigfield, and VonSecker, 2000; Iyengar and Lepper, 1999; see Ryan and La Guardia, 1999). These findings are consistent with sociological theory and organizational studies suggesting that alienation, not engagement, is produced by work situations that create feelings of powerlessness (see Blauner, 1964).

A large body of primarily experimental studies demonstrates that emphasis on rewards and other extrinsic reasons for engaging in an activity can undermine intrinsic interest in the activity (see reviews by Cameron and Pierce, 1994; Deci and Ryan, 1985; Kohn, 1993; Ryan and Deci, 2000b; Tang and Hall, 1995). For example, reminding students that they need to complete assignments because a passing grade depends on it, rather than pointing out what they will learn, focuses their attention on the extrinsic reasons for doing schoolwork and thus promotes the feeling that they are doing it because they have to, not because they want to do it. Students need to know the criteria for evaluation and the consequences of their behavior, and some students may need extrinsic incentives to get started. But constant reminders of the extrinsic consequences of their behavior are usually unnecessary and are likely to undermine high levels of cognitive engagement.

Other practices that undermine the desire to engage in activities were articulated by some of the urban youth interviewed by Davidson and Phelan (1999). The students in their study expressed feelings of alienation associated with authoritarian discipline policies, policies that limited their academic options or ability to make decisions, rigid and distrustful teachers, and teachers who did not encourage students to express their perspectives and opinions in class. One student suggested that authoritarian policies promoted rebellion, not academic engagement: "This year, [with] our new administrator guys it's like we're in a prison or something . . . as a result, I think people are more rebellious. Because he won't trust you with anything" (Davidson, 1996, p. 46).

Giving students some choice and autonomy is not the same as eliminating structure. To the contrary, students need to have limits, and choices need to be given in the context of clear expectations. The importance of structuring students' learning experiences was made clear by the urban ninth graders interviewed by Yowell (1999). Nearly all of the mostly Latino students in her study expected to go to college. Despite these high aspirations, they reported that they often skipped school and did not do their homework. Ironically, they blamed their behavior in part on their teachers. Referring back longingly to elementary school, one student explained, "teachers made sure we finished our homework and made sure we turned it in" (p. 18). Some students complained that in contrast to elementary school, their high school teachers said little when they didn't do their work, and rarely informed their parents of problem behavior. Parents usually did not hear of their truancy, for example, until they had missed more than 20 classes and it was too late to make up the work. Ninth graders may require more attention than students in the later grades of high school, but many older students also need assistance and support in completing their work. Taken together, research evidence suggests the value of choice, but within a structure. It does not support either a free-for-all or a military approach.

Research also provides evidence on what makes learning experiences more enjoyable, thus motivating to students. Making school more interesting and fun may be a powerful strategy for engaging students—or at least increasing attendance. In the most recent MetLife (2002) survey of 7th through 12th graders, the most frequent explanation for both skipping school (37 percent) and dropping out of school (76 percent) was that "school was boring." A summary follows of the particular qualities of activities that engage students' interest and enthusiasm (see also Stipek, 2002). It is noteworthy, and probably not coincidental, that these same qualities have been shown by cognitive scientists to promote deep, conceptual understanding (see National Research Council, 1999).

Emphasis on High-Order Thinking

Research on learning shows that students become cognitively engaged when they are asked to wrestle with new concepts, when they are pushed to understand—for example, by being required to explain their reasoning, defend their conclusions, or explore alternative strategies and solutions (National Research Council, 1999). When asked to provide reasons for being unengaged in schoolwork, many of the economically disadvantaged students in the Davidson and Phelan (1999) study complained that they had little opportunity to convey or address conceptual misunderstandings. After describing a math class in these terms, one urban student added, "I was smart in math until I got her and I got stupid" (Davidson, 1999, p. 355). In contrast, when describing a particularly motivating teacher, another student explained: "You ask him a question, and he . . . gives you the clues, and then you have to figure it out yourself. . . . I like that, because he makes you think" (Phelan, Davidson, and Yu, 1998, p. 136).

Challenging work, mentioned earlier as being important for promoting feelings of competence, also has been shown to promote greater interest and enjoyment. Research evidence contradicts a common stereotype of urban youth—that they prefer easy work that requires little effort. In a study by Turner et al. (1998), for example, students used a daily log to rate each task they were given on how skillful they were in completing the task, how challenging the task was, and how they felt about the task. They reported the highest levels of engagement on tasks for which they rated both their skills and challenge as high. When level of challenge was rated as lower than their skills, students were not very intrinsically motivated or engaged. Accountability and a focus on learning were also important. In observations of the students' classes, the researchers found that teachers in classes rated as high in challenge and high in intrinsic motivation were more likely to hold students accountable for understanding.

In another study, high school students rated classes that challenged them as being more engaging (Newmann, 1992). Furthermore, observers' ratings of the level of challenge and the degree to which high-order thinking was required in classes were strongly correlated to their ratings of student engagement. When students were asked to identify, independently, the most interesting and worthwhile class they took in the past year and the class that made them "think the hardest," nearly 60 percent named the same class. The association was especially strong for students from low-income families.

Active Participation

Students enjoy and exert more effort when they are active participants than when they are passive. Over the long term, they are more likely to engage when they are asked to conduct rather than read about experiments; to participate in debate and role playing rather than listen to a lecture; or to create a model and complete projects rather than answer questions about how a process works (Davidson, 1999; Guthrie et al., 2000; Mitchell, 1993). In the Public Agenda (1997) telephone survey of 1,000 high school students, 67 percent claimed that they would learn a lot more if their teachers used "hands-on projects and class discussion," compared to 14 percent who claimed they would learn more if their teachers lectured.

When students in Boaler's (2002a) study of British students who experienced different approaches to mathematics instruction were asked what they like about mathematics, the most popular response given was "activities." They were also able to explain why they enjoyed activities more than the textbook and workbooks they often used. A prominent theme was being able to work autonomously and take pride in their achievement: "you learn more by doing something on your own" (p. 38); "you feel more proud of the projects when you done them yourself. If it's just working through the book, you can't feel proud" (p. 38); "because you had to work out for yourself what was going on, you had to use your own ideas" (p. 68).

Variety

In explaining her distaste for a particular English class, a student in the Davidson and Phelan (1999) study explained:

> . . . we read, read, read and that's all we do. It's like every week it's the same routine. On Mondays you come in and do your vocab—definitions. And then Tuesdays you read the story, Wednesday keep on reading the story, Thursday answer the questions, and Friday you do a test. . . . It's boring to do the same thing every day . . . we should have like more discussions of the stories that we read and have group work. That would make the class more interesting. Plus that each week have a different class project (p. 258).

Her attendance was directly affected. She had 62 absences in this course, compared to 28 in her science class, which involved more active learning.

Students in Boaler's (2002a) study also complained about instruction that was repetitious. As one student explained: "The books are a bit boring, the chapters . . . repeat the same questions over and over again, like when they explain something they do the question and then you have to do about 20 of them at the same time" (Boaler, 2002a, p. 37). When another student was asked how he would change math lessons in his class, he said he would: " . . . have one lesson a week on the booklets, one on activities, one where you get a problem and you have to solve it—just a variety" (p. 37).

Collaborative Activities

Most students enjoy working together (Davidson, 1999; Johnson and Johnson, 1985; Mitchell, 1993). Individual accountability is important, but students' engagement in the learning process can be enhanced by allowing them to work in pairs or small groups on activities that require sharing and meaningful interactions. Students are also more receptive to challenging assignments when they can put their heads together rather than work in isolation. Collaborative work also can help students develop skills in cooperation. Furthermore, it helps create a community of learners who have responsibility for each other's learning, rather than a competitive environment, which is alienating to many students, particularly those who do not perform as well as their classmates (Cohen, 1994).

One challenge to successfully implementing a collaborative learning activity is the inherent status inequities that arise in the social system of the classroom. Those students who are seen as having high academic status typically do more talking and often control the group tasks in a collaborative learning activity, while the low-status students will have a hard time being heard or persuading the other members of the group to even listen to them (Cohen, 1997). Cohen and Lotan (1997) address these "status conditions" of students in the underlying principles of "complex instruction"—a model of pedagogy that involves students actively and equitably in meaningful, challenging group work. These principles include: (1) constructing tasks that are open ended; (2) incorporating multiple intellectual abilities; (3) bolstering group interdependence and enforcing individual accountability; and (4) connecting activities through central concepts and big ideas of the disciplines (Lotan, 1997, p. 107). In this model of collaborative learning, teachers delineate the multiple intellectual abilities a group of students must bring to each task, emphasizing that each student will have his or her own strength to contribute to the group process. Another model for collaboration that increases the chance of equal contributions is the "Jigsaw Classroom," which has been shown to improve the learning, engagement, and enjoyment of low-performing students at all grade levels (Aronson, Stephan, Sikes, Blaney, and Snapp, 1978). The model creates interdependency among students in a group by giving each member a critical element of the task.

Meaningful Connections to Students' Culture and Lives Outside School

Students enjoy learning more, and they learn better, when topics are personally interesting and related to their lives (Meece, 1991). A high school English teacher gives the following example of connecting the curriculum to students' experiences: "when we began *To Kill a Mockingbird,* I asked them to remember their childhood and was there anyone on their block they were afraid of" (McLaughlin and Talbert, 2001, p. 28). A math teacher describes another meaningful connection: "Graphing skills for example. I make up a bunch of crazy data like compare the profits of Metallica versus Billy Idol. . . . And I get a 90 percent return rate on homework" (p. 29).

Giving choices increases the likelihood that students will work on something of personal interest. Another strategy for making schoolwork more relevant and interesting is to invite students to express opinions. Describing a class that she found particularly engaging, one urban high school student explained, "Like if you read something and everyone interprets it differently, she [the teacher] wants to hear everyone's opinion. . . . You learn different points of view and how to analyze different things. . . . It's not just memorizing facts and then spitting them back to the teacher" (Davidson, 1999, p. 349).

Providing opportunities for students to take responsibility and engage in work they believe offers value to their communities also enhances the personal meaningfulness of school (McLaughlin, 2000). As one adolescent commented on the experience of community service:

> It gives me a sense of responsibility, like what you've got to be [when you have a job]. . . . You've got to be there on time, work hard at it, and get done what needs to get done. That's why I am part of this [program] because I needed that responsibility (p. 6).

Promoting a Sense of Belonging

Wentzel (1997) provides evidence on the kinds of behavior that adolescents interpret as caring. She asked students: "How do you know when a teacher cares about you?" and "How do you know when a teacher does not care about you?" In their responses to the former question, students described teachers who tried to make classes interesting; who talked and listened to them; who were honest, fair, and trusting; and who showed concern for them as individuals by asking whether they needed help, making sure they understood what was being taught, and asking them if something was wrong. In response to the second question, students described teachers who were boring or off task; who continued to teach when students weren't paying attention; who ignored, interrupted, embarrassed, insulted, or yelled at students; and who showed little interest in them personally by forgetting their name, not doing anything when they did something wrong, and not trying to explain something when the student didn't understand. In a second study by Wentzel (2002), students' perceptions of how fair their teacher was predicted their interest and enjoyment and their desire to learn. Negative feedback (e.g., scolding) was associated with low engagement in the form of disruptive behavior and violation of rules.

Newmann (1992) suggests that a sense of fair treatment is also critical to feeling connected to school. He cites studies suggesting substantial inequities related to race and income in some schools in expectations, quality of instruction, and due process. Such inequities are likely to disengage students who are treated unfairly. Adolescents who perceive differential treatment by teachers and counselors based on race are also less likely to value school (Roeser, Eccles, and Sameroff, 1998).

In the Davidson and Phelan (1999) study, students stressed two types of teacher behaviors that were important to them—learning something about their lives outside of school and communicating directly and regularly with them about their academic progress. They mentioned subtle behaviors that demonstrated concern about their academic success, such as stopping to clarify a point when a student appeared confused and asking why they had missed school. One student noted, "You go in and you're not there for a day and they notice and they say, 'Why are you tardy?' And they care" (p. 250). One adolescent explained in a study in which urban high school students were asked what advice they would give to a new teacher: "If there's confusion on my face I want you to see it. If there's disagreement

I want you to say, You disagree? Why?" (Cushman, 2002, p. 2). Another student complained about a particularly unmotivating teacher: " . . . he's just writing things on the board . . . He don't look at the class—like, Do you understand?—he's just teaching it to us. He sees that a couple of students understand it and he moves on. He doesn't make a space for us to ask" (p. 8). Students also mentioned humor, which seemed to lessen the social distance between teacher and student. Another theme in their comments concerned fair and respectful disciplinary practices that included student input.

Why does a caring teacher promote student engagement? One student explained that teachers' concern made students want to give back: "We owe her something now, now it's like we can't say 'we don't know this.' . . . We gotta do it [our work], we owe her that, you know" (Davidson, 1999, p. 346). Another student, who had highly variable attendance for different classes, attributed her regular attendance in one class to the teacher caring about her as a person, explaining:

> Like whenever I'm absent or whenever we plan to cut or whatever, I say "No, I have to go to fifth period," all I care about is fifth period. . . . I have to go to that class (p. 347).

Some evidence suggests that a sense of belonging may, under some circumstances, be associated with the degree to which a student's own ethnic background is similar to that of other students. Finn and Voelkl (1993) found that "at-risk" (mostly minority) students in their study rated the school community (quality of teacher-student relationships and whether the school has "real school spirit") more positively when they attended schools with relatively high proportions of minorities. Using a nationally stratified sample of high school students (AddHealth), Johnson et al. (2001) similarly found that students reported greater attachment to school (feeling close to people at school, feeling a part of their school) when they attended schools with proportionally more students of their own race. School racial composition was not, however, associated with students' reports of their engagement in academic work.

In brief, students feel like they belong in educational settings in which they are treated fairly and with respect, and in which adults show they care about them as people. One way that students judge how much teachers care is by whether they hold them to high expectations and make an effort to ensure they are learning.

BEYOND THE CLASSROOM

No teacher, however good or committed, can engage students in academic work in a school context that does not support the kinds of practices described in this chapter (see Chapter 4). Feelings of incompetence and no control over outcomes produce the same disengagement in teachers as in students (Tschannen-Moran, Hoy, and Hoy, 1998). To protect their own sense of competence, teachers often attribute poor student performance to external factors over which they have no control, such as low student capacity, unsupportive homes, and lack of resources. Some teachers give up hope and stop trying. School administrators need to apply what is known about maintaining confidence and feelings of control and belonging in students to create supportive settings for teachers.

Teachers' efforts in individual classrooms can also be undermined by school organization and policies. For example, tracking diminishes students' choices and the access of relatively low-skilled students to peers with positive academic values. Highly competitive school environments in which only high-performing students are recognized publicly undermine many students' sense of competence. Students are not likely to develop a sense of belonging in schools that are organized in ways that make it difficult for teachers to know and develop personal relationships with students, or in schools that tolerate racism or bullying. Schools that do not promote a sense of community and shared purpose among teachers are not likely to provide clear expectations and goals or to promote a sense of connectedness and belonging among students. If teachers spend all of their workday engaged directly with students, they will not have sufficient time to prepare appropriately challenging and culturally meaningful instruction and activities that involve collaboration and higher order thinking. Teaching that engages students takes much more time to plan than the repetitive textbook teaching that many teachers resort to because of the other demands on their time.

School policies also affect the degree to which students feel encouraged and supported in their learning. For example, a policy of contacting parents after only a few unexplained student absences, providing additional help for students who fall behind, and helping students gain access to community resources to meet basic physical and psychological needs conveys to students that people care about them and want them to learn. Efforts to make school a comfortable and accessible place for parents are also important; one example is translating information into languages that parents speak (see Chapter 3, this volume). Efforts to increase student engagement therefore must involve the whole school. We elaborate on school-level policies and practices in Chapter 4.

BEYOND THE SCHOOL

Student motivation is affected by policies made beyond the school as well as in the school. For example, policies at the state or district level related to curricula, textbooks, and resources for science laboratories and technology have direct implications for the kind of instruction teachers can offer.

Recent policies that promote greater accountability and stricter standards may have particularly powerful implications for student engagement (Hanushek, 1997; National Research Council, 1996). In 2001, 17 states required students to pass a state-administered exit examination in order to graduate, and 7 more had committed to implementing graduation exams within the next several years. Four states required students to pass a statewide exam as a condition for grade promotion, and four more were in the process of implementing this policy. Other states (e.g., Alabama and Florida) used participation in extracurricular activities as an incentive for students to maintain a specified grade point average (Education Week, 2002); 19 states take students' driving privilege away or refuse to grant a license based on failure to attend school or poor academic performance (Martinez and Bray, 2002). Similar policies have been implemented by a number of school districts, including New York City, Chicago, Philadelphia, and Boston.

Studies have not examined the effects of high-stakes testing for promotion or graduation on student motivation and engagement, and research assessing the effects on achievement is mixed (Bishop, 2002; Frederickson, 1994; Jacob, 2001). The evidence is clear, however, that they increase the likelihood of retention (Jacob, 2001; McDill, Natriello, and Pallas, 1986; Roderick and Engel, 2001). For example, during the 1999-2000 school year, more than half of all ninth graders entering Boston's comprehensive high schools could not read well enough to learn at the high school level. In an effort to rectify this problem, Boston Public Schools required, for the first time, that 9th graders pass a reading examination in order to be promoted to 10th grade. Although many students made sufficient progress during the school year to be promoted to 10th grade, more than one-third of the 1999-2000 freshmen had to repeat 9th grade the following year.

Accountability approaches that increase retention have a serious downside. The evidence is mixed on whether retention improves academic performance (Alexander, Entiwisle, and Dauber, 1994; McCoy and Reynolds, 1999; Pierson and Connell, 1992; Sheppard and Smith, 1989), and virtually all the empirical studies to date suggest that retention, even in the lower elementary grades, significantly increases the likelihood of dropping out (Balfanz, McPartland, and Shaw, 2002; Fine, 1991; Goldschmidt and Wang, 1999; Grissom and Shepard, 1989; Jimerson, 1999; Kaufman and Bradby, 1992; Neild and Balfanz, 2001; Roderick, 1994; Roderick, Nagaoka, Bacon, and Easton, 2000; Rumberger, 1995; Rumberger and Larson, 1998). For example, Rumberger (1995) found that students who were retained in grades 1 to 8 were four times more likely to drop out between grades 8 and 10 than students who were not retained, even after controlling for socioeconomic status, eighth-grade school performance, and a host of background and school factors.

Emerging evidence suggests that exams required for entering and graduating from high school may also promote dropping out (Balfanz and Letgers, 2001; Haney, 2001; Lee, 2001; Mizell, 2002; New York City Board of Education, Division of Assessment and Accountability, 2001). In Chicago reports are beginning to document students dropping out at a younger age, as well as in higher numbers (Lee, 2001). These negative effects of high-stakes testing appear to be stronger for students of color (Balfanz and Legters, 2001; Haney, 2001).

In addition to their more direct effects on student engagement and motivation, school accountability and high-stakes testing can have indirect effects on students through their teachers. A study of school reform in a Texas school district (Berends, Chun et al., 2002) indicates that high-stakes testing can undermine the willingness and ability of teachers to engage students in meaningful learning. This occurs because teachers feel compelled to teach what is on the test, which often results in broad, superficial coverage. The multiple-choice format of typical tests promotes the teaching of isolated facts and skills rather than conceptual understanding and critical thinking. In an effort to raise test scores, some schools are imposing double period test preparation sessions and requiring teachers to "teach to the test." Although such practices may improve high-stakes testing results, their effects on student motivation are questionable at best.

Although systematic studies are not available on the effects of high-stakes testing on student motivation, the research on motivation described in this chapter provides clues about what we can expect. The key concepts are perceptions of competence and control. Most likely, high-stakes testing has little effect on the motivation of the highest achieving students who are confident they will achieve ambitious educational goals. High-stakes testing should increase the motivation of students who are just getting by, but know they could do better. The risk of being retained in grade or denied a high school diploma may lead them to exert more effort on schoolwork than they would otherwise (National Research Council, 1996; Roderick and Engel, 2001), but only if they believe they have the capacity to succeed.

These positive effects, however, may come at the expense of students performing at the lowest level. As Roderick and Engel (2001, p. 221) suggest, high-stakes testing may benefit some by "making sacrificial lambs of the most vulnerable." Many students, especially in urban schools in economically disadvantaged communities, have experienced years of failure in school, and their skills lag far behind even minimal standards. Simply asking them to achieve higher standards without providing them with the assistance and support they need is more likely to discourage than to motivate them. Research on motivation has shown clearly that people do not exert effort when they do not expect their efforts to lead to success. To the contrary, a perception that success is out of reach leads to helplessness and withdrawal.

Standards and high expectations are critical, but they must be genuinely achievable if they are to motivate student engagement. The committee's endorsement of challenging work and high standards does not imply endorsement of high-stakes testing. If it is implemented, however, it is essential that it is accompanied by a great deal of support and resources devoted to helping students achieve the standards. We base our conclusion primarily on achievement motivation research that does not involve high-stakes testing. But there is some evidence from research at the middle grades that high-stakes testing for promotion may lead to improved student achievement when it is combined with extra instructional resources for low-achieving students (Roderick and Engel, 2001). Raising standards without providing this kind of support will be counterproductive.

A WAYS TO GO

Research on factors that motivate students to be engaged in academic work is not definitive, but it provides a solid foundation that can be used to guide practice. Currently, the practices supported by research are least likely to be observed in schools serving the students who need them most. Many developmental studies have shown substantial declines in achievement motivation and engagement in learning as children progress through school (Jacobs et al., 2002; Stipek and MacIver, 1989). Steinberg, Brown, and Dornbusch (1996) also found a decline from 7th to 9th grade in the number of students who claimed to feel a part of their school or close to people at their school. Perhaps not coincidentally, studies comparing educational practices at different levels suggest that the practices known to promote motivation are also less likely to be seen at the secondary than at the elementary level. For example, at the point that autonomy needs are most powerful—in adolescence—school environments usually become more controlling (Eccles and Midgley, 1989). Perhaps this is why all of the 56 Latino 9th graders that Yowell (1999) interviewed named an elementary school teacher when asked who their favorite teacher was. Furthermore, the schools serving adolescents who are at greatest risk of becoming seriously disengaged from school are the most likely to be large, impersonal, and highly controlling, and to convey low expectations for academic success.

Although examples of schools that promote high levels of engagement and achievement for low-income youth and students of color are few and far between, they are the proof we need to move forward with some confidence that progress can be made. The MetLife (2001) survey mentioned earlier, found that even among the low-income students in their sample, 89 percent claimed that the statement "I really want to learn" applied to them. In the 2002 survey, 84 percent of the students claimed that they worry about doing well in school (MetLife, 2002). The remaining chapters in this volume give further guidance for creating high schools that maintain students' desire to learn and to succeed by showing how the general principles of motivating contexts described here look in real schools.

3

Teaching and Learning

The nature and context of instruction are what matter most in engaging students in learning. Although policies at the school level and beyond affect what goes on in classrooms, classroom instruction—how and what teachers teach—is the proximal and most powerful factor in student engagement and learning. In this chapter we discuss what is known about engaging teaching, with special attention to the needs of students in economically disadvantaged urban settings.

Teaching at the high school level is challenging in part because students are expected to master discipline-specific knowledge that does not have obvious relevance to real-life settings. What does the reading of a John Donne poem or solving an algebraic equation have to do with adolescents' lives or even their anticipated roles as workers and parents in adulthood? The challenges are particularly daunting in low-income urban communities, where many students enter high school with low skill levels and limited English proficiency, and lack stable resources in the form of family income, housing, or health care. Any of these risk factors can increase the likelihood that students will be unmotivated to engage productively in the intellectual demands of the high school curriculum.

Research on teaching is vast, but concentrated on the elementary level. Consequently, although a fair amount is known about effective pedagogy for adolescents, the research base is meager compared to that which is focused on younger children. Concentrating on studies involving students in urban high schools limits the empirical base even further.

Despite the relative scarcity of studies on subject-matter teaching at the high school level, there is evidence that can be used to guide instructional planning (Alvermann and Moore, 1991). We discuss in this chapter what is known about effective teaching in literacy and mathematics, focusing especially on research involving urban low-income students and students of color. We selected these two subject areas because they are considered core and they are instrumental to learning other subject matter. In the final section of the chapter we discuss research on school organizational factors and conditions of teaching that best enable the kind of teaching that research suggests is most effective.

LITERACY

The teaching of reading, writing, and speaking at the high school level ideally takes place in every subject matter. Students are expected to read literature and write essays and creative pieces in English-language arts, and to read textbooks and occasionally primary source documents in history, social studies, and science. Although there tends to be little reading in mathematics, mathematical literacy is required to understand and evaluate public arguments (often in newspapers and magazines and on television programming) and forms of advertising where numerical data are used as evidence (Paulos, 1990, 1995). Many students come to high-poverty schools with poor proficiency in reading and writing, and few urban high schools are prepared to address the double challenge of meeting students' basic literacy needs while teaching them to tackle the complex reading and writing tasks of the disciplines (Finders, 1998-1999; Jimerson, Egeland, and Teo, 1999; Roderick and Camburn, 1999).

Gains have been made in mathematics achievement over the past decade, but not in reading. On the National Assessment of Educational Progress (NAEP), 17-year-olds today read no better than their counterparts a decade ago. Scholastic Aptitude Test (SAT) scores also have remained flat. Furthermore, huge gaps exist among different ethnic groups. African-American and Latino 17-year-olds taking the NAEP read about as well as and have vocabularies roughly equivalent to those of white 13-year-olds (NCES, 1999b; Phillips, Crouse, and Ralph, 1998). Reading problems are particularly pronounced in the high schools of large urban districts in low-income communities (Campbell et al., 2000; Dreeben and Gamoran, 1986; Education Trust, 1999; Guiton and Oakes, 1995). In the 35 largest central cities in the country, more than half of entering 9th-grade students read at the 6th-grade level or below (Grosso de León, 2002).

The poor progress in developing literacy skills may be explained in part by adolescents' low participation in literacy activities. Based on NAEP survey data, 25 percent of 17-year-olds currently report reading fewer than five pages per day for both schoolwork and homework (see Education Trust, 2001).

What Is Involved in Reading?[1]

Reading is a form of problem solving (Olshavsky, 1976-1977).[2] When good readers first encounter a text, they search for clues about topic, theme, or perspective. They search their long-term memory for models or explanations that can provide a filter for understanding the rest of the text. For example, if the reader sees the word "bat" in the title or first sentence, she searches her prior knowledge and reads on to find out whether this story will be about baseball or animals that fly.

An abundance of research in reading documents the powerful role that prior knowledge plays in reading comprehension. For example, if the title of a story has the word "sine," and the reader has no clue what a "sine" is, he will have difficulty making sense of the text. Readers need knowledge of topics, vocabulary, and the structure of words, sentences, paragraphs, and texts (e.g., stories versus expository texts). Stories may be structured as mysteries, science fiction, magical realism, or satire. The structure of expository texts may be extended definition, comparison-contrast, or problem-solution. Consideration of these kinds of prior knowledge that students bring from their lives inside and outside of school is crucial to teaching reading comprehension.

Readers must actively construct their understanding of texts from word to word within sentences, from sentence to sentence, from paragraph to paragraph, from section to section, and even across texts. Whereas a literary reading may emphasize searching for multiple, nuanced meanings of words, phrases, and whole texts, reading a scientific report does not involve such degrees of freedom. Knowledge in scientific writing may be communicated through words, mathematical formulas, graphs, or illustrations of patterns and cycles. Concepts are often communicated through technical vocabulary that has very specialized meaning in the particular scientific domain. For example, the word force may mean one thing in physics from the perspective of the Theory of Relativity and something qualitatively different from the perspective of Quantum Theory. Reading primary source documents in history requires the reader to question the potential biases of

---

[1]In order to address one area with some depth, we have elected to focus on reading, rather than on the challenges of teaching written composition or speaking.

[2]For thorough reviews of what research says about what is involved in the process of comprehending written texts, see the following: Kamil, Mosenthal, Pearson, and Barr (2000). For more succinct reviews of the research on reading comprehension, see the following: Fielding and Pearson (1994); Pearson and Dole (1987); Pressley (2000).

the author and to search across multiple texts to find other perspectives. The structure of sentences in both historical documents (such as the Declaration of Independence, the Narrative of Frederick Douglass, the essays of Francis Bacon) and older literary works can be difficult to parse because they are long and complex. Very different evidence is required to make cogent arguments in support of Darwin's theory of evolution in contrast to the claim that the character of Sethe in Toni Morrison's novel *Beloved* was justified in killing her baby to keep the baby from being taken back into the horrors of the African Holocaust of Enslavement. These are just a few examples to illustrate the complexity of the task of reading in the disciplines.

The extraordinary access to information in this new information age also has important implications for our definition of literacy and the skills that need to be taught. The World Wide Web makes information available, including technical information, that nonspecialists previously could not easily access. But the information available on the Web is often not accurate or objective. More than ever, students need to be taught to critically evaluate information, consider its source and possible biases, and compare and contrast claims from various sources. A literate citizen must now have a higher level of critical and analytic skills than was true even a decade ago.

These forms of critical evaluation, reasoning, and making sense of different kinds of texts in different subject matters should be the object of literacy study at the high school level. But most secondary teachers, regardless of subject matter, have little formal training in the teaching of reading, nor specifically in the problems of reading in the subject matters they teach (Anders, Hoffman, and Duffy, 2000). Literacy skills are not taught in part because many teachers believe that they are teachers of subject matter not teachers of reading (Anders et al., 2000; O'Brien, Stewart, and Moje, 1995; Romaine, McKenna, and Robinson, 1996), or they assume that students with poor reading skills cannot tackle difficult texts. Rather than provide instruction on how to develop the skills students need, teachers often give them watered down textbooks (Alvermann and Moore, 1991).

Literacy needs to be taught in urban high schools, both to ensure that students have access to subject matter instruction and to develop their literacy skills in various subject matters. By implementing existing knowledge of motivation and effective pedagogy, we can provide instruction that engages students and helps them achieve high levels of literacy (Oldfather and Dahl, 1995; Oldfather and McLaughlin, 1993; Oldfather and Thomas, 1998; Verhoeven and Snow, 2001). We summarize evidence on effective strategies for teaching reading, then illustrate these teaching principles by describing some exemplary programs.

Effective Pedagogy

Literacy Teaching and Student Engagement

Few empirical studies explicitly link particular approaches to literacy instruction with student engagement and even fewer studies include large samples of ethnically diverse, low-income high school students (Verhoeven and Snow, 2001). Consistent with the general principles of motivation discussed in Chapter 2, correlational studies reviewed by Guthrie and Wigfield (2000) indicate that students who believe they have some control over achievement outcomes and have a sense of competency are relatively more motivated to read. Furthermore, studies have shown that students who read outside of school become better readers (Anderson, Wilson, and Fielding, 1988; Fielding, 1994; Guthrie, Schafer, Wang, and Afflerbach, 1995). Most of the latter studies, however, have been with elementary-aged children.

In one of the few large-scale studies of adolescents, Cappella and Weinstein (2001) examined reading resilience, using a cohort of 1,362 students in the National Educational Longitudinal Study (NELS) of 1988. Resilience was operationally defined as turning around low reading achievement in the 8th grade by the 12th grade. They distinguished between distal risk factors (e.g., low socioeconomic status, single-parent household) and proximal risk factors (e.g., school environment, curriculum). By the 12th grade, only 15 percent of the students who had been at risk for continued low achievement in reading in the 8th grade had advanced to intermediate or advanced reading proficiency, so the resilient group was small. As has been found in the achievement motivation studies discussed in Chapter 2, students' beliefs predicted their resilience. Students who believed they had the power to affect outcomes were more likely to show significant improvement in their reading skills. In a similar vein, eighth-grade educational expectations predicted resilience 4 years later, in conjunction with taking rigorous academic courses.

In the next section, we will describe the features of literacy instruction that appear to promote learning. Although the studies reviewed do not assess engagement directly, it seems safe to assume that improved achievement involved increased engagement. The features discussed include forms of task structure, task complexity, grouping practices, evaluation techniques, motivational strategies, and quality of student-teacher and student-student relationships.

Features of Effective Pedagogies for Literacy

The instructional approaches supported by research on literacy learning are dramatically different from what is usually seen in low-performing urban high schools. The high school English-language arts curriculum usually involves disconnected lists of books and readings of the same authors (Alvermann and Moore, 1991; Applebee, 1993, 1996; Applebee and Purves, 1992), and teaching remains largely "frontal" lecturing (Applebee, Burroughs, and Stevens, 2000; Hillocks, 1999). Reading in the content areas tends to be limited to textbooks and is not characterized by strategy instruction (Alvermann and Moore, 1991; Bean, 2000). Although more innovative instructional practices and uses of technology are being implemented in many schools, they are less common in urban high schools serving low-income students and students of color (Irvine, 1990; McDermott, 1987; Pillar, 1992).

Based on the accumulated research findings regarding the teaching of reading comprehension (Education Trust, 1999; Moore, Bean, Birdyshaw, and Rycik, 1999; National Reading Panel, 2000; Pressley, 2000; Roehler and Duffy, 1991; Snow, 2002), we abstract the following features of successful pedagogy in literacy:

- Personalized relationships
- Authentic tasks
- Capitalizing on cultural knowledge
- Use of multiple resources
- Rigorous and challenging instruction
- Explicit instruction
- Frequent feedback from assessments
- Integrated curricula

We elaborate on each of these features.

As discussed in previous chapters, the term *personalized relationships* refers to the nature of relationships between and among adults and students. The nature of interpersonal relationships may be socialized through classroom structures such as small-group and whole-class instruction through the norms for who can talk and about what. In addition to facilitating social connections, researchers have found that providing students with opportunities to interact with each other, such as by debating important ideas and working in small groups, increased the amount of reading and thinking about texts in which students engaged (Alvermann and Hynd, 1989; Guthrie et al., 1995). The task of creating personalized relationships between adults and adolescents can be more complex in low-income urban schools, where many adolescents carry out adult-like roles (as parents, caregivers for siblings, financial support for families) while expected to fulfill more child-like roles at school, but may be more important for these students than for more affluent students (Burton, Allison, and Obeidallah, 1995).

Authentic tasks involve reading and writing activities that have some meaning in the world outside of school. Students who have been disengaged from academic work often do not see why the reading and writing they are asked to do in school matters—for their personal development, for their future adult roles, or for the communities in which they live. Authentic tasks that require the application of complex reasoning in real-world settings are more motivating and produce higher academic achievement (Lee, Smith, and Croninger, 1995). Ideally, authentic tasks also must be fundamentally linked to problems and modes of reasoning within the academic subject matter.

Studies also suggest the value of capitalizing on students' *cultural knowledge*. All knowledge is cultural. The question is whose cultural knowledge is privileged or made accessible in instruction (Moll and Greenberg, 1990). The lack of congruence between students' life experiences and instruction in most schools has been well documented, especially for low-income students, students of color, and English-language learners (Banks and Banks, 1993; Delpit, 1988; Gay, 1988; Hilliard, 1991-1992; Nieto, 1992; Philips, 1983). We also know that prior knowledge is crucial to all acts of learning and especially to reading. Students sometimes have difficulty understanding texts that are not related to their personal experiences and cultures because they lack the appropriate prior knowledge of the topic, or they do not know how to tap into relevant knowledge they do have.

Lee (1995a, 1995b, 2001) addresses this challenge in her work with low-income African-American high school students with histories of low achievement in reading. She designed a framework for culturally responsive curriculum and instruction related to literature, although the framework is applicable to other reading and problem solving in other subject matters. Lee's Cultural Modeling Framework for teaching literature identifies categories of problems in the high school literature curriculum that are considered generative. These include recognizing symbolism, irony, satire, using unreliable narrators, and using specific strategies for rejecting a literal interpretation and reconstructing a figurative interpretation (Rabinowitz, 1987; Smith and Hillocks, 1988). The approach involves using students' cultural knowledge to learn technical literary concepts. For example, students learn figurative language by analyzing familiar literary forms, such as oral genres of African-American Vernacular English, rap lyrics, and film clips. Lee argues that speakers of African-American Vernacular English already have a tacit understanding of these language forms, but do not activate that knowledge in school-based contexts. Using culturally familiar material and a specially designed curriculum, Lee's intervention was successful in getting students with low standardized reading scores to tackle complex works of literature. The conventions for instructional talk in Cultural Modeling classrooms included the productive use of African-American Vernacular English discourse norms. Similar approaches to discipline-specific and culturally responsive pedagogies in literacy have been reported elsewhere (Ball, 1992, 1995b; Foster, 1987; Mahiri, 1998).

The value of allowing students to use *multiple resources* or sources of help to gain mastery was discussed recently by Gutiérrez, Baquedano-Lopez, and Tejada (1999) and is supported by an abundance of research on learning (see National Research Council, 1999). Such resources may include support from peers, from competencies in languages other than English, and from tools such as computers. Examples of drawing on multiple-language competencies include English-language learners using their knowledge of their first language to help them read and write in English, or using skills in African-American Vernacular English to interpret literary problems (Lee, 1993, 1997). Other resources may include access to multiple modalities (reading, writing, speaking, drawing, performing) for problem solving or to represent knowledge (Gardner, 1993).

The value of being able to use a native language is suggested by a study by Jimenez, Garcia, and Pearson (1996). They examined the reading strategies of a small sample of sixth- and seventh-grade bilingual students who were successful English readers. These successful bilingual readers demonstrated substantial knowledge about similarities and differences in the structure of English and Spanish. They actively used this knowledge, for example, in looking for Spanish cognates in English words to help infer word meanings. They also translated across languages as an aid in constructing meaning. Perhaps most importantly, these successful bilingual readers held a different conception of the purposes of reading than their less successful counterparts. Jimenez (2000) reports that successful readers saw reading as a process of making sense of text, and they believed they could draw on multiple-language competencies to do this. Less successful bilingual students saw reading as saying the words correctly in English.

Moll, Estrada, Diaz, and Lopes (1980) found that students demonstrated greater levels of participation in instructional talk as well as more complex thinking when the organization of classrooms encouraged students to draw on their competencies in both English and Spanish. Lucas, Henze, and Donato (1990) identified eight characteristics of high schools that are successful with language-minority students, all focusing on ways that the school systematically structures opportunities to help students use both languages as tools for their learning.

A key idea is that what a student can do with support is always greater than what he or she can do alone (Cole, 1996; Rogoff, 1990; Vygotsky, 1981). The goal is to provide students with as many sources of support as possible. In some cases, the task is simply to encourage students to identify and use the resources they have. Students who work through problems of

BOX 3-1
A Study Guide for Chapter 1 of *A Separate Peace*

1. Carefully study the following quotation which is found on p. 11, and then translate it into your own words: " . . . considered authority the necessary evil against which happiness was achieved by reaction, the backboard which returned all insults he threw at it."
2. List *five* authorities who impact your life in some way.
3. Reflect on situations in which you personally have reacted to authority. Write a paragraph in which you describe the authority, the situation, and your reaction.
4. Reread the quotation above and explain why Phineas felt this way.

SOURCE: Applebee et al. (2000, p. 420). Reprinted with permission.

academic reading and writing while drawing on multiple sources of support should also develop confidence in their ability to learn (Alvermann, Hinchman, Moore, Phelps, and Waff, 1998).

The *rigor and challenges of the literacy curriculum* (across subject matters, not just the English-language arts) refers to whether students are asked to learn new constructs from reading texts and writing about what they read (rather than simply to remember facts), whether they are asked to apply what they learn from reading and writing to novel tasks, and whether they are expected to make connections across bodies of readings. Box 3-1, taken from Applebee et al. (2000), provides an example of a rigorous assignment in English-language arts. The assignment illustrates a rigorous curriculum because:

- it focuses attention on a portion of text that is central to understanding the internal state of a character and by extension to examining the themes of the work as a whole.
- there are no simple right or wrong answers to the questions, but there are constraints on a warrantable response based on the text itself and the life experiences of the students.
- it asks students to make connections between their own life experiences and those of a key character in ways that help to explicate the themes of the work as a whole.
- it asks students to read, think critically, and communicate their reasoning in written form.

Explicit attention to strategies for problem solving is another feature of effective literacy pedagogies (National Reading Panel, 2000; Pearson and Dole, 1987; Pressley, 2000; Snow, 2002). Although there is an abundance of research on the effectiveness of explicit teaching of reading comprehension strategies in elementary school, much less attention is paid to this issue at the high school level.

Strategies for teaching both reading comprehension and composing need to be different at the high school level from what is effective at the elementary level. In addition to generic reading, high school students need to know discipline-specific strategies for asking questions, making and testing predictions, summarizing, drawing inferences, using prior knowledge, and self-monitoring (Beck, McKeown, and Gromoll, 1989; Dole, Duffy, Roehler, and Pearson, 1991; Lemke, 1998; Rabinowitz, 1987; Wineburg, 1991; Wineburg and Wilson, 1991). Examples of discipline-specific reading skills include understanding symbolism in literature, reliability in primary source documents in history, and argumentation in the sciences. In addition to generic reading, most students need explicit instruction to achieve such competencies, as well as to feel competent, which is a critical factor in engagement.

Providing explicit supports for students to engage in complex reasoning that involves reading, writing and speaking, comprehending and critiquing difficult texts, and producing sophisticated texts are more effective than scripted lessons or decontextualized drills. Scripts and drills are useful for memorizing, but not for the complex reasoning required of reading in the content areas (National Research Council, 1999). Strategies for teaching discipline-specific literacy skills, however, have not been well studied.

Finally, students need *frequent feedback* from assessments to be able to observe their progress and to self-correct. Feedback on progress toward mastery can contribute to students' sense of competence and control, and teachers need the feedback from assessments to plan instruction. Assessments at the most local level—schools and classrooms—generally give the most useful information because they are tailored to the curriculum and the skills of the students at hand. Classroom assessments have the power to be diagnostic and to provide students with immediate feedback on what they can do and what they need to learn. Assessments at the departmental or course level in high school provide opportunities for teachers to learn from their practice and to target larger issues of curriculum and instruction.

The instructional approaches that teachers use can be facilitated or constrained by the curriculum, which is often defined at the school or even the district level. Applebee and colleagues (2000) describe curricula in which the content (for example, texts selected for reading) is disconnected and unrelated, and the relationships across texts are not well defined (for example, survey literature or history courses organized solely by chronology).

BOX 3-2
An Integrated World Cultures Course

In the Perspectives unit, French [the teacher] provided students with a matrix with which to analyze myths, folktales, and proverbs. Throughout the year students returned to this method of analysis to compare myths and tales across cultures. . . . Studying Nigerian culture, French began with Nigerian creation myths, moving to Nigerian proverbs, folktales consisting of trickster tales, dilemma tales, and orphan tales. She then moved into folklore from another African country to contrast tales. Running concurrently with the proverbs and folktales were other genres that she emphasized: novels, short stories, poetry. Most importantly, the frameworks for analyzing the tales became a way for students to see patterns across the whole year's course. . . .
The multicultural texts they read reflected the cultures they studied as well as the multicultural composition of their own classroom.

SOURCE: Applebee et al. (2000, p. 411). Reprinted with permission.

The kinds of instructional strategies described in this chapter are most likely to be found in schools that implement what Applebee and colleagues call "*integrated curricula*," in which students continuously revisit the core questions of the discipline across lessons and units of instruction within a year as well as across years. (See Box 3-2 for an example.)

We turn now to four studies of literacy instruction at the middle and high school levels to illustrate the implementation of these features of effective literacy pedagogies. The studies were conducted in urban communities where students had very low skills when they entered high school. Three of the four examples examine whole-school approaches to literacy instruction across multiple sites; all four include schools in urban districts with ethnically diverse and low-income student populations. Each reflects some national effort, either through an intervention that is national in scope or through analysis by a national or regional research center. Furthermore, all four include a large sample size and provide empirical data regarding student outcomes in reading (at least) as well as process data regarding how each feature was enacted. The findings of these studies are also corroborated by many smaller studies of individual or small clusters of classrooms or teachers. Although an evaluation of these four programs is limited by possible selection biases (of students, staff, or both), the major finding across these studies is that the implementation of literacy pedagogies cannot be limited to specific instructional activities. Instead, they require a coherent adherence to a core set of principles.

Effective Literacy Programs

Literacy Instruction in High-Performing Schools in Low-Income Communities

Under the direction of Langer (2001), the Center for English Learning and Achievement (CELA) conducted a groundbreaking study of middle and high schools across the nation that "beat the odds" in terms of indicators of achievement in reading. A total of 24 schools were selected from Florida, New York, Texas, and California based on district-level high-stakes assessments. Fifty-eight percent of the schools had 45 to 84 percent of students who received free or reduced-price lunches. Over a 2-year period, CELA researchers studied 44 teachers working in 25 schools involving 2,640 students, with 528 students as student informants. They observed classrooms, shadowed and interviewed teachers across their various professional activities in the school, interviewed case study students, and analyzed classroom and school-level documents.

Based on classroom and school-level data, teachers were placed into one of three categories: (1) exemplary teachers in high-achieving schools; (2) exemplary teachers in schools that were typical for their districts; and (3) typical teachers in typically performing schools. Langer and her colleagues found common features in the instructional practices of exemplary teachers in both exemplary and typical schools that are similar to those we have described.

Successful teachers gave explicit instructions in reading and writing and they created opportunities for students to learn and practice skills in the context of authentic reading and writing tasks. In contrast, teachers in at least half of the typically performing schools taught skills in isolated lessons that were not connected to larger units of instruction.

High-achieving schools integrated test preparation into the routines of classroom instruction across the school year, rather than providing test preparation as an isolated activity apart from the curriculum. High-achieving teachers and schools tended to analyze the demands of high-stakes assessments and to structure units of instruction so that students had multiple opportunities over time to develop conceptual understanding and skills as well as test-taking competencies. They used their analyses of test performance and of student work to make adjustments in the curriculum.

Exemplary teachers created connections within and across lessons. They also created connections between school learning and students' experiences outside of school. By contrast, teachers with lower rates of achievement had disconnected and uncoordinated lessons; they focused on an initial level of mastery of a given skill and moved on to the next skill, without giving students an opportunity to integrate and apply skills and knowledge they had developed.

All of the exemplary teachers explicitly taught the skills and strategies students needed to comprehend and compose complex texts across genres. They developed rubrics that made explicit the criteria for evaluation of both the processes that students employed and the quality of the products that students produced. Explicit instruction in strategies, skills, and concepts helped students develop both procedural knowledge (how to do it) and meta-cognitive knowledge (how to monitor one's understanding and self-repair when comprehension breaks down). By contrast, 83 percent of typical teachers in lower achieving schools asked students to analyze text or create a composition without any instruction in how to accomplish these difficult tasks.

Successful teachers also helped students develop deep conceptual understanding. To promote this level of understanding, students were asked to apply concepts and strategies across multiple texts. Whole-class instruction was often used, but students were also encouraged to work together in groups to explore and evaluate problems from multiple perspectives. These peer interactions often involved rich discussions in which students initiated and elaborated on one another's ideas. Nystrand (Nystrand, 1997; Nystrand and Gamoran, 1997) found similarly that successful teachers engaged students in authentic discussions, with students asking questions that required conceptual analysis.

Although some of the instructional practices we have described were found in lower achieving schools, their presence was intermittent. This study shows that individual exemplary teachers can make a difference, even in schools that do not support schoolwide productive practices and professional development. For students who enter high school already significantly behind, however, sporadically excellent teachers are not sufficient to overcome their risks for continued underachievement.

Coalition Campus Schools Project

The second large-scale study involves the Coalition Campus Schools Project (CCSP), the collaboration between the New York City Board of Education and the Center for Collaborative Education. This study (Darling-Hammond, Ancess, and Ort, 2002) involved 11 small schools that replaced 2 large high schools in New York City. Curriculum in these small schools was structured on the model of New York alternative schools serving low-income students, which have achieved success far surpassing district-level averages (see Chapter 5, this volume).

The first cohort of six small schools began during the 1993-1994 school year. There is good objective evidence of their success in engaging students in learning. Although they enrolled larger percentages of low-income students and English-language learners than city averages, these high schools had higher graduation rates, higher attendance rates, and fewer rates of discipline problems than city school averages. In the area of reading achievement, based on both SAT and New York Regents exams, results were mixed for the first several years. However, by 1996-1997, 11th-grade general education students in three of the schools substantially outperformed similar schools on the New York State Regents exams in reading and writing. Consistent with other findings, these data collected by Darling-Hammond and colleagues support the proposition that changing school instructional cultures is difficult (all of the schools did not show strong positive effects) and takes time (it took several years for positive effects to show).

The instructional practices used in the Coalition schools correspond closely to what other lines of research, described earlier, have shown to be effective. Personalized relationships were achieved by reducing teaching loads for teachers and creating longer instructional blocks of time. Intellectual rigor was achieved by encouraging complex reasoning across subject matters. In all core subjects (with a possible exception of mathematics), this necessitated extended reading and writing of complex texts. For example, students read works across national and cultural boundaries by authors such as Isabel Allende, Bertolt Brecht, Henrik Ibsen, Gabriel Marquez, Toni Morrison, William Shakespeare, and Richard Wright. Students studied complex topics in the social studies and the sciences. Portfolios requiring in-depth study and evaluations of the quality of student understanding contributed to the level of intellectual rigor in these schools. Authentic tasks were evident across sites. Projects, portfolios, and internships outside of school involved reading, writing, and research. Structured opportunities to help students reflect on and evaluate their work in these authentic experiences were also characteristic across sites. Students were asked to identify problems, make plans, do field work, and write up their conclusions. For example, in one class project, students identified tree samples for Central Park rangers, who were understaffed. Explicit instruction in strategies was given and incorporated into evaluation procedures, which included detailed rubrics that made public the criteria by which students' works were judged. Students had access to multiple resources for learning through collaborative projects, internships outside the school, and seminars and assignments that involved reflections on what and how they were learning. Multiple supports also included tutoring before and after school that involved peers and adult mentors. Finally, a flexible and responsive assessment system required students to think deeply during complex, authentic tasks as well as to take more traditional tests. Students were encouraged to reflect on their learning and they were given feedback and supports to bolster areas of weakness. As was found for effective teachers in the CELA study, students were not given isolated lessons on test preparation, but rather assessment was integrated into the instructional routines across the school year.

Strategic Literacy Project

The third set of examples comes from the Strategic Literacy Project (SLP) with a home base at the West Ed Lab (Greenleaf, Schoenbach, Cziko, and Mueller, 2001; Schoenbach, Greenleaf, Cziko, and Hurwitz, 1999). The Strategic Literacy Project takes on the challenge of teaching reading at the middle and high school levels. The project attends to reading across subject matters, addressing the social dimensions of learning, the personal dimensions of students' identities as readers, the cognitive dimensions of reading strategies that characterize better readers, and a knowledge-building dimension that involves expanding repertoires in knowledge of topics, vocabulary, genres, and text structure that readers need as resources for constructing meaning while reading.

A study of 9th graders in a high school serving a substantial population of low-income students and students of color (including those in special education and English-language learners) showed significantly greater than a year's growth at the 9th-grade level. Rates of growth did not vary as a function of the teacher, or by the students' ethnicity or language background. This study involved a specially designed freshman course in academic literacy, preparing students for the demands of reading across content areas (Greenleaf et al., 2001).[3]

Descriptions of classroom interactions document how students were able to draw on multiple resources to support learning, rigorous authentic work, assessments that provided students with timely and useful feedback, personalized relationships among all participants, and explicit attention to modeling and scaffolding strategies. In relation to the motivational potential of this work, the researchers also surveyed students before and after the freshman course regarding their conceptions about reading as a process and about themselves as readers. Students reported doubling the number of books they read over the year. In the postsurvey, students described explicitly an array of strategies available to them to make sense of what they read.

---

[3]Although this reported rate of growth is laudable, it must be noted that in order for students who are significantly behind in reading to "catch up," they must achieve greater than a year's growth for a year of instruction. Although there is evidence of such rates of growth at the elementary school levels, there are few examples, especially of any large scale, of such rates of growth at the high school level. This may be due, in part, to the increased demands of subject matter reading required at the high school level.

School Achievement Structure

The School Achievement Structure (SAS) was founded by Dr. Barbara Sizemore as a model for whole-school reform based on her earlier work in low-income schools in the Pittsburgh Public Schools. The Ten Routines of SAS (Sizemore, 1995) are consistent with the pedagogical principles we have outlined. SAS is based on the Effective Schools Models (Edmonds, 1979; Sizemore, 1985) and emphasizes the reorganization of the whole-school climate. Consistent with the pedagogical principles described in this chapter, SAS emphasizes 5-week assessment routines that are aligned with standards to which schools are accountable. Schools identify concepts and strategies to be mastered and pace instruction so that skills are distributed across the school year. Students are grouped flexibly so that individual student needs are addressed. Data-driven decisions about reteaching, regrouping, and retesting are made by teachers across the school year. Designing literacy instruction to be culturally responsive to students' prior knowledge and experiences is also central to SAS routines.

SAS has worked since 1992 with a number of schools in Chicago placed on academic probation, including 14 high schools with long histories of very low achievement. Before the intervention began in 1993, SAS high schools had 17.2 percent of their students reading at or above national norms. The number increased in SAS high schools to 37.2 percent in 2000. Another indicator of the value of this model is the percentage of students scoring in the bottom quartile in reading comprehension: in 1994, 73 percent; in 2000, 38 percent. These figures are particularly important because SAS schools involve no selection biases in terms of staffing or students (Sizemore, 1995).

Although the research is not extensive, what is available provides persuasive evidence that it is possible to engage and increase the literacy skills of urban youth. Looking across studies, the evidence reveals considerable overlap in the instructional approaches that appear to have been most effective. We turn now to mathematics, where the research provides additional evidence for the value of similar strategies.

MATHEMATICS

Achievement in mathematics has serious consequences for life opportunities, earning potential, and the ability to participate fully in society. On a daily basis, people encounter information (e.g., election results, interest rates, unemployment trends, weather reports, medical risks) that they need to interpret. With the increasing use of technology in the workforce, people who cannot manipulate symbols and the language of computers will be at a significant disadvantage.

The evidence is clear that students in urban schools are not faring well in mathematics. In 2000, 40 percent of 12th graders in central cities scored "below basic" on the National Assessment of Educational Progress (National Center for Education Statistics, 2001a), compared to 32 percent in urban fringe (suburban) and large towns and 35 percent in rural and small towns. The picture is actually worse than these data suggest because the proportion of students who have dropped out by the 12th grade is much higher in urban than in suburban schools (see Chapter 1, this volume). The gap between students of color, who are disproportionately in urban schools serving low-income youth, and white students remains substantial. As was found for reading, in 1999 African-American and Latino 17-year-olds scored about the same on the NAEP math test as did white 13-year-olds (NCES, 1999b).

Gender differences on standardized tests in mathematics also have been found, but they are modest compared to the gender differences found in the beliefs that mediate engagement discussed in Chapter 2. Compared to males, on average females typically rate their math competencies lower (even though they often get higher grades), have lower expectations for success, and consider math less relevant to their future. Perhaps not coincidentally, females are less likely to persist in the mathematics curriculum or to aspire to mathematics or science-related careers (Eccles, 1984, 1994; Eccles et al., 1983; Eccles, Barber, and Jozefowicz, 1998). Because most studies that examine gender do not also look at race, we do not know whether the gender differences found apply to all ethnic groups.

Contributing to the relatively poor performance of urban high school students is their poor access to high-quality mathematics teachers. Many studies suggest the value of both a solid background in mathematics and teacher training for student learning (e.g., Darling-Hammond, 1996, 1999; Ferguson, 1991; Ferguson and Ladd, 1996; National Commission on Mathematics and Science Teaching for the 21st Century, 2000). A national survey found that in schools where 60 percent or more of the students served were eligible for free lunches, approximately one-third of the mathematics teachers and nearly 20 percent of the science teachers did not hold an undergraduate or graduate major or minor in their main teaching field (National Center for Education Statistics, 1999c). Oakes (1990) reports huge differences in the qualifications of teachers in schools serving nonwhite students compared to those serving white students. White students had a 69-percent chance of getting a math or science teacher with a college degree in the subject, whereas nonwhite students had only a 42 percent chance. White students had an 86-percent chance of having a teacher certified to teach math or science; the comparable figure for nonwhite students was 42 percent According to data gathered by the National Commission on Teaching and America's Future (1996), 40 percent of students in high-poverty schools (greater than 49 percent eligible for free lunch) had math teachers who had not even minored in mathematics.

Having a strong background in mathematics does not ensure effective teaching, but a deep knowledge of the subject matter is necessary for teachers to engage students in activities that go beyond rules and procedures (Ball, 1992; Ma, 1999). Not knowing mathematics can severely limit the repertoire of instructional strategies on which teachers can draw. The lack of a strong mathematics background, common among teachers in urban schools, may thus contribute to the frequent use of textbooks, worksheets, drills, and teaching that emphasizes disconnected rules as opposed to a web of interrelated concepts (National Research Council, 2001).

What Mathematics Involves

Most people think of mathematics as procedures that children need to develop fluency in applying. But much more is involved. Mathematics is the science of patterns, including mental or visual, static or dynamic, quantitative or qualitative, practical or recreational, real or imagined (Dehaene, 1997; Devlin, 2000). Balance in the architecture of buildings, the repeat nature of limb branching in trees, and even the dispersion of milk poured into a cup of coffee reflect mathematical properties. Doing mathematics requires being able to see similarities in features of problems that allow one to apply previously proven rules.

Educational researchers and mathematicians define mathematical proficiency as having five components: (1) *conceptual understanding* (comprehending mathematical concepts, operations, and relations); (2) *procedural fluency* (being able to carry out procedures flexibly, accurately, efficiently, and appropriately); (3) *strategic competence* (being able to formulate, represent, and solve mathematical problems); (4) *adaptive reasoning* (being able to think logically, reflect, explain, and justify); and (5) *productive disposition* (being inclined to see mathematics as sensible and useful, while also believing in diligence and one's own efficacy; National Research Council, 2000).

Consistent with this multidimensional definition of mathematics proficiency, the National Council of Teachers of Mathematics (NCTM, 2000), the leading professional organization for researchers and practitioners concerned with mathematics education, stipulates that students should understand mathematics from a number of perspectives and be able to communicate that knowledge in a number of ways. Consider, for example, the simple linear function: $y = 3x + 9$. Rather than expecting students to merely plug numbers into algebraic equations to get answers (the traditional two-column chart), students should be able to understand that the notation represents a relationship between two objects (X and Y). They should also be able to represent the equation in graphical and verbal forms and understand the relationship between these forms. Students should be able to describe in everyday words what the function looks like (e.g., a straight line increasing from left to right, like a ramp on a loading dock), what some of its properties are (e.g., linear), and how the graphical version relates to the symbols used to represent the function in the equation shown (e.g., noting that the slope is represented by the number 3 and the point at which it crosses the y-axis is when x equals 0, or where the ramp would enter the ground if it continued).

To gain a deeper understanding of concepts, students need to be able to move back and forth between different representations of data and ways of proving conjectures, not just completing exercises. For example, if students are never asked to relate the abstract symbols of math to something in their real world, they are deprived of the resources (e.g., real contexts, personal experiences) for problem solving. In this case, math remains a disconnected set of facts rather than an intricate web of concepts. Students should be expected to understand the following: What shifts the function upward and downward on the y-axis (as if the floor on which the ramp rests was raised or lowered)? What shifts the function left and right on the x-axis (as if the ramp could be pulled in one direction or another across the floor)? What increases or decreases the slope of the function (the angle of the incline of the ramp)? What other groups of functions share similar properties? Technology (e.g., graphing calculators) can make this learning more efficient by visually modeling changes in the function without students having to develop a separate table of values and then a graph for every trial set of points they decide to pursue. With the help of java applets, students have the ability to change two variables at the same time and watch how they affect the shape and other properties of the function.

Features of Effective Pedagogy

NCTM has grappled with the task of defining strategies for making mathematics instruction engaging to students. The framework NCTM (2000) developed on the basis of research in mathematics learning provides us with a vision for what mathematics instruction should look like:

> [Students] draw on knowledge from a wide variety of mathematical topics, sometimes approaching the same problem from different mathematical perspectives or representing the mathematics in different ways until they find methods that enable them to make progress. Teachers help students make, refine, and explore conjectures on the basis of evidence and use a variety of reasoning and proof techniques to confirm or disprove those conjectures. . . . Alone or in groups and with access to technology, [students] work productively and reflectively, with the skilled guidance of

> their teachers. Orally and in writing, students communicate their ideas and results effectively. (p. 3)

This vision of school mathematics differs considerably from what many of us experienced (and were uninspired by) as high school students, when we learned equations and rules that the teacher wrote on the chalkboard, and practiced their application on sets of similarly formatted problems. Traditional math instruction has not typically engaged students actively in mathematical thinking and problem solving. The active grappling with math ideas described in the NCTM standards, in contrast, is consistent with what motivation researchers have found to engage students (see Chapter 2, this volume).

Although educators and researchers continue to debate the best approaches to teaching (e.g., "direct instruction" versus "inquiry oriented," "teacher centered" versus "student centered," "traditional" versus "reform"), quality mathematics education is more complex than can be captured in simple dichotomies. For example, effective teachers are student centered in the sense that they build on student's understanding, engage them in active problem solving, and connect math learning to their experience outside of school. They are also directive in the sense that they determine the mathematical concepts to be learned, select most (although not all) of the problems students work on, guide students' thinking, assess their knowledge, and create opportunities for them to practice their understandings and to develop fluency.

Notwithstanding some dispute about the value of particular practices, there is a fairly good body of research supporting some practices over others, to which we now turn. Because engagement, as it is defined in Chapter 2, is usually not measured in studies of math teaching, we focus on three indirect indicators of student engagement: (1) participation in the school mathematics sequence (taking a relatively large number of mathematics courses—usually more than three—during high school); (2) participation in advanced levels of school mathematics (e.g., trigonometry, precalculus, discrete/finite mathematics, statistics, calculus); and (3) mathematics achievement on standardized tests. The three indicators are interrelated. For example, both the number of courses taken in high school mathematics and participation in advanced levels of mathematics are associated with higher achievement scores (Lee, Croninger, and Smith, 1997; National Center for Education Statistics, 2001a; Rock and Pollack, 1995).

Caution is called for in interpreting the effects of instruction on standardized achievement tests because the tests often do not match the school curriculum (Stake, 1995; Zevenbergen, 2000). For example, mathematics teaching that emphasizes understanding over memorizing does not always produce increased scores on tests of basic skills, but does appear to increase scores on tests that also emphasize mathematical concepts (Carpenter, Fennema, and Franke, 1996). Indeed, standardized tests in mathematics rarely match the forms of instruction most researchers find to be effective. For example, most students are not tested on problem solving or reasoning, but rather on their ability to identify the appropriate rule and apply it to achieve a correct answer. Few tests include open-ended questions, instead relying on multiple-choice answers that reinforce students' belief that getting the correct answer is more important than the strategy behind solutions.

The tests used also can underestimate some students' competencies. When Boaler (2002b) altered the content on a mathematics test to eliminate confusing contexts and language for word problems, low-income Latino students were able to demonstrate significantly higher levels of mathematics understanding than their standardized test scores suggested.

Looking across studies, we see support for the features of engaging and effective practices in mathematics that are listed below. The features found to be effective in research on teaching mathematics are remarkably similar to the features of engaging literacy instruction, although they are chunked into slightly different categories. As was true for literacy, it is difficult to identify in studies the specific practices that enhance engagement. More likely, sets of practices work synergistically either to promote or undermine student engagement and learning. The features of effective instruction are as follows:

- Personally relevant
- Access to native language
- Authentic, open-ended problems and involvement in mathematical discussions
- Peer collaboration
- Rigorous and challenging instruction with frequent assessment and feedback
- Access to technology

The value of making mathematics *personally relevant* is suggested by a study of nine high school mathematics departments (Gutiérrez, 2000b). In schools where students showed significant gains in mathematics achievement between grades 9 and 12 and where they took more mathematics and higher levels of mathematics than their peers, teachers were more likely to report using activities that drew on the everyday knowledge and interests of their students (e.g., National Basketball Association standings, African-American voter registration in southern states, and ages of actors and actresses when nominated for Academy Awards) to provide a context for mathematical concepts and representations of data. Teachers in these effective settings were also more likely to offer students some choice in topics for projects or activities.

As has been found in research on literacy teaching at the high school level, studies have demonstrated the value of giving students *access to their native language* in mathematics courses. Mathematics is a language unto itself. Therefore, although everyone who learns math must negotiate the translations between everyday language and formal mathematics, students whose native language is not English encounter greater cognitive demands in making sense of mathematical terms. Although most of the research conducted is at the elementary level, there is good evidence that effective mathematics teachers of English-language learners show respect for their students' culture and language, and encourage students to draw on their native language to master mathematical concepts (Gutiérrez, 2002a; Moses and Cobb, 2001). Studies also suggest the value of allowing students to work and collaborate with each other in their native language, and providing materials for them in their primary language (Khisty and Viego, 1999; Silver, Smith, and Nelson, 1995).

Explaining or teaching something to someone else consolidates and deepens the understanding of the subject matter by the person in the teaching role. This is one of the reasons why experts in mathematics instruction recommend that students be given *authentic open-ended problems* and opportunities to be involved in mathematical discussions, such as by asking them to discuss and justify the strategies they use to solve problems. In one national study, 12th-grade students who reported talking with others about how to solve mathematics problems at least weekly scored higher than those students who reported talking with other students monthly or never[4] (National Center for Education Statistics, 2001a). Moreover, in both national (e.g., Moses and Cobb, 2001; Silver et al., 1995; Somerton, Smith, Finnell, and Fuller, 1994) and small-scale studies (e.g., Gutiérrez, 2002b), students who were active in mathematical discussions tended to persist in the mathematics sequence or score higher on mathematical exams.

Boaler (2002b) compared the instruction in British classrooms in which students were highly engaged and claimed to be enthusiastic about math to classrooms in which students claimed to be mostly bored and didn't particularly like math. One of the most prominent differences between the engaging and boring classrooms was the nature of the problems students were asked to solve. In the engaging classroom students were given open-ended problems that had multiple solutions or strategies and that allowed students to take initiative and be creative. (See Box 3-3 for an example.)

[4]This trend was true in both 1996 and 2000; however, only in 1996 was this difference shown statistically.

BOX 3-3
Example of Open-Ended Math Problem

Teacher What does it mean to divide 1 by 2/3? I don't want to know the rule, I want to know how to make sense of the problem.

Student I think it's 6.

Teacher And you think it's 6 because . . . ?

Student Because $^1/_3$ goes into 1 three times and then 2 × 3 is 6.

Teacher All right. Other thoughts about this? Claire?

Claire Um, I got $1^1/_2$ because I made the 3 in the numerator and the 2 the denominator.

Teacher You used the reciprocal of $^2/_3$. Why?

Student Because that's what we did on the other one.

Teacher So right now we have two different answers. We have the answer of 6 and Leslie's saying it's because there's 3 in 1 and 2 × 3 is 6. And then we have the other theory that the answer is $1^1/_2$, but we don't know why except it's a rule. Does Leslie's answer make sense? I don't want the rule, I want to know why it makes sense. I want every group to come up with what makes sense and some reason why. Put those heads together.

Students talk in groups of 3-5 students; teacher walks around room having individual conversations

Teacher On this side of the room that I talked to, about half of the people think it was 6, and about half thought it was $1^1/_2$. Sam is willing to make an argument for $1^1/_2$. Sam, would you go to the board and draw your picture?

Sam *(draws a circle divided into three parts)* Well, if you have this one whole, let's pretend these two parts are shaded and that's $^2/_3$, right? Now you still have the $^1/_3$, and $^1/_3$ is half of $^2/_3$, so you just add $^1/_2$ to the 1. And that's what I was thinking.

Teacher Now remember the day we talked about convince yourself, convince a friend, and convince a skeptic? Anyone want to challenge Sam or push on his thinking a little.

Students had to use what they knew about mathematics in novel contexts, often deriving the rule from their own efforts rather than being told the rule before they began the problem. Students in the boring classrooms worked primarily from textbooks, learning rules and procedures to use on sets of similar problems. When students encountered difficult or multidimensional problems, teachers often broke them down into small pieces that could be solved by applying a learned procedure.

A related teaching strategy that appears to promote engagement in mathematics is *peer collaboration*. Treisman (1990) found that when African-American and Latino students were taught to work with others to complete homework assignments or to study (a strategy that was spontaneously adopted consistently by Asian students), they scored better on course exams and standardized tests. Similar success was seen by a college professor who used group work to teach mathematics to African-American college students. The opportunity appeared to promote interest in more mathematics coursework and mathematics-related careers (Anderson, 1990).

To be sure, merely "talking" with classmates does not ensure mathematical engagement or learning. The emphasis on reasoning (about particular strategies for solving problems) and developing justifications for arguments seems to be most fruitful (Boaler, 2002b). Moreover, some students (e.g., English-language learners) may be less inclined to participate in a discussion-oriented format than in traditional paper-pencil tasks (DeAvila, 1988; Moschkovich, 1999; Secada, 1996). Students who are not confident in their abilities may also have difficulty with such formats, especially in a competitive classroom context. Murrell (1999) studied 12 urban middle school students and found that open-ended, discussion-oriented classes did not increase African-American male students' understanding of mathematical concepts. These students participated in the conversation, but they shied away from substantial engagement with mathematics for fear of making mistakes. This pattern aligns with other studies of African-American students who, when put in the spotlight, may perceive a threat of fulfilling a stereotype (e.g., that African Americans are intellectually inferior to other groups) and show reduced performance on measures of achievement (Steele, 1999). Opportunities to talk about mathematical problems with others appears to benefit students only when the teacher skillfully focuses the discourse squarely on mathematics, establishing norms that uncertainty is good and is a prerequisite for complex reasoning (see Boaler, 2002b).

Students are more engaged in mathematics when they receive *challenging, rigorous instruction* (Gutiérrez, 1996; Lee and Smith, 1995). Researchers have attributed the relatively high standardized test scores among students in Catholic schools, controlling as best as possible for potential confounds, to the college preparatory courses all students take (Bryk et al., 1993; Lee et al., 1993). In contrast, the mathematics curriculum in most public urban high schools is composed substantially of lower track and lower level mathematics courses (e.g., business math, consumer math, math explorations, prealgebra), with students having little access to calculus, which is an important gate to college majors in mathematics and science (Mullis, Jenkins, and Johnson, 1994; Oakes, 1990). Further evidence that students in urban schools often get less than rigorous instruction comes from a study of urban schools in California and New York conducted by Gamoran, Porter, Smithson, and White (1997). They describe low-track courses in which "instruction is weak and growth is shallow"—courses that serve as a "dead end for students' mathematical careers" (p. 333).

Frequent assessment of student understanding is a critical accompaniment to rigorous instruction. Black and Wiliam (1998) reviewed 250 research studies and concluded that student learning (especially that of low achievers) is promoted by teachers who focus on formative assessment when making judgments about teaching and learning. Although formal paper-and-pencil assessments are useful strategies for gauging student learning, they provide limited information. Because students exhibit what they know differently under different conditions, teachers also need to gather information about their students (both procedural skills and conceptual understanding) frequently and using varied techniques, such as observations, conversations, interactive journals, and careful examination of student work—making sure not to confound judgments about students' mathematical knowledge with their language skills or writing ability. This kind of information gathered and considered collectively by teachers can help them make critical decisions about when to review material, when to move on, how to revisit a difficult concept, and how to adapt tasks for struggling students or enrich tasks for students who have mastered the material.

Finally, evidence suggests that urban youth may be more engaged in mathematics when their teachers employ *technology* to help convey concepts (Dildine, 2000; Gutiérrez, 1996; Moses and Cobb, 2001). For example, in a study of nine U.S. high schools by Gutiérrez (1996, 2000b), graphing calculators and computers were used on a regular basis in the schools in which students actively participated in the mathematics curriculum, took more advanced mathematics courses such as precalculus and calculus, and scored better than predicted on standardized tests. Specifically, students used algebra and geometry software and graphing calculators to collect and represent data in different forms. In one analysis of NAEP data, 12th-grade students who reported using graphing calculators regularly scored higher on standardized tests than those students who reported using them less frequently (National Center for Education Statistics, 2001a). The direction of causality cannot be determined from existing studies, but they suggest the value of further investigation.

Consideration also must be given to *how* technology is used. Research on motivation suggests that using technology to simulate or to apply mathematics concepts to real-world problems is likely to engage students' interest. But studies of the use of technology suggest that this is not how technology is typically used in urban schools. A recent report indicated that although approximately the same proportion of white students reported using computers primarily for simulations and applications (31 percent) as for drills and practice (30 percent), far more African-American students used computers primarily for drills and practice (52 percent, compared to 14 percent for simulations and applications; Wenglinsky, 1998). The difference was also strong when comparisons were based on student poverty.

Students in Title 1 schools were much less likely to use computers primarily for simulations and applications (13 percent) than students in schools that did not receive Title 1 funds (30 percent).

The practices described in this section can be implemented in any setting, but it is difficult, as we will explain later, for an individual teacher to use these ambitious approaches to teaching mathematics without a great deal of training and ongoing support. Professional development programs and support systems have been developed to meet this need. Next we provide examples of comprehensive programs that are based on the general principles of effective instruction that we have summarized and include support for teachers.

Effective Mathematics Programs

Using the three measures of student engagement in mathematics mentioned earlier, we highlight three programs designed specifically to engage low-income urban students in mathematics. All three of these programs promote practices that are consistent with the findings from the achievement motivation literature reviewed in Chapter 2. They are based on the belief that learning is maximized when it involves meaningful relationships with caring adults who have high expectations, where students work with others, where the focus is clearly on mathematics, and where connections are made to adolescents' knowledge and personal experiences.

The Algebra Project

In 1982 Robert Moses developed The Algebra Project to engage African-American inner-city and rural youth in mathematics (Checkley, 2001; Moses, Kamii, Swap, and Howard, 1989; Moses and Cobb, 2001). To date, more than 22 sites involve students in grades 7, 8, and 9 in 13 states, in cities such as Chicago, Milwaukee, Oakland, Atlanta, Indianapolis, San Francisco, and Los Angeles.

Some key features of the program are providing professional development to teachers so they can come to see themselves as learners (focusing on joint learning with students and other teachers); employing adults who have enough contact with adolescents inside and outside of school to develop meaningful relationships; abolishing ability grouping and getting students to work effectively in both individual and small-group learning situations; using curricular materials that focus on the way people create and use mathematics in the real world; and letting students experience a cultural event (e.g., riding the subway) that generates data to be used in exploring mathematical concepts.

A key premise of The Algebra Project is that learning must be tied to students' personal experiences. Therefore, students learn to translate everyday life experiences into the symbolic language of mathematics. Four key components of the curriculum that teachers follow are

1. Physical Events (e.g., students take a trip—a ride on a metropolitan transit system, a bus tour, or a walking tour of their community)
2. Pictorial Representation/Modeling (students are asked to draw pictures that visually model the event)
3. Intuitive Language/"People Talk" (students are asked to discuss and write about the physical event in their own language)
4. Structured Language/"Feature Talk" (students isolate features of the event—such as start, finish, direction, distance—on which they can build mathematics)

The Algebra Project takes seriously the NCTM claim that students need to be able to represent and communicate data in a variety of forms (algebraic/symbolic, graphical, verbal, tabular). Thus, when students are asked to represent the physical trip with a picture, it is similar to graphing. When they are asked to use "people talk," they are being asked for a verbal description of their graph. When they seek features of the event that can be translated into structured mathematics language, they are being encouraged to use mathematics as symbols.

Unfortunately this approach has not been rigorously evaluated. The evidence suggests, however, that the approach has some value. The first group of students who graduated from the project enrolled in high school in geometry and many have gone on to medical school and other graduate schools. In Arkansas, 7 out of the 11 cohorts of students that were followed showed at least a 10-point increase in mean scaled scores on the SAT-9 a year after being in the program. In all 12 Arkansas sites, there was a greater than 10 percent increase in the number of students scoring at or above proficiency on the state exam, whereas students at 8 out of the 9 control sites stayed at their previous levels or declined (West and Baumann, 2002).

MESA Program

A comprehensive outreach program, Mathematics Engineering Science Achievement (MESA), has been engaging Latino (primarily Mexican-American) and African-American students throughout California since 1970 (Somerton et al., 1994). The program is outside of the students' regular school curriculum, but nevertheless provides evidence of the value of particular approaches to engaging urban youth in mathematics. Students sign up for the program if they are enrolled in or willing to take algebra in 9th grade, and they continue to take rigorous mathematics courses throughout high school. Most students earn average grades when they start, but they have an interest in careers in science or engineering.

Currently, MESA helps prepare nearly 20,000 students of color each year for mathematics- and science-based careers. More recently expanded to include sites throughout the nation, MESA takes regular mathematics and science teachers and turns them into advisors who offer courses alongside the traditional mathematics/science curriculum offered by schools. In addition, 6-week summer enrichment programs and Saturday academies help students deepen their understanding and prepare for college courses in mathematics and science.

MESA is founded on the idea of partnering with parents, business professionals, and community members to provide additional role models and to mentor students. Using hands-on instruction (e.g., where students build models of mathematical structures and processes), adults and older students in the MESA program become resources for adolescents, helping them model and visualize mathematics and science in ways that build a solid foundation for college instruction. The MESA curriculum focuses on themes that cut across disciplines (e.g., probability, measurement, matter, environment), with the goal of preparing adolescents for a rapidly changing environment. Students are also given leadership roles to develop their skills in obtaining summer internships and jobs in the field. As an incentive, the program pays a small stipend to students who earn a 3.0 or greater grade point average while in high school.

MESA high school students are remarkably successful on traditional measures of achievement, including SAT scores and college attendance (Somerton et al., 1994), although it is not possible to ascertain to what degree these positive outcomes are a result of the program itself. There is clearly a selection bias in who enters the program, and research with an appropriate control group would provide much clearer evidence of the program effects. The achievement of the students in the program, however, is so remarkable that it is highly unlikely that participating students would have done as well without it. Although the program is designed as an adjunct to the regular high school, most components of the program could be implemented in the regular mathematics curriculum.

The QUASAR Project

The Quantitative Understanding: Amplifying Student Achievement and Reasoning (QUASAR) Project is designed for middle school students. Since the fall of 1989 the QUASAR Project has been implemented in six economically disadvantaged communities in California, Georgia, Massachusetts, Oregon, Pennsylvania, and Wisconsin (Doty, Mercer, and Henningsen, 1999; Silver et al., 1995).

Key components of the project are curriculum development and modification (e.g., developing activities for particular classes); staff development and ongoing teacher support (e.g., opportunities for teachers to continue to learn mathematics); classroom and school-based assessment design (e.g., focusing on students' thought processes, not just the answers they produce); and outreach to parents and the school district at large. With respect to pedagogy, a classroom emphasis is placed on building communities of learners (cooperative groups, supporting mathematical thinking and collaboration); learning to question and coming to understand others; building communities of linguistically diverse learners; and enhancing the relevance of school mathematics (building on students' experiences, relating mathematics to students' interests, and connecting mathematics to students' cultural heritage). To try to connect mathematics to cultural knowledge, for example, students in the QUASAR Project are encouraged to tell stories that model the mathematics they are learning (fitting the oral tradition of some cultural groups). In sites with a substantial African-American population, students have been asked to write essays on Egyptian numerals and the life of Benjamin Banneker. Mathematical discussions are promoted by asking students to debate mathematical assertions and use mathematical argumentation to support differing positions.

The evidence suggests that these strategies increase student engagement and learning. In schools across the nation, the QUASAR Project has seen significant gains in student engagement in classroom discussions and in standardized achievement scores (tests of basic skills as well as conceptual understanding; Silver and Lane, 1995).

As was found for literacy, a fair amount is known about the qualities of instruction that engage high school students, and evidence from a few programs suggests that these strategies might be applied effectively in urban schools. There is still much to learn, particularly about implementing programs at scale in urban high schools. But the existing evidence provides no support for the traditional textbook and worksheet instruction seen in most schools serving low-income students and students of color.

SPECIAL NEEDS OF URBAN YOUTH

Our conclusions about effective teaching in literacy and mathematics are based in part on studies conducted in urban high school settings, giving us some confidence in their applicability to the students of concern in this volume. There are, however, particular circumstances related to teaching in schools that serve economically disadvantaged students, which need to be considered in any effort to increase students' engagement in learning.

We have discussed the importance of connecting new knowledge in literacy and mathematics to students' own interests, experiences, and culture. In urban low-income communities, effective pedagogy also requires attention and sensitivity to the out-of-school challenges that many students face—including racism, homelessness, violence, and lack of sufficient resources to address mental and physical health problems. (See Chapter 7 for an extended discussion of this topic.)

At the core of The Algebra Project (Moses and Cobb, 2001) and Lee's Cultural Modeling (Lee, C.D., 2000) is the goal of attending wholistically to the developmental, cognitive, and emotional needs of students. These models address the complex agenda that Ladson-Billings (1997, 2001) articulates in her call for culturally responsive pedagogy. They require attention to the very real risks and challenges faced by urban adolescents. In the MESA program, for example, students are given opportunities to develop their skills in dealing with foreign and sometimes hostile environments (e.g., summer jobs in scientific laboratories where personnel are not accustomed to people of color).

In addition to helping students cope with the challenges they face in urban environments, teachers can empower students by helping them develop leadership roles to promote change (Spencer, 1991, 1995, 1999; Spencer, Cross, Harpalani, and Goss, in press; Spencer, Noll, Stoltzfus, and Harpalani, 2001). Ladson-Billings (1994) writes eloquently on the impor tance of encouraging activism and political awareness in any effort to engage low-income urban students in school.

What we are recommending expands the role of the teacher substantially, from someone who focuses just on subject matter to someone who focuses on students, including the larger context in which they live (Foster, 1994). This requires a commitment to addressing social injustices (Hilliard, 1991, 1995). Teachers' philosophy related to their role may be as important as their lessons or the curriculum (Bartolome, 1994; Beauboeuf-Lafontant, 1999; Gustein, Lipman, Hernandez, and de los Reyes, 1997; Ladson-Billings, 1995; Lee, 1994; Shujaa, 1994). There is some evidence that teachers who are philosophically committed to equity and racial justice are less likely to have low expectations and more willing to adjust their instruction to meet the needs of their students while maintaining academic rigor (Ball, 1995b, 2000a, 2000b; Lightfoot, 1973; Stodolsky and Grossman, 2000).

Although no studies have shown the independent effects of a social justice orientation, there is evidence that suggests its possible value. In an evaluation of his National Science Foundation-supported (Mathematics in Context) curriculum supplemented with units on social justice, Gutstein (in press) found that 18 of his 24 7th-grade Latino urban students passed city entrance exams for competitive magnet schools and all went on to take algebra in 9th grade. His students averaged a gain of 1 month's grade equivalent in mathematics for every month they spent in his class. Similar success of students persisting in the mathematics sequence or enjoying mathematics has been found by mathematics professors who hold a strong social justice stance (Anderson, 1990; Frankenstein, 1990, 1995).

Another challenge that is especially prominent in urban schools serving low-income youth is the low level of skills with which many students enter high school. Although there is good evidence that even students who are far behind when they begin high school can master the high school curriculum and achieve high standards, these students are the exception. The programs described in this chapter were all designed for students in schools serving predominantly low-income students and students of color, and they show promise of improving on traditional remedial methods. (See also Chapter 5.)

In summary, it is important to acknowledge that teaching in economically disadvantaged urban schools involves special challenges; it is equally important not to fall into a trap of low expectations, which often breed formulaic teaching and restricted conceptions of subject matter (Boaler, 2002b). There are far too few examples of urban high schools that hold their students to challenging standards and engage them in mastering difficult disciplinary concepts and strategies, but such schools exist, and provide the proof that schools can become such institutions. Complexity is no excuse for retreat.

SUPPORTING TEACHERS

Teachers in urban schools face students who are trying to cope with an array of challenges in their lives outside of school and struggling to learn the skills assumed by most high school curricula. These teachers also often face difficult working conditions—large class sizes, little preparation time, scarce resources, and now, pressure from high-stakes tests that are often not aligned with their instructional program and goals. Teachers also have to confront their own stereotypes related to race and social class. Given these conditions and challenges, it is not surprising that the kind of ambitious pedagogy described in this chapter has not taken root in most urban schools. This kind of teaching requires considerable skill and sustained support. Because of the sheer complexity of teaching and the special challenges of urban schools, the need for strong professional communities of teachers is critical. Indeed, building teacher capacity and providing teachers with ongoing, expert support may be the most critical factor in creating urban high schools that engage all students in learning.

The same motivation principles that apply to student engagement are relevant to teachers as well. For example, just as self-efficacy promotes engagement in students, Stodolsky and Grossman (2000) saw relationships between teacher' sense of efficacy and their willingness to adapt to the needs of their students. Ball (1995a, 2000a, 2000b) has developed an effective program to help groups of teachers grapple with their assumptions about diversity and about what it means to learn. Collaboration and group work are most likely necessary for teachers to develop both the commitment and the sense of efficacy to pursue rigorous standards in the often difficult circumstances of urban school teaching.

Many studies have shown the value of a culture of collaboration in fostering effective teaching practices (e.g., Coburn, 2001; Desimone, Porter, Garet, Yon, and Birman, 2002; Hiebert, Gallimore, and Stigler, 2002). For example, Louis, Marks, and Kruse (1996) found that teachers in schools that had a strong teaching professional community (defined by a shared sense of purpose, collaborative activity, collective focus on student learning, and reflective dialogue) engaged in higher quality teaching, and their students performed higher on NAEP mathematics and reading assessments when compared to teachers in schools with weak professional communities. (See also Louis and Marks, 1998.)

Some mathematics experts tout the value of "lesson study," a strategy used in Japan for teacher collaboration. Stigler and Hiebert (1999) suggest that mathematics achievement in the United States might be raised by giving teachers time and support to form teacher workgroups to plan, experiment with, analyze, and revise lessons. For example, teachers can videotape and analyze lessons they have planned together. The approach has been introduced in some U.S. elementary and middle schools, and might be adapted to be useful at the high school level as well.

In the area of literacy, there are many excellent examples of local professional communities of teachers working in urban districts. Perhaps the longest existing national model is the National Writing Project, which promotes collaboration among individual teachers across school sites. Organized, funded projects, such as QUASAR, The Algebra Project, and MESA, provide the practical training and social support required to implement effective and engaging mathematics teaching (Gutiérrez, 2000a). There are also many examples of strategies implemented at the city, district, school, and department levels to develop the kind of sustained, professional communities that support effective teaching.

Many studies point to the importance of the subject matter department in high school teachers' ability to teach and to adapt to the needs of their students (Gutiérrez, 1996; Lieberman and Miller, 2001; Little, 1993; McLaughlin, 1993; McLaughlin and Talbert, 1993, 2001; Siskin, 1994; Talbert and McLaughlin, 1994). Effective subject matter departments involve teachers in collective goal setting; in aligning curriculum, pedagogy, and assessment; in engaging particular students in certain content; and in finding ways of addressing students' overall needs. These collaborative efforts at the department level are associated with positive learning and achievement for students (Ancess, 2000; Freedman, Simons, Kalnin, Casareno, and the M-Class Teams, 1999; Greenleaf and Schoenbach, 1999; Lee, 2001).

Gutiérrez (1996, 1999, 2000b, 2002b) has studied successful urban high school mathematics departments and found that certain forms of structural organization and normative cultures (including beliefs) are associated with teachers' willingness and ability to engage diverse learners. She found that mathematics departments whose teachers did not view mathematics as a static subject, used a rigorous mathematics curriculum, discussed lesson plans and students, rotated course assignments, had a commitment to equity, and observed each other teaching tended to have students who were actively engaged in the mathematics curriculum and scored well on standardized tests. Although they do not report data on student outcomes, Stodolsky and Grossman (2000) likewise found in their survey of teachers in 16 U.S. high schools that mathematics and English teachers who experimented with the curriculum in order to engage diverse learners in the classroom tended to work in departments that were collaborative and focused on professional development (see also Coburn, 2001; McLaughlin and Talbert, 2001).

A strong sense of community at the department level may also diminish the alienation that teachers often experience in large, urban, bureaucratic schools. Talbert (1995) proposes that collaboration among teachers can serve as a catalyst for increasing a school's commitment to meeting the needs of students who otherwise have low priority (also see Wehlage et al., 1989). Talbert and McLaughlin (1994) found in their analysis of survey data—for 253 teachers in 36 academic departments in 8 public high schools—that teachers' participation in a collaborative, innovative professional community predicted their expectations for student achievement and their caring for students, controlling for their subject preparation and overall job satisfaction. Gutiérrez (1996, 1999, 2000b, 2002b) and Stodolsky and Grossman (2000) observed further that the teachers who engaged students best were in professional communities committed to equity. Thus, a teacher's workplace setting is critically important in supporting the kinds of practices that engage students in learning.

Practices in schools and the broader community are also important. For example, Valerie Lee (2000) found that high schools that had a communal focus (reformed instruction, shared authority, collective commitment to the personal development of students) produced considerable gains in student achievement and nearly eliminated social class differences between students. The school community is so critical to successful mathematics teaching that in choosing its sites, the QUASAR Project requires a school climate that supports teacher innovation.

Schools also have norms regarding what it means to teach and to learn, which can have powerful effects on instruction in classrooms and student engagement. Researchers have examined, for example, norms for instructional conversations: "the kinds of questions to be asked . . . , the concepts to be explored, the vocabulary through which these concepts were expressed, the relevance of personal knowledge and experience, and the nature of acceptable argument and evidence" (Applebee et al., 2000, pp. 413-414; see Cazden, 1988, 2001; Lee, C.D., 2000; Marshall, Smagorinsky, and Smith, 1995; Mehan, 1979; Nystrand and Gamoran, 1991, 1992; Tharp and Gallimore, 1988). These norms often vary for different tracks. Studies show that the students in lower track classes have significantly fewer opportunities to elaborate on ideas, to weigh evidence from multiple and sometimes conflicting points of view, or to generate propositions (McDermott, 1987; Nystrand and Gamoran, 1997; Oakes, 1985)—the kind of active participation in rigorous learning experiences that motivation researchers have found to be most engaging. As Rosa, a 9th-grade student from the Strategic Literacy Project (Greenleaf et al., 2001, p. 101), describes:

> Um, usually in like a regular history class, like the one I had last year? Which was just pretty much all writing? Okay, "read from page so-n-so to so-n-so, answer the red square questions and the unit questions and turn them in." And he corrects them and says, "You did this wrong, you did this right. Okay, here you go." And that was pretty much the basic way every single day has gone. So, from day one to the end of the year, that's pretty much all we did. Answer the red square questions. And pretty much it's been like that since I got to middle school. . . ."

Urban schools serving low-income students are capable of much more, as is illustrated in a real instructional dialogue that reflected disciplined norms for reasoning in response to literature (see Box 3-4).

As efforts are made to improve the support and circumstances teachers encounter in urban high schools, parallel efforts need to be made to recruit teachers with expertise in their subject matter. The best of circumstances will not overcome deficiencies in knowledge of subject matter, of how people learn, and of the developmental needs of adolescents. Realistically, the kind of teaching described in this chapter is not likely to be implemented on a large scale until teaching is made more attractive in terms of working conditions that support career-long professional development, especially in urban schools. Equally important are improvements in preservice teacher education that address preparation for the quality of teaching that this chapter has described. Teacher training is beyond the scope of this volume, but it is clearly a critical piece of any effort to improve teaching in urban high schools.

BOX 3-4
Class Discussion of *Beloved* by Toni Morrison

		Commentary
Victor	When it came out of the water, she sat in on the tree all day and night, resting her head on the trunk.	Student notices an important literary detail without prompting by the teacher.
Prof. Lee	Ooooh! Ahhhh! *(the class says in unison).* Wow!	The other students value the literary insights of Victor.
Michelle	What did he say?	
Janice	He put something under the tree.	
Victor	Beloved is a tree.	Victor has made a crucial and difficult inference, namely that the woman coming out of the water is the baby that Sethe had killed.
Prof. Lee	Victor *(students are all talking at the same time)*, hold up. Victor, please explain that. That's powerful.	The cross-talk is an indicator that the other students are engaged with Victor's provocative thesis.
Victor	Let me find it exactly. *(Victor opens his book and begins to find the page in the novel where he has found his evidence.)*	The classroom culture clearly values textual evidence to support claims as Victor opens his book to locate text to support his claim, without being asked by the teacher.
Victor	Let me find it exactly.	
Prof. Lee	All right, Victor. Tell us the page.	The teacher invites the class community to examine together Victor's evidence.

CONCLUSIONS

The findings from research on effective teaching of literacy and mathematics are strikingly similar. The evidence suggests that the instructional program must be challenging and focused on disciplinary knowledge and conceptual understanding. It needs to be relevant to and build on students' cultural backgrounds and personal experiences, and provide opportunities for students to engage in authentic tasks that have meaning in the world outside of school. Engaging instruction gives students multiple learning

Victor	*(reading from the novel)* ". . . walk down to the water, lean against the mulberry tree all day and night, all day and all night she sat there with her head rested on the trunk . . . *(inaudible)* enough to crack the brim in her straw hat."	Victor cites appropriate text to support his literary claim.
Prof. Lee	She's not only resting on a tree, but she seemed to be abandoned on this tree. Oooh, this is good. Now, so alright, David, a little bit louder so everybody can hear you. Charles Johnson, are you listening? David, a little louder.	Evidence of this as a learning community is that the teacher herself has gained new insights into this passage from Victor's claim. The teacher creates a classroom culture that presumes everyone is responsible for partici pating as evident when she asks Charles Johnson if he is listening.
David	This book is connected to trees like tree is Sweet Home, tree on her back, tree in her yard.	David extends and elaborates Victor's claim about the significance of the symbol of the tree. David makes intratextual links by noting the presence of the tree as a symbol across multiple sections of the novel.
Prof. Lee	Ahhhh!	
David	Tree on this. Tree on that. . . .	
Joe	Dr. Lee, can I just say something real fast?	

NOTE: This dialogue is taken from a class of high school seniors with histories of low reading scores.

SOURCE: From Lee, Cultural Modeling Project. See Lee (2001).

modalities to master material and represent their knowledge, and allows them to draw on their native language and other resources.

This kind of teaching is not possible if teachers do not have a deep understanding of their subject matter, of how people learn, and of how to address students' developmental needs. In addition, teachers need opportunities to collaborate with colleagues, and access to ongoing, expert guidance to advance their own knowledge and skills. Effective pedagogy also needs to be supported by a coherent school curriculum and school norms that support student inquiry and active involvement in their learning, interest in students as individuals, and respect for their cultural backgrounds.

Our intent is not to argue that simply providing "good" pedagogy is sufficient. Our point is that "good" pedagogy is engaging and motivating. We do not assume that if you offer rigor students will come. We are confident, however, that if schools offer rigor and explicit supports for learning that are responsive to the developmental needs and cultural backgrounds of students, the majority of students will enter the academic game.

4

Climate, Organization, Composition, and Size of Schools

Moving from the classroom to the school, in this chapter we summarize the conclusions of various domains of research on how school climate, organization, composition, and size are related to student engagement in learning. The social and economic circumstances of students' families and neighborhoods greatly influence student engagement, and as mentioned earlier, schools cannot "do it all." But the evidence is clear that schools can make a significant difference, and that their effects on students' engagement, learning, and future opportunities depend substantially on how they structure the learning environment, and on the values they communicate to students and their families.

We chose to examine school climate, organization, composition, and size in part because there was, for each, a fairly substantial research base suggesting effects on student engagement or learning, and because all are amenable to change. As in other chapters, we cast a broad net for evidence and did not limit ourselves to studies that measured student engagement directly. The inclusion of studies that focused on student achievement as the outcome is based on the assumption that gains in achievement imply increased engagement.

SCHOOL CLIMATE

Conceptualizing School Climate

School climate refers to the values, norms, beliefs, and sentiments associated with routine practices and social interaction in schools. Theorists and researchers have used a wide variety of terms to refer to aspects of school climate—including atmosphere, culture, environment, morale, school community, and school ethos. Accompanying divergent conceptualizations are different measurement instruments (cf. Gottfredson, Hybl, Gottfredson, and Castandeda, 1986). Although the design of the qualitative and correlational studies reviewed in this chapter limit the degree to which causal conclusions can be drawn, the evidence is consistent enough to give substantial confidence in a conclusion that qualities and factors related to school climate can affect student engagement and learning. Research-based judgments about desirable practices, however, require a careful examination of the specific definition and measurement of school climate in studies.

Investigations of school climate date back as far as Willard Waller's (1932) classic treatise on the sociology of the school, which he conceived as a miniature society as well as a formal organization. Following in Waller's footsteps, Hollingshead's (1949) case study of a small, midwestern community and its school system, and Gordon's (1957) account of "Wabash High" several years later portrayed the social system and organizational culture of single high schools.

James Coleman's study of the "value climates" of ten midwestern high schools in the late 1950s, summarized in *The Adolescent Society* (Coleman, 1961), claimed to document the pervasive influence of the adolescent subculture on students' academic values, performance, and social activities. In this provocative book, Coleman concluded that in the typical high school, the adolescent social system channels the energies of students into nonacademic directions, and that the system provides a set of social rewards and punishments that supports athletics and other social activities and discourages intellectual pursuits. Coleman's study prompted a wealth of commentaries, subsequent empirical studies, and debate on the antecedents, nature, and consequences of the "adolescent society" in contemporary America (Boocock, 1966, 1972; McDill and Rigsby, 1973).

In 1979, Michael Rutter and colleagues published a study of 12 nonselective, inner-city, secondary schools in London, which established the notion of "ethos" as an important quality of schools (Rutter et al., 1979; see also Grant, 1988, and John Dewey, 1900, who referred to the school as a small society). A school's ethos concerns the coalescence among practices, beliefs, values, and norms, as Driscoll (1995, p. 217) explains:

> The concept of school ethos . . . is far more than an aggregate collection of individual variables. Rutter et al. recognized that it is the interaction of social processes and not merely their sum that explains the variance in the performance outcomes measured . . . the "ethos" of an effective school is in large measure a reflection of general, schoolwide expectations of consistent values and norms that permeate the institution. The ethos of an effective school is characterized by generally shared high expectations of

> teachers and respect for them; positive models of administrators and other teachers for teacher behavior that reflects concern for one another; and some system of feedback through which teachers can evaluate their work.

Rutter's study was in part a reaction to an earlier highly publicized study conducted by Coleman and colleagues (Coleman et al., 1966), which concluded that nonschool variables, especially the racial background and economic circumstances of students, accounted for the vast majority of differences in educational outcomes among schools, not differences among schools themselves. Rutter criticized Coleman's survey methods and his focus on tangible resources, arguing that the study had underestimated the magnitude of school effects because it had not considered the social climate and organization.

With the 1980s came the concept of "the school as a community." Implicit in both the ethos and "communitarian" conceptualizations is an assumed synergism in the operation of the school—the notion that the whole of a good school is more than the sum of its parts. New concepts like community, democracy, and "an ethic of caring" (Noddings, 1988) emerged, based on the assumption that students' attachment to school and their academic achievement are contingent on first satisfying teachers' and students' social and personal needs (Phillips, 1997).

Descriptions of communal or communitarian schools are strikingly similar to descriptions of out-of-school environments that appear to support healthy adolescent development (e.g., McLaughlin, 2000; National Research Council and Institute of Medicine, 2002). According to a recent review of evidence related to out-of-school environments (National Research Council and Institute of Medicine, 2002, pp. 90-91), students are most engaged when the social context promotes physical safety; provides some structure and opportunities for youth to develop new skills in the context of warm, supportive relationships; and promotes positive social norms.

A relative newcomer to conceptualizations of school climate is the notion of "academic press." In a series of publications, Shouse (1996a, 1996b, 1997) and Phillips (1997) address an ongoing debate related to what appeared to be competing visions for increasing student engagement and learning—a communitarian climate, as already described, versus a climate characterized by academic press, defined succinctly by Shouse (1996a, p. 175) as "the degree of normative emphasis placed on academic excellence by members of the organization" (see also McDill et al., 1986). The notion of academic press is related to what has been referred to in the literature as high expectations for success, and which has been shown to predict relatively high achievement (e.g., Evans, 1997; Hoy and Sabo, 1998; Marks, Secada, and Doane, 1996; Newmann, 1992).

The evidence we will review suggests that these two conceptualizations of school climate are not, in fact, incompatible.

Effect of School Climate on Engagement and Learning

Building on previous research on private and public high schools (Coleman, Hoffer, and Kilgore, 1982), which had been highly criticized for not addressing problems of selection bias, Coleman and Hoffer (1987) studied school communities in private and public schools using the second wave of data from the High School and Beyond Longitudinal Study (National Center for Education Statistics, 1982). They reported Catholic high schools as having higher average achievement than public schools, lower dropout rates, and greater success in placing their graduates in some type of post-secondary institution. Although selection bias could not be ruled out altogether, they controlled for the variables most likely associated with selection bias, and attributed the better outcomes in Catholic schools in part to a strong, positive, disciplinary climate and conforming student behavior.

Also using data from the High School and Beyond Longitudinal Study (National Center for Education Statistics, 1982), Bryk and Driscoll's (1988) subsequent study examined in greater detail the elements of a communally organized school, and demonstrated the importance of the school community to the quality of both public schools and Catholic schools. In contrast to much of the earlier literature, it provided quantitative evidence on the effects of school community and has served as the prototype for many of the more recent efforts to demonstrate the importance of school climate for adolescents' school attachment, engagement, and achievement. The authors posited three crucial components of communally organized schools: (1) a shared value system that pervades the school and derives from a shared history; (2) a common agenda for school members involving coursework, activities, rituals, and traditions that function as a unifying factor; and (3) an ethic of caring that permeates relationships among students and staff and between staff and students. Bryk and Driscoll's most important finding was that communally organized schools (schools with these three sets of qualities), whether public or private, had better attendance, higher morale, and better mathematics achievement.

Using data from the National Education Longitudinal Study of 1988 (NELS 88), Lee with Smith (2001) examined whether reforms promoting communally organized schools were associated with indicators of student engagement and achievement. The NELS 88 database includes information on 800 high schools and a nationally representative sample of 25,000 students. These students were first studied when they were in eighth grade in 1988. Follow-up data were collected for the cohort in 10th grade and

12th grade.[1] Additional data from the students' teachers and on the characteristics of their high schools also were collected and used in this study.

Using hierarchical linear modeling in part to control for possible confounds, the research design compared traditional "bureaucratically" organized schools with communally organized schools. According to Lee with Smith (2001, p. 103):

The bureaucratic structure of most high schools relies on affectively neutral social relationships to facilitate the administration of standardized rules and procedures. Strong personal ties among adults, or between adults and students, make it more difficult for staff to comply with standard practices and procedures.

Communal schools, in contrast, were structured to facilitate the creation of emotional bonds between teachers and students and also among teachers. Lee with Smith (2001, p. 104) describes the characteristics of communally organized schools as follows:

> Rather than formal and affectively neutral relationships, members of communally organized schools share a common mission. Staff and students interact outside the classroom; adults see themselves as responsible for students' total development, not just for the transmission of lessons. Teachers share responsibility for students' academic success, often exchanging information and coordinating efforts between classrooms and across grades.

Analyses revealed that communal schools had better outcomes than bureaucratic schools for both teachers (satisfaction, morale, absenteeism) and students (less class cutting, less absenteeism, lower dropout rates; see also Marks, 2000). Lee also found that disparities in these outcomes associated with ethnicity and class were smaller in communally structured schools than in others. Additional studies suggest that supportive and caring schools may be especially beneficial for disadvantaged students (Battistich et al., 1995; Battistich et al., 1997; Bryk and Driscoll 1988; Bryk et al., 1993).

Lee with Smith (2001) examined alternative explanations of the advantages she observed of communally structured schools, such as differences in the curriculum and instruction. The most potent predictor of student outcome differences was teachers' collective responsibility for learning (see also Lee, Dedrick, and Smith, 1991). This factor reflects teachers' views on their students' abilities and willingness to learn, their sense of responsibility for the learning of their students, whether teachers believe they can "get

---

[1]25 percent of the 8th grade student participants in the study were not surveyed 4 years later when their cohort reached 12th grade because they either had been retained in grade or had dropped out of school.

through" to even the most difficult students, whether teachers assess their own effectiveness, and whether they change how they teach depending on whether their students are learning. In schools where teachers assumed collective responsibility for their students' learning, students learned more, and differences associated with race and class were less prominent. Schools that had developed practices associated with the communal model were relatively high on the measure of teachers' collective responsibility for learning, but the causal order between school restructuring and collective responsibility is unclear. The authors point out that schools may be able to implement particular reform practices effectively because their teachers have these attitudes. Whether teacher collective responsibility (or self-efficacy) is a consequence or a cause of communal practices, evidence from many studies suggests its value in promoting student engagement and learning (e.g., Bandura, 1993, 1997; Lee, Dedrick, and Smith, 1991; Tschannen-Moran et al., 1998).

Findings from Bryk and Schneider (2002) support Lee's findings regarding the importance of teacher attitudes for student outcomes, and focused attention on another aspect of a communal social climate (see also Marks, 2000). In a longitudinal study documenting the effects of school reform in Chicago between 1991 and 1997, Bryk and Schneider found that "relational trust" was essential to school improvement. The extent to which relational trust was present in hundreds of Chicago schools was determined by teacher responses to survey questions about their interactions with the principal, fellow teachers, and parents. The questions addressed issues such as respectfulness, belief in each others' competence and the willingness to fulfill obligations, caring about each other professionally and personally, and putting the interests of kids first.

Bryk and Schneider found that in schools with the highest achievement, nearly all teachers reported strong relational trust characterizing their interactions with the principal; three-fourths reported strong relational trust with fellow teachers, and 57 percent reported trusting relationships with parents. In bottom-quartile schools, fewer than half had trusting relationships with the principal, only a third with fellow teachers, and 40 percent reported trusting relationships with parents. Schools with strong relational trust had a 50-50 chance of making significant advances in mathematics and reading achievement; only one in seven schools with weak relational trust made similar advances. Relational trust was higher in small schools (fewer than 350 students) and in schools in which administrators, teachers, and students chose to be there instead of having been assigned.

A few findings suggest strategies for promoting relational trust. In the study by Lee with Smith (2001), teachers in schools high on communality were likely to have a common planning time and to work in interdisciplinary teams. Opportunities to work collaboratively may have contributed to respectful, trusting relationships among teachers and between teachers and administrators. The high levels of parent involvement in communally organized schools may have promoted more trusting relationships with teachers and administrators, although parent involvement is also likely to be a result of feelings of trust.

Studies of alternative high schools created for students at risk of dropping out provide additional support for the value of a communal social climate. These programs operate either within regular schools or as separate, alternative schools. They generally provide a complete, but alternative, educational program separate from the one found in regular, comprehensive schools.

There have been several evaluations of alternative programs for at-risk students at the secondary level that bear on the importance of the educational climate. Stern, Dayton, Paik, Weisberg, and Evans (1988) evaluated 10 within-school academy programs in California high schools; Wehlage et al. (1989) evaluated 12 alternative and 2 comprehensive schools; and Dynarski and Gleason (1998) evaluated 3 within-school and 6 alternative schools. Although the programs differed in the types of students they enrolled, the curricula and services they provided, and the way they were structured, there appear to be several common features among programs with relatively low dropout rates:[2]

- a caring and committed staff who accepted personal responsibility for student success;
- a school culture that encouraged staff risk taking, self-governance, and professional collegiality; and
- a school structure that provided for a low student-teacher ratio and a small class size to promote student engagement.

Taken together, the evidence suggests that student engagement and learning are fostered by a school climate characterized by an ethic of caring and supportive relationships; respect, fairness, and trust; and teachers' sense of shared responsibility and efficacy related to student learning. The evidence is clear, however, that a communitarian climate is not sufficient to increase academic engagement and learning. Equally important is a focus on learning and high expectations for student achievement, or "academic press."

---

[2]Effective programs were programs in which there was a statistically significant difference in dropout rates between program participants and those in the control group computed at the 10 percent level. For example, dropout rates for participants in the Seattle Middle College program were 27 percent compared to 42 percent for students in the control group (regular high school students).

The term "academic press" does not mean "pressure." Press means focusing students' attention on genuine learning (rather than simply going through the motions). Teachers "press" students to learn by encouraging them, by paying attention to their work and giving constructive feedback, by not accepting low or half-hearted effort, by holding them accountable, by providing assistance when they need it, and by not giving up on them. Simply having informal conversations with students about college and career goals is a form of academic press.[3]

A strong press for achievement might seem to contradict the notion that engagement is promoted by a supportive, communal school climate. But the evidence suggests that the combination is both achievable and desirable. Shouse (1996a, p. 184) explains:

> Any achievement effects associated with a sense of community stem primarily not from consensus and cohesion, but instead from the strength and transmission of particular organizational values related to the importance of academic endeavor. Without such commitment, commonality of beliefs, activities, and traditions and care for students as individuals are unlikely to affect achievement levels in positive ways, and may even work to impede them. An important corollary follows from this, however: the most powerful impact on student achievement should occur when a school's sense of community is built around a solid structure of academic press.

Consistent with this hypothesis, Shouse, using NELS:88 data on high schools serving economically disadvantaged children, found that achievement effects were particularly strong when high communality was accompanied by high academic press (Shouse, 1996a, 1996b, 1997; see also Marks, 2000; Phillips, 1997). Boyd and Shouse (1997) conclude, "average achievement in low-SES [socioeconomic status] schools having high levels of both academic press and communality, in fact, rivaled that of schools serving more affluent students; the least academically effective low-SES schools were those that combined strong communality and weak academic press."

Lee and Smith (1999) also assessed the relative effects of the communal organization model (social support for learning) and academic press (focusing on content reform directed at increasing academic standards) on student engagement in school and achievement in math and reading. They

---

[3]Students in a national study who claimed that this occurred frequently in their school had, on average, higher educational expectations for themselves and higher postsecondary education participation (Wimberly, 2002). Compared to white students, African-American students claimed that such conversations occurred less frequently in the schools they attended.

analyzed 1994 data from the Annenberg Institute for School Reform, which included 30,000 sixth- and eighth-grade students in 304 public elementary schools (K-8) in Chicago. The findings indicated that the relationships between social support and performance on standardized achievement tests in mathematics and reading were stronger in schools with greater academic press (Lee and Smith, 1999, pp. 934-935). The authors conclude:

> Our point is that reforms that focus on both the academic and the social domains are important. . . . To succeed in schools that press them to learn, students need support from the people with whom they interact (Lee and Smith, 1999, p. 935).

The findings of the complementarity of academic press and a communitarian school context provide important guidance for efforts to make urban high schools more engaging and effective as learning environments. These findings on school climate, moreover, are consistent with research on achievement motivation, discussed in Chapter 2, which reveals that students are more engaged in contexts in which they feel socially connected and in which they are held to high standards. Taken together, the evidence suggests that high schools need to convey a clearly articulated and coherent set of values that focus on learning and achievement in the context of close and caring relationships with adults and peers.

Policies for "Trouble-Makers"

Policies for how to deal with behavior problems have direct implications for the school climate as well as for the trouble-making students' own engagement—especially their persistence in school. An understandable response to adolescents who violate the rules, undermine a climate focused on learning, and threaten students' and teachers' feeling of safety is to remove them—to suspend them for some number of days or to expel them altogether. This form of disengagement has been described as "discharge"; "students drop out of school, schools discharge students" (Riehl, 1999, p. 231).

The students who are asked to leave are typically low performers with poor attendance (Lee and Burkam, 1992; Rumberger and Larson, 1998). Being prohibited from attending school puts them further behind, and makes it more likely that they will drop out (Lee and Burkam, 1992; Rumberger, 1995; Rumberger and Larson, 1998; Swanson and Schneider, 1999). Moreover, being suspended or expelled may not seem like much of a punishment for students who are already disengaged from school. Thus, although suspension and expulsion may create a more hospitable environment for the teachers and students remaining in school, they are more likely to exacerbate than to help the disengagement of the students who are misbehaving.

Students in urban schools are more likely than others to be suspended. Nationwide, more than 3 million students were suspended from school during the 1997-1998 school year, nearly 7 percent of all students (Office for Civil Rights, 2000). But suspension rates vary widely among students and schools, even schools within the same district (The Advancement Project and The Civil Rights Project, 2000). Black students are more than twice as likely to be suspended as white students nationwide (13.2 percent versus 5.5 percent). As a result, urban schools, with high concentrations of students of color, generally have higher suspension rates than other schools. The recently growing policy of zero tolerance for violations of school safety rules is likely to increase the number of students who are forced to disengage from school (Skiba and Peterson, 1999), and these policies are more often applied in urban schools serving low-income students than in schools serving more affluent students (Kaufman et al., 2001, Table A1).

One strategy that has been used to deal with seriously misbehaving students is to send them to alternative schools. But this too can aggravate any inclination towards disengagement. In their longitudinal study of 100 Latino high school students in Austin, Romo and Falbo describe the "special" schools the school district created for difficult students. Youth who had broken school rules were mixed in these schools with those who had committed serious, even violent crimes. In the district's own evaluation, staff reported that students who attended these special schools were more likely to drop out of school than were comparable students who stayed in the regular high school (Romo and Falbo, 1996, p. 87).

Clearly prohibiting students from attending school, either for some fixed amount of time or permanently, will not increase their engagement in school. From this perspective, the policy makes little sense. When alternative arrangements are made for students who have difficulty functioning in a regular school or are making it impossible for other students to be engaged, care must be given to the composition of the alternative arrangements, and attention needs to be paid to the social climate of these schools in which the students are the most in need of a caring, communally oriented context focused on achievement.

"Zero-tolerance" policies and alternative school programs for disruptive students do not address the day-to-day challenges related to discipline that classroom teachers in many urban schools encounter. To a substantial degree, implementing the kind of engaging instruction described in Chapter 3 in a caring, respectful social context should reduce discipline problems.

Consistent with the notion of creating a respectful social context, recent efforts to develop effective discipline strategies have emphasized collaboration instead of authoritarian, punishment-oriented approaches—with students having an active voice in deciding on matters of classroom management (Charles, 2000, 2002). An emphasis on democratic classroom principles and student responsibility—moving students from being "tourists" in the classroom to being "citizens" (Freiberg, 1996, p. 32)—is also being touted. Creating a climate of trust also has been proposed as a proactive strategy for maintaining order and cooperation (Charles, 2000). Charles (2002, p. 9) suggests that to be effective in today's classroom, teachers need to make "all students feel welcome, replacing reward and punishment with strong values, asking students to contribute ideas for resolving problems . . . moving beyond the usual conception of discipline in favor of developing a sense of community in the classroom."

There is currently no evidence on the effectiveness of these more egalitarian approaches to student discipline. They are, however, compatible with findings suggesting that students are more engaged in academic tasks when they are in a trusting, caring and respectful social context.

SCHOOL ORGANIZATION

By organization we mean how teachers and students are sorted and how instruction is delivered. The way high schools are organized can affect engagement in learning by the messages the organization conveys and by the opportunities it creates for students to experience a climate that promotes engagement.

High schools are currently experimenting with many aspects of school organization to facilitate closer relationships and more personalized teaching, in part by enabling teachers to see fewer students and students to see fewer teachers each day. One organizational feature that is touted by many experts is scheduling some courses in longer blocks (at least 90 minutes) to allow deeper and more sustained engagement and more individualized pacing. These courses are often multidisciplinary and team taught. A second feature is referred to as "looping"—teams of teachers working with cohorts of students for at least two continuous years. Looping allows more sustained relationships to develop among teachers and students, as well as more individualized instruction.

These organizational changes are usually embedded in efforts to convert large high schools into smaller units or to create new small high schools. Consequently, it is impossible to untangle the effects of any particular organizational feature. As a package, however, they seem to have considerable value.

The Coalition Campus Schools Project (CCSP), for example, redesigned two large and very troubled New York City high schools, Julia Richman High School in Manhattan and James Monroe High School in the Bronx (see Darling-Hammond et al., 2002). The design was derived from successful schools launched earlier—Central Park East Secondary School, International High School, and the Urban Academy. Teachers work in interdisciplinary teams with a group of 40 to 80 students, and block scheduling and looping are implemented. The schools were able to create smaller teacher-student ratios by putting a relatively high proportion of their resources into hiring teachers, and by having students take fewer and longer courses each day.

Analyses of 7 years of student data conducted by Darling-Hammond et al. (2002) suggest that this package of organizational changes, along with a small size and curricular reforms that included individualized programs and portfolio-based, authentic assessment, substantially improved students' attendance rates, lowered the incidence of disciplinary problems, increased performance on reading and writing assessments, and increased graduation and college-going rates, despite serving a more educationally disadvantaged population of students than the high schools they replaced. Variations of these design features are currently being encouraged by the Gates Foundation, and implemented in many small high schools throughout the country.[4] Although they are relatively new to the world of secondary education, they show considerable promise of achieving the kind of school climate and learning environments that the evidence suggests should engage students in academic work.

Another organizational feature of high schools, tracking, has been studied extensively. Tracking is particularly relevant to motivation because it is likely to convey the message that some students can achieve at high levels and some cannot. If tracking is rigid, in the sense that each year in a lower track makes it more difficult to move to a higher track, students may learn that they are not really expected to improve their academic status. Short of a clear-cut tracking system, course requirements can also limit students' opportunities. For example, some courses, such as 9th-grade algebra, can serve as gate-keeper courses; without them, students are prevented from ever getting into college preparatory courses.

Taking low-track or lower level courses also disadvantages students because they are likely to get the least experienced, least expert teachers. McLaughlin and Talbert (2001) report from their case studies of high schools that teachers' subject expertise was often matched to students' competence in the subject. The best-prepared teachers were assigned to the high-achieving students and the least prepared teachers taught the classes with students having the most academic difficulty (see also Oakes, 1990). Using High School and Beyond, Talbert and Ennis (1990) found that teacher

---

[4]For further information on these design features, see http://schoolredesign.net; http://www.lab.brown.edu/public/pubs/ic/block/block.shtml (for information on block scheduling); and http://www.lab.brown.edu/public/pubs/ic/looping/looping.shtml (for information on looping).

tracking (some teachers teaching almost exclusively low-track courses and some teachers teaching almost exclusively classes with relatively higher achieving students) was more extensive in schools with relatively high proportions of low-income and minority students (see also Lucas, 1999). Moreover, low-track teachers reported significantly lower levels of administrative support, control over instructional choices, and influence over school decisions. Finley (1984), similarly, reports also that the low-track teachers in her study were accorded less respect by their peers and were less involved in professional development.

A few studies have examined the effect of tracking on student engagement. Ethnographers in both Great Britain and the United States have concluded that tracking polarizes students into positive and negative academic attitudes and behavior (see Berends, 1995). It is possible, however, that the differences in attitudes existed before students entered a tracking system.

Wiatrowski, Hansell, Massey, and Wilson (1982) analyzed attitudes toward school in a longitudinal data set and found no differences, based on students' track, in 12th graders' attachment to and misbehavior in school, after controlling for social background variables and initial attitudes. Using High School and Beyond longitudinal data from 1980 to 1982, however, Berends (1995) found modest but significant effects of track placement on students' college expectations, absenteeism, disciplinary problems, and engagement to school (reported interest in school and time spent on homework), with students in the academic track showing more favorable outcomes.

Coleman and Hoffer (1987) attributed the lower dropout rates and higher average achievement that they found in Catholic schools to less curricular tracking. Similarly, in their study of 4,450 sophomores in 160 public and Catholic high schools from the High School and Beyond data set, Bryk and Thum (1989) found that students were more likely to persist in schools that had less curricular differentiation and more students in academic programs, even after controlling for the academic and social class background of students. In their study of 11,794 sophomores in 830 high schools from the NELS:88 data set, Lee and Smith (1995) found that schools where more students took advanced coursework had higher levels of student engagement, defined in terms of attitudes and self-reported effort, after controlling for student academic and social class background. A few other studies suggest that being in a low track reduces the likelihood of students taking challenging, college-preparatory classes, even after controlling for socioeconomic status and previous achievement (Braddock and Dawkins, 1993).

Low-track courses may undermine students' motivation unnecessarily. In mathematics, for example, most teachers believe that there is a clear sequence for learning, and that students cannot process high-level concepts, such as algebra, until they have mastered basic computational skills (Grossman and Stodolsky, 1994, 1995; Stodolsky and Grossman, 2000). As a consequence, students who enter high school with poor basic skills are likely to receive drill in basic concepts rather than more motivating instruction that engages them in challenging, open-ended problem solving. Research discussed in Chapter 4 shows clearly that even students who have relatively poor skills can engage in instruction that allows them to engage in deep analysis, and there is considerable evidence now that algebraic and other mathematical concepts can be introduced at many levels and at almost any age (RAND Mathematics Study Panel, 2002).

Formal and comprehensive tracking is less common now than in the past. High schools more often offer courses that are differentiated by level of achievement or perceived ability of students. High-achieving students take honors and Advanced Placement courses, but they are not distinguished formally as being in a college-bound track.

A common strategy to make advanced courses accessible to low-income students and students of color who have in the past been disproportionately placed in remedial or vocational tracks is to give students the choice of taking more advanced courses. Although choice theoretically provides opportunities for all students to be held to high expectations and to be engaged in challenging learning experiences, in reality, students end up being sorted, or they sort themselves along the same class and ethnic lines that applied to more formal tracking structures. For 3 years Yonezawa, Wells, and Serna (2002) studied 10 racially and socioeconomically mixed secondary schools that had voluntarily implemented detracking, giving students the choice of taking more advanced courses. Few of the Black and Latino students took advanced classes for a variety of reasons, including lack of information, failure to meet prerequisites, and a lack of encouragement from counselors or teachers. One student in their study described a counselor's weak encouragement (p. 52): " . . . she said . . . 'Who knows, if you work real hard, you can probably . . . keep up.' " Some of the most significant barriers were psychological. The students themselves often did not take advantage of opportunities because they had experienced too many years of being perceived to have low skills, and they lacked the confidence to take advanced courses, or they were anxious about being uncomfortable in classes with predominantly white and Asian and more affluent students. They feared being uncomfortable or disrespected in classrooms where they were different from the other students. Some also expressed concerns about the burden of demonstrating their own capability as well as countering racial stereotypes. As one student in an honors math class explains (p. 56):

> I was like, "Oh man, I don't even belong in here," because it was like 30 Caucasian kids and one African student. I felt like I had to prove myself and prove that Blacks aren't stupid. [I felt like] if I were to get a problem wrong and raise my hand, they would look at me and say, "Ah, that Black." I was always under pressure, so . . . I transferred to just [the] advanced level.

Although eliminating a rigid tracking system is a step in the right direction, allowing choice is not enough to eliminate the status quo with course-taking patterns differentiated along social class and race lines. To be effective, such a policy decision would need to be accompanied by concerted efforts to create a social climate that informed and encouraged low-income students and students of color to participate in a rigorous and challenging curriculum. Special efforts also would have to be made at the classroom level to ensure that all students felt valued, respected, and included.

Most important, strategies would need to be implemented to ensure that all students in a class are able to handle the material covered and the academic demands of the course—a difficult task in a class of students who have dramatically different skill levels. One organizational strategy that has been used successfully at the college level for students who are not proficient in English is to link tutoring and small-group learning, often with a specialist in reading or English as a Second Language (ESL), to a regular class (Benesch, 1988a). Thus poor readers or English-language learners have the advantage of being integrated in regular classes, but with the extra support they need to master the material. In one program at University of California, Los Angeles (UCLA), English-language classes were linked to content courses (e.g., in political science or psychology; Snow and Brinton, 1988). The language class assisted students in developing reading, writing, and study skills that were directly related to the content course. City University of New York created a block of three linked courses—freshman social science, ESL reading, and ESL writing (Benesch, 1988b). Like the UCLA program, the links were designed to help students develop basic skills in the context of developing content knowledge. Hostos Community College in New York connected small tutor-led groups to content courses, such as biology, business, and early childhood education (Hirsch, 1988).

Although we did not find examples of this strategy being applied at the high school level, the approach addresses some of the problems of the typical strategy of creating remedial or ESL courses that isolate low-skilled students and English-language learners from high-skilled and native English-speaking peers. The strategy gives students access to regular courses, and special instruction designed to help them master the material of the course. Although not proven, the approach merits some experimentation in urban high schools.

A key concern in classrooms with cultural, linguistic, and academic diversity is that students create social rankings within the classroom based on "status" differences, including academic ability (Cohen, Lotan, and Leechor, 1989). Differences in literacy resources at home, the use of standard English, and knowledge of academic discourse are often perceived by both students and teachers to reflect intellectual ability. These perceptions can be translated into a status hierarchy, which can influence students' individual behavior and contributions to the group. For example, those students with high academic status typically talk more and express their opinions more freely, while "low-status" students defer to their leadership (Cohen, 1997).

Cohen and Lotan's model of "complex instruction" (a model of collaborative learning) was designed to address these status differences in the classroom (Cohen and Lotan, 1997). Their studies suggest that teachers can reduce the influence of academic status by publicly recognizing the contributions and value of many different kinds of intellectual competencies in the classroom and by emphasizing that every student brings valuable and different strengths which are required for the group's success. Although most of the research on complex instruction has been done at the elementary level (Cohen and Lotan, 1997), Bower (1997) found that students in 11th-grade social studies classes in which the approach was used gained more in achievement than the control group. In summary, although the evidence suggests that tracking and other policies that limit students' access to a rigorous curriculum have negative effects on some students' engagement, simply eliminating tracking or formal prerequisites is not sufficient. These organizational changes need to be supplemented with others that provide students with the encouragement, support, and structures they need to be able to achieve success.

SCHOOL COMPOSITION

Policy decisions at the district level can affect the distribution of students among schools, and the evidence suggests that those policies affect student engagement and learning. Although we know little about the mechanisms involved, correlational evidence suggests that the social composition of students in a school influences student achievement above and beyond the effects of student characteristics at an individual level . Student composition may also influence achievement indirectly, through its relationship with other school characteristics, such as resources and practices.

Kahlenberg (2001) proposes that school composition affects student learning in part by influencing three different peer mechanisms—the influence of peers on learning through in-class and out-of-class interactions (e.g., cooperative work-groups, study groups), the influence of peers on the motivation and aspirations of fellow students, and the influence of peers on the social behavior of other students (Kahlenberg, 2001; see Chapter 3 for a more detailed discussion of peer effects). Student composition might also affect some of the climate variables discussed earlier, such as teachers' expectations for student learning and the degree to which they press for excellence or develop supportive, personalized relationships with students.

Research has shown that several aspects of student composition are associated with student performance: the average socioeconomic status of the students in the school, their average academic skills, and the schools' racial and ethnic composition. Schools serving relatively more students from high socioeconomic backgrounds and with high academic skills have lower school dropout rates, lower absentee rates (Bryk and Thum, 1989), and lower student mobility rates , after controlling for the individual effects of student background characteristics. An analysis of 26,425 sophomores attending 968 schools from the High School and Beyond data indicated that the effect of school socioeconomic composition on dropout rates was about one-third to one-half as strong as the effect of individual socioeconomic status (Mayer, 1991).

Because the extent and quality of resources, such as the proportion of qualified and experienced teachers, are confounded with the proportion of low-income students, it is not possible to untangle these confounds from the effect of the student body composition itself on student engagement. In future research it will be important to identify the reasons for the effects of the student body composition on student engagement and learning. We suspect that in addition to differential resources, differences in standards, expectations, and in the curriculum mediate school composition effects.

SCHOOL SIZE

The research evidence on small schools suggests that reducing substantially the size of schools is a promising strategy for achieving the kind of personalized education that engages youth. Definitions of "small" for the purpose of research varies, with some studies considering a high school enrolling 400 or fewer students as "small" (Howley, 2002) and others considering "small" to be any number up to 1,000 students (e.g., Lee, 2001). Howley (2002) suggests that the terms "smaller" and "larger" are more useful, allowing for relative comparisons to be made (see also McLaughlin and Drori, 2000). Researchers studying school size also use many different definitions of academic engagement—including attendance, persistence, graduation rates, and sense of belonging—and some use standardized test scores. Despite some inconsistencies in definitions and findings, a careful review of the evidence supports three tentative conclusions: (1) smaller school size is associated with higher achievement under some conditions; (2) smaller schools improve achievement equity; and (3) smaller schools may be especially important for disadvantaged students (Howley, 2002).

One of the first challenges to the effectiveness of large, comprehensive high schools in the United States came from Roger Barker and Paul Gump's 1964 book, *Big School, Small School: High School Size and Student Behavior*. Their study of more than 200 schools revealed that a much higher proportion of students participated in school activities in smaller schools than in large ones. In the nearly 40 years since Barker and Gump's book was published, many researchers have sought to examine the effects of school size on student engagement and achievement. Barker and Gump's original challenge to the assumption that bigger is better has been supported and expanded, and although questions remain about school size, we can conclude that bigger usually is not better.

Whereas some studies find no difference between the achievement levels of students in large and small schools (e.g., Caldas, 1987 [Louisiana schools]; Haller, Monk, and Tien, 1993 [10th graders in math and science]; Melnick, Shibles, Gable, and Grzymkowski, 1986 [nonurban Connecticut schools]), many studies find students in small schools doing better than those in large schools (e.g., Eberts, Kehoe, and Stone, 1982 [national data sample]; Eichenstein, 1994 [10 New York City public high schools]). In a relatively large study of the approximately 300 high schools in New Jersey, Fowler and Walberg (1991) found that students in smaller high schools performed better on achievement tests than students in larger schools (see also Walberg and Fowler, 1987; Walberg, 1989, 1992). Data tracking students from large schools in Philadelphia that converted into small schools suggest that small schools can also increase attendance, course passage, persistence, and graduation rates (McMullan, 1994). Wasley and colleagues (2000) likewise found more persistence in small schools in Chicago, in restructured existing large schools as well as autonomous, free-standing small schools. Fetler's (1989) study in California similarly reported lower dropout rates as well as higher achievement in smaller schools.

In contrast to these studies, which found a linear relationship between school size and achievement, Lee's analyses of the National Education Longitudinal Study of 1988 (NELS 88) showed a curvilinear relationship (Lee, 2001; see also Lee, V. E., 2000). Schools of about 300 to 900 students performed better than both larger and smaller schools. The advantages of being small appeared to diminish substantially below a threshold of about 300 students. We suspect that the national data set, which included a substantial number of very small (<300 students) schools, explains why Lee found a curvilinear relationship when other researchers found a linear relationship. The data sets used by researchers who studied relatively populated states such as California and New Jersey may not have had enough very small high schools to affect the statistical findings. Taken together, the findings suggest that smaller might be better up to a point, but below that point small schools may have disadvantages, such as in course offerings and other resources, which affect student achievement.

The evidence suggests that relatively small schools may also promote achievement equity. A few studies have shown dramatically higher levels of academic engagement among poor and working-class youth of color in small schools relative to their peers in large schools (e.g., Ancess, 2000; Fine, 1994; Lee and Smith, 1995, 1997; Meier, 1998; Wasley et al., 2000; for reviews see Fowler, 1995; Gladden, 1998; and Raywid, 1998). Lee (2001) likewise found that disparities in achievement gains based on SES were smallest in the three smallest categories of school size (up to 1,200 students). With regard to promoting equity, being very small did not appear to create any disadvantages.

The evidence on greater achievement equity in small schools suggests that school size may be especially important for economically disadvantaged students. Taking a somewhat different approach to examining possible differential effects of school size on students from different economic backgrounds, Howley and Bickel (2000) found that small school size reduced the impact of poverty on student achievement. In their analysis of data from three states (Texas, Georgia, and Ohio), they found that "the lower the income in the community, the more student achievement is benefited by smaller schools" (p. 4). They describe a possible "differential excellence effect," an interaction effect of socioeconomic status and school size, in which larger sizes are particularly harmful in low-income communities.

Schools-Within-A-School

Findings suggesting the benefits of small schools have stimulated the creation of schools-within-a-school (SWAS)—dividing schools into small learning communities, sometimes associated with academic or vocational themes (see Chapter 6, this volume). The research supporting the advantages of this structure is not as strong as research comparing whole schools that vary in size (e.g., Cotton, 1996; Howley, 2002; Meier, 1995). The evidence does, however, show some benefits for students in small learning communities with regard to both academic achievement and attitudes toward school. In an evaluation of the Kansas City SWAS program, Robinson-Lewis (1991) found that achievement test scores for SWAS students increased during their years in the SWAS program. Students also showed improved attendance and grades, and believes the program had helped them improve their basic skills. In a similar evaluation, Levine and Sherk (1990) found evidence of benefits for the SWAS programs in Kansas City,

New York, and Orlando urban middle and high schools. Students in all three metropolitan areas showed improved reading comprehension during participation in the SWAS programs. Finally, Eichenstein (1994) evaluated the Project Achieve program for at-risk students in New York City public high schools. She found that restructuring existing schools into "houses" (averaging 250 students) was associated with improved attendance, student responsiveness, and student satisfaction.

Inside Small Schools—What Really Matters?

Smallness by itself is not likely to promote greater engagement (Darling-Hammond et al., 2002). More likely a smaller number of students makes it easier to implement policies and create the kind of climate that studies suggest are conducive to high levels of engagement.

Achievement motivation theory and findings discussed in Chapter 2 provide some clues as to why small schools might typically engage youth better than large schools. For example, small schools should facilitate meaningful faculty-student relations, a sense of belonging and attachment, more individualized instruction that can create optimal levels of challenge for all students, and opportunities for both students and teachers to exercise autonomy. In the absence of these effects, we suspect smallness in itself has little value.

Very few studies have documented directly these kinds of possible mediators of the effect of size on student engagement. One exception is a study of Chicago elementary schools, in which students in small schools were more likely to report "academic press" (the feeling that teachers challenged them to reach high levels of academic performance), "peer academic support" (their friends tried hard to get good grades, attended classes, believed paying attention in class was important, treated homework assignments seriously, and followed school rules), positive "classroom behavior" (classmates treated each other with respect and care), and "safety" (perception of personal safety in and around school; Sebring et al., 1996).[5] Lee with Smith (2001) also found that a communal climate is more likely to be seen in small schools, which, according to the research discussed earlier, supports student engagement.

Small schools that do not also adjust their organization and instruction may have few advantages. Note that in studies finding positive effects of small schools on student engagement and learning, the schools also imple-

---

[5]Two federally funded studies are currently under way, looking for the "active ingredients" in effective small learning communities (Gambone, Klem, Moore, and Summers, 2002).

mented a variety of other innovations, such as block scheduling, looping, multidisciplinary courses, and teachers seeing fewer students and students seeing fewer teachers (Darling-Hammond et al., 2002).[6] A noteworthy and probably essential component of small schools that produces learning gains is a great deal of attention to instruction—including developing a curriculum that challenges students to understand concepts deeply, adjusting modes of teaching to individual students' skills and learning styles, and providing extra supports for students who need them to succeed.

The small schools that are most effective with respect to academic engagement, persistence, and graduation rates have also developed and implemented thoughtful and rigorous alignment of curriculum, pedagogy, and assessment systems in which youth and faculty are held publicly accountable to high standards (Fine, 1994; Wasley et al., 2000). The small schools that are least effective are those that are simply small in size, but have developed neither curricula nor assessment systems that demand rigorous engagement and performance by all (Wasley et al., 2000).

Some caution in interpreting the research on school size is in order because selection bias most likely contributes to the positive findings discussed. Many small schools are open to all students within a district or geographical area larger than the existing neighborhood high school, and require students and families to apply or at least put themselves into a lottery. Some make particular requirements of families and students, and admit students to some degree on a judgment about whether the "fit" is good. Teachers and administrators also often choose to teach in small schools, and some small schools are able to select from among a large pool of teachers and administrators. Selection bias also can be relevant in studies of schools within schools, because these are sometimes theme based and attract students who have interests that match the school theme. Tracking also occurs, although not necessarily by design, with low- or high-achieving students systematically self-selecting into different schools or learning communities.

Although selection bias may play a role in some studies of the effect of school size on students' engagement and learning, we suspect that it does not explain all of the differences that have been found. Studies do show that small schools have advantages for students who typically perform very poorly in school, and if selection played a role, it may not be entirely because of "creaming," but because choice and matching have their own benefits. We recommend, however, that future researchers pay careful at-

[6]Intensive experimentation with small high schools sponsored by the Gates Foundation has resulted in 10 design principles for effective small schools; see http://www.stanford.edu/dept/SUSE/csrn.

tention to the possible role of selection bias of students, teachers, and administrators.

CONCLUSIONS

A review of the evidence presented in this chapter provides convincing, if not conclusive, evidence that school climate, organization, composition, and size can have important effects on student engagement and learning. Effective schools communicate high expectations for their teachers and students in the form of academic press and an atmosphere of trust and caring relationships among teachers, administrators, parents, and students. To achieve this kind of climate, teachers need opportunities to develop relationships with each other and with their students. Promising strategies for promoting caring relationships include decreasing the size of schools and the number of students seen by each teacher and the number of teachers seen by each student, block scheduling, and looping.

Research on school organization suggests that tracking undermines engagement for students in the lower tracks, but that merely offering more choices to those students does not eliminate differential course taking. Students who have a history of poor achievement or who were previously excluded from challenging courses often do not have the confidence to take the more challenging courses. Teachers and administrators will need to overcome these psychological barriers by providing strong encouragement and eliminating the option of watered-down courses. In addition, they need to make sure that supports are provided for students to be able to succeed in challenging courses.

Student composition within a school is associated with student engagement; the more high-achieving and high-SES students in a school, the more individual students are engaged and learning. Special efforts need to be made to increase the resources of schools serving a high concentration of low-income students and to maintain a climate that is conducive to high engagement. To the degree that there is diversity in students' economic backgrounds, efforts should be made to mix students from different backgrounds.

There is also convincing evidence that small schools can confer an advantage for those students most at risk, and may help achieve greater equity in achievement outcomes. But the committee does not recommend creating small schools without consideration of the qualities of schools that have been shown to promote student engagement and learning—challenging and clear standards, personalization, meaningful and rigorous pedagogy and curriculum, and professional learning communities. Moreover, it is not clear from the evidence that these qualities can be achieved only in small schools, although it appears more difficult to achieve them in large schools. We do not yet know whether the school-within-a-school strategy will show the same benefits that are seen in some studies of autonomous small schools. But the evidence suggests that this is a strategy worth investigating, and studies are underway that will provide useful information on the potential of this school reform strategy.

5

Family, Community, and Peers

High schools can increase students' engagement in learning by creating personalized, supportive contexts focused on academic achievement. But schools cannot achieve the high levels of engagement and standards for learning currently asked of them by themselves (e.g., Cohen and Ball, 1999; Comer, 1997; Epstein, 2001b; Gold, Simon, and Brown, 2002; Hill, Campbell, and Harvey, 2000; Shirley, 1997; Steinberg, 1997). Patricia Graham (1995, p. 22) makes this point vividly:

> The battleship, the school, cannot do this alone. The rest of the educational flotilla must assist: families, communities, government, higher education, and the business community. Only then will all of our children be able to achieve that which by birthright should be theirs: enthusiasm for and accomplishment in learning.

In some respects it makes little sense to discuss what schools can do to engage students in learning without considering the settings in which both schools and students live. Ideally, schools would build on the knowledge and interests youth develop at home and in the community and create opportunities for students to extend and apply school-learned skills in contexts outside of school. They would take advantage of resources and supports for learning in the community and be a positive force in the community for developing an environment that supports positive youth development.

Elsewhere in this volume we discuss how schools can expand curriculum offerings by embedding learning opportunities in authentic work environments (Chapter 6), and how they can collaborate with health and social service providers from the community to address the nonacademic needs of students (Chapter 7). In this chapter, we focus on how schools can increase students' engagement in learning by involving their families and connecting with the community. Also discussed in this chapter are strategies for fostering positive peer influences. Peers are often viewed as the enemy when it comes to persuading adolescents to focus on academic pursuits. Research suggests, however, that peer effects on school engagement can be as positive as they can be negative, and that adults can affect the nature of that influence by the way they structure the peer world.

SCHOOL-FAMILY-COMMUNITY CONNECTIONS

Many efforts to improve schools are "school-centric" in the sense that they focus exclusively on school resources and programs (Honig, Kahne, and McLaughlin, 2001). Although school-focused efforts are certainly necessary to improve student engagement, they may not be sufficient. Too many of the factors that shape students' behavior in school are based in their experiences outside of school. This observation does not let schools "off the hook." But it does have important implications for the kinds of school reforms that are likely to have substantial positive effects (Cibulka and Kritek, 1996; Honig et al., 2001; Kahne, O'Brien, Brown, and Quinn, 2001; Wehlage, Smith, and Lipman, 1992).

Advocates of school reform initiatives that emphasize families and communities as partners generally view schools as part of a wider social ecology that includes neighborhoods, community organizations, and families (National Research Council and Institute of Medicine, 2002). They seek to marshal the energy, resources, and support of families and communities to promote learning and positive youth development. We will discuss evidence suggesting the value of deep, institutionalized connections among schools, families, and the community. Be forewarned that the kind of connections advocated by many experts require fundamental changes in most schools—in how they are organized, how decisions are made, and even how instruction is implemented (see Comer, 1980; Connell, Gambone, and Smith, 2000; Giles, 1998; Gold, Simon and Brown, 2002; Heckman, 1996; Honig et al., 2001; Lewis, 1996; Murnane and Levy, 1996a; Wehlage et al., 1992).

Consistent Messages

Adolescents need many sources of support, and they need consistency in the messages they receive from the important people in their lives. Lawrence Cremin (1976) is among the many educators and researchers who over the years have described the school as but one educating institution among a multiplicity of institutions that educate (see also Delgado-Gaitan, 1987; Mehan, Hubbard, and Villanueva, 1994; Phelan et al., 1998). Cremin (1976, p. 22) noted, for example, that every family has a curriculum "which it teaches quite deliberately and systematically over time." Religious institutions also socialize youth to certain values and beliefs, as do workplaces, radio and television, and youth organizations. The fundamental question is whether, in Cremin's words, "The relationships among the institutions constituting a configuration of education may be complementary or contradictory, consonant or dissonant" (1976, p. 31; see also Phelan et al., 1998).

A growing body of research underscores the importance of consistent messages emanating from these settings (Jessor et al., 1998; for a review, see Aber, Gephart, Brooks-Gunn, and Connell, 1997). Findings from a study by Steinberg, Darling, Fletcher et al., (1995), for example, suggest the value of congruence between parent and peer support for academic matters. In their study of nine high schools in Wisconsin and Northern California, students who received academic encouragement from both parents and peers performed better in school than those who received encouragement from only one source (see also Lee and Smith, 1999).

Darling and Steinberg's (1997) findings on social integration illustrate both the value of coherence in the messages adolescents receive and the importance of positive messages. They measured "social integration" using a questionnaire that assessed the extent to which adolescents had an opportunity for nonteacher adult contact, and parents had the opportunity to meet their adolescents' friends and their parents. The undesirable effects of coherent negative messages were just as strong as the desirable effects of coherent positive messages. The authors explain (pp. 128-129):

> Family social integration was associated with adolescent school engagement and lower levels of substance use only in communities where other adolescents were engaged in school and were not involved in substance use. In contrast, social integration was associated with lower engagement and more substance use when community adolescents were more deviant and less involved in school. In other words, social integration exaggerated the potentially negative influence of living in a community with poorly adjusted peers.

These findings suggest the value of creating social connections between families and school staff and of involving families in school activities that facilitate social interactions with parents who have strong educational values. In addition to promoting consistency in the messages youth receive at school and at home, school-initiated activities can help families build the social networks that have been shown to support youth development and learning.

Connections to Families

Creating strong linkages between schools and families may support student engagement in other ways, as well as by fostering congruence in the values adolescents are exposed to at home and at school. Although most studies are correlational, making it difficult to establish the direction of causality, research findings are generally consistent with the proposition that children benefit from their parents' involvement in their school (e.g., Ames, Khoju, and Watkins, 1993; Baker and Soden, 1998; Booth and Dunn, 1996; Clark, 1983; Dornbusch and Ritter, 1988; Eccles and Harold, 1996; Epstein, 2001a; Lee, 1994; Lee and Croninger, 1994; Morgan and Sorensen, 1999; Scott-Jones, 1987; Steinberg, Lamborn, Dornbusch, and Darling, 1992; Stevenson and Baker, 1987; Tocci and Englehard, 1991). In one of the few studies that used a longitudinal design, Steinberg (1997) was able to examine cause-effect more directly. He concluded that although parents appeared to be more involved as a consequence of their adolescents doing well in school, their involvement also appeared to contribute to better performance.

The value of parent involvement is also suggested by dropout studies. In their study of 14,217 sophomores in 913 public, Catholic, and private schools from the National Education Longitudinal Study of 1988 (NELS 88), Rumberger and Palardy (2002) found lower dropout rates in schools in which parent involvement was high. Parent involvement predicted dropout rates after controlling for the academic and social-class background of students as well as school resources (e.g., student-teacher ratio, proportion of teachers with advanced degrees) and structural characteristics (e.g., size and urbanicity).

Parental involvement is almost universally considered desirable by parents, educators, and policy makers (Epstein, 2001a), and at least nominal parental involvement has been required in some federally supported educational programs since the mid-1960s through legislation authorizing Title I (Keesling and Melargano, 1983). Parental involvement was listed as a major national educational priority in the 1994 Goals 2000 Educate America Act, as well as in some local legislation, such as the 1988 Chicago School Reform Act. The Chicago legislation mandated that parents and community leaders be involved in their local school's budget making, hiring, and firing decisions, and in the development of school improvement plans (Bryk and Schneider, 2002; Bryk, Sebring, Kerbow, Rollow, and Easton, 1998).

Studies reporting the benefits to students of parent involvement involve mostly elementary and middle-school children, and often do not differentiate among different kinds of parent participation, such as volunteering in activities at school; at-home involvement in children's learning; participating in school decisions through parent-teacher organizations and other venues; communicating about children's educational progress and plans; obtaining advice from school personnel about child-rearing or parenting practices; and working with the school to collaborate with other community organizations (Baker and Soden, 1998; Epstein, 2001a, p. 409). A notable exception is Epstein's work over the past 20 years, in which she differentiates six types of teacher-parent collaboration (e.g., parenting, learning at home, collaboration with the community) and shows that different parent behaviors are linked to different educational outcomes (Epstein, 2001a). Steinberg (1997) also differentiates the varied forms of involvement in his study of adolescents. He found that the most common types of involvement—checking homework, encouraging their children to do better, and overseeing their academic program from home—did not appear to contribute to performance, perhaps because they were parental responses triggered by academic problems and thus experienced by the student as controlling. A more powerful predictor of student performance was the type of parental involvement that drew parents into the school physically—to attend teacher conferences and school programs such as back-to-school nights and extracurricular activities. Other studies, however, indicate that students who rate their own parents' involvement and encouragement at home as high have higher academic self-concept, greater motivation, and more positive attitudes toward school (e.g., Sanders, 1998; Wiest, Wong, Cervantes, Craik, and Kreil, 2001; Wong, Wiest, and Cusick, 2002).

Despite general agreement about the desirability of parental involvement, there is a dearth of research at the high school level. Longitudinal research that makes it possible to examine the direction of causality is also needed, and studies that differentiate particular kinds of parent involvement would be useful to identify the kinds of involvement that are most beneficial.

What is clear from extant research is that parental involvement in schools decreases markedly during middle school and high school (Baker and Stevenson, 1986; Epstein and Dauber, 1991) and that low-income and poorly educated, single and minority parents have relatively low rates of involvement in their children's schools (Comer, 1988; Epstein, 2001a; Hoover-Dempsey, Bassler, and Brissie, 1987; Lareau, 1987, 1989; Leitch and Tangri, 1988).[1] There is also considerable evidence that school practices and policies affect the level of parent involvement (Cole and Griffin, 1987; Comer, 1980; Dauber and Epstein, 1993). One recent comprehensive study of parent involvement, using data from the eighth grade of the NELS study (Sui-Chu and Willms, 1996), examined what student-level and school-

[1]For case studies about what schools do and don't do to promote parental involvement of ethnic minorities, see Delgado-Gaitan (1991).

level factors influenced four types of parental involvement—home discussion, home supervision, school communication, and school participation—and the impact of these measures on 8th-grade school achievement. The study found that schools had influence on school participation, although not on other forms of parental involvement that there were substantial differences among ethnic groups in these four parental involvement measures, and that home discussion of school activities was the most strongly associated with student achievement. Epstein (2001a, p. 45) concluded from a review of research: "Teachers' practices to involve families are as or more important than family background variables such as race or ethnicity, social class, marital status, or mother's work status for determining whether and how parents become involved in their children's education." School practices may therefore explain, in part, the relatively low participation rates of parents with children who are most at risk of school failure.

Schools may not facilitate the involvement of low-income parents as much as they do more affluent parents. Jordan and Plank (2000) found that parents of low socioeconomic status (SES) were a little more than half as likely as high-SES parents to have been contacted by their adolescent's high school about course selection decisions, postsecondary education, or career plans. This finding suggests that less effort was made to involve low-SES parents than more advantaged parents. But low-SES parents in their study were also less likely to attend a school-sponsored program on postsecondary educational opportunities and financial aid, suggesting that they did not take as much advantage of opportunities the school did provide.

We can only speculate about why some low-SES parents might be less likely to take advantage of opportunities for involvement. The evidence does not suggest less interest or concern about their children's school achievement, and most parents want to be more involved (Epstein, 1990; MetLife, 1987). We speculate that language and culture play a role. For example, immigrant parents who do not speak English may feel less comfortable in school contexts and have more challenges in participating. Social class differences between parents and teachers could produce another psychological barrier. Work schedules, babysitting needs, transportation, and neighborhood safety may also come into play (e.g., Heymann and Earle, 2000).

Some of these obstacles can be overcome through various measures, such as having communications to parents written in the languages spoken by parents and providing translators at school events; making the school physically and socially hospitable to the families; and providing transportation and babysitting. Because the obstacles to parent involvement most likely vary among communities, high schools need to assess the needs of their own parent community and identify local resources to address the obstacles they find. One study suggests that including information on family involvement programs and their implementation, as well as strategies for overcoming barriers to involvement, in teacher education improves teachers' confidence in their ability to involve parents in their children's education (Morris and Taylor, 1998).

Communication is probably a first and necessary step to involving parents in their adolescents' education. Teachers' perceptions of the educational values and goals of parents often are different from the values and goals expressed by the parents, and some teachers complain that they do not understand what information parents would like from them (Dauber and Epstein, 1993). Parents, in turn, report that they do not fully understand what teachers are trying to do (Epstein, 2001a). Improved communication among parents, teachers, and students about educational objectives and strategies might lead to greater participation by parents as well as foster congruence between messages and supports for learning at home and at school (see Darling and Steinberg, 1997; Lamborn, Brown, Mounts, and Steinberg, 1992; Moll and Greenberg, 1990; Rosenfeld et al., 2000).

Special efforts may be required for schools to connect with some parents, but the evidence supports the value of such efforts. A number of studies at the elementary and middle school levels have documented the benefits of teachers' efforts to collaborate with single- and low-income parents, and other parents perceived as hard to reach (e.g., Clark, 1983; Comer, 1980; Epstein, 1990; Epstein and Dauber, 1991; Rich, Van Dien, and Maddox, 1979; Scott-Jones, 1987). Moreover, teachers who find ways to work with low-income and single parents are much less likely than teachers who do not work with those parents to hold stereotypic views of them. For example, they are less likely to believe that parents don't care about their children's education or do not want to be involved with the school in activities that will lead to better outcomes for their children (Becker and Epstein, 1982; Epstein, 1990). Presumably the breakdown of such stereotypes contributes to better communication and connections between teachers and parents.

Given the importance of families in adolescents' development, ignoring parents and other adults who have caretaking roles seriously limits the effects of even the most inspired school reform. Most parents want to be involved, and schools that reach out aggressively to parents and reduce obstacles to their involvement amplify their own efforts to improve student engagement and learning.[2] Murnane and Levy (1996b) suggest that an outside "agent" (e.g., community organization) can sometimes help schools

---

[2]For an example of how schools can connect with parents and other caretaking adults, see the description of First Things First's family advocacy system in Chapters 6 and 8.

connect with low-income parents. Some organizations that work with groups of parents to increase connections between parents and the school have created the National Coalition of Advocates for Students (see Murnane and Levy, 1996b). An example of a high school that used a coalition of local churches to help make connections to parents is discussed later in this chapter.

Connecting with Communities

Several national, and many state and local, organizations now provide support and guidance for school-community partnerships.[3] The types of connections vary greatly, as they should to be responsive to the local needs and resources of schools and communities. Our goal here is to give a flavor of the kinds of activities that might be considered. Some of these examples involve tinkering around the edges—improving communication and building bridges to community organizations—which can serve as the starting point for serious reforms. School-community collaborations that have substantial impact on youth engagement in school, however, involve changes at the core, in how schools define their role and how they function.

In addition to linking with community agencies that provide services to meet students' nonacademic needs (see Chapter 7, this volume), schools can develop close connections to after-school and other youth-serving programs. Involving students in well-organized after-school and summer activities may promote positive attitudes about school shared by groups of students because organized activities are consistent with the values and norms of the school. They can provide a positive social context for youth to demonstrate their competence and experience a sense of belonging; furthermore, participants simply have less time to "hang out" with each other in unsupervised activities where they could develop shared beliefs and attitudes that are different from, and possibly in opposition to, those of the school (Lamborn et al., 1992; McLaughlin, 2000; National Research Council and Institute of Medicine, 2002).

High schools can also involve community members and create support by serving as a resource for the community. Many high schools provide evening courses for adults in everything from carpentry and computers to Spanish and sewing. Athletic facilities can be made available and performances can be advertised throughout the community. School personnel and students can show their commitment to the community by participating in

[3]Examples include Coalition for Community Schools (http://www.communityschools.org) and the National Community Building Network (http://www.ncbn.org).

clean-up and beautification projects, inviting community members to activities, such as fairs and pancake breakfasts, and taking their performances out into the community. Parents and other community members can be invited to spend a Saturday helping to improve the physical plant of the school. Community members can be enlisted to advocate for school resources, and school personnel and students can assist in efforts to bring resources to the community.

School-community connections can also be established to enrich the instructional program. College faculty, students, and local business people can come to the school to work directly with students or participate in classroom instruction. Local artisans and artists can visit classes to demonstrate their craft and to work directly with students. Students can expand their knowledge and learn how to apply new skills by working as interns or volunteers in community settings.

More powerful strategies for school-community connections transform schools so that they become one among many coordinated settings in which youth are educated. We will explain what this means through examples. The first example involves a sustained collaboration between a school and a community organization that integrates the academic program with service to the community. The second is a description of a school-community collaborative in Houston, Texas, which became the basis of a national school reform model called Project GRAD. The third example illustrates the growing practice of service learning. All three examples address some or all of the principles of engagement described in this volume and they all promote productive links between schools and their communities.

El Puente Academy for Peace and Justice

The El Puente Academy for Peace and Justice was established in 1993 by the El Puente community organization with support from New York City's New Visions initiative. An after-school program is so well connected to the academic curriculum of the school that it is difficult to differentiate where one ends and the other begins. Teachers and youth organization staff collaborate with each other and work with youth both during and after the regular school day.

Students learn basic skills in part through projects. For example, as part of a math and science unit, they spent afternoons and weekends creating a community garden in a vacant lot. The activity was designed to teach math skills in the context of planning and budgeting and science skills in the process of selecting and growing plants. In another activity students developed writing skills in the context of producing a community newspaper. The program was created to give students opportunities to express their own values and concerns and to build leadership skills by assessing community needs and making decisions about where to invest their time. One group of students decided to organize an immunization drive for young children. Another group surveyed 500 residents and subsequently developed a walking tour that included historic, economic, and environmental analysis of the south side of the city. Although not a formal evaluation, it is noteworthy that 92 percent of the first graduating class of 33 seniors attended college, a figure far above what would be expected given the students' backgrounds.

Project GRAD—USA

Based on an educational collaborative developed at Jeff Davis High School in Houston, Texas, Project GRAD (Graduation Really Achieves Dreams) is a national program promoting school-community collaboration and the vertical integration of reform efforts, from kindergarten through college. In 2002, Project GRAD was serving 80,000 students attending urban schools with a history of poor performance in eight cities across the United States. Among its goals are to ensure that 80 percent of entering 9th graders in Project GRAD high schools go on to graduate and that 50 percent of graduates enter and complete a program of postsecondary education.[4]

A brief history illustrates the many ways a high school can be connected to and benefit from the resources of the community. Since 1981 Jeff Davis High School had been involved in a business partnership with Tenneco Corporation, which was located near the school. The partnership provided Davis with tutors, mentors, and some college scholarship money. But when Emily Cole arrived as principal in 1989, Davis High School had all the problems associated with an urban, high-poverty, low-achieving school. Students were wandering the hallways and absenteeism was rampant. Nearly 20 percent of Davis students dropped out every year, and fewer than 10 percent of its graduates went on to college. That year, 65 Davis students became pregnant. It was clear that much more needed to be done.

Cole made a number of changes at the school, which serves a predominantly Hispanic and low-income community. Internally, she looked for ways to implement research-based programs and practices reflecting the child-centered philosophy of education she previously had found successful as an elementary school principal. To personalize relationships of students

[4]For further information on Project GRAD, see http://www.projectgradusa.org.

to adults, she adopted block scheduling, restructured the ninth grade to create small learning communities, and restructured the administrative team. To increase students' responsibility for learning, a well-researched cooperative discipline program was adopted.

But Cole believed that to make a significant difference in education outcomes and the lives of her students, she also would need the help of parents and members of the community. She initiated changes in school governance that allowed parents and teachers to be involved in decision making about the school reform process. With the addition of new partners and new outreach strategies, the high school's business partnership with Tenneco was transformed into a much broader community collaborative.

Among the new partners was "Communities in Schools,"[5] which provided on-site staff at Davis to help students stay in school by connecting them with whatever social services they needed (see Chapter 7, this volume). Another was the University of Texas Health Science Center, which provided medical services and worked to help cultivate students' interest in the health professions.

Also joining the collaborative was The Metropolitan Organization (TMO), a coalition of local churches. Their goal was to help Davis High School to improve communication with parents and also to garner support from Hispanic business professionals, church groups, and other key elements of the local community. With guidance and assistance from TMO, Davis High School implemented its first "Walk for Success" in 1989. Davis staff, including Cole and TMO volunteers, visited the home of every Davis freshman to explain the college scholarship opportunities ($1,000 per year for up to 4 years) and their requirements. Parents were asked to sign an agreement outlining the requirements, one of which was that their high school student attends two summer institutes at the nearby Downtown campus of the University of Houston. TMO volunteers made follow-up contacts with parents to help them monitor their children's progress.

Since these collaborative activities with the community were implemented, there has been slow but steady improvement in educational outcomes for Davis students. Annual dropout rates from the school have decreased, and college enrollment has increased markedly. The percentage of students who graduate on time has improved, as have standardized test scores. The coordinated educational reform strategy in Davis' feeder elementary and middle schools that was begun in 1993 is gradually increas-

[5]Communities in Schools is a national model with local affiliates around the country. Its purpose is to connect community resources with schools to promote student learning and healthy development and to prevent students from dropping out (http://www.cisnet.org).

ing the number of entering students who have the skills needed to succeed in their 9th-grade classes, and beyond. Davis' efforts demonstrate the promise, the complexity, and the need for patience and persistence in school reform.

Service Learning

Service learning is another strategy for creating ties between schools and their communities and making the instructional program relevant to students' lives outside of school.[6] Students are placed in various community-serving organizations in ways that are directly connected to the curriculum (for example, in science, civics, or social studies). A 1999 study by the National Center for Education Statistics found that nearly half of all U.S. high schools use service learning as part of the curriculum (Pearson, 2002; Skinner and Chapman, 1999).

Like work-based learning (see Chapter 6, this volume), service learning provides students with different experiences and information that can make schooling more meaningful and help them to formulate future options. It is based in part on research showing that learners become more motivated when they perceive that what they are learning may be useful to others (Cognition and Learning Technology Group of Vanderbilt University, 1998; McCombs, 1996; National Research Council, 1999; Pintrich and Schunk, 1996). Advocates for service learning focus on four kinds of student engagement: civic engagement, social engagement with the communities they serve, personal engagement with individuals they serve, and academic engagement, which teachers mention as one of their principal reasons for using service learning (Ammon et al., 2002).

The evidence on the effects on school engagement, although sparse, is positive. Melchior's (1997) national study showed greater self-reported engagement (attention, effort, positive emotions) among students whose teachers included service learning than among students whose teachers did not. A large portion of the service learning students (87 percent) reported having learned a new skill that they believed would be useful in the future. In addition, statewide studies in Florida and California showed increased school attendance among students while they were engaged in service learning, compared to the previous semester or year, when they were not participating in service learning (Follman and Muldoon, 1997; Weiler, LaGoy,

---

[6]Service learning is distinguished from community service in that service learning, although it may meet community needs, is deliberately designed to develop skills and understanding of academic content.

Crane, and Rovner, 1998). The authors concluded that service learning makes the curriculum more interesting and more relevant for students and has the potential to motivate students to engage more genuinely in classroom activities.

The Teen Outreach Program that combines structured community service experiences with classroom discussions about careers and relationships has been studied more than most service learning programs. Studies using matched comparison of students in 35 states (Allen, Philliber, and Hoggson, 1990) as well as experimental designs at 25 sites (Allen, Philliber, Herrling, and Kupermine, 1997) found advantages of program participants in rates of school suspension, school dropout, school failure, and even pregnancy.

Honig et al. (2001) summarize other studies that provide clues about why service learning might be a particularly effective strategy for engaging youth in school. They suggest that students are more motivated in part because they are applying learning in contexts (hospitals, construction sites) that are personally meaningful. They also suggest that the academic skills youth develop in these settings build their confidence as learners, and that they develop social, emotional, and other nonacademic competencies and greater personal and social responsibility, which facilitate success in school.

Three qualities of service learning programs appear to contribute to their success (Honig et al., 2001). First, they are most effective when students have regular structured time to discuss the content and the process of their practical experiences. Second, successful programs give students opportunities for personal agency—to develop their own ideas and pursue their own interests. Third, effective service learning programs are closely linked to the academic curriculum.

It's Not Easy, But It's Worth the Effort

Documentation of efforts to develop and sustain school-family-community connections indicates that they are difficult to achieve (Honig et al., 2001; Kahne et al., 2001; White and Wehlage, 1995). Differences in cultures, competition for resources and control, limitations in time, mistrust, bureaucratic and funding barriers, and other obstacles need to be overcome. Short-term collaborations and activities are easier, although the payoff in terms of enhancing youth engagement in school and promoting positive development are not likely to be as great as sustained, coordinated efforts.

The evidence suggests that creating such linkages is worth the effort. The effects of the kinds of community partnerships we have described are difficult to isolate for many reasons, including the need to identify an appropriate control group and disentangle the effects of initiatives to collaborate with families and the community from the effects of other initiatives being implemented at the same time. Most program evaluations fall short of standards for rigorous scientific evidence, but looking broadly, the relevant evidence suggests the value of such initiatives.

The Coalition for Community Schools compiled information on 49 evaluation reports of school-community programs (Dryfoos, 2002). The programs varied substantially in the nature of the activity involved and the level of implementation (e.g., national, state, local school district). Taken together, the programs evaluated showed evidence of achievement gains, improved behavior (with fewer suspensions), reduced high-risk behavior (e.g., drug use), improved parenting practices and parent involvement in school, and lower neighborhood violence rates.

Clearly, programs vary in their value and effects on students. Honig et al. (2001, p. 1019) summarize succinctly evidence on the qualities of school-community connections that engage youth and promote positive development. Effective programs are

- focused on each youth in a holistic sense;
- focused on all youth;
- strengths-based, prosocial, and developmental;
- responsive to specific youth and neighborhoods;
- youth-centered; and
- filled with expanded opportunities to learn from adults in and out of school.

Having reviewed the evidence, the committee is convinced that until all organizations, including schools, see themselves as partners in supporting positive youth development, efforts to increase student engagement in school will have limited success. Moreover, organizations, models, and lessons learned from previous efforts are available now to assist schools and communities in developing useful collaborations.[7]

PEERS

The social world of peers, like that of the family, can promote engagement in learning to the extent that the social relationships in those settings are emotionally supportive and cultivate values consistent with those of the

[7]A source for such models and lessons learned is the National Network of Partnership Schools at Johns Hopkins University, which has documented many research-based, goal-oriented approaches to improving family and community involvement in the schools. The network offers many ideas for school and district personnel to implement that have successfully increased family and community participation, such as after-school tutoring programs, parent surveys, and back-to-school picnics (http://www.partnershipschools.org).

school (Comer, 1980; Connell, Gambone, and Smith, 2000; Giles, 1998; Gold et al., 2002; Heckman, 1996; Lewis, 1996; Murnane and Levy, 1996a; National Research Council and Institute of Medicine, 2002). Because peer interactions take place inside of schools as well as in community settings, many if not most peer relationships among adolescents are with other students. Educators, therefore, have some effect on whether peer groups and friendships support or undermine engagement in learning. Just as they can reach out to parents to make the familial environment more supportive of learning, they also can influence the social world of peers.

Peer influences are as complex and multilevel as the peer social world itself. To better understand how peers affect adolescents' engagement in learning, we review four lines of research—on peer cultures, peer crowds, gangs, and friendship groups.

Peer Cultures

Casual observations of adolescents' behavior may appear to support Coleman's (1961) claim that they are more concerned about being popular with peers than about achieving academically. Even if this is true, it does not mean that adolescents are not concerned about academic achievement. More recent research suggests that the norms of the peer group in most high schools support, at least at some modest level, academic achievement rather than disengagement (for a review, see Brown, 1990). For example, urban high school students in one study reported that their peers generally encouraged them to study their school subjects rather than not to do so (Brown, Clasen, and Eicher, 1986).

Fordham and Ogbu (1986) have proposed that an antiacademic peer culture is common among Black adolescents.[8] They based their thesis on an ethnographic study of a Washington, D.C., high school where nearly all of the students were Black and many were from low-income families. They observed that "peer groups discourage their members from putting forth the time and effort required to do well in school and from adopting the attitudes and standard practices that enhance academic achievement. They oppose adopting appropriate academic attitudes and behaviors because they are considered 'white' " (p. 183; see also Chapter 2, this volume).

Steele (1992) also has argued that African-American students believe they have to give up value priorities, preferences, and styles of speech and appearance to master mainstream (predominantly white) culture, and that

---

[8]Ogbu has also applied his notion of oppositional culture to Mexican-Americans (e.g., Ogbu, 1989; see also Romo and Falbo, 1996, and Valenzuela, 1999).

some prefer instead to disidentify with mainstream culture. He notes "once disidentification occurs in a school, it can spread like the common cold. . . . One's identity as an authentic Black is held hostage, made incompatible with school identification" (p. 75).

Other qualitative studies provide further evidence that some Black students have peer groups that maintain norms against high achievement. In a study of 10 schools engaged in voluntary detracking, some of the Black students interviewed were apprehensive about taking honors classes because they feared being ostracized by Black peers (Yonezawa et al., 2002). A few reported that Black students called Black peers names like "sellout" or "whitewashed" to deter them from developing relationships with white students. Fordham (1996) also found that some Black students in the high school she studied expressed concern about losing their ethnic identity as the result of becoming a successful student.

Additional data relevant to the issue of the value students place on academic success is found in two studies of sixth through eighth graders in economically depressed areas of Los Angeles (Graham, Taylor, and Hudley, 1998). When asked to name classmates whom they admired, respected, and wanted to be like, the African-American boys in these studies named more low-achieving classmates than high-achieving classmates. By contrast, African-American girls named more high-achieving than low-achieving classmates as peers whom they admired, respected, and wanted to be like. The data for girls are inconsistent with Fordham and Ogbu's (1986) hypothesis because their ethnographic study suggests that both boys and girls experience a peer culture that devalues academic achievement. Even for boys, the data do not clearly demonstrate that the African-American boys devalued academic achievement, because low-achieving African-American boys might have nominated low-achieving classmates not because they devalued academic achievement, but because they had a positive view of classmates whom they perceived as similar to themselves. Nevertheless, the study suggests that the African-American boys in the sample did emulate peers who were low achieving.

Survey evidence contradicts Fordham and Ogbu's (1986) hypothesis. Peer culture was indirectly examined in analyses of the data obtained from nearly 17,000 high school sophomores who participated in the first follow-up of NELS (Ainsworth-Darnell and Downey, 1998; see also Downey and Ainsworth-Darnell, 2002). One of the questions the study asked was whether African-American high school students who were high in academic achievement were unpopular with their peers. Most of the students who participated in NELS were white, but the sample included more than 2,000 African-American students. In the sample as a whole, students who reported that their classmates regarded them as very good students were also likely to report that they were popular, socially active, and among the social leaders in the school. Moreover, the relationship between academic achievement (i.e., being a very good student) and popularity was even stronger for African-American students than for white students.

Also using NELS data, Cook and Ludwig (1998) found no difference, when controlling for socioeconomic background, in the proportion of Black and white 10th graders who expected to go to college, or the amount of time they spent on homework, or rates of absenteeism—variables they claim should have been higher for Black students if they were disproportionately alienated from high school.

Ferguson (2002) found in his survey of ethnically mixed suburban schools that more of the Black students than those from any other ethnic group checked "very important" to a question about how strongly friends would agree with the statement, "It's important to study hard to get good grades." In a MetLife (2002) national survey of youth from 7th to 12th grades, more students (64 percent) claimed to have one or more friends who liked school than claimed to have friends who thought that doing well in school was not "cool" (24 percent). The students' ethnicity and their parents' education level were only modestly associated with their responses to these questions. Black students were slightly more likely (67 percent) to report that they had friends who liked school than were white (62 percent) or Hispanic (64 percent) students. Teachers' beliefs about students' friends were, in contrast, strongly associated with the demographic characteristics of the school population. In schools with high minority (more than 66 percent) enrollment, teachers expected about 45 percent of their students to "hang out with people who believe that doing well in school is not 'cool'," compared to 30 percent of the students in schools with 34-66 percent minority students, and 20 percent of the students in schools with less than 34 percent minority students.

Taken together, the findings from these and other studies (e.g., Arroyo and Zigler, 1995; Cook and Ludwig, 1997, 1998; Downey and Ainsworth-Darnell, 2002; Farkas, Lleras, and Maczuga, 2002; Spencer, Cross, Harpalani, and Gross, in press; Spencer et al., 2001) suggest that the hypothesis of a distinctly oppositional peer culture in high schools with large numbers of students of color is not pervasive. Although such antiacademic subcultures have been observed in ethnographic work, the quantitative survey data suggest that they are not the norm for African-American students.

Viewed from a different perspective, however, the peer culture may be somewhat antiacademic for high school students from all ethnic groups.[9]

---

[9]For examples of cultural subgroups that foster or at least reflect poor school attitudes, see Valenzuela, 1999.

In particular, the norms of the high school peer group are likely to be different from the norms of the students' parents. Ethnographic studies suggest that parents of urban high school students think their children should spend more time studying and doing homework than their children think they should spend (e.g., Fordham, 1996). Quantitative studies of differences between adolescents' and their parents' values are rare because few researchers assess both students' and parents' views about academic achievement and even fewer use comparable measures for both. There is, however, some relevant evidence. Coleman (1961) reported that more parents wanted their children to be remembered as brilliant students in high school than their children did. In another study conducted in junior high schools (Berndt, Miller, and Park, 1989), students said their parents would be less accepting of misbehavior in class than they were. Ethnographic reports and survey data suggest that many students believe their peers have a negative view of students with high academic achievement (Arroyo and Zigler, 1995; Fordham, 1996).

In summary, there is no question that an antiacademic orientation can be found among some students, although large-scale empirical data do not support claims that an antiacademic orientation is pervasive among African-American students. The existence of such an orientation among some groups of students, especially in urban high schools serving low-income communities, and its negative effects on engagement and learning, suggest the importance of investigating its origins and how schools can address the problem. It is unlikely that those students who demonstrate an antiacademic orientation actually wish to fail in school. A possible explanation is that they perceive the demands of academic work as threatening, perhaps because they are asked to carry out academic tasks they do not understand or because they do not perceive the value of carrying out the tasks to be worth the effort required. Whatever the reason and however small the numbers, special attention needs to be given to preventing the development of such values that undermine engagement.

A major limitation of the research on peers is that the majority of studies are on white middle-class youth, and few studies examine subgroup differences. In addition, the effect of the school climate, as discussed in Chapter 5, on the peer culture has not been studied extensively. An important exception is the research of McDill and Rigsby (1973), which showed that whether or not peer influence "mediated" the effects of the normative school climate on student academic behavior depended on the measure of peer influence used, and how the constructs are operationalized. As McDill and Rigsby's work suggests, it is likely that the positive effects of high school climates characterized by high expectations and a press for academic achievement are partly explained by the effect of such a climate on students' own values related to learning and achievement and the values their peers espouse. More research is needed on how the climate promoted by adults affects peer norms—distinguishing among different groups based on gender, class, ethnicity, and cultural backgrounds.

Peer Crowds

When given opportunities to interact with peers, adolescents typically choose peers who are similar in clothing, hairstyles, ethnic background, social class, and other attributes, including academic achievement, school engagement, extracurricular activities, and activities outside of school. Collections of friendship groups that share a number of attributes are found across multiple settings. These are referred to as "crowds." Crowds are reputation-based collectives of similarly stereotyped individuals who may or may not spend much time together (Brown, 1990). Thus, a crowd is defined by its reputation in the entire peer group for certain characteristic activities or attributes. Some crowds such as the "druggies" are defined by their primary activities. Other crowds are defined by personal attributes such as ethnicity (in ethnically diverse schools; e.g., "Mexicans"), social status (e.g., "populars"), or academic achievement (e.g., "brains"). Because crowds are defined by reputation rather than social interaction, not all members of the same crowd interact socially. In a large high school, some members of the same crowd may not even know one another.

Students who belong to different crowds typically differ in their academic achievement. For example, in one major study of peer crowds that included thousands of high school students from ethnically diverse rural and urban high schools (Brown, Mounts, Lamborn, and Steinberg, 1993), students named five crowds to which their classmates belonged: brains, populars, druggies, outcasts, and jocks. Students in the brain and popular crowds generally had high grades; students in the druggie and outcast crowds had low grades, and the jock crowd was in the middle.

Belonging to a particular crowd could influence high school students' behavior, but perhaps not exactly as common sense might suggest. Because members of the same crowd do not necessarily interact with one another, there may be no direct influence of crowd members on one another. Moreover, students may belong to the same crowd because they have independently developed certain patterns of behavior, not because other crowd members encouraged them to initiate those behaviors.

The most powerful influence of crowd membership may be an indirect result of the treatment received by adults and members of different crowds (for illustrations of this differential treatment, see the case studies by Fine, Valenzuela and Bowditch, 1993). The status hierarchy of crowds within a school is strongly reinforced by the adults there. Principals and teachers favor the members of high-status crowds because those students typically are vocal in their support for school activities and they bring positive forms of attention to the school. For example, adults in the school are usually delighted when athletic teams succeed in high-profile interscholastic athletic events. Members of low-status crowds, in contrast, are less revered because they are more difficult to manage and they sometimes bring negative forms of attention to the school.

Most students know in which crowds their peers place them and where their crowd falls in the status hierarchy (O'Brien and Bierman, 1988), and the relationships between high-status and low-status crowds are often hostile (Coleman, 1961; Eckert, 1989). Consequently, high school generally is not a supportive setting for students in low-status crowds. They often are disliked by their teachers and rejected by their higher status classmates. Not surprisingly, many are disengaged from school or actively hostile toward students and teachers. Stated colloquially, they can see that they are not wanted, and they drop out at the first opportunity (Brown, 1990; Eckert, 1989).

The school organization can reinforce the effects of crowd membership, or it can minimize them. Academic tracking, for example, makes differences in students' social status highly visible. Tracking can also exacerbate negative peer influences by isolating students with low academic achievement from peers who are academically engaged and value achievement. Adults can reinforce status difference by being harsher, more authoritarian, and less supportive and encouraging of low-status students.

Rather than reinforce a status hierarchy that adolescents create, schools need to make concerted efforts to counteract a social context that fosters disengagement among low-status students. Eliminating tracking is one strategy for making differences among students' skill levels less visible. Another strategy is to create activities that involve students from different crowds that are affirming and decrease the salience of the status hierarchy. Such activities can contribute to a school climate that is cohesive and supportive of individual students and of academic values.

Recognizing students for various talents and achievements can also raise the status of students who do not perform well on conventional measures. Some students who are neither high achievers nor jocks have artistic talents (e.g., drawing, break-dancing) and skills (e.g., woodwork, restoring cars) that can be encouraged, publicized, and built on to improve academic engagement. In classes, students' status can be raised by giving them responsibilities in cooperative learning activities, by arranging for them to tutor younger children, and by drawing out their unique experiences and cultural knowledge. In these and other ways, adults in schools can reduce the negative effects of crowd stereotypes on students in low-status crowds, and thus encourage their sense of belonging and commitment to school.

Gangs

Gangs are a form of peer group that does not promote academic engagement. In many urban high schools, members of youth gangs use their clothing and behaviors to signal their membership to others, especially students in rival gangs (Howell and Lynch, 2000). Even if school administrators make rules to eliminate these signals (e.g., not allowing baseball hats to be worn on school grounds), gang members usually find a way to identify themselves.

Gang members are typically described by their peers as belonging to crowds characterized by drugs and violence, but a gang is qualitatively different from a crowd. Gangs are social organizations that have unique rules (e.g., about what clothes to wear) and norms (e.g., about what to do when someone teases you). These organizations can have a powerful influence on adolescents' behavior, particularly by promoting criminal behavior, drug abuse, and other deviant behaviors (Battin-Pearson, Thornberry, Hawkins, and Krohn, 1998).

In addition to promoting antisocial as well as antiacademic behaviors, gang presence in schools can undermine the ability of all students to be engaged in academic work (Flores-Gonzalez, 2002; Howell, 1998). Disruptions caused by fights, for example, are common, and occasionally nongang members are caught in the crossfire. National surveys have shown that students who report gang activity in their high schools also report that they do not feel safe at school (Howell, 1998; Howell and Lynch, 2000), a feeling that is hardly conducive to a focus on academic work.

Interventions, some implemented in school-based curricula, have been designed to reduce the problems associated with youth gangs, but their effectiveness is rarely evaluated systematically (Howell, 1998). The focus of some interventions is on decreasing the number of students who join gangs. Other interventions focus on reducing the level of gang violence or encouraging students to leave a gang and join more socially sanctioned peer groups.

The committee speculates that an isolated program intervention approach to preventing youth involvement in gangs is less likely to be successful than comprehensive changes in the school climate and instructional program. Adolescents' experiences in school are highly predictive of whether they join a gang. Youth who join gangs are typically low achievers in low-status crowds—those least likely to experience high school as a personally supportive social context in which they feel valued. In a prospective longitudinal study of 800 youth in high-crime neighborhood Hill, Lui, and Hawkins (2001) found that the highest risk factor (along with availability of marijuana in the neighborhood) was a learning disability. Students with learning disabilities were 3.6 times more likely to join a gang than were students without learning disabilities; students with low academic achievement were 3.1 times more likely to join gangs compared to better achieving classmates. Not feeling attached (twice as likely) or committed to school (1.8 times as likely) were also strong predictors of joining a gang. These findings suggest that creating high schools that help students learn in a caring, respectful, and supportive social climate may be the best strategy for preventing gang involvement. Adolescents join gangs to meet social and psychological needs that are not being met elsewhere (Padilla, 1992). To the degree that schools can better meet these needs, their students will be less likely to try to meet them in potentially destructive peer groups.

Friendship Groups

Most adolescents report that they have a few best friends (Berndt, 1996, 1999). An adolescent's best friends are usually friends with each other; thus, they constitute a friendship group. Adolescents spend more time with the members of this close friendship group than with other peers. They also feel closer and share more intimate information with their best friends than with other peers (Newcomb and Bagwell, 1995).

For decades, researchers used estimates of the similarities between friends on specific characteristics, including academic achievement, as an index of how much friends influence one another (e.g., Ide, Parkerson, Haertel, and Walberg, 1981). Influence, however, cannot be assumed from similarity (e.g., Kandel, 1978, 1996). The old saying, "birds of a feather flock together," applies well to friendships (McPherson, Smith-Lovin, and Cook, 2001). Friends have similar characteristics partly because adolescents with similar characteristics become friends, not simply because adolescents who have become friends influence one another so that they become more similar.

More recent longitudinal studies, however, provide credible evidence that adolescents are influenced by their best friends, more so than by any other peers. Berndt and Keefe (1995) used a longitudinal design to examine the influence of best friends on the school adjustment of junior high school students. In the fall of a school year, the students named their best friends and reported their positive involvement in school and their disruptive behavior in the classroom. Their teachers also reported on their involvement, disruption, and report-card grades. Because most students listed friends who were also participating in the study, the students' scores could be matched with their friends' scores. These assessments were repeated in the spring of the same school year. Analyses showed that students' adjustment was fairly comparable in the fall and the spring. Most students who were high in involvement and academic achievement and low in disruption in the fall showed a comparable profile in the spring. Some students' adjustment changed, however, and the direction of the changes were predicted by the fall adjustment level of their friends. In particular, students who had friends who were rated relatively high in the fall in involvement, disruption, or grades increased on these dimensions from the fall to the spring. These data strongly suggest that the students' adjustment to school was influenced by the adjustment of their friends. Similar data from studies with diverse samples of high school students suggest that their positive engagement and disruptive behavior are influenced by the engagement and behavior of their friends (Epstein, 1983; Hallinan and Williams, 1990; McFarland, 2001; Steinberg, Brown, and Dornbusch, 1996).

The longitudinal studies of friends' influence also imply that friends can have either a positive or a negative influence on high school students' engagement, depending on the friends' characteristics. In a variant of the usual longitudinal design, Epstein (1983) identified students in the elementary through high school grades who were relatively high or low in academic achievement and who had friends who were relatively high or low in achievement. One year later, she assessed the students' achievement again. She found that students who initially were high in achievement but whose friends were low in achievement decreased in achievement. Conversely, students who initially were low in achievement but whose friends were high in achievement increased in achievement. Most important, the positive influence of high-achieving friends was roughly equal to the negative influence of low-achieving friends. This large-scale study demonstrates that friends' influences on students' engagement in school can be as strong in the positive direction as in the negative direction.

High school students tend to form friendships within their academic track or set of courses (Oakes, Gamoran, and Page, 1992). The negative effect of friends suggests the importance of avoiding organizational structures and programs that create concentrated groups of academically disengaged students. Catterall's (1987) observation of a dropout prevention program that increased the dropout rate among program participants is consistent with this view. Attempts to explain this unexpected outcome revealed that students in the program had many opportunities for social interaction, which led to the formation of friendships among them. After the program ended, some students decided to drop out of school, and when they did so, their friends usually dropped out, too.

After reviewing the results of many dropout prevention-intervention programs, Dishion, McCord, and Poulin (1999, p. 762) concluded, "there is reason to be cautious and to avoid aggregating young high-risk adolescents into intervention groups." Unless attention is also paid to the friends' characteristics, these interventions may inadvertently strengthen the negative influence of friends with negative characteristics. In particular, interventions of this kind with urban high school students could strengthen negative attitudes toward school, tendencies to drop out of school, and other facets of school disengagement.

Again, the research points to potential harmful effects of tracking and other policies that isolate students at risk of becoming disengaged and prevent them from having opportunities to interact and develop friendships with peers who are more committed to schooling. The strength of peer networks and youths' need for peer support, however, make it difficult to promote curricular mixing. In the Yonezawa et al. (2002) study of detracking discussed in Chapter 5, students of color resisted taking advanced and honors courses with white students in part because they did not want to give up the supportive networks of peers they had developed in their lower-level courses. Apparently providing more student choice in the courses they take is not sufficient to achieve substantial mixing of students from different backgrounds and crowds. Concerted efforts need to be made to ensure that students who have previously not had access to a challenging curriculum are made to feel psychologically safe and comfortable in such courses.

CONCLUSIONS

Schools can increase adolescents' engagement by harnessing the resources of families and the larger community. The evidence reviewed in this chapter suggests the value of efforts to improve communication and coordination among adults in the various settings where adolescents spend their time—including schools, homes, religious institutions, as well as the various organized extracurricular activities sponsored by schools and community groups. To the extent that adults in these settings collaborate to ensure that the various environments where adolescents interact with each other in the community are inclusive, informed by positive values, and supportive of the healthy development of young people, productive engagement in school-based learning is likely to be promoted (Connell and Klem, 2000; Connell, Gambone, and Smith, 2000; National Research Council and Institute of Medicine, 2002).

Both parent and peer influences can be positive or negative, and school policies and activities affect the direction of these influences. Parents are more likely to be involved, and thus to reinforce the messages from school, in schools that reach out and make proactive efforts to include them. Peer influences likewise do not occur independent of the behavior of adults or the organization of schools, community organizations, and other settings where youths interact. Adults can work to structure school environments that are affirming, supportive, and deliberately designed to make all students feel that they are valued members of the school community. This can be achieved by heterogeneous grouping for classes, collaborative learning activities in and out of class that bring together students with different levels of achievement, activities that are based on shared interests rather than academic competence, and in many other ways. Careful attention needs to be given to how class assignments and activities promote student interactions. Because students will naturally seek others like themselves, self-conscious, proactive strategies to "mix" students are required.

6

Meeting Students' Nonacademic Needs

Students who come to school hungry, tired, chronically ill, depressed, or preoccupied by family problems cannot engage fully in the academic curriculum. Pregnancy and drug and alcohol addiction can also interfere with attention to schoolwork. Youth from families living in poverty are often burdened with financial responsibilities that require them to work, with the care of siblings and grandparents, and with other roles that middle-class youth typically do not assume until they are older. As a society, we need to be concerned about all aspects of youth development. But even if our only objective is to engage adolescents in schoolwork, we could not neglect aspects of their lives that interfere with their ability to participate productively in school.

Distractions that result from poor nutrition, absence of health care, homelessness, and violence are common in low-income, urban communities. Other distractions, such as pregnancy and drugs, are common in middle- and upper class neighborhoods as well. Permanent and pervasive solutions to the effects of culture and poverty lie beyond the reach of educators; they require a fundamental reshaping of economic and social conditions in this country. While acknowledging that we can make limited progress working within high schools, we still cannot wait for the problems of poverty and other negative cultural influences to be resolved. We must reform high schools to better meet adolescents' needs while we develop economic and social policies that reduce inequality and minimize the consequences of poverty. Effective reforms that increase the engagement of urban youth in school will require a new vision of how high schools address students' nonacademic needs.

This chapter begins with a description of traditional approaches to meeting high school students' basic social, emotional, and physical needs. These usually involve a combination of professionals, such as guidance counselors, social workers, and nurses, working in high schools with a panoply of separate programs. The programs tend to focus on physical and mental health, sex education and pregnancy prevention, drug and alcohol problems, and life skills. Existing programs vary according to students' needs, funding limitations and opportunities, proclivities of principals and teachers, the availability of appropriate services, and the capacity and interest of the local community.

The new vision that we advocate in the second part of this chapter shifts attention from and exclusive focus on the individual student to a focus on the larger high school context, reconceptualizes the roles and responsibilities of all adults in the school, and makes the high school part of a network (and sometimes the hub) of community resources rather than an independent organization.

THE TRADITIONAL APPROACH

The roles of adults in traditional high schools are highly differentiated. Teachers teach; counselors and social workers focus on students' nonacademic needs. Even within the counseling domain, roles are usually differentiated into career counseling, academic counseling, and psychological counseling. Special education provides specific, individualized, or small-group services to students who qualify, and experts or packaged programs are brought in to address issues such as pregnancy prevention and alcohol and drug abuse. School nurses and occasionally doctors may attend to students' physical health on site, or students may be referred to community clinics for physical as well as mental health problems.

Some evidence is available on how well these traditional approaches meet high school students' nonacademic needs. We review briefly evidence related to the functions of career and academic counseling, and mental health and other support services in high schools.

Career and Academic Counseling

In the early 20th century, counseling originated in efforts to help students make vocational decisions. Today, career counseling has been substantially displaced with academic and college counseling (Krei and Rosenbaum, 2001). Relatively few resources are devoted to counseling. A decade ago the ratio of students to counselors was around 500:1 nationally (Chodzinski, 1994). A more recent estimate of 1,000:1 (with a 2,500:1 ratio for school psychologists or social workers) suggests that resources may be declining (Kuperminc, Leadbeater, and Blatt, 2001). These ratios contrast with recommendations of 50:1 for at-risk students (Commission on Precollege Guidance and Counseling, 1986), between 100:1 under ideal conditions, and 300:1 as a maximum (American School Counselor Association, 1988).

Given current ratios, individual students receive relatively little attention of any kind and few students are able to form close relationships with their counselors. Furthermore, the time that counselors can spend with students has been severely diminished by administrative paperwork, including record keeping, monitoring progress, documentation, and class scheduling (Hardesty and Dillard, 1994; Lee and Ekstrom, 1987; Louis, Jones, and Barajas, 2001).

Access to even these meager resources is not evenly distributed among students. Although college advising and guidance counseling are especially important to students from low-income and minority families who may have fewer informational resources, counselors often spend more time with college-bound, middle-class white students (Chapman, O'Brien, and DeMasi, 1987; Lee and Ekstrom, 1987).

When counselors do find time for counseling, they tend to combine academic counseling focused on progress through the high school with cognitive-behavioral strategies to improve students' defeatist attitudes and perceptions of low ability (Trusty, 1996). In Rosenbaum's study of counselors in Midwestern high schools, counselors were leery of providing any career direction for fear of discouraging college plans or being perceived as steering or tracking students. The dominant strategy was to preach "college for all," advising all students to prepare for college and providing them with the information necessary to meet college requirements (Rosenbaum, 2001).

When counselors do engage with students in any form of career planning, they typically use the trait and factor approach, in which counselors help students uncover their own preferences and personality traits (often through interest and personality inventories), then provide them with information about occupations suited to their interests and abilities—a process sometimes belittled as "test 'em and tell 'em," or the "information dump."[1] Other approaches to counseling stress the acquisition of decision-making

[1]See, for example, Table 10.a in Herr and Cramer (1992), in which three of the top five services provided are occupational information, educational information, and individual assessment information.

"skills,"[2] based on the implicit assumption that decision making is a simple skill that can be easily learned.

In particular, current strategies do not serve the needs of students who do not have other adults in their lives to help them access information and make important decisions (Grubb, 2002). Students need to be able to assess the accuracy of the information they receive, and weigh present and future possibilities and the tradeoffs among them. They need to be able to make decisions about educational and occupational alternatives with different probabilities of success, and to consider a wide range of alternatives, including formal schooling, which they may not be able to consider in a balanced way because of negative experiences. Finally, decisions about jobs and careers involve deeply rooted dimensions of identity, and the development of career identity is a long, complex process. Decision making—reasoning about the relation between preferences and opportunities—is a multifaceted "competence" in its own right, which conventional guidance and counseling do not address. In the absence of effective career and academic counseling, students are all too often left (as described by Schneider and Stevenson, 1999) "ambitious but directionless," with high ambitions for the future but no understanding of the connection between schoolwork and their occupational goals.

One way to evaluate current approaches to counseling is in terms of how well they reflect the conditions necessary for enhancing motivation and engagement, as described in Chapter 2. Our analysis suggests serious deficiencies. Resources in guidance counseling are so limited that few students and counselors get to know each other well. The dominant approaches to career and academic counseling fail to offer students any active role in learning about or weighing postsecondary education and employment options. Partly because of limited resources, guidance and counseling in most high schools is a hit-or-miss affair; the idea of a coherent program, with a set of activities designed to introduce students systematically to the education and employment options they face, is absent from most high schools.

In addition, the independence of guidance and counseling from classroom activities means these activities are usually poorly integrated with learning. The dominance of college for all means that most students are counseled into only one option. Although this approach avoids charges of bias or tracking, it also fails to provide much information about alternative routes to meaningful employment and self-sufficiency. Furthermore, the

---

[2]The British, with their longer history of choice mechanisms in schools, have clarified that information may be necessary but is rarely sufficient. See Hodkinson, Sparkes, and Hodkinson (1996), especially Chapter 8 on technical versus pragmatic rationality, and Reay and Ball (1997) on class differences in conceptions of choice.

lack of sustained academic and career counseling means that programs in most high schools do not help students understand the role of school in expanding or constricting their future options. Indeed, the large numbers of students who fail to understand college entrance requirements, or who leave high school without any clue about their postsecondary options, is testimony to the ineffectiveness of high schools in helping students develop potential pathways (Schneider and Stevenson, 1999). Thus the current structure of guidance and counseling in most high schools violates every one of the precepts that support motivation and engagement.

Only a little direct evidence exists on the effects of guidance and counseling; well-designed outcome-based evaluations are almost nonexistent (Green and Keys, 2001). Borders and Drury's (1992) summary of the literature concluded that well-designed group counseling can have positive effects on academic persistence, achievement, attendance, classroom behavior, self-esteem, self-concepts, and attitudes toward school. Group counseling programs that have shown promise are typically structured, time-limited groups with a developmentally appropriate curriculum that enables students to support each other, share strategies, give each other feedback, and challenge each other (Borders and Drury, 1992). The positive effects on academic and personal outcomes held for various groups, including low-achieving students, disruptive students, learning disabled students, and those from divorced families. In another review, Whiston and Sexton (1998) examined outcomes from several studies of both academic and personal counseling and found positive effects on student achievement, career planning, and social skills. They found tentative support for career planning, group counseling, social skills training, and peer counseling—all models that, except for individual career planning, display the positive features outlined by Borders and Drury (1992).

In addition, there is now substantial evidence that well-designed mentoring programs—in which mentors are systematically taught about their potential roles and carefully matched and supervised—can help students in several ways (Grossman, 1999; Mecartney, Styles, and Morrow, 1994; Morrow and Styles, 1995; Tierney, Grossman, and Resch, 2000). Students themselves value mentors: Wirth-Bond, Coyne, and Adams (1991) noted that a counselor was identified more than 50 percent of the time by high-risk students who claimed to have a "significant other" at their school who supports and understands them. To the extent that individual counselors can serve in close mentoring roles, they may be effective in enhancing motivation, progress, and completion, but such roles are currently limited by high ratios of students to counselors.

Overall, the evidence about the effects of guidance and counseling is quite thin. It is difficult to disentangle the effects of such services from other elements of a high school, and it is nearly impossible to avoid the suspicion that self-selection affects all these evaluations.[3] But the evidence that is available suggests that a well-designed and well-placed program with adequate resources can have positive effects on students, but also that most high schools lack such well-designed programs.

In high school youth must make choices that can set them on particular trajectories that can be difficult to reverse. If we fail to support them in making those decisions, students who do not have resources in their homes or community will remain bewildered about the purposes of schooling. Lacking this understanding, they have little reason to be actively engaged in the high school curriculum. Our current approach is not working, and not simply because resources are too scarce. Although additional resources may be necessary, we will suggest later in this chapter alternative uses of those resources.

Mental Health Counseling

During the 1920s counselors in schools began to give greater attention to "personal adjustment" (Gysbers, 2001), an old-fashioned term reflecting an enduring notion that students need to adjust to school conditions rather than vice versa. By the 1940s personal counseling was as much a part of the high school counselor's role as was vocational and academic guidance. Now, however, no matter what their labels, counselors describe their own roles as largely confined to scheduling, monitoring progress, and paperwork (Wilson and Rossman, 1993). Even those who are able to carve out time to provide mental health services tend to focus on crisis intervention and not on individual or group work (Borders and Drury, 1992; Keys and Bemak, 1997).

Although estimates vary depending on the definition used, it is clear that emotional difficulties and mental health problems are common among students whose academic performance is poor and who drop out of school, suggesting the importance of addressing emotional problems in any effort to increase student academic engagement (Adelman and Taylor, 1998; Roeser, Eccles, and Strobel, 1998). Knitzer, Steinberg, and Fleisch (1991) estimate that nearly two-thirds of the country's dropout population has some kind of behavior or emotional problem. Other studies show that two-

---

[3]In a study of community college students, Grubb (1996, chap. 3) detected a kind of triage situation: The students most sure of themselves and their programs did not go to counselors except perhaps for a final verification of the in-course plans, and the students least sure of their plans also failed to use counselors because they were unsure of what to ask. A group in the middle, with some direction but not clear plans, seemed the most likely to see guidance counselors.

thirds of all children and youth identified with behavioral or emotional disorders function below grade level and have histories of repeated grade failures; nearly half of them (42 percent) end up dropping out of school (Friedman et al., 1988; Wagner and Shaver, 1989). Findings from the National Co-Morbidity Study (Kessler, Foster, Saunders, and Stang, 1995) show that 14.2 percent of high school dropouts have a history of psychiatric disorder, compared to only 5 percent of high school graduates who do not go on to college. In the most recent cohort surveyed, 23.6 percent of the male dropouts and 22.7 percent of the female dropouts had histories of earlier mental health disorders (Kessler et al., 1995).

The links between mental health and school engagement are supported by correlational research. Roeser, van der Wolf, and Strobel (2001) found that students who had either internalized (e.g., anxiety, depression) or externalized (e.g., anger) problems had relatively low expectations for academic success. Depressive symptoms have been associated with impaired cognitive performance, lower expectations for success, lower academic self-efficacy, and avoidance of challenge in the classroom, as well as with lower achievement on standardized tests and lower grades.[4] Externalized distress has been associated with social rejection, disruptive and refusal behaviors in class, and aggression, as well as with poor achievement and dropping out of school.[5]

In Roeser, Eccles, and Sameroff's (1998) longitudinal study of middle school students, mental health (absence of emotional distress, depression, anxiety, anger) was positively associated with academic motivation (perceptions of competence, academic values) and achievement at the beginning of seventh grade and at the end of eighth grade. Positive mental health in seventh grade predicted adolescents' academic performance in eighth grade, suggesting a reciprocal relationship between mental health and academic engagement.

Many mental health providers and policy analysts agree that young people with mental health problems are inadequately served. Approximately 20 percent of the U.S. students experience social, emotional, or behavioral problems that interfere with daily functioning in and out of school (Institute of Medicine, 1994; Weist, 1997). Estimates show, however, that less than one-third of this group receive any type of mental health services

---

[4]In a large literature, see Blechman, McBaron, Carolla, and Audette (1986); Brackney and Karabenick (1995); Kendall and Dobson (1993); Kovacs (1989); Nolen-Hoeksema, Girgus, and Seligman (1986); Roeser and Eccles (1998); Roeser, Eccles, and Sameroff (1998); and Roeser et al. (2001).

[5]See Cairns, Cairns, and Neckerman (1989); Hinshaw (1992); Parker and Asher (1987); Roeser and Eccles (1998); Roeser, Eccles, and Sameroff (1998); and Roeser et al. (2001).

(Adelman and Taylor, 1998; National Advisory Mental Health Council, 1990; Office of Technology Assessment, 1991). Local studies are consistent with these national estimates. For example, in a survey of parents and teachers in a northeastern school district, Zahner, Pawelkiewicz, DeFrancesco, and Adnopoz (1992) found that 38.5 percent of children were at risk for developing psychiatric disorders, but only 37 percent of these children had received any treatment at school. (An additional 24 percent received care in a nonschool setting.) Goodwin, Goodwin, and Cantrill (1988) found that approximately 15 percent of students in a Colorado school district who were qualified to receive mental health services were not receiving them.

Most mental health services in schools are currently limited to students in special education (Duchnowski, 1994), but even many students who have been diagnosed to have special needs do not receive appropriate services. Moore, Strang, Schwartz, and Braddock (1988) estimate that 58 percent of all school districts provide no counseling services on their own; of those students who do receive counseling, 60 to 70 percent receive five or fewer sessions. Weist (1997) points out that the availability of services to address children's emotional and behavioral problems decreases as they advance through the grades, and thus high school students have the least access to such programs.

Like academic counselors, school psychologists spend only a small percentage of their time in direct services with youth or their families (Conoley and Conoley, 1991; Knitzer et al., 1991). They do not engage in long-term counseling or therapy; instead they refer students to out-of-school community or private mental health services (Borders and Drury, 1992; Keys and Bemak, 1997; Weist, 1997).

In addition, a familiar inequity plagues mental health services. Despite their greater needs and the overrepresentation of mental health problems among dropout populations (e.g., Knitzer et al., 1991; Trusty, 1996; see also Chapter 3, this volume), low-income and minority students are underrepresented in counseling (Brinson and Kottler, 1995). Many reasons have been suggested for this inequity, including the possibility that such students are more likely to drop out of counseling prematurely because they do not believe their needs are being addressed, or because they lack accurate information about available services. In addition, a basic incongruence between mainstream and minority perceptions about mental health, the lack of ethnically similar counselors, the lack of culturally sensitive treatment approaches, and the focus on individual rather than on environmental factors may contribute to low rates of utilization (Atkinson, Jennings, and Leongson, 1990; Atkinson, Morten, and Sue, 1989; Brinson and Kottler, 1995; Locke, 1992; Sue and Sue, 1990).

Despite the overall lack of services related to mental health, the limited data available indicate that students do benefit from counseling when they receive it. Weist, Paskewitz, Warner, and Flaherty (1996) showed increases in students' self-concept and decreases in depressive symptoms after school-based individual or group counseling. In a sample of minority urban youth, the length of mental health treatment was positively correlated with grades (Nabors, Weist, Reynolds, Tashman, and Jackson, 1999).

Current debates over the future of mental health services focus less on how their effectiveness could be improved through changes in how they function, and more on the level of resources to support whatever mental health professionals do in the schools. For example, the American Counseling Association has recommended an increase in resources to raise the number of counselors from the current range of between 500:1 and 1,000:1 students to counselors to the range of 100:1 to 300:1 (American School Counselor Association, 1988); the Commission on Precollege Guidance and Counseling (1986) has recommended a ratio of 50:1 for at-risk students. Increased services to students would also require addressing the multiple roles counselors play. Their current absorption in administrative duties unrelated to personal counseling means that increasing the numbers of counselors might not increase the support available for mental health issues.

Because children who gain access to mental health services typically do so through schools, without the school connection most of them would not receive any services (Armbruster and Lichtman, 1999). Whether services are at the school or in the community, schools must be part of the solution to adolescents' needs for mental health services. Most schools now refer students to community-based mental health services and other community institutions, an approach that takes advantage of different funding streams rather than relying on scarce educational funds, and makes use of existing expertise rather than duplicating such expertise in school-based programs. The disadvantage is that referral to outside agencies makes it difficult to coordinate mental health personnel with professionals, including teachers, who see adolescents in school. To address these problems, some schools have hired school social workers or school psychologists specifically to create bridges between schools and community-based organizations. But the availability of these professionals is inadequate and highly variable, and like counselors they are often overwhelmed with other administrative duties.

Well-designed mental health services provided in schools have the potential advantage of providing a single point of access to students and their families; the elimination of many barriers to accessing mental health services in the community; a familiar environment in which students already participate; improved capacity to provide preventive services to the entire school population; the ability to see students in multiple contexts and over long periods of time; the availability of experts to help teachers detect early signs of mental health problems and to support teachers in handling problems in the classroom; the potential for reduced stigma attached to receiving services; and fewer referrals to special education (Weist, 1997). On the other hand, the resources for mental health programs are usually not available in education budgets. Some students do not experience schools as supportive environments and may be concerned about confidentiality, and on-site services add to the supervisory burdens of principals and other administrators[6] who are already pulled in many directions. In the absence of more fundamental change (as we advocate later in this chapter), and without greater understanding about how well either school- or community-based services work in a widely diverse range of communities and local circumstances,[7] we believe that using community-based services with liaisons such as school social workers seems a promising way to meet the mental health needs of students without diluting the educational focus of schools.

Other Support Services

High school students have a significant array of problems and conditions, in addition to mental health problems, that undermine their academic engagement. A recent report based on the National Longitudinal Study of Adolescent Health shows that more than 10 percent of males and 5 percent of females have committed a violent act; about 18 percent of adolescents say they drink alcohol more than monthly; 25.2 percent have smoked marijuana at least once, and 12.7 percent have smoked at least once in the past month; 49.3 percent of high school students have had sex; and 19.4 percent of high school women who have had sex became pregnant. The authors concluded that "while most teenagers are doing well, many young people face a constellation of problems that undermine their well-being today and will threaten their health in the future" (Blum and Rinehart, 1998, p. 14). These problems are in addition to common consequences of living in poverty, such as hunger, homelessness, exposure to violence, lack

[6]See, for example, Archer (2002) is based on a focus group with six principals. Although empirical research has not been done on trends in how principals use their time, there is considerable consensus that administrative jobs have become much more demanding and that the requirements of noneducational duties, including special education, increasingly have drawn principals away from educational concerns.

[7]See Armbruster and Lichtman (1999), who found the benefits of school-based and clinic-based mental health services to be comparable for students in inner-city schools. They argue that school-based services therefore have the potential for bridging the gap between need and utilization by reaching low-income urban students who otherwise would not have access to services.

of adult supervision, and primary care-taking responsibilities for younger siblings.

Usually, specific programs are designed to meet particular needs. Programs include health clinics, substance abuse programs, the federal school breakfast and lunch programs (widely underutilized in high schools), sex education and pregnancy prevention programs, and drug and alcohol prevention and rehabilitation programs. In most high schools, principals and other administrators create a variety of ad hoc arrangements with local community-based organizations, hospitals, public health agencies, and social service providers, funded with a patchwork of public and private funds. As a result, the services available vary tremendously from school to school, and are typically unstable and poorly coordinated. Moreover, problems are dealt with in isolation when in reality, most are highly interrelated.

Despite the efforts of those who work to promote greater coherence and integration of existing services, in practice the same barriers often emerge: inadequate funding; a tendency for services to become absorbed in the local school bureaucracy, thereby losing the authority to operate services independently of the district; a tendency to consume the time and attention of school personnel; negative perceptions by parents and students who have had poor school experiences; and the impossibility of reaching students who formally or informally have dropped out of school (U.S. General Accounting Office, 1993; Wang, Haertel, and Walberg, 1997).

Nevertheless, a few studies have found positive effects. For example, Jessor et al. (1998) found evidence that availability of services improved graduation rates and decreased the prevalence of problem behaviors.

Weaknesses of Traditional Approaches

Although the need for support services remains widely acknowledged, and despite some evidence that they *can* have positive effects on student engagement, the current status of students' academic and nonacademic well-being persuades us that conventional approaches to providing these services are not achieving their purposes.

First, most available services are not good matches with the needs of high school students, especially low-income students, no matter where the services are located. Available services tend to be rigidly limited by the constraints of categorical programs, despite the fact that students' needs are interrelated. The services are often provided by professionals who know little about the special needs of adolescents or the conditions of living in poverty and in poor neighborhoods. Typically services are provided in settings that do not allow providers the time or opportunity to develop trusting relationships with adolescents, even though their needs are met most effectively in the context of trusting, respectful relations and communities of support.

Second, when schools try to compensate for the weaknesses of existing services in the community, they are likely to be unsuccessful. Distinguishing effective from ineffective services, let alone creating effective services where none exist, is not something that educators are likely to have the expertise to do; they certainly lack the funding. Although a few energetic school leaders have been successful in creating ad hoc relations with community-based organizations, they may be making their improvements at the expense of other schools with less aggressive or ingenious principals. Such efforts are also likely to distract teachers and administrators from their educational objectives.

We conclude that the means to address students' nonacademic needs available in most high schools—career and academic counseling, mental health services, and a range of other problem-oriented services—are inadequate in amount and quality, and inequitable for both low-income and minority youth. These services are outside the core academic activities and marginalized within schools themselves, subject to cutting in every fiscal crisis. When services are provided by public and private institutions outside the school, they create less of a burden for the school, but they become more difficult to coordinate.

Clearly, vast improvements could be made within the dominant models of service provision. Additional resources in counseling might help, particularly if they enabled young people to know a counselor well enough to find consistent support and develop a trusting relationship. A greater ability to identify and treat a variety of mental health issues would be better than the current situation in which many serious problems go untreated. Improving the patchwork of other services would provide more access by students who are now becoming pregnant, using drugs and alcohol, and otherwise showing up in the conventional statistics of despair. At a minimum, given the magnitude of the underlying problems, appropriate assessments of the comparative effectiveness of alternative strategies would provide better information about promising approaches.

Recommendations for more, better quality, and better coordinated services, although entirely warranted, have been frequently made and just as frequently ignored. We are dubious that another effort to document the inadequacy of these services will achieve more than previous attempts. More importantly, we are convinced that more and better services will not be enough to significantly improve academic engagement. Although the availability of counselors to connect with students seems to be effective for those students reached, the traditional model of counseling has failed to ensure that all students, particularly those at risk, receive the adult attention and guidance they need. Systemic change, rather than merely an increase in the number of counselors, is a more promising avenue for improving student achievement. We therefore propose a substantially new way of thinking about strategies for meeting high school students' nonacademic needs.

Our focus in the second part of this chapter on what high schools can do should in no way obscure the importance of addressing simultaneously the circumstances of poverty, racism, and social norms and values that make it difficult for many adolescents to be productively engaged in school. Although the reforms we propose could reduce some of the barriers to academic engagement, we must not forget that efforts to address only the barriers within the high school are seriously limited.

A DIFFERENT VISION

Current strategies to meet students' physical, social, and emotional needs are not accomplishing their purposes not only because they are underfunded and poorly organized. They are more fundamentally flawed for the following reasons.

First, no intervention or services offered on the side are potent enough to promote high levels of academic engagement in a dysfunctional, unsupportive school. Although we recognize that some students have serious physical and mental health problems that require far more intensive individual attention than they are now receiving, we believe that at least as much weight must be given to the broader school context.

Second, because students as learners cannot be divorced from students as people with social-emotional, physical, and mental health needs, strict distinctions among the roles of school personnel in all of their relations to students do not make sense. We recommend restructuring the roles of all school personnel, eliminating the notion that only counselors, social workers, and nurses are responsible for identifying and addressing students' nonacademic needs.

Third, although schools cannot ignore students' nonacademic needs, taking responsibility for meeting these needs can distract them from their central mission, which is to engage students in academic work. We strongly endorse strategies that link high schools to a larger network of service providers and supports. The community must be encouraged to assume some responsibility for students' developmental needs, as neither the school nor the family can do this alone.

Fourth, we recommend a reframing of our approach to addressing adolescents' nonacademic needs to achieve a sharper focus on strategies for building assets rather than on interventions designed to address problems that have already developed.

These four recommendations and the rationale for each are discussed in the following sections.

Focusing on School Environments

The service model of individual referrals to school-based or community-based services deals with problems one student at a time, one diagnosis at a time. This problem-oriented approach views students as needing to be "fixed." In some cases this is appropriate, especially for conditions that may have some organic origin and require medical intervention. In many other cases, students' problems are rooted in poverty, neglect by adults, poor housing conditions, or neighborhood violence. Although personal counseling and mental health services may help students cope, these approaches are simply palliatives for much deeper social problems.[8]

Urban schools can be counted among the culprits because they contribute to as well as suffer from the consequences of students' nonacademic problems. Large, impersonal environments in which students feel that "nobody cares" do not produce the feelings of control over outcomes, or the social connectedness that promotes both mental health and academic engagement. Similarly, when instruction is beyond students' reach and they are not provided the help they need to master the curriculum, they will not be confident in their ability to succeed and therefore will not be engaged. School climates characterized by pervasive low expectations for student engagement and learning do not promote confidence and enthusiasm for learning in students. The negative effects of an unsupportive school climate are more likely to be exacerbated than overcome when high-stakes tests are imposed by districts or states without the resources that would help students meet the new standards. The day-to-day experience of failure in classrooms and low expectations conveyed by teachers cannot be overcome by counseling or pull-out programs designed to make students feel confident about themselves or to raise their self-esteem.

In contrast, evidence from the National Longitudinal Study of Adolescent Health indicates that students in schools that foster feelings of social connectedness and being cared for by teachers, peers, and families are less

---

[8]See, for example, the voluminous *Guidebook of the Center for Mental Health in Schools*, which divides problems into Type I problems caused by the environment, Type II problems from a combination of environmental and intrapersonal sources, and Type III problems caused primarily by pathology within the person (Common Psycho-social Problems of School-Aged Youth: Developmental Variations, Problems, Disorders and Perspectives for Prevention and Treatment, available from the Center for Mental Health in Schools, University of California at Los Angeles).

likely to experience emotional distress, use alcohol and drugs, engage in violent or deviant behavior, or become pregnant (Blum, McNeely, and Rinehart, 2002). Furthermore, the evidence is clear that self-confidence, feelings of control, and high levels of engagement are fostered in academic contexts that provide challenging but manageable instruction and tasks and hold students to high but achievable standards (see Chapter 2, this volume). Although mental health and other services surely have their independent roles to play, reforming high schools with an eye to improving the connectedness of students and providing appropriate and engaging instruction are likely to reduce the need for special services.

In other chapters of this volume, we discuss strategies for improving connectedness, including making changes related to classroom management, reducing school size, avoiding harsh and punitive discipline policies, expanding participation in extracurricular activities, and encouraging positive social connections and support among peers. Many of these reforms have been shown to enhance engagement and motivation directly, and to promote positive social, emotional, and mental health. We also make suggestions for providing students with instructional programs that enhance their competencies and promote positive beliefs about their ability to control outcomes and to succeed. Reforming pedagogy to give adolescents greater opportunities for their own explorations of alternative paths to becoming a productive adult (as in the school-to-work reforms outlined in Chapter 7, this volume) might also reduce the sense of purposelessness that often results in the need for mental health services as well as disengagement. A preventive policy, one that attempts to strengthen the settings in which young people live, would reduce the incidence and thus the need to redress emotional and mental health problems.

We conclude, therefore, that it is inadequate merely to add to the array of services offered at or near high schools, although these services may be needed and may bring benefits. Addressing the nonacademic barriers to student engagement requires reforming high schools themselves as well as improving and strengthening services designed to meet individual needs.

Restructuring Roles and Responsibilities

Fundamental changes are needed in how adults and students relate to one another in high schools. Every student needs to be known well by at least one adult who can monitor progress and communicate to specialists and parents when difficulties emerge, who can identify needs for special services and talents that should be recognized and developed, and who can listen to, encourage, and advocate for the student. Substantial increases in the number of specialized personnel in high school will not achieve the personalized connections and climate of caring that youth need. A meaningful change in the climate requires the participation of all adults in the school.

Many schools are currently experimenting with organizational structures to achieve these kinds of personalized connections. One model is for every adult—including teachers and sometimes nonprofessional staff—to be assigned to a small group of students and given opportunities to connect with those students individually and in small groups. The National Association of Secondary School Principals (NASSP, 1996, 2002) recommends that no adult should serve as an advocate for more than about 20 students, and that the same adult should follow a student throughout his or her years in high school, with weekly meetings. Although this individual is not expected to provide services that require specific expertise, he or she is expected to call attention to problems as they become apparent, and assist a student in finding needed services. This person also has the broad view of the student's needs, and can play a role in ensuring some coordination among services and service providers, and between them and academic personnel. The NASSP (2002) also suggests that the adult advocate play the role of facilitating students' relationships with other adults and students in the school by identifying problems that should be discussed with counselors, mediating conflicts with teachers and peers, and visiting students' homes.

Ongoing support for people in mentoring roles is essential, as is time to take on these additional responsibilities. Specialized staff such as counselors, social workers, and nurses can provide training and support for the adults who serve as advocates, in addition to providing specialized services to students. As with any reform in the way schools operate, there must be some buy-in among the staff for this kind of a change; a top-down mandate can create resentment that could result in more harm than good for students.

One example of this kind of restructuring of roles is the Family Advocacy System that is included in the First Things First's school reform approach (see Chapter 8, this volume). In this system all teachers, administrators, and specialized and qualified support staff in the high school are assigned a group of students (typically 12 to 17), and remain connected to the same student as long as the student is at the school. These "family advocates" meet with each student for at least 5 minutes each week, and at least an hour a week is set aside for them to meet with students individually and in groups. They initiate monthly contact with parents or other caregivers by phone, mail, e-mail, or face to face to "touch base" and discuss students' accomplishments and challenges. They also meet with each student and his or her family member(s) twice a year for at least 30 minutes to review student progress and develop action plans, including possible referrals and follow-ups to additional support services.

Family advocates are given initial training by First Things First staff and experienced participants from other school districts. They are also provided support services (e.g., translation services, transportation, security), and ongoing training by teams of district employees (e.g., counselors, social workers, parent liaisons, school improvement facilitators) in identifying students who need services, in making appropriate referrals, and in handling troubled and troubling students.

Although an adult advocate model has many benefits, there are other ways to enhance relationships between adults and students, and other opportunities for adults to show an interest in and to support positive and productive behavior in students. Wimberly (2002), for example, recommends school-sponsored activities that connect students and adults, such as special projects and school-community programs. Students and adults might also collaborate on performances and artistic activities.

In addition to involving teachers and other adults in counselor roles, the committee supports efforts to embed high school counselors more directly in the educational mission of the school. The Puente Program provides an example of the proposed expansion of counselors' roles. The program was created to help Latino students become eligible for public colleges and universities in California.[9] It includes a half-time counselor for 120 students who consults with English and math teachers to diagnose academic problems and devise ways to solve them. Counselors work with students in groups on many topics, including college entrance requirements, study habits, SAT preparation, and financial aid. They arrange trips to local colleges to familiarize students with college both as a place and as an idea. They organize parent groups, partly to educate parents about college and its requirements and partly to convince Latino parents to "let go" of their children. Puente generally succeeds in creating a school within a school, in enhancing the quality of instruction, in strengthening parent participation and support, and in giving students the information necessary to fulfill the single-minded goal of having all students go to college, using counselors as central participants with multiple roles.[10]

Similarly, the school-to-work reforms described in Chapter 6, which have integrated broadly occupational content and applications into their

[9]For more information on the Puente program and its effects, see Gándara, Mejorado, Gutiérrez, and Molina (1998); regarding the role of counselors, see Grubb, Lara, and Valdez (2001). A Puente-like program also exists for African-American students at the community college level.

[10]A similar program was designed in Los Angeles as a supplemental yet comprehensive programmatic approach to dropout prevention: the "Achievement for Latinos through Academic Success" or ALAS program (Gándara, Larson, Rumberger, and Mehan, 1998; Larson and Rumberger, 1995).

programs, have been forced to confront the need to educate students about their options, and consequently have strengthened their career and academic counseling. Sometimes this is done in conventional ways, by having representatives of career academies or majors talk to ninth graders about options. In many cases, however, a much more elaborate program of experience, experimentation, and choice has been developed. In one high school in the Pacific Northwest, for example, students may choose among six different majors or clusters. In the 9th grade and the first half of 10th grade, they take a 9-week minicourse in each of six clusters, learning the technologies, methods, and careers associated with a broad range of occupations. Then each student chooses two of the six clusters for a second 9-week period of experience, at more advanced levels. Finally, they choose one of those two clusters for their program in 11th and 12th grades. All students experience every cluster the school offers and learn about occupational alternatives both through experience and through conventional reading and teaching; they make two choices, with substantial but not irreversible consequences.[11] In these programs the guidance and counseling function is broadly distributed among counselors, occupational instructors, academic instructors who may tailor their assignments and projects to be consistent with the theme of an academy or cluster, the experiences within workshops, and for students with work placements, supervisors and co-workers.

Another promising effort in reconceptualizing the roles of counselors is the National School Counselor Training Initiative, which envisions moving counselors away from one-on-one (or small group) counseling to participating in more central ways in academic reforms designed to enhance achievement.[12] Counselors become diagnosticians and reformers, responsible for collecting information about substandard performance, diagnosing problems, and working with teachers to develop solutions that may involve changes in a teacher's instructional practices and treatment of students. Thus, instead of pulling out students to "fix" them so they will be engaged in the classroom, they help to create more engaging classrooms for

[11]Individuals working in such integrated programs usually say that only 25 percent of students stay with their high school major or cluster after high school. This practice is not, therefore, the German or Swiss practice of forcing students to make irreversible career decisions in ninth grade, but it does give students practice in making decisions.

[12]This initiative is being supported by the Metropolitan Life Foundation and the Education Trust (see http://www.edtrust.org/main/school_counseling.asp). We have also benefited from discussions with Reese House at The Education Trust and with Linda Miller of the Louisville, KY, schools, one of the districts participating in this initiative. The initiative's motto is "College Begins in Kindergarten," leading us to suspect that the basic message of its efforts will be college for all.

students having difficulties. In this initiative, counselors would also operate as advocates for poor and minority students and others who have historically fared poorly in schools. This conception of a counselor's role also requires different training than is typically provided, as well as the support of principals, teachers, and district officials.

We are not endorsing any particular model of restructured roles; rather we are proposing that the roles of all adults in schools be reconsidered so that all students' needs are given greater attention and there is coordination among those who are directly involved in the education and life of any particular student. Much more development is necessary before these kinds of reforms become well-accepted parts of high schools, but extant programs suggest some clear alternatives to conventional guidance and counseling. In both Puente and the National School Counselor Training Initiative, academic counselors are central to school changes rather than peripheral service providers. They arrange a wide variety of activities and their work is closely connected to that of teachers. We suspect that developing these and similar alternatives that integrate counseling into the high school curricula would be more effective in engaging students in academic work than simply promoting more resources in conventional academic and career counseling.

Connecting High Schools to the Community

High schools are ideally suited to serve as the primary location for identifying students' nonacademic as well as academic needs, and for connecting students to the resources they need to meet those needs. But high schools cannot do it all without becoming overly distracted from their primary mission. We have recommended stronger connections between high schools and their communities in several chapters (see especially Chapter 5, this volume), and do so again here. Connections to the community are especially critical for addressing students' nonacademic needs.

Arrangements will vary considerably, depending on funding sources, community resources, and even the availability of space. Some schools are able to offer on-site services that are funded through and administered by other agencies. The evidence shows that school-based clinics are well used, and that they are associated with positive outcomes, including lower use of drugs, better school attendance, lower dropout rates, and reduced course failures and disciplinary referrals (Kisker and Brown, 1996; McCord et al., 1993; Pearson, Jennings, and Norcross, 1998).

In creating a system of support services—whether on site or in the community—it is critical to attend to issues of coherence and sustainability. Students' problems rarely come in neat, circumscribed packages. Poor physical health often leads to depression and other mental health problems. Anxiety disorders are associated with alcohol abuse; depression is linked to unplanned pregnancy; students with low self-esteem are more likely to engage in antisocial behaviors. Homelessness, poor nutrition, unstable parenting, and being exposed to violence are associated with a variety of physical and mental health problems (Dryfoos, 1990).

Despite this co-morbidity, we typically treat problems and needs—if we treat them at all—as though they were isolated. We have programs to prevent drug abuse and programs to prevent teen pregnancy, even though the same adolescents are at risk for both. A social worker may see a student who is homeless without communicating with the doctor who is treating his asthma or a teacher who has kicked him out of class for abusive behavior. Because of the differentiation of professional roles in school, and the absence of any one individual who gets to know students as whole people, supports designed to address nonacademic needs are fragmented and disconnected from the academic program.

The committee recommends that schools, school districts, and communities develop different kinds of communication links. Creating small schools and learning communities helps provide adults with more opportunities to know their students well and to become aware of the range of issues they face. Some schools have used school social workers or school psychologists in a caseworker role to keep track of students with serious nonacademic needs and create bridges to community services. Technology also offers some opportunities to create databases that can be used to collect information on individual students from various sources and to facilitate communication among individuals who care for students' different needs.

An increasing number of communities are working to respond to the prevalence of students' unmet nonacademic needs with "full-service schools" and "community schools." These models—and their predecessors of the past 20 years—have sought to provide a comprehensive array of services, and to use case management to identify the problems of particular students, to determine the appropriate services, and to follow up with the student to determine whether services were effectively provided (U.S. General Accounting Office, 1993). Some comprehensive programs have provided client-focused integration activities, linked families to these services, and made efforts to share information across different service agencies and to develop joint planning.

In recent years, community schools have been growing—in size, number, and popular support. The Coalition for Community Schools describes community schools as a set of partnerships that together create a set of conditions linked to learning. It identifies these conditions as follows:

- The school has a core instructional program with qualified teachers, a challenging curriculum, and high standards and expectations for students.

• Students are motivated and engaged in learning—both in school and in community settings, during and after school.

• The basic physical, mental and emotional health needs of young people and their families are recognized and addressed.

• There is mutual respect and effective collaboration among parents, families and school staff.

• Community engagement, together with school efforts, promote a school climate that is safe, supportive and respectful that connects students to a broader learning community (Blank, Melaville, and Shah, 2003).

The Coalition also reports on 18 evaluations which, taken together, found that participation in community school activities was associated with varying combinations of improved grades in school courses and/or scores in proficiency testing; improved attendance; reduced behavioral or discipline problems and/or suspensions; greater classroom cooperation, completion of homework and assignments, and adherence to school rules and positive attitude; and increased access to physical and mental health services and preventive care. The Coalition concluded that the community school approach achieves improved student performance when it builds on sufficiently high quality teaching and curriculum to meet the needs of young people when they are ready to learn (Blank, Melaville, and Shah, 2003).

To achieve coherence within schools—regardless of how services are provided—it will be necessary to address the incoherence of funding streams and mechanisms at the federal, state, and local levels, and between public and philanthropic sources. Rules related to eligibility, access, and accountability can create nightmares for the most expert administrator.

Developing Assets

We also suggest a more positive approach to supporting student social-emotional and mental health than is reflected in the current "fix-the-problem" strategy. Our assumption, which has some support in research and reflects the rich experience coming out of the youth development field, is that if youth are involved in activities that meet their basic needs to be competent, autonomous, and meaningfully connected to adults, they are less likely to develop maladaptive or self-destructive behaviors. Students' engagement in school should be higher if they are given opportunities to learn new skills, to develop social skills with peers and adults, to develop self-confidence and social responsibility—overall, to develop in multiple ways, along multiple paths, with multiple competencies or "intelligences" (Gardner, 1993).

Service learning, discussed in Chapter 5, is one strategy that high schools have used to provide these kinds of opportunities. They can also be provided in after-school programs. Current interest in after-school programs in urban areas reflects the recognition that students growing up in poverty have poor access to youth-serving organizations as well as to school-sponsored extracurricular activities sponsored by schools themselves—sports teams, band and orchestra, clubs and organizations—many of which have been cut in financially strapped high schools. Their supporters hope they will "provide a safety net for children who are at high risk for depression, substance abuse, early sexual activity, teenage pregnancy, and violence," and can thereby promote long-term academic success.[13]

Although after-school programs vary enormously, most seem to provide a variety of activities and experiences that provide positive alternatives to just hanging out with peers, including sports and recreation, dance, computer work, school-based enterprises, and school-related tutoring (including practice on high-stakes exams such as exit exams). The novel element in after-school programs is that rather than (or in addition to) providing access to problem-oriented support services, they can offer an array of activities that are not provided within most schools and that may offer their own educational and developmental value. They are supported by the research of Jordan and Nettles (1999), who found that participation in structured activities (including religious activities) and time spent interacting with adults during 10th grade had positive and significant effects on educational outcomes by grade 12, whereas time spent hanging out with peers was consistently associated negatively with educational outcomes.

On the other hand, after-school programs have run up against the same barriers as school-linked services, including lack of funding; general tensions between school and after-school staff about student behavior, equipment, and classroom use; lack of available space; the need for excessive attention from overextended principals; and the "capture" of after-school programs by the school's agenda, sometimes leading to an extension of "skills and drills" teaching—hardly a way to motivate students already doing poorly in school. It is still too early to judge the promise of after-school programs because most have started quite recently; they offer some new directions, but they also remain limited by familiar barriers that seem to plague every effort to develop nonschool activities that support the high school's missions.

---

[13]See "Urban Seminar on After-School Time," The Urban Seminar Series on Children's Health and Safety, John F. Kennedy School of Government, Harvard University (undated), available online at http://www.ksg.harvard.edu/urbanpoverty, and Perry, Teague, and Frey (2002). The major federal funding for after-school programs—the Community Learning Centers—explicitly includes high schools, while state funds are not always available to high schools.

Certainly after-school programs are becoming part of the solution, but they cannot substitute for what remains the primary task: to create environments and opportunities—both in high schools and in the community—that give urban youth the same chance that their more affluent peers have to develop competence and a sense of control and social connectedness.

An asset orientation is not restricted to out-of-school activities. There should be many opportunities in high schools for all students to make choices that contribute to their sense of control, to provide opportunities that contribute to their sense of importance and responsibility, and to develop and be recognized for skills and talents that contribute to their sense of competence.

CONCLUSIONS

The committee recognizes the many ways in which unmet nonacademic needs can interfere with students' engagement in school. We understand the difficulty of teaching a student who is hungry, abused, or neglected. Neither educators nor citizens should, however, use students' unmet nonacademic needs as an excuse for complacency. We disagree with opinion leaders, as well as school teachers and administrators, who do not support efforts to improve the quality of education because other factors in students' lives limit the effects of school reform (see, for example, George Will's column headlined "Can't Fix Education Until We Fix Families," The Washington Post, January 4, 2002).

In the vision we hold, instruction is appropriately challenging and students are given the support they need to achieve high standards. The school climate is career and college oriented, and the roles of school personnel are reconsidered so that all adults in the school are aware of students' nonacademic as well as academic needs. All students should have one adult who knows them well, who communicates regularly with their families, and who serves as a resource and advocate for special services. Coordination among those who are directly involved in the education and life of any particular student is essential, and specialists—such as counselors, social workers, and nurses—need to be well connected to teachers and administrators, providing training and guidance and assisting them in creating environments that support positive development.

The school reforms that we recommend as particularly promising represent substantial departures from conventional practices. Although the evidence on the effects of such reforms is just beginning to become available, indirect evidence and theory suggest that they should promote positive social-emotional development and mental health, and by doing so, reduce many barriers to engagement in high school work.

7

Education Through Theme-Based Learning Communities

Creating schools with occupational themes is a promising new school reform strategy for making the curriculum more relevant and personally meaningful to students. This approach is also likely to enhance motivation by offering students choices among several themes.

In schools that have tried this approach, the theme often has a broad occupational focus—for example, health occupations rather than nursing; industrial production rather than welding; agriculture rather than farming—that is elastic enough to encompass a variety of types of learning, including standard academic subjects. This strategy is different from that of traditional vocational education, which has been designed to prepare individuals for specific entry-level jobs. Although an occupational focus provides distinct benefits, a theme does not need to be occupational. Some schools focus on international trade and others examine urban issues or the environment. Current common themes for magnet schools include technology, the arts, science, health, agriculture, or (in the case of Aviation High School in New York, for example) a range of related occupations.

The theme-based approach has various roots and appears under different names. Some have labeled the thematic approach to high school education as the "new" or "emerging" vocational education, to distinguish it from traditional vocational education; others refer to school-to-work or school-to-career programs, invoking the School-to-Work Opportunities Act of 1994 (now ended).[1] Some proponents describe thematic programs as

[1]The School-to-Work Opportunities Act added work-based learning to earlier efforts to integrate academic and vocational education and to incorporate "tech prep," but many people have adopted the school-to-work label for programs with an occupational focus even though they lack any work-based learning.

"college and career" programs, stressing the dual outcomes possible,[2] and others have labeled them forms of "education through occupations," recalling John Dewey's argument that "education through occupations consequently combines within itself more of the factors conducive to learning than any other method."[3] We will use these terms interchangeably, despite differences in emphasis.

This type of reform provides substantial opportunities to integrate academic content with occupational applications. Integration strategies include teaching the conceptual prerequisites for occupational activities in academic classes, examining occupational applications in math or science classes, analyzing a particular phenomenon from the perspectives of several disciplines, and creating projects that span several classes. One intent is to replace the current high school curriculum—made up of independent, disconnected courses—with a more coherent program that allows students to see how subjects are related. The extent of integration varies among schools and depends substantially on teacher planning time. Successful examples occur in schools that have eliminated conventional divisions between academic and vocational instructors.

Thematic programs usually stress preparation for college, or for work after high school, or for a combination of college enrollment and employment. These programs are different from traditional, terminal vocational education programs designed previously for students not bound for college. The emphasis on "college *and* careers" conveys a range of options that is broader than is typically found in traditional vocational education or "general education" tracks or an academic track, with its single-minded pursuit of "college for all."[4] Sometimes the route to college is structured through "tech prep" or "2 + 2" programs that integrate a high school program with nearby community college classes. These efforts involve a view of high school as part of a longer K-16 continuum.

This approach to high school education sometimes incorporates forms of learning outside of school, including projects in the community or the work world, job shadowing and internships, and cooperative education that integrates substantial amounts of work-based learning into the curriculum. Once a school has been reorganized to include occupational "majors" or schools within schools, the links to work-based opportunities are easier

---

[2]See especially Stern (1999) and Urquiola et al. (1997).

[3]See Dewey (1916, p. 309), especially Chapter 23, on "Vocational Aspects of Education." The historical background of the practices examined in this chapter is reviewed in Grubb (1995b).

[4]On the power and limitations of "college for all," see Boesel and Fredland (1999) and Rosenbaum (2001).

to make. The most thorough approaches to "education through occupations" require a substantial change in the ways communities and employers work with schools; both students and the community can benefit.

The thematic approach to educating students usually develops within small schools, or schools within schools, capitalizing on the advantages of the closer relationships among teachers and students.[5] The three most common organizational forms are career academies, high schools with majors, and high schools with themes.

Career academies are schools within schools with 200 to 250 students and a group of teachers who teach core subjects such as English, math, science, or history, as well as the occupational or intellectual area that gives an academy its focus (see Institute for Research and Reform in Education, 2002). Students stay with each other and with these teachers for 2, 3, or 4 years, and instructors integrate their courses in various ways. Academies usually establish close connections with employers, who may provide resources and opportunities, such as representatives who visit the school, summer jobs, internships, or employment after high school.

Academies were the earliest examples of thematic high schools. Notable examples are the Electrical Academy developed in Philadelphia in 1969, the network of Partnership Academies funded by the state of California, and finance and tourism academies supported by American Express. Networks have been formed to strengthen and extend the academy model.[6] The occupational focuses of existing academies include traditional vocational subjects—electricity, automotive occupations, and health occupations—as well as more modern occupations, including electronics, computers, communications or journalism, and engineering. As schools within schools, career academies have the advantage of requiring the cooperation of fewer numbers of teachers. Thus the scale of the reform is considerably smaller than most of the reforms described in this volume, in which entire faculties of large high schools must all work together in new ways.

High schools with majors, or clusters, require every student to choose a focus, usually during 10th grade, from a roster of choices. The extent to which the major dominates a student's curriculum varies. In some cases students take the majority of their courses within a cluster; in others, a two-

---

[5]This aspect of "education through occupations," which began at least with the first career academies in 1969, considerably predates the recent interest in small schools, often dated to Meier (1995).

[6]Regarding academies, see Stern, Raby, and Dayton (1992) and Stern, Dayton, and Raby (2001). Current networks include the Career Academies Support Network at the University of California at Berkeley, the National Academy Foundation at http://www.naf.org/ and a network of 38 Junior ROTC academies sponsored by the U.S. Departments of Defense and Education.

period block of time (e.g., the afternoon) is spent within a major, while other courses are conventionally taught. The ideal, as in academies, is to encourage the integration of curriculum across subjects and to provide links to employers and the outside world. A number of districts have developed individual high schools with majors or clusters; for example, Oakland, California, has been transforming all of its high schools into cluster schools. A number of the New American High Schools have followed this model, and the Talent Development High School at Johns Hopkins University also includes majors or clusters, with a ninth-grade "Success Academy" to prepare students for the choice of majors.[7]

Some high schools adopt a theme or focus for all students. Examples include schools emphasizing the arts or the performing arts; health-related high schools; an agriculture high school in south Chicago; magnet schools emphasizing areas such as computers, business, and communications; High Tech High in San Diego, with an emphasis on technology and project-based learning in all classes; and Aviation High and the High School of the Performing Arts in New York. Invariably, these are relatively small high schools with 400 to 800 students. The extent to which the focus permeates the curriculum varies: Some infuse a focus into virtually every class; others are more like conventional high schools, with some afternoon classes in the area of focus.[8]

The reforms described in this chapter reshape the high school as a whole, and require rethinking its purpose, structure, and relation to the outside world. Perhaps most importantly, the reforms serve as an alternative to the traditional monolithic high school, dominated by the academic courses of the college prep curriculum. The traditional high school has provided relatively little choice to students, except for a limited array of electives, and it does not link school to the world of work or the community in the way that schools with a theme or focus do.

The challenge is to see whether theme-based high schools enhance motivation and engagement, or any of its correlates, including persistence, graduation, or measures of learning. We review three kinds of evidence: (1) analysis of whether its practices are consistent with what is known about motivation and engagement in general; (2) the perceptions of teachers and students who have been engaged in these reforms; and, most importantly,

[7]Regarding high schools with clusters, see Grubb (1995a); regarding the Talent Development High School, see Legters (1999) and McPartland, Balfanz, Joan, and Legters (1998).

[8]Considerably less has been written about such high schools, but see Katz, Jackson, Reeves, and Benson (1995). However, many magnet schools have a theme or focus.

(3) evidence related to outcomes. Unfortunately, outcome evidence is still scant because few reforms have been in place long enough to be evaluated.

Overall, the different kinds of evidence suggest that various forms of "education through occupations," if carefully implemented in accordance with the basic precepts about motivation and engagement described in Chapter 2, have many potential benefits and few negative effects. Because these reforms are relatively new, their real benefits may not have developed yet. However, their success depends critically on the details of implementation, which we examine in Chapter 9.

PRACTICES ENHANCING MOTIVATION AND ENGAGEMENT

One way to evaluate the potential effects of programs with occupational themes is to examine their consistency (or inconsistency) with what is known from existing research about motivation and engagement. An analysis of the motivational qualities of programs also serves as a guide for creating programs that engage students in learning. We concentrate on six such conditions, recognizing that, although some programs may meet these conditions, others may not. Although this summary represents an idealized version of schools with occupational themes, it does reflect the goals of most programs.

First, programs motivating students allow for close adult-student relationships. The research summarized in Chapters 2 and 4 supports the value of social contexts for learning that are accepting and supportive and that facilitate personal connections.[9] The recent "movement" for small schools, described in Chapter 5, builds on these findings. Most programs with occupational themes follow this precept in creating smaller learning communities within the high school, academies, and clusters or majors where students remain with other students and with a few teachers over 2 to 4 years. In addition, most themed high schools are relatively small.

Several related practices should further enhance the motivational value of these approaches. Thematic programs usually develop work teams and projects involving students collectively—including the cooperative forms of learning that have always been part of vocational education (Achtenhagen and Grubb, 2001), and sometimes mimicking the social nature of work (Lave and Wenger, 1991; Wenger, 1998). In addition, programs with occupational themes that include work placements give students opportunities

---

[9]See Ames (1992) and Stipek (2002). See also the February 2002 issue of *Principal Leadership* for testimonials about the value of small schools, small learning communities, and career academies.

to make connections to fellow workers and supervisors. The national school-to-work evaluation found that students value these one-to-one connections (Hershey, Silverberg, Hamison, Hudis, and Jackson, 1998). Another review concluded that practices such as small class sizes and weekly seminars helped build relationships among teachers, students, and worksite personnel, creating a "family-like atmosphere" (Pedraza, Pauly, and Kopp, 1997; Stern et al., 1992). Not all work settings have "family-like" environments or educative and supportive cultures; thus, work settings must be carefully chosen and monitored. Kemple and Snipes (2000) found that interpersonal supports are needed to maximize the positive effects of career academies. Programs that did not structure opportunities to build relationships with adults and to provide career awareness actually disengaged students from school. Hamilton and Hamilton (1997) and the Institute for Research and Reform in Education (2002) recommend using a private case management or advocate approach that offers each student personal assistance and academic support.

Second, engagement increases in environments where students have some autonomy in selecting tasks and methods, and in which they can construct meaning, engage in sense-making on their own, and play an active role in learning, rather than the passive role typical of teacher-centered classrooms (Ames, 1992; National Research Council, 1999; Ryan and LaGuardia, 1999; Stipek, 2002). Students are usually offered a choice—either in which thematic school they attend or in which theme they participate among an array offered in their school. Research on motivation suggests that having an opportunity to choose promotes feelings of self-determination and thus engagement.

"New voc" programs typically foster autonomy and active roles in several other ways. They are more likely to use projects and other forms of direct investigation, both in occupational classes and in activities that involve several classes. Usually, students have some choice about their projects, and some, particularly senior projects or "capstone" projects, can occupy considerable amounts of time (Tsuzuki, 1995). According to motivation research, challenging projects that require sustained effort promote feelings of competence and pride, which motivate further efforts (Stipek, 2002). In addition, proponents of vocational education have always promoted the benefits of "hands-on" learning, which usually refers to some features of adept instruction in the workshop:[10] the process of showing and

[10]The pedagogy of vocational education is in many ways more complex than that of academic instruction, though it has received little attention in the English-language literature. These results are drawn from Grubb and colleagues (1999, Chap. 3) and from the review of the German and English literature in Achtenhagen and Grubb (2001).

doing, with the student practicing what the instructor has shown; the development of visual, manual, and interpersonal skills; the development of teamwork, communications, and problem-solving skills; opportunities for one-on-one instruction, as teachers circulate to help individuals or groups of students in the workshop or lab; and opportunities for feedback from errors, as some projects that fail to work "right" provide their own correctives. Students are often engaged in workshops in an experimental mode under the guidance of the instructor, a process close to the cognitive apprenticeship model described by Collins, Brown, and Newman (1989).

In addition, the work-based component of some programs with occupational themes provides other settings in which students can exercise autonomy and engage in active learning. In case studies of three career-related programs, Stasz and Kaganoff (1998) noted that students in school settings rely on the teacher for information, while in work settings the same students often determine on their own how to obtain information they need to solve problems.

Third, motivation and engagement are enhanced in well-structured educational environments with clear, meaningful purposes. Programs following the logic of "education through occupations," by using a broadly occupational theme, can be both well structured and clear in their purposes because they are linked both to future employment opportunities and to subsequent educational enrollment. In addition, high schools with clusters and theme high schools often dispense with the electives and extracurricular activities of the "shopping mall high school" (Powell et al., 1985) because no time is left over after fulfilling academic, occupational, and work-related requirements. Thus these reforms can improve the coherence of the comprehensive high school, where courses are typically unrelated to one another and where the curriculum is not clearly related to future goals aside from college entrance.

Fourth, motivation is enhanced in settings with a challenging curriculum, high expectations, and a strong emphasis on achievement. Theme-based programs often replace the watered-down offerings in the general track. For example, the Talent Development High School model and the Southern Regional Education Board reforms replace the general track with more demanding integrated programs. Carefully structured workshops also are designed to enhance learning and are integrated with classroom instruction involving applications. This approach improves on traditional vocational education's tendency to simplify content and to become largely avocational—boys working on cars, girls styling hair, and students developing pictures in darkrooms.

Work-based placements provide another setting that supports learning, especially if these work opportunities are integrated with school-based learning through "connecting activities."[11] The students in Ryken's (2001) academies learned different but complementary competencies in school and work settings: Work tended to teach the procedures in biotechnology production, while school components taught the theories underlying these procedures. Many forms of nonschool learning can emerge from work settings, including the ability to work on a team.

Fifth, motivation and engagement are enhanced when students have multiple paths to competence. Research summarized in Chapter 2 indicates that students are most engaged when they feel competent. This requires diverse opportunities to develop and demonstrate mastery. "Education through occupations" can provide multiple avenues for success, including artistic success, success in making and repairing devices, and success in developing competencies related to employment as well as formal schooling.

Programs with occupational themes often include individualized workplace activities that allow students to master additional kinds of skills. The national evaluation of school-to-work programs (Hershey et al., 1998) found that students valued internships and job shadowing more than other career development activities (such as career education courses). Similarly, evaluations of career academies found that jobs related to the academy theme motivated students to succeed both on the job and in school because they knew they might be dropped from the program if their schoolwork lagged (Stern et al., 2001). The students in Ryken's (2001) biotechnology program stressed the value of internships in providing opportunities to develop new lab skills critical to entering the biotechnology workforce.

The value of work placements as an avenue to mastery recalls a savage criticism of the high school by Goodman (1956) in *Growing Up Absurd.* He asserted that the problem youth faced was that they did not have anything serious to do—nothing approaching adults' activities that define adult status. High school for many students is an infantilizing activity in which they are told what to do at every step, even while they are exploring newly found freedoms in other arenas. The construction of a long adolescence, when youth might explore the identities available to them, also has disconnected them from adult life and real experience, a frequent complaint about high school.[12] Carefully constructed work experiences provide op-

---

[11]See also the well-designed cooperative programs in the Cincinnati area devised with complementary school- and work-based components, described in Villeneuve and Grubb (1996).

[12]See also Stern (1989) and the various commission reports of the 1970s that complained about the isolation of high school students from the worlds of adults: Carnegie Council on Policy Studies in Higher Education (1980), National Commission on Youth (1980), National Panel on High School and Adolescent Education (1976), Panel on Youth of the President's Science Advisory Committee (1974), and Timpane, Abramowitz, Bobrow, and Pascal (1976).

portunities for youth to do meaningful work, rather than the menial work of "youth jobs." Without abandoning adolescence as an experimental and transitional period, occupational themed high schools can provide opportunities for youth to do something real and adult-like, consistent with the importance of multiple paths to competence.

Finally, helping students develop education and career pathways can enhance their understanding of school and their motivation to participate fully. Students are unlikely to be highly engaged in schoolwork if they do not understand its relevance to their future goals (Schneider and Stevenson, 1999). Programs with occupational themes can help students envision various future careers, develop direct information about careers, and understand related educational requirements. Both Crain et al. (1999) and Pedraza et al. (1997) reported that school-to-work programs provided a clear work-related identity for participants. Similarly, Ryken (2001) found that biotechnology students began to understand the structure of the biotechnology industry with some sophistication, with different levels of understanding developed in high school, in work placements, and in the college component. Their varied experiences helped them envision a career in science and the steps required to create a science career.

High schools offering majors and career academies use a variety of strategies to connect students' educational programs to professional goals. For example, in one school offering six majors, students in 9th and 10th grades first complete a 9-week "exploratory" in each of six majors, then choose two for a second and more intensive "exploratory," and then choose a major from those two—providing two choice nodes with serious (but still reversible) consequences. In addition, students in programs with occupational themes usually have a choice of work placements and an opportunity to match their interests to placements.

If carefully implemented, programs with occupational themes may be a substitute for weak high school guidance and counseling programs. As we proposed in Chapter 6, such active approaches are preferable to conventional guidance counselor practices, including passive activities sometimes derided as "test 'em and tell 'em" or advising "college for all."

Programs with occupational themes can improve student motivation and engagement, but the advantages we have described are not automatic. Theme-based high schools need to be carefully structured to include well-integrated opportunities to develop a wide range of competencies. In schools where notions of "old" vocational education dominate, or in urban high schools with outdated equipment and poor prospects for meaningful work placements, implementation may be more difficult. Work-based learning is especially fragile. Although carefully structured opportunities can motivate students and have more positive effects than most of the work students find on their own,[13] poor work placements can do just the opposite.[14] The most engaging and educative work experiences also require the most careful planning and development.

PERCEPTIONS OF STUDENTS AND TEACHERS

A different kind of evidence about theme-based education comes from the comments of teachers, students, administrators, and other participants. Most of this kind of evidence available is fraught with potential bias; it is often unsystematic, and sometimes merely anecdotal. Advocates often record positive comments, but not negative ones. A few studies, however, have interviewed students and faculty systematically.

In an analysis of two career academies, Ryken (2001) interviewed 22 students (as well as teachers and work supervisors), and profiled 10 students in greater depth. There was no comparison group; implicitly, students compared their academy experiences to those in other high schools. These students corroborated many elements related to engagement and motivation: the diverse settings for learning and the importance of career and labor market knowledge embedded in these programs. They praised the support from their teachers both in school and in their work settings. They commented on the value of working one-on-one with supervisors and being able to ask many more questions that even small school settings allow.

As part of Crain's analysis of career-oriented magnet schools (Crain et al., 1999), Heebner (1995) interviewed 70 students and 60 adults in four schools. There was no comparison group; implicitly, most students compared their experiences in magnet schools to their earlier experiences in nonmagnet schools. Students said they valued internships, after-school programs, co-op placements, and other opportunities to learn and practice skills in real or simulated workplace environments. Developing useful skills enhanced their interest in college preparation classes that were relevant to workplace skills, suggesting that occupational content can reinforce motivation in academic programs. Finally, the career magnets stimulated active planning for the future, often for multiple job and career options. Students also related drawbacks, including inadequate academic preparation for high

---

[13]Students who find positions through their school programs—compared to those who find "youth jobs" on their own—have access to more diverse workplaces, receive more training time, get more feedback about their performance, and see more links between school studies and their job requirements (Hershey et al., 1998).

[14]See the discussion in Villeneuve and Grubb (1996) on the differences in work placements between employers with a "grow your own" philosophy and those who view interns as a source of low-cost labor.

school, a lack of role models among teachers and administrators from minority backgrounds, and overloaded teachers.

In the early stages of a random assignment evaluation of 10 academies, Manpower Demonstration Research Corporation (MDRC) researchers distributed questionnaires to students and teachers in both the academy group and the control group, who were in the same high school but not in the academy. Academy students consistently ranked their schools and their teachers more highly than did nonacademy students, reporting more personalized attention, more help with personal problems, higher expectations, and more concern about their performance and their futures. Students also reported that their peers were more engaged: They paid attention; they tried to get good grades; they were more likely to think that doing well in school paid off; and they were less likely to be bored and to think that cutting class is cool. The ratings of collaboration among students were also higher for academy students compared to nonacademy students (Kemple, 1997, Tables 3.2 and 3.3). Similarly, academy teachers reported more collaboration with their colleagues, more adequate resources, a greater influence over instruction and administrative policies, more opportunities to learn, more colleagues who emphasized personalized attention to students, and generally higher levels of job satisfaction and efficacy (Kemple, 1997, Table 4.2). Overall, these results describe academies as communities of support and learning for both students and teachers.

In an evaluation of the Talent Development High School replications in Philadelphia, researchers interviewed 185 students and 34 teachers and administrators at three replication sites. The students reported high levels of satisfaction, including improved relations with their teachers. Students praised the separation of ninth graders from older students, and overwhelmingly approved of the Freshman Seminar (where career planning, study skills, and work habits were developed). Furthermore, students valued the longer class periods of 90 minutes, described the school as orderly, and said their coursework was challenging rather than a repetition of what they had learned earlier. Teachers liked being part of a team. Their negative comments concentrated on the difficulty in meeting with other teachers, and the varying (and sometimes inadequate) assistance from curriculum coaches.[15] In addition, the teachers in one school suffered from the instability of teams (Goldwasser et al., 2001).

Stasz and Kaganoff (1998) carried out one of the few studies of student

---

[15]See "Philadelphia's Talent Development High Schools: Second-Year Results," from the Philadelphia Education Fund, available online at http://www.philaedfund.org. More details about these interviews with students are available in Corbett and Wilson (2001); more details on teachers are available in the implementation study of Goldwasser, Yoshida, Christman, and Reumann-Moore (2001).

perceptions of work components. Overall, students were satisfied with work experiences, even though they did not find them very challenging. Work seemed to enhance social skills and positive attitudes toward work, but it did not affect basic academic or problem-solving skills. Few students in either program used higher level reading, writing, or math skills. The links between school and work were perceived to be weak, despite practices intended to facilitate cooperation. Finally, students reported some conflict with school, including having less time to do homework and thinking they might be more likely to quit as a result of the work component. Two obvious implications are that work placements need to be carefully selected and structured so that they are challenging and reinforce academic competencies, and that they may compete with schooling if not well connected to the academic program (Greenberger and Steinberg, 1986).

EVIDENCE FROM OUTCOME EVALUATIONS

Although interview studies suggest that teachers and students are generally positive, this kind of evidence is always suspect. Teachers and students may feel positive about reforms without improvements in their performance, learning, persistence, or understanding. Even if motivation is improved, students will not benefit if other conditions are not met—if, for example, the "new" vocationalism has not moved away from the low-level content of the "old" vocational education.[16] Most outcome evaluations have examined career academies rather than high schools with majors or occupational high schools, simply because academies have been around the longest.[17] Findings generally favor academies over comparison schools, but caution is called for in interpreting the findings because students were not randomly assigned to academies and there are complex selection procedures in some cases that influence the results in both positive and negative directions.

Some of the earliest evaluations were conducted for the California academies. Evaluators found annual dropout rates of 2 to 4 percent in academies, compared to 10 to 11 percent among a comparison group matched by race, gender, and achievement test scores (Stern et al., 1992, Chap. 5). Overall, 94 percent of academy students graduated, compared to 79 percent from the comparison group. A later evaluation of academy replications found a 3-year cumulative dropout rate of 7.3 percent in acad-

[16]High schools that have developed from traditional vocational programs tend to look more like vocational programs with more academic content, while those that have emerged from conventional academic high schools tend to look like academic schools with a little occupational content added.

[17]For another review of the effects of career academies, see Stern et al. (2001).

emies and 14.6 percent in the comparison group for the first cohort, of 6.6 percent and 14.3 percent in a second cohort, and of 2.8 percent and 2.2 percent in a third. While they were enrolled, academy students showed better attendance, failed fewer courses, earned more credits, and obtained better grades than did the comparison students—all indirect evidence of better motivation and engagement.

The effects of the academies on employment were mixed. (In contrast, a nonexperimental evaluation of Philadelphia academies found that graduates were more likely to be employed, and to have been employed longer, compared to a matched comparison group—benefits that may be attributed to careful selection of students.) The earliest California evaluations found higher rates of college attendance (62 percent versus 47 percent) for academy graduates, though subsequent evaluations found only that academy graduates were more likely to enroll in 4-year rather than community colleges.

Another evaluation of academies was conducted in a school district that has incorporated multiple academies into every high school (Maxwell and Rubin, 2000). These evaluations compared academy and nonacademy students, controlling for demographic variables that included gender, race, English proficiency, special education status, and 10th-grade achievement. In both uncontrolled and controlled results, academy students rated their program higher on several dimensions related to motivation and engagement, including supporting good study habits, maintaining positive attitudes toward schooling, being prepared for their current education, and being self-motivated. In addition, academy students were more likely to report that their program was related to their current job or future education, prepared them for their current or most recent job, helped them to meet work deadlines, and helped them see the relationship between schooling and work. Academy students also had higher grade point averages (GPAs) and were more likely to attend 4-year (but not 2-year) colleges. All of these differences were significant in analyses that controlled for demographic variables. Being in an academy did not significantly increase graduation once GPA was considered, but the effect of academies on GPAs did increase graduation rates indirectly—as was also true for both 2-year and 4-year college-going.

Ryken's (2001) study of two high-quality biotechnology academies provides some results on persistence, although the lack of a control group limits the conclusions that can be drawn. In both schools, the graduation rate was 100 percent among academy students starting in the junior year. In contrast, the 12th-grade dropout rate among nonacademy students at one of the high schools was 12 percent for Latino and African-American students and 7 percent for Asian-American students. (At the other school it was 0 percent.) Students without summer internships were much less likely to persist from grade 11 to grade 12, indicating the potential power of work placements. In one school, 57.6 percent of students attended the community college component of the program, 21.2 percent planned to attend 4-year college, and 13.6 percent planned to enter another 2-year college. Comparable figures for the second school were 48.3 percent, 38.3 percent, and 6.7 percent. Although judging these figures is difficult, they clearly indicate that a majority of students persisted in the program to the community college, and more than half received a certificate within a year. Students cited the value of having a clear progression from high school to college to employment.

Because it is impossible to control for all the possible differences among students that might account for differences between academy and nonacademy students in nonexperimental evaluations, considerable attention has been paid to a random assignment evaluation conducted by the MDRC starting in 1993. The first set of outcome results was consistent with previous studies suggesting the positive effects of academies, particularly for students at the greatest risk of dropping out who chose to attend the academies. Dropout rates for this group were lower than those in the control group (21.3 percent versus 32.2 percent) and average attendance was higher (81.5 percent versus 76 percent). Academy students earned more credits overall and more credits in selected college preparation subjects, and they were more likely to earn 3 or more vocational credits (58.3 percent versus 37.7 percent), confirming that academy students took more academic and more vocational courses than nonacademy students. High-risk academy students were more future oriented in several ways. They were more likely to have researched college options, to have taken the SAT or ACT, and to have submitted college applications. Academy students, however, did not have better math and reading scores than nonacademy students. Based on these results, academies appear to enhance the motivation and engagement of high-risk students, improve completion rates, and enhance their planning for the future, although not the academic skills assessed by standardized achievement tests (Kemple and Snipes, 2000, especially Tables 3.1, 3.2, 3.3, 3.5). The results for students in the medium- and low-risk groups were more mixed. Although most comparisons favored academy students, few of these were statistically significant, and a few were in the "wrong" direction.

Given the overall positive effects of academies on engagement, especially for high-risk students who choose to attend academies, the most recent results in the series of MDRC reports have been disappointing. The high school completion rates for academy and nonacademy students were virtually the same (87.2 percent versus 86.7 percent),[18] as were their enroll-

---

[18]A somewhat negative finding is that academy students were more likely to complete high school by receiving a GED (7 percent versus 5 percent, though this difference was not statisti-

ment rates in postsecondary programs (54.8 percent versus 54.6 percent). Although high-risk academy students appeared to have higher graduation rates than high-risk nonacademy students (77 percent versus 73 percent), to be more likely to graduate on time (56 percent versus 50 percent), and to be more likely to enroll in postsecondary education (41 percent versus 37 percent), these differences were not statistically significant—though small sample sizes (of 80 and 56, respectively) may be to blame. The high-risk group was also significantly more likely to complete a basic academic core (63.8 percent versus 48.2 percent), and all three risk groups were more likely to complete a basic academic core plus a career-oriented focus—the emphasis of academies (Kemple and Snipes, 2000, Table ES.2, Figure 8, Table 3, Figure 9).

Overall, the MDRC study suggests that academies can have positive effects on motivation and engagement. Furthermore, there are no obvious problems with occupationally oriented academies. The broad occupational focus does not decrease students' rates of taking academic courses, applying to college, or going to college. There is no evidence of substituting employment for a college orientation, as has been true for traditional vocational education.

The Talent Development High School model also has been assessed, both at its initial implementation site at Patterson High School in Baltimore and at its replication sites in two Philadelphia schools. Attendance at Patterson rose by 10 percentage points during the 2 years of implementation, while it declined in other Baltimore high schools by 3.2 percentage points. During the same time frame, the proportion of students missing 20 or more days improved by 10 percentage points, the proportion passing the Maryland State Functional Exams increased by 28 percentage points, and the school's performance index—a state-specified composite of climate, attendance, promotion, and academic achievement—rose by 7 points, while the next best Baltimore school improved by only 3.2 points. Other high schools averaged a decline of 0.2 points. Student reports of safety, rules, state of the bathrooms, and the overall school were substantially better than other Baltimore schools (McPartland et al., 1998). The Talent Development High School model was developed to bring a large, out-of-control high school back into control through the development of schools within schools; evidently this goal was largely met.

---

cally significant). Although findings are mixed, some studies have found that the GED does not provide the same level of access to employment or postsecondary education as the conventional diploma (see Cameron and Heckman, 1993; Murnane, Willett and Boudett, 1995).

The evaluations of the Philadelphia replications compared their results to two matched high schools. In the Talent Development High Schools, the proportion of freshmen passing core academic courses increased from 24.1 percent to 55.8 percent, much greater than the improvement in control high schools, from 33.2 percent to 38.9 percent. The proportion promoted to 10th grade increased substantially, from 43.8 percent to 73 percent in one school, and from 41.5 percent to 75 percent in the other, compared to small decreases in control schools. The increases in math scores on the Stanford-9 achievement tests were substantially higher than control schools (3.5 normal curve equivalents versus a 0.2 NCE decline), though reading scores worsened (although not by as much as in control high schools). In the second year, the school climate continued to improve, with substantial drops in arrests and suspensions and increases in attendance; the proportion passing the three core academic subjects was about 20 percentage points higher than at the control site. Though the study design can be faulted for being nonrandom, in every dimension of performance the Talent Development High Schools outperformed the control high schools.[19]

An evaluation of magnet high schools with broadly occupational themes also generated interesting, if ambiguous, results. New York City established magnet high schools in which half of the students were admitted by lottery, while the remaining half were chosen by the school in a competitive process. The lottery thus created a random assignment opportunity. Evidence from four magnet schools—one in health, one in business, one in business communications, and one in engineering—indicated that completion rates were worse for those students in magnet schools: 25 percent of lottery winners graduated at the end of the fourth year, compared to 31 percent of lottery losers. The authors (Crain et al., 1999, Chap. 2) attributed this result to the fact that the career magnet schools were more academically demanding than the comprehensive schools, and the career magnet schools enforced standards by limiting the occupational program to only a fraction of students they admitted, thereby increasing dropouts. The real benefits of these magnet schools came in the long term. Interviews with both lottery winners and losers indicated that graduates of the career magnet earned more college credits and were more likely to have chosen a college major in their first or second year after high school graduation. The career magnet students were more likely to report that they had become "really good at something," and to have developed a career identity during their high school years, a result consistent with Heebner's (1995) findings that magnet

[19]For these results, see "The Talent Development High School: First-Year Results of the Ninth Grade Success Academy in Two Philadelphia High Schools 1999-2000" and "Philadelphia's Talent Development High Schools: Second-Year Results," both from the Philadelphia Education Fund, available online at http://www.philaedfund.org.

students engaged in "parallel career planning," developing both employment and postsecondary education goals. Overall, the authors concluded that the success of career magnets depends on orienting students toward future college and career decisions.

Finally, we note some intriguing statistical findings by Arum and Shavit (1995), based on the High School and Beyond data collected on sophomores in 1980 and followed through 1986. They focused on the effects of academic, vocational, and general tracks, but also included a "mixed" track with academic and vocational courses. Students in the vocational track were less likely to attend college, but those in the mixed track were just as likely as students in the academic track to enroll in postsecondary education.[20] Furthermore, for those who were not still in school, students from the mixed track were more likely to be employed than those from the academic track. The mixed tracks were not necessarily the programs we have described as theme-based high schools because such programs barely existed in the early 1980s. However, these results indicate that a mix of academic and occupational courses does not necessarily reduce postsecondary enrollment, and can increase employment for those who do not go to college.

CONCLUSIONS

Compared to traditional high schools, the reforms associated with theme-based high schools are, in theory, more consistent with general conditions necessary for student motivation and engagement—small size, environments where students can play a greater role in their own learning, clearly structured, coherent curricula, relevance to the outside world, and other criteria reviewed in Chapter 2. Of course, certain programs may not adhere to some of these precepts: The New York magnet schools, for example, are not always small learning communities, and some reforms may slight learning about careers and their connections to schooling. But, in theory, these reforms have promise for improving American high school student engagement.

Both students and teachers report positive experiences in these settings more than in traditional high schools. Students value smaller learning com-

---

[20]These results recently have been replicated in part by Plank (2001, Figures 4A–4D) using National Education Longitudinal Study of 1988 (NELS 88) data. He found that 87 percent of academic concentrators enrolled in postsecondary education, compared to 79 percent of dual (academic and vocational) concentrators, with much lower proportions for general students (69 percent) and vocational concentrators (56 percent)—a higher differential between academic and dual concentrators than Arum and Shavit found, but still implying that mixed programs lead to relatively high postsecondary enrollment.

munities and the variety of instructional settings; they appreciate information on careers and future options, and the possibility of "parallel career planning" has advantages over the previous dichotomy between college-bound and non college-bound students. In programs incorporating work-based learning, students report that they learn in different ways in different settings, although the quality of work placements is crucial. Some students find these integrated programs are not for them, especially if they are in an occupational area they do not enjoy. Some teachers report that they do not have enough time for collaboration. Overall, however, the level of satisfaction with these reforms seems high.

The effects on motivation and engagement appear to be relatively strong and consistent. In most cases, attendance is improved, engagement with school seems to go up, and negative behavior seems to be reduced. The effects of the Talent Development model in establishing an orderly climate conducive to learning is especially remarkable. The detailed results in Ryken's (2001) study of a high-quality academy reveal the attachment and learning that can take place in programs with several different learning environments. These results, as well as those from the New York magnet schools, suggest the value of "education through occupations" in orienting students toward future opportunities in both employment and education. Even in the most rigorous random assignment study (the MDRC study), students report more personalized attention, more teacher support with schoolwork, and more engaged peers.

The conclusions about outcomes, however, are more mixed. The quasi experimental studies of academies typically report higher grades and higher rates of college-going. But there is little evidence of any positive influence on direct measures of learning. The recent findings of the MDRC random assignment study indicate academy students are not even more necessarily likely to complete high school or enroll in postsecondary education. The differences between academies and other schools on measures of engagement and motivation evidently do not necessarily lead to clearly improved academic achievement or the increases in educational attainment that would be expected if higher achievement levels were observed.

The lack of effects on learning has important implications for practice. Even when the strategies described in this chapter increase motivation, they may not increase learning if a reform does not also pay attention to the quality of instruction. The reforms we have described focus more on *what* is taught than on *how* teaching was done, with the exception of more opportunities for learning in real-world settings. Taken together, research on theme-based schools and research on instruction (Chapter 3, this volume) suggest that the implementation of a theme needs to be combined with efforts to improve the quality of teaching.

Finally, consistent with MDRC findings (Kemple, 1997, 2001; Kemple and Snipes, 2000), any good idea can be undermined by mediocre implementation, and some evaluation results have been affected by weaknesses in programs as implemented. Academies vary in the extent to which instructors can construct integrated curricula and in their connections to employers and postsecondary institutions. The New York magnet schools seem to include relatively little occupational coursework, and have not developed small learning communities within these large high schools. The Talent Development model has struggled with getting districts and unions to free up sufficient time for teacher preparation, and in some cases been plagued by instability of teachers and administrators. In addition, the availability and quality of work-based learning, and more generally of connections between school and the wider community, vary substantially.

The good news is that the kinds of negative effects academically oriented critics might expect of schools with occupational themes have not been found. There is no evidence of lower grades, lower test scores, or lower rates of college-going. A judicious summary might be that there are no obvious problems in theme-based education in the contexts in which they have been studied and there is the potential for substantial improvements in school climate, motivation, and other outcomes. Because this approach to high school reform began seriously only about 20 years ago, it is too soon to know its true potential.

8

Comprehensive High School Reform Designs

The previous chapters describe the key features of high schools that are necessary to engage students from challenging backgrounds. Implementing any one of these features will have modest effects at best on student engagement. The evidence suggests that narrowly construed interventions addressing isolated aspects of school functioning and student experience are not sufficient to move students toward high levels of engagement and achievement. Implementing some of the suggestions made in this volume without consideration of the larger picture could even undermine student engagement.

Comprehensive school reform models have been created to guide whole-school, sometimes whole-district, efforts to improve student engagement and learning. The goal is to put all the pieces together—to create a set of reforms that will support and reinforce each other and be sufficient to improve substantially student engagement and learning. Designers of school reform models also create organizational structures that provide ongoing assistance for implementation on a broad scale.

As a movement, comprehensive school reform has existed for some time. A few reform models that exist today began as long as two decades ago. The movement gained substantial momentum, however, in 1997 when Congress approved $150 million to support implementation of comprehensive school designs in school districts nationwide. An additional $134 million for comprehensive reform was approved in fiscal year 1999, enabling more than 2,000 schools to receive grants of at least $50,000 to implement reforms over 3 years. Most recently, reform of secondary schools has begun to receive attention from other federal and private philanthropic sources. The U.S. Department of Education has appropriated more than $125 million for reform of large comprehensive high schools[1] and several foundations, such as the Bill and Melinda Gates and the Carnegie Foundations, also have made major investments.

In this chapter we summarize a group of comprehensive school reform models available to high schools. The central features of the various design models overlap considerably, and one goal is to show the high level of consensus that has evolved regarding the features of effective secondary schools. A second goal is to provide examples of strategies that have been developed to reorganize high schools in ways consistent with the specific, research-based recommendations made in this volume.

Designs included in this review of comprehensive reform initiatives are limited to those that:

- are being implemented in high schools serving economically disadvantaged communities in more than one locality;
- are supported by national technical assistance organizations;
- include elements addressing all three broad areas covered in the earlier chapters of this volume: pedagogy (curriculum and how it is being taught); school organization, climate, and policies; and connections to the outside world;
- ground key features of the design in research on what increases high school students' engagement and learning; and
- articulate strategies for getting these research-based features implemented.

The annex to this chapter provides a brief description of each initiative included in this review.

First, we examined the degree to which comprehensive models that met our criteria include some of the key features of engaging high schools suggested by the research reviewed in this volume—high standards for both academic learning and student conduct, personalization, meaningful and engaging pedagogy and curriculum, and professional learning communities.[2] Using materials provided by developers of each design, we assessed

---

[1]U.S. Department of Education grant 84-215L.

[2]Some of the other features suggested by the committee's review of the literature, such as changing the way counseling is conducted in schools and connecting schools to families and communities, are found less consistently in the current comprehensive design models. Therefore, we did not include them in this analysis.

whether these four features were (1) not included, (2) recommended and supported by the design, or (3) central to and required by the design. Table 8-1 summarizes this analysis. As the table demonstrates, there is considerable consistency in the presence of these four features in the description of the models, although not necessarily in all schools that have attempted to implement the models. A few models do not explicitly include high standards for student conduct, and one does not address personalization of the family's experience. Only three models (Edison Schools, First Things First, and Talent Development High School) include all four of the features as central and required elements. Notwithstanding these variations, the conclusions regarding some of the qualities of engaging schools discussed in this volume are remarkably well represented in national school reform models.

Although in theory the models are consistent with empirical evidence on engaging schools, efforts to implement the models are still works in progress. For many reasons related to resources, the availability of credible and qualified technical assistance providers, and support and consistency in policies at the district and state levels, implementing these models in the real world is difficult. We return to some of the most common obstacles later in the chapter.

Another approach to whole-school reform that incorporates principles of engagement is the movement to create small schools. The specific goals and findings related to small schools are discussed in Chapter 4. Although creating small schools is a prominent reform strategy, it does not fit the criteria for a comprehensive reform design because of the variability in objectives and design. Small schools are also often new schools rather than reformed existing schools with existing staff, administrators, and students.

FROM THE WHAT TO THE HOW: IMPLEMENTATION STRATEGIES

Having found such consistency across models in the key features of high school reform, we now turn to the means proposed by the models to put these features in place. Table 8-2 summarizes the strategies used by the comprehensive school models that met our criteria. Most of the strategies that are included in the models are based on research that has been discussed in this volume.

All of these reform models are designed to raise expectations for student academic performance and ensure equity of opportunity to meet these higher standards. Some models explicitly state what students are expected to know and be able to do by subject areas and by grade levels. The support organizations associated with some of the reform models hire staff to help

TABLE 8-1 Selected Comprehensive School Reform Models: Key Features Leading to Student Engagement and Learning

Reform Model	High and Clear Standards		Personalization of School Experience		Meaningful and Engaging Pedagogy and Curriculum	Professional Learning Communities for Adults
	Academic	Conduct	Student	Family		
America's Choice (AMCH)	•	—	•	•	•	•
ATLAS Communities (ATLAS)	•	o	•	•	•	•
Coalition of Essential Schools (CES)	•	o	•	•	•	•
Community for Learning (CFL)	•	—	•	•	•	•
Co-NECT (CON)	•	—	•	o	•	o
Edison Schools (EDS)	•	•	•	•	•	•
Expeditionary Learning/Outward Bound (ELOB)	o	o	•	o	•	•
First Things First (FTF)	•	•	•	•	•	•
High Schools That Work (HSTW)	•	—	o	o	•	•
Modern Red Schoolhouse (MRSH)	•	o	•	•	•	•
Paideia (PAD)	•	o	•	—	•	o
Talent Development High School (TDHS)	•	•	•	•	•	•

KEY: • Critical feature is explicit and required in the model.
o Critical feature is implicit in the model or recommended but not required.
— indicates that the model does not address that critical feature.

schools align what is being taught and the evaluations of student learning with the higher standards.

Many reform models do not incorporate specific strategies for improving student conduct, although most work to improve behavior by providing more personalized, rigorous, and engaging experiences for students, including greater access to higher quality student and family services. For models that explicitly address how to improve behavior, staff work with small teacher learning communities to help them develop more effective disciplinary approaches that are consistent with existing policies.

The models propose a variety of strategies for personalizing student and family experiences. Some models involve reorganizing larger schools into smaller units (often called small learning communities or academics) where the same students and teachers stay together for longer periods during the school day ("block" scheduling) and over at least two school years ("looping"), as described in Chapter 4. In some cases the smaller units have themes based on career or academic interests (see Chapter 7), which give students and their families some choice in the noncore curriculum.

One of the goals of creating smaller learning units is for teachers to have fewer total students to know and to teach and for students to see fewer teachers. This is also achieved sometimes by using resources to involve more adults in teaching roles, thus reducing the student-teacher ratio (see Chapter 4). Another strategy that is common in comprehensive reform models is to provide an advisor, mentor, or advocate to each student, as described in Chapter 6. In some models, this person also communicates with students' families and helps identify students' nonacademic needs and connect students to services in the school or in the community to meet those needs.

All of the comprehensive reform models address how teaching is done and what is being taught, although they vary considerably in how prescriptive they are. In most cases schools are expected to create schedules and staff assignments that increase instructional time and, in some designs, to reduce student-to-adult ratios, especially in language arts and math. Some of the reforms also include more specific guidelines for students who are substantially behind their grade level.

The use of technology and project learning, cooperative learning, learning opportunities that are embedded in real-world contexts, and other strategies to involve students actively in the learning process are endorsed and supported by all models. Furthermore, all models refer specifically to the importance of connecting schoolwork to students' own interests, experiences outside of school, and culture. A curriculum that crosses traditional discipline boundaries is also common in the reform models.

All of the comprehensive reform models recognize the importance of supporting teachers and helping schools build a community of adult as well

TABLE 8-2 Common Strategies Used by Comprehensive High School Reform Designs to Implement the Key Features

High and Clear Standards	Personalization of School Experience	Meaningful and Engaging Pedagogy and Curriculum	Professional Learning Communities for Adults
Academic	*Student*		
Ensure that clear and rigorous content and performance standards are linked to high-stakes assessments.[a]	Reorganize schools into smaller groups of teachers and students.	Infuse student interests, background, and experience into teaching process.	Provide common planning time for staff to meet and discuss their work.
Align existing or new curriculum materials to standards and assessments; create content standards, benchmarks, and indicators that are available both as formative, ongoing measures of student progress and as summative evaluations of student mastery.[b]	Provide choice to students among smaller units around student and staff interests.	Introduce project-based learning within and across disciplines emphasizing application and content knowledge.	Expect and support teachers to improve instruction through training, practice, dialogue, and coaching, and through access to high-quality learning activities and content knowledge "refreshers" linked to their teaching responsibilities.
Make sure all students are expected to take and have access to high-level courses and curriculum (detrack).	Require same groups of teachers to stay with students across the school day and school years.	Develop and provide internships, apprenticeships, and service learning opportunities.	Use student performance results and student work to drive instructional decisions.

Increase instructional time for students to meet higher standards through block scheduling, more instructional time in schedule, extended school day and school year.	Create opportunities for lower student-to-adult ratios during core classes.	Expect and equip staff to use instructional approaches that maximize students' active engagement (e.g., cooperative learning structures, Socratic methods).	Flexibly allocate available resources (time, people, money, facilities) to groups of teachers to meet their students' needs.
	Have individual teachers and other staff act as student advisors, mentors, or advocates.	Use high-quality, high-interest instructional materials for below-grade-level readers.	Ensure collective responsibility for student outcomes within groups of teachers sharing students.
	Provide customized and responsive school- and community-based services to students to meet wide range of academic and nonacademic needs.	Use technology to enrich curriculum and pedagogical approaches	
Conduct Ensure that district and school disciplinary policies are clearly communicated and consistently carried out by all adults.	*Family* Include parents and other adults from students' communities on school decision-making body (e.g., steering committee).		
	Have teachers and other staff act as family advocates.		

[a]This strategy is controversial and not supported by all model developers.

[b]The order of the development of standards, assessments, and curricula varies. Ideally, curricula and assessments are developed after clear and rigorous content and performance standards are set, but assessments are often imposed on model developers by the state or district.

as student learners. One of the purposes of the designs that reorganize large high schools into smaller units is to create teams of teachers who share the same students. All of the models include opportunities for teachers to meet with one another to discuss their instruction, student progress, and governance and policy issues affecting the school community.

Some reform models work with schools to provide small learning communities with individual and disaggregated student data that are used to develop strategies to improve student achievement. All designs provide professional development opportunities, and some provide in-class and ongoing coaching. The relative emphasis on project-based learning, new teaching strategies, curriculum development and implementation, team building, and leadership training vary considerably among the reform models.

A remarkable degree of overlap exists among the features and strategies stressed in comprehensive reform models and those the committee found evidence to support in its review of the research literature. Admittedly, many of the conclusions about effective practices are based on soft and incomplete evidence. Nevertheless, there is substantial convergence in the conclusions drawn by different people who have examined existing research and craft knowledge—both about what needs to be done and promising strategies for getting it done.

We turn next to evidence on the success of comprehensive school designs to improve student learning. Because most of the models are relatively new, and because some require two or more years to be fully implemented, the data here are both new and thin. Moreover, most of the designs described in this chapter are still in the research and development phase. Because they are changing in response to their emerging results, evaluations are often studies of moving targets. Studies discussed next, however, suggest that extant comprehensive school reform models show some promise of improving student engagement and learning.

RESEARCH EVIDENCE

An extensive array of research studies has been conducted on comprehensive school reform models in the past decade. However, the majority has focused on elementary and middle schools (Berends et al., 2002; Kirby, Berends, and Naftel, 2001; McCombs and Quiat, 2000; Supovitz and Poglinco, 2001; Wenzel et al., 2001). The little evidence that does exist on the efficacy of the high school designs included in this chapter is consistent with evaluations of elementary and middle school reform efforts: When the school and its external partners are successful in implementing the reform's key features (see Table 8-1), the results are positive. For example, research on the most long-standing high school reform designs[3] as well as more recent data emerging from internal studies of new high school designs[4] indicate that when levels of personalization increase, so do levels of attendance and parent involvement, and disciplinary problems decline (Ancess and Wichterle, 1999; Berends, Kirby, Naftel, and McKelvey, 2001; Boykin, 2000; Fine, 1994; Hamilton and Gill, 2001; Institute for Research and Reform in Education, 2000, 2002; Legters, Balfanz, Jordan, and McPartland, 2002; MacMullen, 1996; Nelson, 2000).

Evaluations of models, without examining the mediators of their effects, suggest that comprehensive school design models show some promise of increasing high school students' engagement and learning. Two models that have examined the crime rate of their students (sometimes considered a measure of disengagement)—Coalition of Essential Schools and Talent Development High Schools—have found decreases in reported crimes after implementation (Ancess and Wichterle, 1999; Boykin, 2000; Legters et al., 2002; MacMullen, 1996). Evaluation studies of high school reform models further show students taking more advanced academic courses[5] (Boykin, 2000; Legters et al., 2002) and having higher levels of enrollment in postsecondary schools[6] (Ancess and Wichterle, 1999; MacMullen, 1996), improved test scores[7] (Ancess and Wichterle, 1999; Berends et al., 2001; Institute for Research and Reform in Education, 2002; MacMullen, 1996), increased persistence and graduation rates[8] (Ancess and Wichterle, 1999; Bottoms and Presson, 2000; Institute for Research and Reform in Education, 2000, 2002; MacMullen, 1996), and decreased dropout rates[9] (Ancess and Wichterle, 1999; Bottoms and Presson, 2000; Boykin, 2000; Institute for Research and Reform in Education, 2000, 2002; Legters et al., 2002; MacMullen, 1996).

In addition to assessing effects on individual and diverse indicators of student engagement and learning and related outcomes, evaluations of com-

---

[3]For example, Coalition of Essential Schools and High Schools That Work.

[4]For example, ATLAS Communities, Edison Schools, Expeditionary Learning, First Things First, and Talent Development High School.

[5]For example, High Schools That Work and Talent Development High School.

[6]For example, Coalition of Essential Schools and High Schools That Work.

[7]For example, Coalition of Essential Schools, Co-NECT, Expeditionary Learning/Outward Bound, First Things First, and High Schools That Work.

[8]For example, Coalition of Essential Schools, First Things First, and High Schools That Work.

[9]For example, ATLAS Communities, Coalition of Essential Schools, Community for Learning, First Things First, High Schools That Work, and Talent Development High School.

prehensive school reform designs also seek to answer the more overarching research question: Is the implementation of the designs sufficient to move schools from graduating half or fewer of their incoming freshmen to graduating nearly all, while preparing them well for postsecondary education or high-quality employment? This question has yet to be answered.

In brief, extant evidence suggests that effective implementation of the school reform models included in this chapter does improve some indicators of student engagement and learning. Whether these models can achieve the ambitious goal of improving high school education on a large scale is yet to be seen.

HOW TO BRING ABOUT CHANGE: THE PROCESS

No two models look alike with regard to what consumers and investors should expect in the planning and implementation process, including what roles various stakeholders (people who are affected by the reform) play in providing supports and pressure to meet expectations. Documentation of these processes is not as thorough or reliable as descriptions of the designs' key features and general implementation goals. Furthermore, conclusive research evidence does not yet exist indicating that one approach leads to deeper and more sustained implementation of reform in high schools than another approach. To organize some information on how these reform models work with high schools, we list guiding questions about the change process itself and examples of how reform models diverge in their answers.

1. *What kind of buy-in does the model seek before committing to work with a high school, and how does the model's organization work with the school to build commitment to the reform by all stakeholders?*

Some reform models require that staff at the school level vote to adopt the design before initiating a partnership. Other models discourage votes in advance, instead encouraging district leaders (including the board and the superintendent), community leaders, and leaders at the school level (including administrators, teachers, students, and sometimes parents) to decide whether the reform design is the best vehicle to meet their goals. The staff employed by the design model program (design staff) then join with these leaders to develop school staff and other stakeholders' commitment to the design through the planning and implementation process.

Designs converge on strategies for building buy-in once the design is selected. Most designs engage staff, students, and parents in study and discussion. They use examples of how the design features have been implemented in other schools and involve stakeholders in shaping local decisions.

2. *What, if any, are the nonnegotiable requirements or fixed expectations that the design staff bring into their relationship with school and district personnel?*

At a minimum, most reform models share the goal of increasing all students' achievement to levels needed for postsecondary education and high-quality employment. Most of the models expect all school staff to participate in study and discussion of the design features and implementation strategies. Beyond these shared expectations, however, models vary greatly in what prospective high school and district administrators are expected to sign up for in advance. Examples of nonnegotiables, taken from various models, include

- committing to a set of general principles about what good schools do;
- implementing a specific curriculum;
- adopting specific assessment practices and student certification procedures;
- ensuring that all students have access to high-level academic courses;
- forming thematic small learning communities; and
- selecting from or creating a variety of school structures to promote personalization.

Differences in what is and is not negotiable weigh heavily in schools' and school districts' decisions on whether to adopt one of these designs and which one to adopt. Some districts value the clarity, credibility, and accountability they purchase with the adoption of a design that sets out in advance both the key features and the acceptable pathways to implementing these features. Other districts and schools are concerned that if major decisions about the key features or the implementation strategies do not reside at the building or the small community level, there will not be sufficient buy-in to sustain the reform over rough patches.

3. *How does the reform design use data of various forms to initiate, inform, monitor, refine, and sustain the reform process?*

All of the reform models make legitimate claims to being research based in the sense that their design features are consistent with research on best practices. However, use of data available from participating districts and schools and the requirements for new data to be collected as part of the reform process vary considerably. For example, data on student performance are used in some designs to give teachers and administrators a sense of urgency about initiating and sustaining reform, to inform instructional decisions, and to strengthen collective responsibility for student outcomes. Extensive data are collected by some designs on current instructional practices, school climate, and student and teacher attitudes and beliefs. These designs use these data for a variety of purposes, including guiding the selection of implementation strategies, assessing and improving the fidelity of implementation strategies, and holding individuals and groups accountable for fulfilling commitments to implement design components.

4. *Where does the change process begin and how much progress is expected in a given time period?*

Even when designs have similar key features and implementation strategies, they may begin the reform process differently (for recent analyses of the reform process, see Berends, Bodilly, and Kirby, 2002; Berends, Chun et al., 2002; Berends et al., 2001). Some designs emphasize leading with structural change that ensures personalization, then turning to instructional and curriculum issues. Others lead with instructional and curricular reforms in literacy, then take on restructuring efforts. Still others begin with self-assessment, then use the results to shape entry points for the reform.

Reform models also vary significantly in whether they set deadlines for decision making and implementation, and if so, how firmly. Although most want to see all of the key features (see Table 8-1) implemented, there is wide variation in expectations related to the rate of implementation.

5. *What role does the design developer play in supporting planning and implementation of the reforms?*

All of the reform models present key design features and strategies for implementing those features. The additional supports provided by the models vary in focus (what they do), intensity (how much they do), and longevity (how long they do it). This variation stems largely from differences in the models' nonnegotiables. Models that require schools to adopt new curricula, fundamentally change teaching strategies, or completely restructure their school into radically different units of work expect to do a great deal to support these changes, to be involved for multiple years, and to provide extensive materials and technical training to staff. Models that encourage schools to decide on the scope, scale, and implementation strategies of the reform can remain more hands off, depart more quickly, and focus more on sustaining and facilitating processes developed at the school level than imparting and supporting predetermined content and processes.

6. *What roles do the following stakeholders play in ensuring the reforms are implemented?*

Teaching staff: Some models provide professional development that exposes teachers to theory, research, and best practices and develops their consensus-building strategies and conflict resolution skills. These models assume that the mix of knowledge and process skills provide the foundation for making good decisions about what needs to be done and then getting it done (e.g., High Schools That Work). Technical assistance providers for other models (e.g., First Things First) combine these kinds of supports with strong encouragement for district and building administrators and teaching staff to implement key features of the reform. A few of the reform models (e.g., Talent Development High School) have prescribed curricula and materials that teachers are trained and expected to use.

Teachers' unions: Like other major stakeholders in school and district reform, teachers' unions can play a pivotal role in launching and sustaining or delaying and undermining high school reform efforts. Districts vary widely in the percentages of teachers represented by unions and associations, the negotiating processes used by districts and these organizations, state law and legislative control over union/management relations, and existing contractual obligations and flexibilities. These factors, the personalities involved, and the histories of relationships between unions and district management can all shape how much and what types of influence teachers' unions have on the course of high school reform in any given district.

School administrator: Reform models also vary in their expectations of and supports for principals. Some models specify only that school administrators are expected to lead by example in all areas of the reform. In other models school administrators delegate management duties to "business directors" and focus on getting the reform under way and in place.

Some of the reform models augment the principal's resources by requiring full- or part-time school improvement facilitators and/or instructional coaches. They support planning and implementation of the reform, but usually rely on the principal to ensure that all staff members are "pulling their weight." Less clear are the models' views of the roles of counselors and assistant principals.

District leaders and personnel: District involvement becomes more critical in high school reform than in elementary- or middle-school reform. First, high schools, especially in smaller districts, are more visible—they are the community's "flagship" schools, where the major athletic and cultural events occur. Second, high schools are saturated with district, state, and federal policy constraints, such as course requirements, teacher certification issues, and specialized programs. Third, high schools face more serious, widespread, and visible disciplinary and social issues than elementary and middle schools. Finally, high schools absorb disproportionate resources because they require more extensive facilities and more administrative and senior teaching staff.

Some reform models view districts strictly as resource providers that help the school carry out the model selected by providing time, professional development, and funding. Other models actively engage district personnel and insist on their commitment to support implementation of the reform design along with the building leadership, most pointedly by clearing away overarching challenges to successful implementation of reform of high schools or any schools in the district. Examples of these challenges are

• district organizational structures where principals and other administrative positions responsible for improving teaching and learning in schools (e.g., curriculum specialists, special education coordinators, instructional coaches) report to different supervisors in the central office;

• evaluation polices for principals and other central office staff that focus on compliance issues more than contributions to instructional improvements at the classroom level;

• resistance from many quarters (teachers, parents, students, elected board officials) to changing long-standing policies that preserve enriched opportunities (lower class sizes, more experienced and well-trained teachers) for small minorities of typically high-performing students and more comfortable teaching assignments for more senior faculty; and

• difficulties in reallocation of positions at the building level to meet the needs of their reform effort (e.g., trading in administrative positions for additional teaching positions to lower student-adult ratios).

What is clear from this brief summary of the implementation approaches is that similarity in goals does not translate into similarity in the change processes employed by models. Some amount of flexibility always will be required in comprehensive school reform models because resources, expertise, the student body, and many other variables need to be considered when implementing a model in a particular school. However, as we move now to our summary and concluding comments on scaling up high school reform, we will reintroduce the need for greater clarity in what high schools need to do in order to engage their diverse student populations (see also Connell, 2002).

Lessons Learned

Little research has been conducted on the change process underlying comprehensive school reform implementation in high schools. Much of the research that does exist blends high school data with middle school and elementary school data (e.g., Berends et al., 2001; Berends, Bodilly et al., 2002; Kirby et al., 2001), looks at a small number of high schools (five or fewer) for a model (e.g., Stringfield et al., 1997), or has information only on initial implementation of the model (Connell, 2002; Gambone, Klem, and Connell, 2002).

Despite these limitations, certain factors emerge as fostering higher quality implementation, including:

1. High levels of support and commitment on the part of the teachers once implementation of the reform is under way (Berends et al., 2001; Berends, Bodilly et al., 2002; Kirby et al., 2001, Stringfield et al., 1997).

2. Clear communication between model developers and schools: Models need to effectively communicate the requirements of the design and not make major revisions to the design mid-course (Berends et al., 2001; Berends, Bodilly et al., 2002; Connell, 2002; Kirby et al., 2001).

3. Effective training:

- consistent training that meets the needs of the teachers as they make radical changes to the way they do business (Berends et al., 2001; Berends, Bodilly et al., 2002; Kirby et al., 2001);
- ongoing follow-up training (Stringfield et al., 1997); and
- training for new, incoming teachers (due to high staff mobility; Stringfield et al., 1997).

4. Strong principal leadership (Berends et al., 2001; Berends, Bodilly et al., 2002; Connell, 2002; Kirby et al., 2001; Stringfield et al., 1997).

5. Few competing demands on time from other reform projects by incorporating existing projects into the design model or removing them (Berends et al., 2001; Berends, Bodilly et al., 2002; Connell, 2002; Kirby et al., 2001).

6. Supportive district with effective leadership that:

- backs the reform and makes the reform central to its improvement efforts;
- dedicates resources to the implementation;
- creates rules and regulations that support the initiative and removes rules that hinder implementation;
- provides the school with autonomy to do what it takes to get the reform in place;
- implements assessment systems that are compatible with those of the design;
- develops a working relationship among school, district, and union staff; and
- has district-level accountability (Berends et al., 2001; Berends, Bodilly et al., 2002; Connell, 2002; Gambone et al., 2002; Kirby et al., 2001; Stringfield et al., 1997).

7. Schools that focus on making changes to classroom instruction in order to improve teaching and learning (Connell, 2002; Stringfield et al., 1997).

SCALING UP HIGH SCHOOL REFORM: PROSPECTS AND CHALLENGES

In this chapter, we have attempted to examine (but not advocate for) a number of comprehensive reform designs now being implemented in urban high schools. Rather than pitting them against one another, we have examined them as a group and extracted important commonalities and differences among them. We found remarkable similarities in the comprehensive school reform models that met our criteria in their commitment to some of the key features identified in the research reviewed for this volume. The evidence reviewed for this report suggests that getting these key features, regardless of the design vehicle, should have positive effects on student engagement and learning.

Documentation of the models' approaches to the change process itself is very uneven, making systematic study of their different approaches problematic. What can be said is that despite the similarities in their basic tenets, there is profound variation among the reform models in the ways they work with schools to get schools moving toward these common goals.

As discussed earlier, we do not yet know whether implementation of these designs is sufficient to achieve meaningful long-term results at the school or district level, such as having 75 percent of a nonselective urban high school's students graduate and perform at levels required for postsecondary education and high-quality employment. Extant research falls far short of identifying the necessary and sufficient conditions to do so.

Scaling up meaningful reform—going from one school to many—in a system as complex as public education requires confronting and addressing a significant set of challenges: diversity within the system of schools and districts and the populations they serve; the multiple levels of financial and political influence on the system; and the "forces of inertia"—discrimination (by race and class), lack of accountability, and inadequate and outdated professional training—that keep in place the current resource inequities and demonstrably ineffective policies and practices. Whereas the "what" of high school reform is becoming clear, the "how"—particularly how to go to scale—remains conjecture at this point. Some progress on the "process" issue has been made at the school level; creating new small schools and restructuring large high schools both show promise as starting points for getting these key features on the ground. The more daunting challenges lurk at the district, state, and national levels, where hundreds, if not thousands, of high schools need major overhauls in their structures and instructional practices.

We see high school reform at a crossroads of opportunity and peril. Opportunity comes in two forms: investments and knowledge. Between the U.S. Department of Education and private foundation initiatives, some dollars are available, at least in the near term, to support work toward improved outcomes for secondary students. Knowledge is also becoming available. This volume and other recent publications and emerging evaluation reports from the Department of Education's research and development grants on secondary reform provide solid information about what high school reform should look like—the conditions that, if put in place, could really make a difference—and some insights into how to do it (see, for example, Institute for Research and Reform in Education, 2002; Lee and Smith, 2001; Legters, Balfanz, and McPartland, 2002; Molnar, 2002).

Even with these opportunities, going to scale with knowledge-based and meaningful high school reform will require additional resources, continuous learning about the necessary and sufficient conditions for the change that needs to occur and how it happens, and time for the reforms to be implemented and studied. We can create the conditions to meet these needs only with additional public and political will and more cohesion within the field itself. We face peril on both fronts.

Public will is waning for any but the most simplistic approaches to "fixing" our poorly performing high schools. From reconstitution and state takeovers to privatization and radical voucher systems, citizens and elected officials are looking for silver bullets and unrealistically fast results. Other fixes to the current system have been proposed as well. Some policy makers believe (or hope) a focus on early and elementary education, specifically in the area of literacy, will steel children and youth against the corrosive effects of large, impersonal, and low-expectation secondary schools. Others believe that standards, testing, and external accountability will bring high schools around to working for all students.

Unfortunately, these expectations run counter to existing research and the experience of reform efforts now underway. Bad secondary schools can undo the best early education and elementary school experience, and high-stakes, repeated testing against high standards in and of itself guarantees only that more students will fail.

What is to be done? At the district, state, and federal levels, expectations and supports around several key issues need to be aligned and implemented.

First, to scale up high school reform, agreement is needed at the federal, state, and local levels on what change needs to occur. For example, at all levels there must be agreement that all students should leave high school above a well-defined and shared threshold level of academic performance, and that high schools in these communities will implement the features identified in this volume to get there.

Second, we need common indicators of what these reforms will look like when achieved in diverse settings and how good is good enough on these indicators. The indicators would need to include acceptable measures of student performance rather than the simplistic measures most states are now using, and there would need to be some assurance that students achieving these thresholds would have equitable access to quality employment and postsecondary education. Measures of how well and how broadly the four key features of engaging high schools are being implemented, and threshold levels of how good is good enough on these measures also would need to be developed and accepted at all levels.

Third, a clear conception of how change is to be implemented is needed. This conception of the process of change will need to have multiple levels and include school, district, state, and federal mechanisms for motivating and initiating reform, for getting through planning and initial implementation, and for sustaining and deepening implementation.

Fourth, this conception of the change process needs to specify what resources (human, economic, and political) are needed to implement changes and how those resources will be provided.

Fifth, a timeline is needed that includes the scale-up gradient and specifies which schools, how many, and when. The timeline also should spell out when interim and long-term outcomes are expected for each school, district, and state as well as across the nation.

Sixth, a public and visible accountability plan needs to be tied to this resource map and timeline. It should specify who is responsible for reallocating and providing those resources and for achieving these interim and long-term outcomes, and it should explain the consequences of not doing so for all involved.

Seventh, there need to be mechanisms for examining progress on the indicators of change, and results should be made public to promote accountability. Indicators should be used to finetune implementation strategies along the way.

Finally, resources need to be made available to allow the kinds of comprehensive changes that will result in real improvements in student engagement and learning. Money is not the answer, but low-budget efforts to improve schools have taught us that, to some degree, "you get what you pay for." Support is needed for both start-up costs and for sustaining constructive changes (see King, 1994).

This is an ambitious list of prerequisites, and it is probably not complete. But if engaging high schools are to become the rule rather than the exception in economically disadvantaged communities, the American public and policy makers at the federal, state, and district levels must tackle this issue comprehensively and with the kind of seriousness this list indicates.

ANNEX TO CHAPTER 8
BRIEF DESCRIPTIONS OF 12 COMPREHENSIVE REFORM INITIATIVES

AMERICA'S CHOICE
http://www.ncee.org/OurPrograms/narePage.html

The America's Choice Comprehensive Design Network (begun in 1989 as the National Alliance for Restructuring Education and in its current incarnation as of 1992) is a program of the National Center on Education and the Economy in Washington, D.C. America's Choice offers an aligned system of standards, assessments, and curriculum. The America's Choice performance standards complement and extend the content standards that the states and many districts have developed. The design includes a strategy for quickly identifying students who are falling behind and bringing them back to standard, as well as a planning and management system for making the most efficient use of available resources to raise student performance quickly. The expectation is that all but the most severely handicapped students will achieve standards in English language arts, math, and science in order to graduate from high school qualified to do college-level work without remediation. America's Choice is a New American Schools design and is currently being implemented in 31 high schools.

ATLAS COMMUNITIES
http://www.edc.org/FSC/ATLAS

The ATLAS Communities approach (Authentic Teaching, Learning, and Assessment for All Students) was formed in 1992 as a partnership of four school reform organizations: the Education Development Center in Boston, the Coalition of Essential Schools at Brown University, Project Zero at Harvard University, and the School Development Program at Yale University. According to the developers, ATLAS builds on a base of research and examined practice drawn from each of the sponsoring organizations. Specifically, the approach draws on essential questions and student exhibitions from the Coalition of Essential Schools; professional development and curriculum development from the Education Development Center; multiple intelligences, authentic assessment, and Teaching for Understanding from Project Zero; and family involvement, school climate, and management and decision making from the School Development Program. A unique feature of ATLAS is the pre-K to 12 "pathway." The "pathway" refers to feeder patterns of elementary, middle, and high schools, which the approach seeks to coordinate to produce a coherent educational program for each student, from the first day of school through graduation. ATLAS is a New American Schools design and is currently being implemented in 18 high schools.

COALITION OF ESSENTIAL SCHOOLS
http://www.essentialschools.org

The Coalition of Essential Schools (CES) was developed in 1984 by Theodore Sizer at Brown University. CES is founded on the Ten Common Principles that guide structural, curricular, pedagogical, and assessment-related change. CES includes a focus on personalized learning, mastery of a few subjects and skills, graduation by exhibition, and creation of a nurturing community. CES is a grassroots reform movement that emphasizes local control and autonomy in interpreting the Common Principles within the cultural and institutional context of each school. Each school's plan is unique, sharing the Ten Common Principles, but actualizing them in ways suited to their school. The approach of the Coalition is to provide staff development assistance to school faculties as they seek to design methods of implementing the principles and to facilitate exchanges among Coalition schools so that teachers may act as "critical friends" to one another as they seek to change their schools. CES is currently being implemented in more than 400 high schools.

COMMUNITY FOR LEARNING
http://www.temple.edu/LSS/cfl.htm

Community for Learning (CFL) was developed at the Temple University Center for Research in Human Development and Education (CRHDE) by CRHDE Director Dr. Margaret C. Wang in 1990. The model is designed to draw communities and schools together to bolster student achievement. Collaboration at all levels is a key goal of CFL. Students learn in a variety of environments, including libraries, museums, houses of worship, higher education institutions, workplaces, and their own homes. CFL links the school to these and other institutions, including health, social services, and law enforcement agencies. The idea is to provide a range of learning opportunities for students, coordinate service delivery across organizations, and foster a communitywide commitment to student success. The emphasis on collaboration extends into the classroom itself, where regular teachers and specialists (such as special education teachers, Title I teachers, and school psychologists) work in teams to meet the diverse academic and social needs of all children. CFL is currently being implemented in 6 high schools, though it has been implemented in as many as 11 high schools at one time.

CO-NECT

http://www.co-nect.com

Co-NECT was founded in 1992 by members of the Educational Technologies Group at the BBN Corporation. Co-NECT is a schoolwide approach that focuses on improving achievement by integrating technology into instruction, organizing lessons around interdisciplinary projects, and reorganizing schools into multigrade clusters of students and teachers. At the core of the Co-NECT design are five benchmarks: shared accountability for results, project-based learning, teaching for understanding and accomplishment, comprehensive assessment for continuous improvement, team-based school organization, and sensible use of technology. (Q: Six benchmarks listed, not five.) The benchmarks help schools evaluate their progress toward meeting the vision of success outlined in their action plan. Co-NECT also offers a set of assessment tools—rubrics—for judging progress within these benchmarks. Co-NECT encourages and supports extensive use of the Internet and other modern technologies—to support student learning, supplement training, and strengthen communication across schools in the network. Co-NECT is a New American Schools design. Information on the number of high schools currently implementing the model is not available.

EDISON SCHOOLS

http://www.edisonschools.com

The Edison Schools design was founded in 1992 as the Edison Project by a for-profit company and began operating in schools in 1995. Edison Schools remain public and are funded by taxpayer dollars after entering into agreements with superintendents and school boards. The local community can terminate the contract if student performance does not meet the terms stated in the contract. According to Edison, the company invests $1.5 million of private capital in a school before it opens. These dollars are earmarked for technology, instructional materials, and professional development. Edison takes responsibility for the day-to-day operation of a school; lengthens the school year by 25 days and the school day by 1 to 2 hours; helps reorganize schools into academies, houses, and teams; provides all Edison teachers with laptops and students in grades 3 and up with home computers; provides a strong liberal arts curriculum guided by high standards; aligns instruction with assessment; and requires students to stay with the same teacher for 3 years. Edison is currently being implemented in approximately 10 high schools.

EXPEDITIONARY LEARNING/OUTWARD BOUND
http://www.elob.org

Expeditionary Learning Outward Bound (ELOB) was established in 1992 as part of the New American Schools network of comprehensive school designs. It is based on two central precepts: students learn better by doing than by listening, and developing character, high expectations, and a sense of community is as important as developing academic skills and knowledge. In ELOB, learning expeditions are at the center of teaching and learning. Learning expeditions are long-term, in-depth investigations of a theme or topic. Students investigate these subject areas through challenging projects that integrate state and local standards. A typical learning expedition takes most of the school day and lasts 8 to 12 weeks or more. Expeditions involve academic work, adventure, and fieldwork. Students complete the expedition with a performance or presentation to an audience. Students in ELOB schools stay with the same teacher for 2 years or more. Schools use the Expeditionary Learning benchmarks to conduct an annual self-review of the school's progress and a periodic peer review from colleagues outside the school. ELOB is currently being implemented in 35 high schools.

FIRST THINGS FIRST
http://www.irre.org

First Things First (FTF) was developed by the Institute for Research and Reform in Education and first implemented in 1996. First Things First provides a clear but flexible framework for reform that districts and schools can adapt to their specific needs. Using the FTF framework, schools and districts focus on three goals: strengthening relationships among students and adults; improving teaching and learning; and reallocating budget, staff, and time to achieve the first two goals. Schools reorganize into small learning communities, create a family advocate system to involve families in supporting student success, and improve instruction through staff development focused on implementing high-quality, standards-based learning activities in every classroom. FTF emphasizes small learning communities as the hub of relationship building, collective responsibility for student outcomes, resource allocation, and professional development activities. Schools and districts are supported to align instruction and curriculum with their standards and use multiple assessment strategies to assess those standards, including those aligned with high-stakes tests. Collective responsibility among students, families, and staff for student success is a fundamental premise of FTF. Over time, schools implementing FTF are expected to prepare all students for success in postsecondary education and high-quality employment. FTF is currently being implemented in 14 high schools.

HIGH SCHOOLS THAT WORK
http://www.sreb.org/programs/hstw/hstwindex.asp

High Schools That Work (HSTW) began in 1988 as a pilot project of the Southern Regional Education Board's Vocational Education Consortium. HSTW is designed to raise the achievement level of career-bound high school students by combining the content of traditional college preparatory studies (e.g., English, mathematics, and science) with vocational studies. It is based on the beliefs that (1) an intellectually challenging curriculum should be taught to all high school students, and (2) students understand and retain academic concepts more readily if they use them in completing projects for their vocational courses. The design provides intensive technical assistance, focused staff development, and a nationally recognized yardstick for measuring program effectiveness. HSTW sets high expectations, identifies a recommended curriculum to meet the expectations, and sets student performance goals benchmarked to the National Assessment of Educational Progress. HSTW is currently being implemented in more than 1,000 high schools.

MODERN RED SCHOOLHOUSE
http://www.mrsh.org

Modern Red Schoolhouse, a New American Schools design, was developed in 1992 by the Hudson Institute, a private nonprofit research organization. William J. Bennett, Secretary of Education during the Reagan Administration, was chairman of the design team at Hudson. The design has since become the Modern Red Schoolhouse Institute, a separate nonprofit organization. Implementation of the design began in 1993. The primary goal of the Modern Red Schoolhouse design is to take the rigorous curriculum, values, and democratic principle commonly associated with "the little red schoolhouse," and combine them with the latest advancements in teaching and learning, supported by modern technology. The approach intends to help schools set high academic standards that are consistent with district and state assessments and cover rigorous core content. Schools are expected to assume increasing responsibility for many items that are traditionally controlled by the district (e.g., budgeting, personnel assignments, curriculum details, scheduling, teacher/student ratios, and time allotted to various subjects). Modern Red Schoolhouse schools use an instructional management system that both tracks student performance and progress and offers continuous reflection on and improvement to the curriculum. Modern Red Schoolhouse is currently being implemented in 20 high schools.

PAIDEIA
http://www.paideia.org

Mortimer Adler outlined the Paideia approach in his 1984 book, *Paideia Proposal: An Educational Manifesto*. The National Paideia Center, housed at the University of North Carolina, Chapel Hill, supports the efforts of educators implementing the Paideia Program through networks, staff development, a newsletter, and other publications. The goal of the Paideia Program is to provide a rigorous liberal arts education in grades K through 12 that will allow all graduates to have the skills needed to earn a living, to think and act critically as responsible citizens, and to continue educating themselves as lifelong learners. Instructional goals are based on acquisition of knowledge, development of intellectual skills, and enlarged understanding of ideas and values. These are addressed through three instructional approaches: didactic instruction, coaching, and small group seminars. Schoolwide restructuring is necessary to fully implement all three instructional pieces, as Socratic seminars often require longer class periods (up to 2 hours), while coaching may call for smaller classes enabling teachers to spend more time with individuals. Paideia is currently being implemented in 10 high schools.

TALENT DEVELOPMENT HIGH SCHOOL WITH CAREER ACADEMIES
http://www.csos.jhu.edu/Talent/high.htm

The Talent Development High School (TDHS) was first implemented in 1994 as a partnership between the Johns Hopkins University Center for Research on the Education of Students Placed at Risk (CRESPAR) and Patterson High School in Baltimore, Maryland. The goal of TDHS is to improve indicators of student achievement and behavior by raising expectations for all students and providing the mechanisms to help them meet those expectations. The model is composed of separate Career Academies for grades 10 through 12 and a Ninth Grade Success Academy. Career Academies are thematic, self-contained "small learning communities" or "schools-within-a-school" that integrate career and academic coursework. The Talent Development High School model asserts that all students can learn in demanding, high-expectation academic settings. Essential components of the model include a demanding common core curriculum based on high standards for all students, a supportive learning environment to encourage close teacher-student relations and an orderly academic climate, career-focused schoolwork, a college-bound orientation, no tracking, and flexible uses of time and resources. TDHS is currently being implemented in 39 high schools.

9

Summary of Findings and Recommendations

Engaging adolescents cognitively and emotionally in school and academic work is a challenge regardless of the social or economic status of the students or the location of their schools. Adolescents are too old and too independent to follow teachers' demands mindlessly, and many are too young, inexperienced, or uninformed to fully appreciate the value of succeeding in school. Academic motivation decreases steadily from the early grades of elementary school into high school, and disengagement from coursework is common at the high school level.

Students living in low-income communities are not alone in being less than enthusiastic about schoolwork. But when students from advantaged backgrounds become disengaged, even though they learn less than they could, they usually get by or they get second chances; most eventually graduate and move on to other opportunities. In contrast, students from disadvantaged backgrounds in environments that provide few quality resources for them, such as those in high-poverty, urban high schools, are less likely to graduate and face severely limited opportunities. In addition to having greater burdens and distractions, the consequences of being unengaged or dropping out of school are more serious for youth who do not have the social and other resources available to cushion the effects of academic failure. Their failure to acquire the basic skills needed to function in adult society, whether or not they complete high school, dramatically increases their risks of unemployment, poverty, poor health, and involvement in the criminal justice system.

Urban high schools are not all alike, and a few, usually small and selective, have excellent records of equipping their students with the skills needed to succeed in postsecondary education and in the workplace. But taken as a whole, urban high schools fail to meet the needs of too many of their students. In many schools with large concentrations of students living in poverty, it is common for fewer than half the students who enter in ninth grade to leave with a high school diploma. Furthermore, dropping out of school is but the most visible indication of pervasive disengagement from the academic purposes and programs of these schools. Many of the students who do not drop out altogether attend irregularly, exert little or ineffective effort on schoolwork, and learn little.

Schools do not control all of the factors that influence students' engagement and motivation to learn. Particularly in disadvantaged urban communities, academic engagement and achievement are adversely influenced by the economic and social marginalization of the students' families and communities. These disadvantages, however, can be mitigated and in many cases overridden by participation in an engaging school community with high academic standards, skillful instruction, and support to achieve educational and career goals.

The evidence reviewed in this volume demonstrates that much has been learned about the conditions in high schools that enhance student engagement. The research base is mostly qualitative, correlational, or quasi-experimental, thus falling short of the random-assignment design that permits strong causal conclusions. But the evidence for the recommendations made is consistent enough to give it credibility.

A common theme among effective practices is that they have a positive effect on the motivation of individual students because they address underlying psychological variables such as competence, control, beliefs about the value of education, and a sense of belonging. In brief, effective schools and teachers promote students' understanding of what it takes to learn and confidence in their capacity to succeed in school by providing challenging instruction and support for meeting high standards, and by conveying high expectations for their students' success. They provide choices and they make the curriculum and instruction relevant to adolescents' experiences, cultures, and long-term goals, so that students see some value in what they are doing in school. Finally, they promote a sense of belonging by personalizing instruction, showing an interest in students' lives, and creating a supportive, caring social context.

This description of engaging schools applies to too few urban high schools in low-income communities. Instead the picture that emerges from both large-scale surveys and case studies is that most comprehensive urban high schools are places where low expectations, alienation, and low achievement prevail. Resources are lacking and services are fragmented. The teachers are the least qualified, and the buildings are the most dilapidated. The curriculum and teaching often are unresponsive to the needs and interests of students—especially students of color, English-language learners, or those who entered high school with weak skills in reading and mathematics. Students often do not get to know or to be known by their teachers. As a result, many students experience schools as impersonal and uncaring. Because few urban schools are closely connected to the communities they serve or to the educational and career opportunities potentially available to their students, many students fail to see how working hard in school will enable them to attain the educational and career goals to which they aspire.

Improving the quality of urban high schools in the United States is critically important, not only to the futures of the students who attend them, but also for the future prosperity and quality of life of cities and for the nation as a whole. Fortunately, knowledge derived from research and practice provides more than a sufficient basis to proceed with urgently needed reforms.

CONCLUSIONS AND RECOMMENDATIONS

The evidence reviewed in this volume leads the committee to the following conclusions and recommendations as a means to achieve the goals of meaningful engagement and genuine improvements in achievement in schools serving economically disadvantaged students. Because our deliberations have revealed significant limits in the available evidence, the committee also specifies directions for future research.

Teaching and Learning

Findings and Recommendations

The evidence is clear that high school courses *can* be designed to engage urban high school students and enhance their learning. The instruction typical of most urban high schools nevertheless fails to engage students cognitively, emotionally, or behaviorally. As typically taught in urban high schools, most subject matter appears disconnected and unrelated to students' lives outside of school. Students spend much of their time passively listening to lectures or doing repetitive, formulaic tasks. Instruction and tasks are commonly very easy or impossibly difficult for many students, and getting right answers is stressed over understanding.

Evidence on teaching indicates that instruction that draws on students' preexisting understandings, interests, culture, and real-world experiences can make the curriculum more meaningful to them. Students are also more motivated when they are actively engaged in problem solving and applying new knowledge to real-world problems than when traditional textbooks and worksheets form the core of instruction. Engagement is relatively high when instruction is varied and appropriately challenging for all students and when teachers allow students to use their native language abilities and other resources to master the material and complete tasks. Research also suggests the value of providing explicit guidance to help students understand and critically analyze, not just memorize, discipline-based knowledge.

Recommendation 1: The committee recommends that high school courses and instructional methods be redesigned in ways that will increase adolescent engagement and learning. This recommendation has many implications, such as for teacher training and accountability practices (discussed below). The evidence reviewed by the committee suggests also that the following strategies can support efforts to create more engaging high school instruction:

- creating schools or small learning communities (clusters or "majors") that have particular academic (e.g., the performing arts, science and math, environmental issues) or occupational (e.g., health occupations, business, biotechnology) foci that capitalize on students' personal interests and connect to the world outside the school while maintaining high academic standards;
- providing service learning and internship opportunities in the community that are directly linked to the academic curriculum; and
- implementing block scheduling (classes meeting in blocks of at least 90 minutes) to allow more sustained attention to a topic.

***

Instruction that is appropriately challenging for all students requires considerable knowledge of each student's understanding and skills. Instructional decisions about tasks and next steps also need to be informed by data on student learning. Standardized testing done annually does not provide useful information for these purposes.

Recommendation 2: The committee recommends ongoing classroom-based assessment of students' understanding and skills. We suggest that teachers monitor continually the effectiveness of curriculum and instructional practices, not only in terms of learning, but also in terms of keeping students engaged behaviorally (e.g., attendance, completion of work), cognitively (e.g., efforts to understand and apply new concepts), and emotionally (e.g., enthusiasm for learning activities). Regular assessments that include daily classroom interactions and analyses of student work, preferably with teachers working in groups to assist each other in making judgments about the meaning of students' work and its implications for curriculum and instruction for those students. Development of these assessments and of engaging instructional strategies in response to their results, are critically important for engaging instruction and a necessary complement to large-scale standardized tests.

***

Teaching that involves active student learning and problem solving requires considerable teacher knowledge about teaching and adolescent learning as well as a deep understanding of the discipline. Implementing engaging instruction and effective assessment also require recruiting and retaining high-quality teachers and strengthening the repertoire of current teachers who are struggling so that all teachers have a range of available strategies to use with their students and who are skilled at adapting instruction to the needs of individual students.

Recommendation 3: The committee recommends that preservice teacher preparation programs provide high school teachers deep content knowledge and a range of pedagogical strategies and understandings about adolescents and how they learn, and that schools and districts provide practicing teachers with opportunities to work with colleagues and to continue to develop their skills. Preservice teacher education programs should provide new teachers with knowledge about student-centered pedagogy that is focused on understanding, and teach them strategies for involving students in active learning. Explicit preparation is also important to prepare new teachers to be effective with diverse, heterogeneous groups of high school students, including English-language learners, students with special disabilities, and students who are substantially behind in their basic skills.

Teachers already working in high schools cannot meet the needs of their students if their own needs for professional development and support are not met. District- and state-level administrators need to provide resources, experts, and opportunities for teachers to continue to develop their teaching skills and school administrators need to provide time for teachers to collaborate with their colleagues and to take advantage of opportunities for professional development.

Suggestions for Research

Far more research on teaching and learning has focused on elementary and middle school than on high school. The committee recommends that more research attention be given to subject matter at the secondary level, including how curriculum and instructional practices can achieve the twin goals of meaningful engagement and authentic achievement. Also recommended is attention to the needs of high school-aged, English-language learners and students who have poor reading skills. There is a serious need for innovative strategies that help students gain access to subject matter while they improve English proficiency. Research is also needed to develop and assess strategies for teaching reading skills to adolescents who reach high school reading at the elementary school level, and for embedding discipline-specific reading instruction in regular courses.

When achievement outcomes are examined in future research, the achievement measures need to be aligned to instructional goals. Too often, studies use generic measures of achievement that do not provide a fair assessment of the instructional program or an accurate assessment of student learning, especially for English-language learners.

Finally, the committee recommends studies that examine the conditions under which effective, engaging teaching occurs—including the effects of different strategies for teacher development and collaboration and state and district requirements related to assessment, curriculum, and curriculum materials.

Standards and Accountability

Findings and Recommendations

Standards and high expectations are critical, but they must be genuinely achievable if they are to motivate student engagement. Students are most likely to be academically engaged when they are challenged with demanding learning goals and when they have opportunities to experience a sense of competence and accomplishment about their learning. Setting high standards and holding students accountable for reaching them can serve as an incentive to exert effort, but only if students believe they can succeed. Simply asking students—especially those at the bottom of the achievement distribution—to achieve higher standards without providing the assistance and support they need is more likely to discourage than to motivate them.

Recommendation 4: The committee recommends that schools provide the support and resources necessary to help *all* high school students to meet challenging standards. Thus, for example, we urge districts and school administrators to provide summer programs and tutoring when feasible to help students who have fallen behind to progress in their skills. While students work toward meeting the high standards ultimately required, teachers need to give students more immediate and proximal individualized goals, calibrated to students' preexisting knowledge and skills.

***

The tests that are used for accountability have substantial impact on curriculum and instruction. It is unrealistic to expect teachers to exert effort to provide a coherent and integrated curriculum and focus on understanding and critical thinking and writing if the tools used to evaluate them and their students measure fragmented, decontextualized, basic skills.

Recommendation 5: The committee recommends that tests used to evaluate schools, teachers, and students assess high-level, critical thinking and that they incorporate a broad and multidimensional conception of subject matter that includes fluency, conceptual understanding, analysis, and application. The committee recognizes the difficulty of creating and the cost of implementing such tests, but the nature of high-stakes tests affect the nature of curriculum and instruction, and thus the level of student engagement. The kind of instructional program that engages youth must, therefore, be reflected in high-stakes tests. We also recommend that whenever stakes are attached to test results, policy makers monitor both intended and unintended consequences, including their effects on student engagement.

Suggestions for Research

Research that examines the nuanced ways in which high expectations and standards are conveyed to students is needed. For example, what kinds of school policies and classroom practices make students feel that they are expected to learn and that they are being held accountable for their learning? How do parents convey high expectations for their adolescents without undermining their sense of autonomy and control?

There is also a critical need for research on the effects of accountability policies, including high-stakes testing, on student engagement in high school, with special attention to unintended consequences, such as dropping out. Research on students' perceptions of the standards and their ability to meet them would be valuable. Studies should also examine how the effects of testing on student engagement are moderated by the supports (individualized instruction, tutoring) available to students to help them succeed on the test.

The committee also recommends research on the effects of high-stakes testing on teaching and on parents' perceptions of their adolescents' future educational opportunities. Does the existence of the test, for example, promote teaching that focuses entirely on answering test items, without consideration for deep understanding of the subject, and does it prompt some parents to give up their hope of their child graduating from high school? Or does it engender stronger commitment in teachers and parents to support student learning?

Creating High School Communities Conducive to Learning

Supportive personal relationships are a critical factor in promoting and maintaining student engagement. Motivation to learn depends on the student's involvement in a web of social relationships that support learning. Most urban high schools are too large and fail to promote close personal relationships and a sense of community between adults and students. As much as possible, high schools should be structured to promote supportive personal relationships among the members of its community; the committee offers several recommendations toward this end.

Recommendation 6: Districts should restructure comprehensive urban high schools to create smaller learning communities that foster personalized and continuous relationships between teachers and students. Restructuring should focus on allowing teachers to see fewer students and students to see fewer teachers than is currently typical in urban high schools. Restructuring can be achieved by starting new schools, by breaking up large schools into new and completely autonomous schools, or by creating smaller connected but somewhat autonomous units in large schools. Block scheduling and looping (teachers staying with the same group of students for multiple years) are promising strategies for promoting deeper and more continuous relationships.

Creating small learning communities may be necessary, but it is not sufficient to improve student engagement. The social climate of the school, in addition to the quality of instruction, are critical variables. Principals and teachers need to make concerted efforts to promote an environment of trust and respect—of each other and of students. They need to model these behaviors and refuse to tolerate disrespectful behavior against peers or adults. A school climate of trust, caring and discipline requires policies that teach students appropriate ways of responding to perceptions of risk or threat. The conditions under which refusals to tolerate disrespectful behavior take place should provide learning opportunities for students and teachers.

Also critical to promoting meaningful student engagement is a social context centered on learning—in which all administrative decisions are made with their effects on student learning in mind and teachers leverage their closer relationships with students to "press" students to challenge themselves and develop deep understanding. This focus can be conveyed through school policies such as recognizing students who step up to academic challenges and intervening quickly and preemptively when problems of poor attendance, failure to complete homework, and poor performance arise.

***

Currently, students who are most at risk of disengaging from school have too little contact with peers who have strong commitments to education and high expectations for success. Groups of students with similar achievement levels are frequently tracked, formally or informally, into different courses, thus isolating relatively low-performing and disengaged students. In addition to preventing poorly engaged students from interacting with high-achieving peers, tracking makes inaccessible to students in the lower academic tracks a rigorous curriculum that prepares them for postsecondary education. Tracked courses, especially at the low achievement levels, can also reinforce lower standards and engender in students the belief that they lack academic competence.

Recommendation 7: The committee recommends that both formal and informal tracking by ability be eliminated. Alternative strategies should be used to ensure appropriately challenging instruction for students who vary widely in their skill levels. Classes that do not prepare but prevent students getting on to rigorous grade-level work should be eliminated, and challenging courses, including Advanced Placement courses, should be as available to students in urban schools serving low-income students as they are in schools serving more affluent students.

A more challenging curriculum with heterogeneous grouping can be successful only if teachers are well trained to address individual student needs. Preservice teacher preparation programs and district and school administrators need to give teachers support in developing instructional approaches that meet the needs of a class of students who vary dramatically in their skill levels. We suggest, in particular, training in individualized and peer group learning strategies that have been shown to be effective in promoting learning in a heterogeneous class. Another strategy, used previously only at the college level but which merits experimentation in high schools, is connecting tutoring and small-group learning with a reading or English-as-a-second-language specialist directly to substantive courses. Thus, rather than isolating students with special needs, the additional assistance that some students need is provided in the context of a regular course with more skilled peers.

The committee also recommends that school administrators create opportunities for low-achieving students to interact with and develop friendships with more academically successful peers and promote a climate in which students feel comfortable venturing beyond familiar peer and instructional contexts. Because adolescents tend to choose to interact with students of similar achievement levels, concerted efforts must be made to create activities that will attract diverse students and make all students feel welcome and comfortable.

* * *

Serious social or psychological problems can interfere with adolescents' own academic engagement as well as undermine a positive learning climate. Currently many problems are unnoticed or untreated. Professionals who have relevant expertise are responsible for far too many students and they have too little time to provide the support and intervention students need.

The problem is especially serious in urban high schools serving low-income youth, where there are limited resources to address students' social and psychological problems.

A climate of learning is also undermined by students' lack of understanding of the consequences of disengagement from school. Many urban high school students are poorly informed about postsecondary educational and career options. In particular, they have only a vague understanding of what they need to learn during high school to have a realistic chance of achieving the ambitious educational and career goals to which many aspire. Because they don't see the connections, students are not motivated to engage in purposeful and challenging academic activities. In most schools, helping students make these connections is the responsibility of guidance counselors who oversee large numbers of students and have little opportunity to know their needs.

Recommendation 8: The committee recommends that school guidance and counseling responsibilities be diffused among school staff, including teachers, who are supported by professionals. A promising strategy is to provide every student and family with a member of the school staff who can act as an adult advocate and who has an expert to consult and to whom students or families with serious problems can be referred. To help students achieve a realistic understanding of how their high school learning experiences and mastery of learning objectives are related to their educational and career options after high school, we suggest also providing students with experiences in work settings, teachers with curriculum materials and instructional supports to integrate rigor and relevance into the core curriculum, as well as close coordination with postsecondary educational institutions.

Suggested Research

The committee recommends research to identify the conditions under which more respectful and mutually accountable relationships that focus on learning can be infused into a school community. What, for example, do principals do in schools that have achieved this climate? What kinds of opportunities do teachers have to connect with each other, and how are parents involved? How is teaching organized and how are classes scheduled in schools that have been successful in creating a socially supportive climate focused on students' learning? The committee also recommends research that examines different approaches to financing schools that will allow lower student-teacher ratios, such as by reducing staff at the district level and increasing the amount of funding that goes directly to schools.

Studies should attempt to assess independently the effects of small size, alone, and the conditions (personal relationships, individualized instruction, close monitoring of student progress and efforts to address nonacademic needs) that small size may facilitate. Careful documentation of effective strategies for transitioning large high schools into small learning communities is also needed, along with more rigorous studies on the effects of school size that include appropriate control groups.

The development and assessment of alternatives to tracking are seriously needed. Heterogeneous grouping poses enormous challenges to teachers, and they need guidance regarding effective strategies for meeting the needs of students with a wide range of skill levels. Studies of innovative strategies for providing tutoring, small-group learning, and other supports to enable students who have low skills to succeed in regular classes would be extremely useful.

Little research on peer influence has included adolescents in high-poverty communities. Future research needs to look carefully at gender, social class, and ethnic differences, and it needs to assess the effects that contextual variables (e.g., whether norms of respect and support for cultural and other differences are present) have on the ways in which peers interact, form friendships, and influence each other's values and behavior. The committee also recommends studies of the effects of district policies related to school choice on the dispersion or concentration of economically disadvantaged students.

Finally, research is needed on alternative models for meeting students' guidance and counseling needs and, more generally, on curricular reform designed to provide students with a better understanding of the relationship between learning in high school and postsecondary futures.

Connecting Schools with Other Resources

High schools cannot, by themselves, achieve the high levels of engagement and standards for learning currently asked of them. Most urban high schools function quite independently of the other adults in adolescents' lives, such as parents, health care providers, and those involved in extracurricular or religious activities. Many efforts to improve schools are too "school-centric" in the sense that they focus exclusively on school resources and programs and fail to take advantage of the resources in the larger community.

Recommendation 9: The Committee recommends that efforts be made to improve communication, coordination, and trust among the adults in the various settings where adolescents spend their time. These settings include homes, religious institutions, and organized extracurricular activities sponsored by schools and community groups.

School administrators and teachers should also expand and enrich the high school curriculum and help students see the real-world meaningfulness of school learning by taking advantage of resources in the community. For example, artists, civic leaders, and community members and parents with cultural or historical knowledge and experiences can be invited to schools to share their knowledge and interact with students. They should also provide students with opportunities to engage in service learning and internships that take them into community contexts.

***

The committee also finds that most urban schools are unable to deal with the many problems (e.g., poor physical and mental health, instability in parenting, substance abuse, homelessness) that some low-income adolescents face and that interfere with their engagement in academic work. Schools cannot be expected to compensate fully for problems associated with economic and social inequalities and the lack of effective policies to address them. However, such problems cannot be ignored by schools in urban communities with high concentrations of poverty. Although personalized, supportive high school communities can help protect adolescents from environments that place them at risk for negative academic outcomes, additional specialized services are needed by some high school students. Policy makers can do more to help students whose personal circumstances interfere with their ability to learn, and school administrators can make better use of the resources that are available.

Recommendation 10: The committee recommends that schools make greater efforts to identify and coordinate with social and health services in the community, and that policy makers revise policies to facilitate students' access to the services they need. School administrators often encounter barriers to partnerships and collaborations with community service providers. Federal, state, and local policy makers should revise policies so that they facilitate greater coordination. Administrators in social service and health agencies and schools should seek ways to improve communication among school personnel and service providers who see the same adolescents.

Suggested Research

The committee recommends research designed to identify the barriers to communication and coordination among the various settings in which adolescents spend their time, and effective strategies for breaking down those barriers.

Research is also needed on effective strategies for involving parents productively in high schools, especially in urban contexts in which there are cultural and language differences between parents and school personnel, and other factors, such as neighborhood safety issues and work schedules, that can impede meaningful connections. Models for connecting schools and community organizations also need to be developed and evaluated. The development and assessment of technological tools for improving communication among the various organizations adolescents frequent would be useful.

Continued research is needed to identify essential resources and the principles underlying the effective mobilization and organization of services that address the multiple, interrelated, nonacademic needs of economically disadvantaged adolescents. Studies that examine ways to translate students' circumstances or problems into needs for specific supports that schools can provide or broker also would be useful. The committee also recommends the development and evaluation of strategies for providing teachers with the support they need to identify students' nonacademic needs and respond to them in a manner that does not detract from the central educational purposes of their task.

CHALLENGES OF IMPLEMENTATION

Although a few schools and districts have made substantial progress toward improving urban students' engagement and learning, most efforts show modest progress at best, and none has been successful on a large scale. Strategies for getting new and effective instructional practices in place at one setting are not easily transported to another (e.g., from elementary to high schools). Guidance for implementing effective curriculum and instructional approaches needs to be specific enough to give direction, but flexible enough to be adapted to local contexts. Guidance for implementation and examples of alternative approaches for adapting the recommended practices to a particular school or district are a critical part of any school reform model.

Although much is known about how certain environmental conditions and educational practices affect student engagement, documentation of strategies for change and the contextual factors that either inhibit or facilitate productive reforms is rare. There is still much more to learn about the necessary and sufficient conditions for reform as they exist in various communities with different sets of opportunities, resources, and challenges. More research is needed on the process of school reform: what schools need to do to implement the knowledge gained from research on effective policies and practices.

The urgency of reform must not lead us to seize upon quick fixes or silver bullets. The research reviewed in this volume illustrates repeatedly that student engagement and learning are directly affected by a confluence of instructional practices in particular schools, by family and community influences, and by a wide range of national, state, and local policies. No single educational policy or practice, no matter how well grounded in research, can be expected to increase students' academic engagement if the policies and practices in which they are embedded are ignored. For example, small, personalized schools may not enhance meaningful cognitive engagement and learning if there is not a strong press for achieving high academic standards and effective teaching; the most engaging teaching practices may have little effect on a student who is homeless, has serious untreated health problems, or faces the chronic threat of violence. Allowing students to choose among different small, thematic learning communities can recreate tracking based on social class, ethnicity, and achievement levels if policies and special efforts are not taken to prevent this from occurring. Furthermore, teachers cannot be expected to provide meaningful and engaging instruction if they do not have deep knowledge of their subject matter.

As this volume has demonstrated, student engagement and learning are affected by a complicated set of nested variables. Some factors affect the motivation of individual students in specific classrooms of specific high schools, while others stem from broad policies at the federal or state level that may affect a large number of very diverse high schools that fall under its jurisdiction. The array of policies and practices that affect student motivation and learning must be aligned so that efforts in one domain (e.g., the classroom) are supported rather than undermined by policies at another (e.g., broader educational and social policies). Although it is neither necessary nor realistic to expect that all potential conflicts be resolved before students can engage productively in learning, educators and policy makers should, at the very least, consider how their policies and practices interact to affect student engagement and learning.

Although the promise of comprehensive school reform models is still unknown, the committee believes there is value in an approach to school change that involves consideration of many aspects of district and school policies and practices—including financing, community involvement, school organization, leadership, teacher professional development, curriculum, accountability, and assessment. Whether school improvements are based on existing reform models, or designed locally, a systemic approach is most likely key to their success.

A fundamental transformation of American high schools and the policy contexts in which high school education is embedded is needed to engage all students in learning and to ensure high standards of achievement. There are no panaceas, and some of the simple solutions that have been proposed, such as raising standards, can alone do more harm than good. Realistically, the reforms that are needed will require greater resources than are currently provided. At the very least, the inequities in resource allocation, with schools serving students with the greatest needs having the fewest resources, will need to be redressed.

The consequences of inaction are severe—for the society and for youth in our urban schools. Ascribing fault and complaining about the larger social-economic and cultural context, government and social institutions, fair or not, will not address the serious challenges we face in giving the nation's youth a realistic chance to succeed in school and in life.

High schools cannot redress all of the problems and inequities of our society. But schools can do better, and a fair amount is known about what they need to do to engage students cognitively and emotionally in learning. For most urban high schools, improvement requires a fundamental rethinking of how they go about their work. Piecemeal reforms will not work. Alone, none of the recommendations made in this volume will have much impact. Real progress will be made only if the pieces fit together, so that policies and practices at one level reinforce policies and practices at other levels.

As a society, we should not fail our youth by failing to hold them, and ourselves, to high expectations. There is more to learn, but, as this volume demonstrates, much is already known about what can be done to increase the engagement of high school students. What is needed now is the will to expect and support the application of this knowledge where it is most needed—in our urban high schools.

Bibliography and References

Aber, J.L., Gephart, M.A., Brooks-Gunn, J., and Connell, J.P. (1997). Development in context: Implications for studying neighborhood effects. In J. Brooks-Gunn, G.J. Duncan, and A.L. Aber (Eds.), *Neighborhood poverty: Context and consequences for children, volume I* (pp. 44-61). New York: Russell Sage Foundation.

Abt Associates. (1993). *Prospects: The congressionally mandated study of educational growth and opportunity*. Washington, DC: U.S. Department of Education.

Abu-Hilal, M. (2000). A structural model for predicting mathematics achievement: Its relation with anxiety and self concept in mathematics. *Psychological Reports*, *86*, 835-847.

Achtenhagen, F., and Grubb, W.N. (2001). Vocational and occupational education: Pedagogical complexity, institutional indifference. In V. Richardson (Ed.), *Handbook of research on teaching, 4th edition*. Washington, DC: American Educational Research Association.

Adelman, H.S., and Taylor, L. (1998). Reframing mental health in schools and expanding school reform. *Educational Psychologist*, *33*(4), 135-152.

Ainsworth-Darnell, J.W., and Downey, D.B. (1998). Assessing the oppositional culture explanation for racial/ethnic differences in school performance. *American Sociological Review*, *63*, 536-553.

Alexander, K.L., Entiwisle, D.R., and Dauber, S.L. (1994). *On the success of failure: A reassessment of the effects of retention in early grades*. New York: Cambridge University.

Allen, J., Philliber, S., Herrling, S., and Kupermine, G. (1997). Preventing teen pregnancy and academic failure: Experimental evaluation of a developmentally based approach. *Child Development*, *64*, 729-742.

Allen, J., Philliber, S., and Hoggson, N. (1990). School-based prevention of teenage pregnancy and school dropout: Process evaluation of the national replication of the Teen Outreach Program. *American Journal of Community Psychology*, *18*, 505-524.

Alvermann, D., Hinchman, K., Moore, D., Phelps, S., and Waff, D. (1998). *Reconceptualizing the literacies in adolescents' lives*. Mahwah, NJ: Lawrence Erlbaum.

Alvermann, D., and Moore, D. (1991). Secondary school reading. In R. Barr, M. Kamil, P. Mosenthal, and P.D. Pearson (Eds.), *Handbook of reading research, volume II* (pp. 951-983). New York: Longman.

Alvermann, D.R., and Hynd, C.R. (1989). Effects of prior knowledge activation modes and text structure on non-science majors' comprehension of physics. *Journal of Educational Research, 83*(2), 97-102.

Amabile, T., and Hennessey, B. (1992). The motivation for creativity in children. In A. Boggiano and T. Pittman (Eds.), *Achievement and motivation: A social-developmental perspective* (pp. 54-74). Cambridge: Cambridge University Press.

American Federation of Teachers. (1998). *Building on the best, learning from what works: Six promising schoolwide reform programs.* Washington, DC: Author.

American School Counselor Association. (1988). *Position statement: The school counselor and comprehensive counseling.* (Adopted 1998, revised 1993 and 1997.) Alexandria, VA: Author.

American Youth Policy Forum. (2000). *High schools of the millennium.* Washington, DC: Author.

Ames, C. (1992). Classrooms, goals, structures, and student motivation. *Journal of Educational Psychology, 84*, 261-271.

Ames, C., Khoju, M., and Watkins, T. (1993). *Parents and schools: The impact of school-to-home communications on parents' beliefs and perceptions.* (Rep. No. 15). Baltimore: Johns Hopkins University.

Ammon, M.S., Furco, A., Chi, B., Middaugh, E. (2002). *Service learning in California: A profile of the CalServe Service Learning Partnerships 1997-2000.* Berkeley: University of California, Service Learning Research and Development Center.

Ancess, J. (2000). The reciprocal influence of teacher learning, teaching practice, school restructuring, and student learning outcomes. *Teachers College Record, 102*(3), 590-619.

Ancess, J., and Wichterle, S.O. (1999). *How the coalition campus schools have reimagined high school: Seven years later.* New York: National Center for Restructuring Education, Schools, and Teaching-Teachers College, Columbia University.

Anderman, E. (2002). School effects on psychological outcomes during adolescence. *Journal of Educational Psychology, 94*, 795-809.

Anders, P.L., Hoffman, J.V., and Duffy, G.G. (2000). Teaching teachers to teach reading: Paradigm shifts, persistent problems, and challenges. In M. Kamil, P. Mosenthal, P.D. Pearson, and R. Barr (Eds.), *Handbook of reading research, volume III* (pp. 719-742). Mahwah, NJ: Lawrence Erlbaum.

Anderson, R.C., Wilson, P.T., and Fielding, L.G. (1988). Growth in reading and how children spend their time outside of school. *Reading Research Quarterly, 23*, 285-303.

Anderson, S.E. (1990). World mathematics curriculum: Fighting eurocentrism in mathematics. *Journal of Negro Education, 59*, 348-359.

Annie E. Casey Foundation. (1997). *City kids count: Data on the well-being of children in large cities.* Baltimore: Author.

Applebee, A. (1993). *Literature in the secondary school: Studies of curriculum and instruction in the United States.* (Rep. No. 25). Urbana, IL: National Council of Teachers of English.

Applebee, A. (1996). *Curriculum as conversation: Transforming traditions of teaching and learning.* Chicago: University of Chicago Press.

Applebee, A., Burroughs, R., and Stevens, A. (2000). Creating continuity and coherence in high school literature curricula. *Research in the Teaching of English, 34*(3), 396-429.

Applebee, A., and Purves, A.C. (1992). Literature and the English language arts. In P. Jackson (Ed.), *Handbook of curriculum research* (pp. 726-748). New York: Macmillan.

Applied Research Center. (2000). *Facing the consequences: An examination of racial discrimination in U.S. public schools.* Oakland, CA: Author.

Archer, J. (2002). Principals: So much to do, so little time. *Education Week, 21*(31), 1, 20.

Armbruster, P., and Lichtman, J. (1999). Are school-based mental health services effective? Evidence from 36 inner-city schools. *Community Mental Health Journal, 35*(6), 493-504.

Aronson, E., Stephan, C., Sikes, J., Blaney, N., and Snapp, M. (1978). *The jigsaw classroom.* Beverly Hills, CA: Sage.

Arroyo, C.G., and Zigler, E. (1995). Racial identity, academic achievement, and the psychological well-being of economically disadvantaged adolescents. *Journal of Personality and Social Psychology, 69*, 903-914.

Arum, R., and Beattie, I. (1999). High school experience and the risk of adult incarceration. *Criminology, 37*, 515-538.

Arum, R., and LaFree, G. (2002). *Educational spending and imprisonment risk: The role of schools as prison gatekeepers.* Paper presented at the 2002 American Society of Criminology Conference, November, Chicago, IL.

Arum, R., and Shavit, Y. (1995). Secondary vocational education and the transition from school to work. *Sociology of Education, 68*, 187-204.

Atkinson, D.R., Jennings, R.G., and Leongson, L. (1990). Minority students' reasons for not seeking counseling and suggestions for improving services. *Journal of College Student Development, 31*, 342-350.

Atkinson, D.R., Morten, G., and Sue, D.W. (1989). *Counseling American minorities: A cross-cultural perspective.* Dubuque, IA: Brown.

Atkinson, J. (1964). *An introduction to motivation.* Princeton, NJ: Van Nostrand.

Augenblick, J., Myers, J., and Anderson, A. (1997). Equity and adequacy in school funding. *The Future of Children: Financing Schools*, 7(3), 63-78.

Baker, A., and Soden, L.M. (1998). *The challenges of parent involvement research.* (Rep. No. 1998-04-00, ED419030). New York: ERIC Clearinghouse on Urban Education.

Baker, D.P., and Stevenson, D.L. (1986). Mother's strategies for children's school achievement: Managing the transition to high school. *Sociology of Education, 59*, 156-166.

Baker, J. (1999). Teacher-student interaction in urban at-risk classrooms: Differential behavior, relationship quality, and student satisfaction with school. *The Elementary School Journal, 100*, 57-70.

Baker, J., Terry, T., Bridger, R., and Winsor, A. (1997). Schools as caring communities: A relational approach to school reform. *School Psychology Review, 26*, 586-602.

Balfanz, R. (2000). Why do so many urban public school students demonstrate so little academic achievement? In M.G. Sanders (Ed.), *Schooling students placed at-risk: Research, policy, and practice in the education of poor and minority adolescents* (pp. 27-62). Mahwah, NJ: Lawrence Erlbaum.

Balfanz, R. (2001). *Preparation to meet high standards: The challenge of high poverty urban high schools.* Prepared for the Hechinger Institute, Columbia University, New York.

Balfanz, R., and Legters, N. (2001). *How many central city schools have a severe dropout problem, where are they located, and who attends them?* Prepared for Dropouts in America: How Severe Is the Problem? What Do We Know about Intervention and Prevention? A forum convened by the Harvard Civil Rights Project, January 13, Baltimore, Johns Hopkins University.

Balfanz, R., McPartland, J., and Shaw, A. (2002). *Re-conceptualizing extra help for high school students in a high standards era.* Prepared for Preparing America's Future: The High School Symposium, Washington, DC, U.S. Department of Education.

Ball, A.F. (1992). Cultural preferences and the expository writing of African-American adolescents. *Written Communication*, 9(4), 501-532.

Ball, A.F. (1995a). Community-based learning in an urban setting as a model for educational reform. *Applied Behavioral Science Review, 3*, 127-146.

Ball, A.F. (1995b). Text design patterns in the writing of urban African-American students: Teaching strengths of students in multicultural settings. *Urban Education, 30*, 253-289.

Ball, A.F. (2000a). Preparing teachers for diversity: Lessons learned from the U.S. and South Africa. *Teaching and Teacher Education, Special Issue on Preparing Teachers for Diversity, 16*, 491-509.

Ball, A.F. (2000b). Teachers developing philosophies in literacy and their use in urban schools. In C.D. Lee and P. Smagorsky (Eds.), *Vygotskian perspectives on literacy research: Constructing meaning through collaborative inquiry*. New York: Cambridge University Press.

Bandalos, D., Yates, K., and Thorndike-Christ, T. (1995). Effects of math self-concept, perceived self-efficacy, and attributions for failure and success on test anxiety. *Journal of Educational Psychology, 87*, 611-623.

Bandura, A. (1993). Perceived self-efficacy in cognitive development and functioning. *Educational Psychologist, 28*, 117-148.

Bandura, A. (1997). *Self-efficacy: The exercise of control.* New York: Freeman.

Banks, J.A., and Banks, C. (Eds.). (1993). *Multicultural education: Issues and perspectives.* Boston: Allyn and Bacon.

Barker, R., and Gump, P. (1964). *Big school, small school: High school size and student behavior.* Stanford, CA: Stanford University Press.

Bartolome, L.I. (1994). Beyond the methods fetish: Toward a humanizing pedagogy. *Harvard Educational Review, 64*, 173-194.

Battin-Pearson, S.R., Thornberry, T.P., Hawkins, J.D., and Krohn, M.D. (1998). *Gang membership, delinquent peers, and delinquent behavior.* (Rep. No. 1-11). Washington, DC: U.S. Department of Justice.

Battistich, V., Solomon, D., Kim, D., Watson, M., and Schaps, E. (1995). Schools as communities, poverty levels of student populations, and students' attitudes, motives, and performance: A multilevel analysis. *American Educational Research Journal, 32*, 627-658.

Battistich, V. Solomon, D., Watson, M., and Schaps, E. (1997). Caring school communities. *Educational Psychologist, 32*(3), 137-151.

Baumeister, R., Twenge, J., and Nuss, C. (2002). Effects of social exclusion on cognitive processes: Anticipated aloneness reduces intelligent thought. *Journal of Personality and Social Psychology, 83*(4), 817-827.

Bean, T. (2000). Reading in the content areas: Social constructivist dimensions. In M. Kamil, P. B. Mosenthal, P.D. Pearson, and R. Barr (Eds.), *Handbook of reading research, volume III* (pp. 629-644). Mahwah, NJ: Lawrence Erlbaum.

Beauboeuf-Lafontant, T. (1999). A movement against and beyond boundaries: "Politically relevant teaching" among African American teachers. *Teachers College Record, 100*(4), 702-723.

Beck, I.L., McKeown, M.G., and Gromoll, E.W. (1989). Learning from social studies texts. *Cognition and Instruction, 6*, 99-158.

Becker, H.J., and Epstein, J.L. (1982). Parental involvement: A study of teacher practices. *Elementary School Journal, 83*, 85-102.

Benesch, S. (1998a). *Ending remediation: Linking ESL and content in higher education.* Washington, DC: Teachers of English to Speakers of Other Languages.

Benesch, S. (1988b). Linking content and language teachers: Collaboration across the curriculum. *In Ending remediation: Linking ESL and content in higher education* (pp. 53-66). Washington, DC: Teachers of English to Speakers of Other Languages.

Berand, B. (1992). Fostering resiliency in kids: Protective factors in the family, school, and community. *Prevention Forum, 12*(3).

Berand, B. (1997). *Turning it around for all youth: From risk to resilience.* (Rep. No. EDO-UD-97-7, ED412309). New York: ERIC Clearinghouse on Urban Education.

Berends, M. (1995). Educational stratification and students' social bonding to school. *British Journal of Sociology of Education, 16,* 327-351.

Berends, M., Bodilly, S.J., and Kirby, S. (2002). *Facing the challenges of whole-school reform: New American Schools after a decade.* Santa Monica, CA: RAND.

Berends, M., Chun, J., Schuyler, G., Stockly, S., and Briggs, R.J. (2002). *Challenges of conflicting school reforms: Effects of New American Schools in a high-poverty district.* Santa Monica, CA: RAND.

Berends, M., Heilbrunn, J., McKelvey, C., and Sullivan, T. (1999). *Assessing the progress of New American Schools: A status report.* Santa Monica, CA: RAND.

Berends, M., Kirby, S.N., Naftel, S., and McKelvey, C. (2001). *Implementation and performance in New American Schools: Three years into scale-up.* Santa Monica, CA: RAND.

Berktold, J., Geis, S., and Kaufman, P. (1998). *Subsequent educational attainment of high school dropouts.* (Rep. No. NCES 98085). Washington, DC: U.S. Department of Education, National Center for Education Statistics.

Berndt, T.J. (1996). Transitions in friendship and friends' influence. In J.A. Garber, J. Brooks-Gunn, and A.C. Peterson (Eds.), *Transitions through adolescence: Interpersonal domains and context* (pp. 57-84). Hillsdale, NJ: Lawrence Erlbaum.

Berndt, T.J. (1999). Friends' influence on students' adjustment to school. *Educational Psychologist, 34,* 15-28.

Berndt, T.J., and Keefe, K. (1995). Friends' influence on adolescents' adjustment to school. *Child Development, 66,* 1312-1329.

Berndt, T.J., Miller, K.E., and Park, K. (1989). Adolescents' perceptions of friends' and parents' influence on aspects of their school adjustment. *The Journal of Early Adolescence, 9,* 419-435.

Bishop, J.H. (2002). *What should be the federal role in supporting and shaping development of state accountability systems for secondary school achievement?* Paper prepared for the Office of Vocational and Adult Education, U.S. Department of Education, Washington, DC.

Black, P., and Wiliam, D. (1998). Inside the black box: Raising standards through classroom assessment. *Phi Delta Kappan, 80*(2)139-148.

Blank, M.J, Melaville, A., Shah, B.P. (2003) *Making the difference: Research and practice in community schools.* Washington, DC: Coalition for Community Schools, Institute for Educational Leadership.

Blauner, R. (1964). *Alienation and freedom: The factory worker and his industry.* Chicago: University of Chicago Press.

Blechman, E.A., McBaron, M.J., Carolla, E.T., and Audette, D.P. (1986). Childhood competence and depression. *Journal of Abnormal Psychology, 95,* 223-227.

Blum, R., McNeely, C., and Rinehart, P. (2002). *Improving the odds: The untapped power of schools to improve the health of teens.* Minneapolis: University of Minnesota.

Blum, R., and Rhinehart, P. (1998). *Reducing the risk: Connections that make a difference in the lives of youth.* Minneapolis: University of Minnesota.

Boaler, J. (2002a). *Experiencing school mathematics.* Mahwah, NJ: Lawrence Erlbaum.

Boaler, J. (2002b). Learning from teaching: Exploring the relationship between reform curriculum and equity. *Journal for Research in Mathematics Education, 33,* 239-258.

Boesel, D., and Fredland, E. (1999). *College for all? Is there too much emphasis on getting a 4-year college degree?* (Rep. No. ED431986). Madison, WI: University of Wisconsin Medical Center.

Boocock, S.S. (1966). Toward a sociology of learning: A selective review of existing research. *Sociology of Education, 39,* 1-45.

Boocock, S.S. (1972). *An introduction to the sociology of learning*. Boston, MA: Houghton Mifflin.

Booth, A., and Dunn, J.F. (Eds.). (1996). *Family-school links: How do they affect educational outcomes?* Mahwah, NJ: Lawrence Erlbaum.

Borders, L.D., and Drury, S.M. (1992). Comprehensive school counseling programs: A review for policymakers and practitioners. *Journal of Counseling and Development*, 70, 487-498.

Boston Plan for Excellence in the Public Schools. (2001). Lessons learned from the Carnegie planning period. In *Proposal to the Carnegie Corporation (Fact Sheet)*. Boston: Boston Public Schools.

Bottoms, G., and Presson, A. (2000). *Finishing the job: Improving the achievement of vocational students*. Atlanta, GA: Southern Regional Education Board.

Bowditch, C. (1993). Getting rid of troublemakers: High school disciplinary procedures and the production of dropouts. *Social Problems*, 40, 493-509.

Bower, B. (1997). Effects of a multiple-ability curriculum in secondary social studies classrooms. In E.Cohen and R. Lotan (Eds.), *Working for equity in heterogeneous classrooms: Sociological theory in practice* (pp. 117-133). New York: Teachers College Press.

Bowman, P.J. (1990). The adolescent to adult transition: Discouragement among jobless black youth. In V.C. McLoyd, and C. Flanagan (Eds.), *New directions in child development* (pp. 87-105). San Francisco: Jossey-Bass.

Bowman, P.J. (1995). Family structure and marginalization of black men: Policy implications/commentary. In M.B. Tucker and C. Mitchell-Kernan (Eds.), *The decline of marriage among African-Americans: Causes, consequences and policy implications* (pp. 309-323). New York: Russell Sage.

Bowman, P.J., and Howard, C.S. (1985). Race-related socialization, motivation and academic achievement: A study of black youth in three generations of families. *Journal of the American Academy of Child Psychiatry*, 24, 134-141.

Boyd, W.L., and Shouse, R.C. (1997). The problems and promise of urban schools. In H. Walberg, O. Reyes, and R. Weissberg (Eds.), *Children and youth: Interdisciplinary perspectives* (pp. 141-145). New York: Sage.

Boyer, E.L. (1983). *High school: A report on secondary education in America*. New York: Harper and Row.

Boykin, W.A. (2000). The Talent Development Model of schooling: Placing students at promise for academic success. *Journal of Education for Students Placed At Risk*, 5(1 and 2), 3-25.

Brackney, B.E., and Karabenick, S.A. (1995). Psychopathology and academic performance: The role of motivation and learning strategies. *Journal of Consulting Psychology*, 42, 456-465.

Braddock, J., and Dawkins, M. (1993). Ability to grouping, aspirations, and attainments: Evidence from the National Educational Longitudinal Study of 1988. *Journal of Negro Education*, 62, 1-13.

Bradley, R.H., Corwyn, R.F., McAdoo, H.P., and Coll, C.G. (2001). The home environments of children in the United States, part I: Variations by age, ethnicity, and poverty status. *Child Development*, 72(6), 1844-1867.

Brinson, J.A., and Kottler, J.A. (1995). Minorities' underutilization of counseling centers' mental health services: A case for outreach and consultation. *Journal of Mental Health Counseling*, 17(4), 371-385.

Bronfenbrenner, U. (1974). The origins of alienation. *Scientific American, 251*, 53-64.

Brooks-Gunn, J., and Duncan, G.J. (1997). The effects of poverty on children. *The Future of Children: Children and Poverty*, 7(2), 55-71.

Brophy, J. (1998). *Motivating students to learn.* Boston: McGraw-Hill.

Brown, B.B. (1990). Peer groups and peer cultures. In S. Feldman and G.R. Elliot (Eds.), *At the threshold: The developing adolescent* (pp. 171-196). Cambridge, MA: Harvard University Press.

Brown, B.B., Clasen, D.R., and Eicher, S.A. (1986). Perceptions of peer pressure, peer conformity dispositions, and self-reported behavior among adolescents. *Developmental Psychology, 22*, 521-530.

Brown, B.B., Mounts, N., Lamborn, S.D., and Steinberg, L. (1993). Parenting practices and peer group affiliation in adolescence. *Child Development, 64*, 467-482.

Bryk, A., and Driscoll, M. (1988). *The high school as community: Contextual influences and consequences for students and teachers.* Madison: University of Wisconsin, National Center on Effective Secondary Schools.

Bryk, A., Lee, V., and Smith, J. (1990). High school organization and its effects on teachers and students: An interpretive summary of the research. In W. Clune and J. Witte (Eds.), *Choice and control in American education, volume 1: The theory of choice and control in education* (pp. 135-226). London: Falmer Press.

Bryk, A., Sebring, P., Kerbow, D., Rollow, S., and Easton, J.Q. (1998). *Charting Chicago school reform: Democratic localism as a lever for change.* Boulder, CO: Westview Press.

Bryk, A.S., Lee, V.E., and Holland, P.B. (1993). *Catholic schools and the common good.* Cambridge, MA: Harvard University Press.

Bryk, A.S., and Schneider, B. (2002). *Trust in schools: A core resource for improvement.* New York: Russell Sage Foundation.

Bryk, A.S., and Thum, Y.M. (1989). The effects of high school organization on dropping out: An exploratory investigation. *American Educational Research Journal, 26*(3), 353-383.

Burton, L., Allison, K., and Obeidallah, D. (1995). Social context and adolescents: Perspectives on development among inner-city African-American teens. In L. Crockett and A. Crouter (Eds.), *Pathways through adolescence: Individual development in social contexts.* Mahwah, NJ: Lawrence Erlbaum.

Cairns, R.B., Cairns, B.D., and Neckerman, H.J. (1989). Early school dropout: Configurations and determinants. *Child Development, 60*, 1437-1452.

Caldas, S., and Bankston III, C. (1997). Effect of school population socioeconomic status on individual academic achievement. *Journal of Educational Research, 90*, 269-277.

Caldas, S., and Banskton III, C. (1998). The inequality of separation: Racial composition of schools and academic achievement. *Educational Administration Quarterly, 34*, 533-557.

Caldas, S.J. (1987). Reexamination of input and process factor effects on public school achievement. *Journal of Educational Research, 86*(4), 206-214.

Cameron, J., and Pierce, W. (1994). Reinforcement, reward, and intrinsic motivation: A meta-analysis. *Review of Educational Research, 64*, 363-423.

Cameron, S.V., and Heckman, J.J. (1993). The nonequivalence of high school equivalents. *Journal of Labor Economics, 11*(1), 1-47.

Campbell, J.R., Hombo, C.M., and Mazzeo, J. (2000). *NAEP 1999 trends in academic progress: Three decades of student performance.* (Rep. No. NCES 2000469). Washington, DC: U.S. Department of Education.

Cappella, E., and Weinstein, R. (2001). Turning around reading achievement: Predictors of high school students' academic resilience. *Journal of Educational Psychology, 93*(4), 758-771.

Carnegie Council on Policy Studies in Higher Education. (1980). *Giving youth a better chance: Options for education, work, and service.* San Francisco: Jossey-Bass.

Carpenter, T., Fennema, E., and Franke, M. (1996). Cognitively guided instruction. *Elementary School Journal, 97*(1), 3-20.

Catalano, R., Berglund, M., Ryan, J., Lonczak, H., and Hawkins, J. (1999). *Positive youth development in the United States: Research findings on evaluations of positive youth development programs.* Seattle: Washington School of Social Work.

Catsambis, S., and Beveridge, A.A. (2001). Does neighborhood matter? Family, neighborhood, and school influences on eighth grade mathematics achievement. *Sociological Focus, 34,* 435-457.

Catterall, J.S. (1987). An intensive group counseling dropout prevention intervention: Some cautions on isolating at-risk adolescents within high schools. *American Educational Research Journal, 24,* 521-540.

Cazden, C. (1988). *Classroom discourse: The language of teaching and learning.* Portsmouth, NH: Heinemann.

Cazden, C.B. (2001) *Classroom discourse: The language of teaching and learning, 2nd edition.* Portsmouth, NH: Heinemann.

Chapman, D., O'Brien, C.J., and DeMasi, M.E. (1987). The effectiveness of the public school counselor in college advising. *Journal of College Admissions, 115,* 11-18.

Charles, C. (2000). *The synergetic classroom: Joyful teaching and gentle discipline.* New York: Longman.

Charles, C.M. (2002). *Building classroom discipline, 7th edition.* Boston: Allyn and Bacon.

Checkley, K. (2001). Algebra and activism: Removing the shackles of low expectations: A conversation with Robert P. Moses. *Educational Leadership,* 6-11.

Chen, C., and Stevenson, H. (1995). Motivation and mathematics achievement: A comparative study of Asian-American, Caucasian-American, and East Asian high school students. *Child Development, 66,* 1215-1234.

Chodzinski, R.T. (1994). Dropout intervention and prevention: Strategies for counselors, a multicultural perspective. In P. Pederson and J.C. Carey (Eds.), *Multicultural counseling in schools* (pp. 1-18). Boston: Allyn and Bacon.

Cibulka, J., and Kritek, W. (Eds.). (1996). *Coordination among schools, families, and communities: Prospects for educational reform.* New York: State University of New York Press.

Civil, M. (2000). *Bridging in-school and out-of-school mathematics.* Paper presented at the Conference on Equity in Mathematics Education, Chicago, Northwestern University.

Clark, R.M. (1983). *Family life and school achievement: Why poor black children succeed or fail.* Chicago: University of Chicago Press.

Coburn, C. (2001). Collective sense making about reading: How teachers mediate reading policy in their professional communities. *Educational Evaluation and Policy Analysis, 23,* 145-170.

Cognition and Learning Technology Group of Vanderbilt University. (1998). Designing environments to reveal, support, and expand our children's potentials. In S.A. Soraci and W. McIlvante (Eds.), *Perspectives on fundamental processes in intellectual functioning, volume 1* (pp. 313-350). Greenwich, CT: Ablex.

Cohen, D.K., and Ball, D.L. (1999). *Instruction, capacity and educational improvement.* (Rep. No. RR-43). Philadelphia, PA: Consortium for Policy Research and Education.

Cohen, E. (1994). *Designing group work: Strategies for heterogeneous classrooms, 2nd edition.* New York: Teachers College Press.

Cohen, E.G. (1997). Understanding status problems: Sources and consequences. In E.G. Cohen and R.A. Lotan (Eds.), *Working for equity in heterogeneous classrooms: Sociological theory in practice* (pp. 61-76). New York: Teachers College Press.

Cohen, E.G., and Lotan, R.A. (1997). *Working for equity in heterogeneous classrooms: Sociological theory in practice.* New York: Teachers College Press.

Cohen, E.G., Lotan, R.A., and Leechor, C. (1989). Can classrooms learn? *Sociology of Education, 62,* 75-94.

Cokley, K.O. (2002). Ethnicity, gender, and academic self-concept: A preliminary examination of academic misidentification and implications for psychologists. *Cultural Diversity of Ethnic and Minority Psychology, 8*(4), 378-388.

Cole, M. (1996). *Cultural psychology: A once and future discipline.* Cambridge, MA: Harvard University Press.

Cole, M., and Griffin, P. (1987). *Contextual factors in education: Improving science and mathematics education for minorities and women.* Madison: Wisconsin Center for Education Research.

Coleman, J.S. (1961). *The adolescent society.* New York: Free Press of Glencoe.

Coleman, J.S., Campbell, E.Q., Hobson, C.J., McPartland, J., Mood, A., Weinfeld, F.D., and York, B.L. (1966). *Equality of educational opportunity.* Washington, DC: U.S. Government Printing Office.

Coleman, J.S., and Hoffer, T. (1987). *Public and private high schools: The impact of communities.* New York: Basic Books.

Coleman, J.S., Hoffer, T., and Kilgore, S.B. (1982). *High school achievement: Public, catholic, and private schools compared.* New York: Basic Books.

Collins, A., Brown, J.S., and Newman, S.E. (1989). Cognitive apprenticeship: Teaching the crafts of reading, writing, and mathematics. In L. Resnick (Ed.), *Knowing, learning and instruction: Essays in honor of Robert Glaser* (pp. 453-494). Hillsdale, NJ: Lawrence Erlbaum.

Comer, J.P. (1980). *School power: Implications of an intervention project.* New York: The Free Press.

Comer, J.P. (1988). Educating poor minority children. *Scientific American, 259*(5), 42-48.

Comer, J.P. (1997). *Waiting for a miracle: Why schools can't solve our problems—and how we can.* New York: Dutton.

Comer, J.P., Haynes, N.M., and Joyner, E.T. (1996). The school development program. In J.P. Comer, N.M. Hayes, E.T. Joyner, and M. Ben-Avie (Eds.), *Rallying the whole village: The Comer process for reforming education.* New York: Teachers College Press.

Commission on Precollege Guidance and Counseling. (1986). *Keeping the options open: Recommendations.* New York: College Entrance Examination Board.

Connell, J. (2002). *Getting off the dime toward meaningful reform.* Report prepared by the Institute for Research and Reform in Education for the U.S. Department of Education Office of Educational Research and Improvement, Washington, DC.

Connell, J., and Wellborn, J. (1991). Competence, autonomy, and relatedness: A motivational analysis of self-system processes. In M. Gunnar and L. Sroufe (Eds.), *Self processes in development: Minnesota symposium on child psychology, volume 23* (pp. 43-77). Hillsdale, NJ: Lawrence Erlbaum.

Connell, J.P., Gambone, M.A., and Smith, T.J. (2000). Youth development in community settings: Challenges to our field and our approach. In P.J. Benson and K.J. Pittman (Eds.), *Trends in youth development.* Boston: Kluwer Academic.

Connell, J.P., Halpern-Felsher, B.L., and Brooks-Gunn, J. (1997). How neighborhoods affect educational outcomes in middle childhood and adolescence: Conceptual issue and empirical examples. In J. Brooks-Gunn, G.J. Duncan, and J.L. Aber (Eds.), *Neighborhood poverty: Context and consequences for children, volume 1* (pp. 174-199). New York: Russell Sage Foundation.

Connell, J.P., and Klem, A.M. (2000). You can get there from here: Using a theory of change approach to plan urban education reform. *Journal of Educational and Psychological Consulting, 11*(1), 93-120.

Connell, J.P., Spencer, M.B., and Aber, J.L. (1994). Educational risk and resilience in African American youth: Context, self, action, and outcomes in school. *Child Development, 65,* 493-506.

Conoley, J.C., and Conoley, C.W. (1991). Collaboration of child adjustment: Issues for school and clinic-based child psychologists. *Journal of Consulting and Clinical Psychology, 59*, 821-829.

Cook, P.J., and Ludwig, J. (1997). Weighing the "burden of acting white": Are there race differences in attitudes toward education? *Journal of Policy Analysis and Management, 16*(2), 256-278.

Cook, P., and Ludwig, J. (1998). The burden of "acting white": Do black adolescents disparage academic achievement? In C. Jencks and M. Phillips (Eds.), *The black-white test score gap* (pp. 375-400). Washington, DC: Brookings Institution Press.

Cooper, H., Lindsay, J.J., Nye, B., and Greathouse, S. (1998). Relationships among attitudes about homework, amount of homework assigned and completed, and student achievement. *Journal of Educational Psychology, 90*(1), 70-83.

Corbett, H.D., and Wilson, B. (2001). *Sustaining reform: Students' appraisal of the second year in Talent Development High Schools in Philadelphia, 2000 2001*. Philadelphia. Philadelphia Education Fund.

Cordova, D., and Lepper, M. (1996). Intrinsic motivation and the process of learning: Beneficial effects of contextualization, personalization, and choice. *Journal of Educational Psychology, 88*, 715-730.

Cornwell, C., and Mustard, D. (2002). Race and the effects of Georgia's HOPE scholarship. In D.E. Heller and P. Marin (Eds.), *Who should we help? The negative social consequences of merit scholarships* (pp. 57-72). Cambridge, MA: Harvard Civil Rights Project.

Cotton, K. (1996). *School size, climate, and student performance*. Portland, OR: NW Regional Educational Laboratory.

Council of Great City Schools. (2000). *Ten year trends in urban education, 1987-1997*. Washington, DC: Author.

Covington, M.V., Spratt, M.F., and Omelich, C.L. (1980). Is effort enough, or does diligence count too? Student and teacher reactions to effort stability in failure. *Journal of Educational Psychology, 72*(6), 717-729.

Crain, R., Allen, A., Thaler, R., Sullivan, D., Zellman, G., Little, J.W., and Quigley, D. (1999). *The effects of academic career magnet education on high schools and their graduates*. (Rep. No. MDS-779). Berkeley, CA: National Center for Research in Vocational Education.

Cremin, L.A. (1961). *The transformation of the school: Progressivism in American education, 1856-1957*. New York: Knopf.

Cremin, L.A. (1976). *Public education*. New York: Basic Books.

Cross, W. (1991). *Shades of black: Diversity in African American identity*. Philadelphia: Temple University Press.

Csikszentmihalyi, M. (1975). *Beyond boredom and anxiety*. San Francisco: Jossey Bass.

Csikszentmihalyi, M. (1988). The flow experience and its significance for human psychology. In M. Csikszentmihalyi and I. Csikszentmihalyi (Eds.), *Optimal experience* (pp. 15-35). Cambridge: Cambridge University Press.

Cushman, K. (2002) *Fires in the bathroom: Advice from kids on the front lines of high school*. Available: http://www.whatkidscando.org/firesinthebathroom.pdf [2002].

Darling-Hammond, L. (1990). Teacher quality and equality. In J.I. Goodlad and P. Keating (Eds.), *Access to knowledge: An agenda for our nation's schools* (pp. 237-258). New York: College Entrance Examination Board.

Darling-Hammond, L. (1996). *What matters most: Teaching for America's future*. New York: National Commission on Teaching and America's Future.

Darling-Hammond, L. (1997). *The right to learn: A blueprint for schools that work*. San Francisco: Jossey Bass.

Darling-Hammond, L. (1999). *Supply, demand, and quality in mathematics and science teaching*. Minutes of the Meeting of the National Commission on Mathematics and Science Teaching for the 21st Century, September 23.

Darling-Hammond, L. (2002). Apartheid in American education: How opportunity is rationed to children of color in the United States. In *Racial profiling and punishing in U.S. public schools* (pp. 39-44). Oakland, CA: Applied Research Center.

Darling-Hammond, L., Ancess, J., and Ort, S. (2002). Reinventing high school: Outcomes of the coalition campus schools project. *American Educational Research Journal, 39*, 639-673.

Darling, L., and Steinberg, L. (1997). Community influences on adolescent achievement and deviance. In J. Brooks-Gunn, G.J. Duncan, and J.L. Aber (Eds.), *Neighborhood poverty: Policy implications in studying neighborhoods, volume II* (pp. 120-131). New York: Russell Sage Foundation.

Dauber, S.L., and Epstein, J.L. (1993). Parents' attitudes and practices of involvement in inner-city elementary and middle schools. In N. Chavkin (Ed.), *Families and schools in pluralistic society* (pp. 53-71). Albany: State University of New York Press.

Davidson, A. (1996). *Making and molding identity in schools: Student narratives on race, gender, and academic engagement*. Albany: State University of New York Press.

Davidson, A. (1999). Negotiating social differences: Youth's assessments of educators' strategies. *Urban Education, 34*, 338-369.

Davidson, A., and Phelan, P. (1999). Students' multiple worlds: An anthropological approach to understanding students' engagement with school. In *Advances in motivation and achievement: Role of context, volume II* (pp. 233-283). Stamford, CT: JAI Press.

DeAvila, E.A. (1988). Bilingualism, cognitive function, and language minority group membership. In R.R. Cocking and J.P. Mestre (Eds.), *Linguistic and cultural influences on learning mathematics* (pp.101-121). Hillsdale, NJ: Lawrence Erlbaum.

deCharms, R. (1976). *Enhancing motivation change in the classroom*. New York: Irvington.

deCharms, R. (1984). Motivating enhancement in educational settings. In R. Ames and C. Ames (Eds.), *Research on motivation in education: Student motivation, volume I* (pp. 275-310). New York: Academic Press.

Deci, E., Nezlek, J., and Sheinman, L. (1981). Characteristics of the rewarder and intrinsic motivation of the rewardee. *Journal of Personality and Social Psychology, 40*, 1-10.

Deci, E., and Ryan, R. (1985). *Intrinsic motivation and self-determination in human behavior*. New York: Plenum Press.

Deci, E., Schwartz, A., Sheinman, L., and Ryan, R. (1981). An instrument to assess adults' orientations toward control versus autonomy with children: Reflections on intrinsic motivation and perceived competence. *Journal of Educational Psychology, 73*, 642-650.

Dehaene, S. (1997). *The number sense: How the mind creates mathematics*. New York: Oxford University Press.

Delgado-Gaitan, C. (1987). Traditions and transitions in the learning process of Mexican children: An ethnographic view. In G.D. Spindler and L.S. Spindler (Eds.), *Interpretive ethnography of education: At-home and abroad* (pp. 333-362). Hillsdale, NJ: Lawrence Erlbaum.

Delgado-Gaitan, C. (1991). Involving parents in the schools: A process of empowerment. *American Journal of Education, 100*, 20-46.

Delpit, L. (1988). The silenced dialogue: Power and pedagogy in educating other people's children. *Harvard Educational Review, 58*, 280-298.

Delpit, L. (1995). *Other people's children: Cultural conflict in the classroom*. New York: The New York Press.

Desimone, L., Porter, A., Garet, M., Yon, K.S., and Birman, B. (2002). Effects of professional development on teachers' instruction: Results from a three-year longitudinal study. *Education Evaluation and Policy Analysis, 24*, 81-112.

Devlin, K. (2000). *The math gene: How mathematical thinking evolved and why numbers are like gossip*. New York: Basic Books.

Dewey, J. (1900). *The school and society*. Chicago: University of Chicago Press.

Dewey, J. (1916). *Democracy and education: An introduction to the philosophy of education*. New York: Free Press.

Dewey, J. (1956). *The child and the curriculum and the school and society*. Chicago: University of Chicago Press

Diener, C., and Dweck, C. (1978). An analysis of learned helplessness: Continuous changes in performance, strategy, and achievement cognitions following failure. *Journal of Personality and Social Psychology, 36*, 451-462.

Dildine, J.P. (2000). *Technology-intensive instruction with high performing and low performing middle school mathematics students*. Unpublished doctoral dissertation, University of Illinois at Urbana-Champaign.

Dishion, T.J., McCord, J., and Poulin, F. (1999). When interventions harm: Peer groups and problem behavior. *American Psychologist, 54*, 755-764.

Dole, J.A., Duffy, G.G., Roehler, L.R., and Pearson, P.D. (1991). Moving from the old to the new: Research on reading comprehension. *Review of Educational Research, 61*(2), 239-264.

Dornbusch, S.M., and Ritter, P.L. (1988). Parents of high school students: A neglected resource. *Educational Horizons, 66*, 75-77.

Doty, R.G., Mercer, S., and Henningsen, M.A. (1999). Taking on the challenge of mathematics for all. In L. Ortiz-Franco, N.G. Hernandez, and Y. De La Cruz (Eds.), *Changing the faces of mathematics: Perspectives on Latinos* (pp. 99-112). Reston, VA: National Council of Teachers of Mathematics.

Downey, D., and Ainsworth Darnell, J. (2002). The search for oppositional culture among black students. *American Sociological Review, 67*, 156-164.

Dreeben, R., and Gamoran, A. (1986). Race, instruction, and learning. *American Sociological Review, 51*, 660-669.

Driscoll, M.E. (1995). Thinking like a fish: The implications of the image of school community for connections between parents and schools. In P.W. Cookson, Jr. and B. Schneider (Eds.), *Transforming schools* (pp. 209-236). New York: Garland.

Drucker, P.F. (1996). The rise of the knowledge society. *Wilson Quarterly, 17*(2), 52-70.

Dryfoos, J. (1990). *Adolescents at risk: Prevalence and prevention*. New York: Oxford University Press.

Dryfoos, J. (2002). *Evaluation of community schools: Findings to date*. Washington, DC: Coalition for Community Schools.

Duchnowski, A.J. (1994). Innovative service models: Education. *Journal of Clinical Child Psychology, 23*, 13-18.

Duncan, G., and Brooks-Gunn, J. (Eds.). (1997). *The consequences of growing up poor*. New York: Russell Sage Foundation.

Dweck, C. (1999). *Self-theories: Their role in motivation, personality, and development*. Philadelphia: Psychology Press.

Dweck, C. (2000). *Self-theories: Their role in motivation, personality, and development*. Philadelphia, PA: Psychology Press.

Dynarski, M., and Gleason, P. (1998). *How can we help? What we have learned from federal dropout-prevention programs*. Princeton, NJ: Mathematica Policy Research.

Dynarski, S. (2000). Hope for whom? Financial aid for the middle class and its impact on college attendance. *National Tax Journal, 53*(3, part 2), 629-661.

Eberts, R.W., Kehoe, E., and Stone, J.A. (1982). *The effect of school size on student outcomes: Final report.* (Rep. No. ED 245 382). Eugene, OR: Center for Educational Policy and Management, University of Oregon.

Eccles, J. (1984). Sex differences in achievement patterns. In T. Sonderegger (Ed.), *Nebraska symposium on motivation, volume 32* (pp. 91-132). Lincoln: University of Nebraska Press.

Eccles, J. (1994). Understanding women's educational and occupational choices: Applying the Eccles et al. model of achievement-related choices. *Psychology of Women Quarterly, 18*, 585-609.

Eccles, J., Adler, T., Futterman, R., Goff, S., Kaczala, C., Meece, J., and Midgley, C. (1983). Expectancies, values, and academic behavior. In J.T. Spence (Ed.), *Achievement and achievement motives: Psychological and sociological approaches* (pp. 75-146). San Francisco: Freeman.

Eccles, J., Barber, B., and Jozefowicz, D. (1998). Linking gender to educational, occupational, and recreational choices: Applying the Eccles et al. model of achievement-related choices. In W. Swann, J. Langlois, and L.Gilbert (Eds.), *Sexism and stereotypes in modern society: The gender science of Janet Taylor Spence* (pp. 153-192). Washington, DC: APA Press.

Eccles, J., Early, D., Fraser, K., Belansky, E., and McCarthy, K. (1997). The relation of connection, regulation, and support for autonomy to adolescents' functioning. *Journal of Adolescent Research, 12*, 263-286.

Eccles, J., and Midgley, C. (1989). State environment fit: Developmentally appropriate classrooms for early adolescents. In R. Ames and C. Ames (Eds.), *Research on motivation in education: Goals and cognitions, volume 3* (pp. 139-186). New York: Academic Press.

Eccles, J., Midgley, C., Wigfield, A., Buchanan, C., Reuman, D., Flanagan, C., and MacIver, D. (1993). Development during adolescence. *American Psychologist, 48*(2), 90-101.

Eccles, J.S., and Barber, B.L. (1999). Student council, volunteering, basketball, or marching band: What kind of extracurricular involvement matters? *Journal of Adolescent Research, 14*(1), 10-43.

Eccles, J.S., and Harold, R.D. (1996). Family involvement in children's and adolescents' schooling. In A. Booth and J.F. Dunn (Eds.), *Family-school links: How do they affect education outcomes* (pp. 3-34). Mahwah, NJ: Lawrence Erlbaum.

Eccles, J.S., and Templeton, J. (2001). *Community-based programs for youth: Lessons learned from general developmental research and from experimental and quasi-experimental evaluations.* (Urban Seminar Series, Urban Health Initiative). Cambridge, MA: Harvard University.

Eccles, J.S., and Wigfield, A. (1992). The development of achievement-task values: A theoretical analysis. *Developmental Review, 12*, 265-310.

Eccles, J.S., Wigfield, A., and Schiefele, U. (1998). Motivation to succeed. In N. Eisenberg (Ed.), *Social, emotional, and personality development handbook of child psychology, volume 3* (pp. 1017-1096). New York: Wiley.

Eckert, P. (1989). *Jocks and burnouts: Social categories and identity in the high school.* New York: Teachers College, Columbia University.

Edmonds, R.R. (1979). Effective schools for the urban poor. *Educational Leadership, 37*, 15-24.

Education Trust. (1999). *Ticket to nowhere: The gap between leaving high school and entering college and high-performance jobs: Thinking K-16.* Washington, DC: Author.

Education Trust. (2001). *Youth at the crossroads: Facing high school and beyond.* Washington, DC: Author.

Education Week. (2002). Quality counts 2002: Building blocks for success. *Education Week, 21*, 17, January 10.

Eichenstein, R. (1994). *Project archive, part I: Qualitative findings, 1993-1994.* (Rep. No. ED 379-388). Brooklyn: New York City Board of Education, Office of Educational Research.

Ekstrom, R.B., Goertz, M.E., Pollack, J.M., and Rock, D.A. (1986). Who drops out of high school and why? Findings from a national study. *Teachers College Record, 87*, 356-373.

Epstein, J.L. (1983). The influence of friends on achievement and affective outcomes. In J.L. Epstein and N. Karweit (Eds.), *Friends in school: Patterns of selection and influence in secondary schools* (pp. 177-200). New York: Academic Press.

Epstein, J.L. (1990). Single parents and the schools: Effects of marital status on parent-teacher interactions. In M. Hallan, D.M. Kle, and J. Glass (Eds.), *Change in societal institutions* (pp. 91-121). New York: Plenum.

Epstein, J.L. (2001a). Perspectives and previews on research and policy for school, family, and community partnerships. In *School, family, and community partnerships: Preparing educators and improving schools* (pp. 38-74). Boulder, CO: Westview Press.

Epstein, J.L. (2001b). *School, family, and community partnerships: Preparing educators and improving schools.* Boulder, CO: Westview Press.

Epstein, J.L., and Dauber, S.L. (1991). School programs and teacher practices of parent involvement in inner-city elementary and middle schools. *Elementary School Journal, 91*, 289-303.

Epstein, J.L., and McPartland, J.M. (1976). The concept and measurement of the quality of school life. *American Educational Research Journal, 13*(1), 15-30.

Escalante, J., and Dirmann, J. (1990). The Jaime Escalante math program. *Journal of Negro Education, 59*(3), 407-423.

Evans, L. (1997). Understanding teacher morale and job satisfaction. *Teaching and Teacher Education, 13*, 831-845.

Farkas, G., Lleras, C., and Maczuga, S. (2002). Does oppositional culture exist in minority and poverty peer groups? *American Sociological Review, 67*, 148-155.

Ferguson, R. (1991). Paying for public education: New evidence on how and why money matters. *Harvard Journal on Legislation, 28*, 465-498.

Ferguson, R. (1998). Can schools narrow the black-white test score gap? In C. Jencks and M. Phillips (Eds.), *The Black-white test score gap* (pp. 318-374). Washington, DC: Brookings Institution.

Ferguson, R. (2002). *Who doesn't meet the eye: Understanding and addressing racial disparities in high achieving suburban schools.* Naperville, IL: North Central Regional Educational Laboratory.

Ferguson, R., and Ladd, H. (1996). How and why money matters: An analysis of Alabama schools. In H. Ladd (Ed.), *Holding schools accountable* (pp. 265-298). Washington, DC: Brookings Institution.

Fetler, M. (1989). School dropout rates, academic performance, size and poverty: Correlates of educational reform. *Educational Evaluation and Policy, 11*(2), 109-116.

Fielding, L.C., and Pearson, D.P. (1994). Reading comprehension: What works. *Educational Leadership, 51*(Feb.), 62-68.

Fielding, L.G. (1994). Independent reading. In A. Purves (Ed.), *Encyclopedia of English studies and language arts.* New York: Scholastic.

Finders, M. (1998-1999). Raging hormones: Stories of adolescence and implications for teacher preparation. *Journal of Adolescent and Adult Literacy, 42*, 252-263.

Fine, M. (1991). *Framing dropouts: Notes on the politics of an urban public high school.* Albany: State University of New York Press.

Fine, M. (1994). *Chartering urban school reform: Reflections on public high schools in the midst of change.* New York: Teachers College Press.

Fine, M., Torre, M.E., Boudin, K., Bowen, I., Clark, J., Hylton, D., Martinez, M., "Missy", Roberts, R., Smart, P., and Upegui, D. (2001). *Changing minds: The impact of college in a maximum security prison*. New York: City University of New York, Graduate Center.

Fine, M., Valenzuela, A., and Bowditch, C. (1993). Getting rid of troublemakers: High school disciplinary procedures and the production of dropouts. *Social Problems, 40*, 493-509.

Finley, M. (1984). Teachers and tracking in a comprehensive high school. *Sociology of Education, 57*, 233-243.

Finn, J., and Rock, D. (1997). Academic success among students at risk for school failure. *Journal of Applied Psychology, 82*, 221-234.

Finn, J., and Voelkl, K. (1993). School characteristics related to student engagement. *Journal of Negro Education, 62*, 249-268.

Finn, J.D. (1989). Withdrawing from school. *Review of Educational Research, 59*, 117-142.

Flores-Gonzalez, N. (2002). *School kids/street kids: Identity development in Latino students*. New York: Teachers College Press.

Follman, J., and Muldoon, K. (1997). Florida learn and serve 1995-1996: What were the outcomes? *NASSP Bulletin, 81*(591), 29-36.

Fordham, S. (1988). Racelessness as a factor in black students' school success. *Harvard Educational Review, 58*, 54-84.

Fordham, S. (1996). *Blacked out: Dilemmas of race, identity, and success at Capital High*. Chicago: University of Chicago Press.

Fordham, S., and Ogbu, J.U. (1986). Black students' school success: Coping with the burden of "acting white." *The Urban Review, 18*, 176-206.

Foster, M. (1987). *"It's cookin' now": An ethnographic study of a successful Black teacher in an urban community college*. Unpublished doctoral dissertation, Harvard University, Cambridge, MA.

Foster, M. (1994). Educating for competence in community and culture: Exploring views of exemplary African-American teachers. In M. Shujaa (Ed.), *Too much schooling, too little education: A paradox of black life in white societies* (pp. 221-244). Trenton, NJ: Africa World Press.

Fowler, W.J. (1995). School size and student outcomes. *Advances in Educational Productivity, 5*, 3-26.

Fowler, W.J., and Walberg, H.J. (1991). School size, characteristics and outcomes. *Educational Evaluation and Policy Analysis, 13*(2), 189-202.

Frankenstein, M. (1990). Incorporating race, gender, and class issues into a critical mathematical literacy curriculum. *Journal of Negro Education, 59*, 336-347.

Frankenstein, M. (1995). Equity in mathematics education: Class in the world outside of class. In W.G. Secada, E. Fennema, and L.B. Adajian (Eds.), *New directions for equity in mathematics education* (pp. 165-190). New York: Cambridge University Press.

Frederickson, N. (1994) *The influence of minimum competency tests on teaching and learning*. Princeton, NJ: Educational Testing Service, Policy Information Center.

Freedman, S.W., Simons, E.R., Kalnin, J.S., Casareno, A., and The M-Class Teams. (1999). *Inside city schools: Investigating literacy in multicultural classrooms*. New York and Urbana, IL: Teachers College Press and National Council of Teachers of English.

Freiberg, H. (1996). From tourists to citizens in the classroom. *Educational Leadership, 54*(1), 32-36.

Friedman, R.M., Silver, S.E., Duchnowski, A.J., Kutash, K., Eisen, M., Brandenburg, N.A., and Prange, M. (1988). *Characteristics of children with serious emotional disturbances identified by public systems as requiring services*. Tampa: Florida Mental Health Institute, University of South Florida.

Futrell, M.H., and Rotberg, I.C. (2002). Predictable casualties. *Education Week, 22*(5), 48, 34.

Gambone, M.A., Klem, A.M., and Connell, J.P. (2002). *Finding out what matters for youth: Testing key links in a community-action framework for youth development.* Philadelphia: Youth Development Strategies and Institute for Research and Reform in Education.

Gambone, M.A., Klem, A.M., Moore, W.P., and Summers, J.A. (2002). *First things first: Creating the conditions and capacity for community-wide reform in an urban school district.* New York: Manpower Demonstration Research Corporation.

Gamoran, A., Porter, A.C., Smithson, J., and White, P.A. (1997). Upgrading high school mathematics instruction: Improving learning opportunities for low-achieving, low-income youth. *Educational Evaluation and Policy Analysis, 19*(4), 325–338.

Gamoran, A. (1992). Social factors in education. In M.C. Alk (Ed.), *Encyclopedia of educational research* (pp. 1222-1229). New York: Macmillan.

Gamoran, A. (1996). Student achievement in public magnet, public comprehensive, and private city high schools. *Educational Evaluation and Policy Analysis, 18*, 1-18.

Gándara, P., Larson, K., Rumberger, R., and Mehan, H. (1998) *Capturing Latino students in the academic pipeline.* Berkeley: University of California, Institute for the Study of Social Change.

Gándara, P., Mejorado, M., Gutiérrez, D., and Molina, M. (1998). *Final report of the evaluation of High School Puente, 1994-1998.* New York: Carnegie Corporation of New York.

Gangi, R., Schiraldi, V., and Ziedenberg, J. (1998). *New York state of mind: Higher education vs. prison funding in the empire state, 1988 1998.* Washington, DC: Justice Policy Institute.

Gardner, H. (1993). *Multiple intelligences: The theory into practice.* New York: Basic Books.

Gay, G. (1988). Designing relevant curricula for diverse learners. *Education and Urban Society, 20*, 327-340.

George, P.S., and McEwin, C.K. (1999). *High schools for a new century: Why is high school changing?* Reston, VA: National Association of Secondary School Principals.

Giles, H.C. (1998). *Parent engagement as a school reform strategy.* (Rep. No. 1998-05-00, ED419031). New York: ERIC Clearinghouse on Urban Education.

Gladden, M. (1998). A small school's literature review. In M. Fe and J. Somerville (Eds.), *Small schools, big imaginations.* Chicago: Cross City Campaign for Urban School Reform.

Glenn, D. (2003). Merit-Aid programs like Georgia's HOPE scholarships can distort students' incentives, scholars say. *The Chronicle of Higher Education,* January 6.

Gold, E., Simon, E., and Brown, C. (2002). *Strong neighborhoods, strong schools: The indicators project on education organizing.* Chicago: Cross City Campaign for Urban School Reform.

Goldschmidt, P., and Wang, J. (1999). When can schools affect dropout behavior? A longitudinal multilevel analysis. *American Educational Research Journal*, 36, 715-738.

Goldwasser, M., Yoshida, H., Christman, J., and Reumann-Moore, R. (2001). *Talent development: A report on the second year of implementation.* Philadelphia: Research for Action for the Philadelphia Education Fund.

Gonzales, P.M., Blanton, H., and Williams, K.J. (2002). The effects of stereotype threat and double-minority status on the test performance of Latino women. *Personality and Social Psychology Bulletin, 28*(5), 659-670.

Goodlad, J.I. (1984). *A place called school: Prospects for the future.* New York: McGraw-Hill.

Goodman, P. (1956). *Growing up absurd: Problems of youth in the organized system.* New York: Random House.

Goodwin, L.D., Goodwin, W.L., and Cantrill, J.L. (1988). The mental health needs of elementary school children. *Journal of School Health*, *7*, 282-287.

Gordon, C.W. (1957). *The social system of the high school.* Glencoe, IL: The Free Press.

Gottfredson, D.C., Hybl, L.G., Gottfredson, G.D., and Castaneda, R.P. (1986). *School climate assessment instruments: A review.* (Rep. No. 363). Baltimore: Johns Hopkins University, Center for Social Organization of Schools.

Gottfried, A. (1990). Academic intrinsic motivation in young elementary school children. *Journal of Educational Psychology*, *82*, 525-538.

Graham, P. (1995). Assimilation, adjustment, and access: An antiquarian view of American education. In D. Ravitch and M. Vovskis (Eds.), *Learning from the past* (pp. 3-24). Baltimore: Johns Hopkins University Press.

Graham, S. (1984). Communicating sympathy and anger to black and white children. *The Journal of Personality and Social Psychology*, *47*, 14-28.

Graham, S., Taylor, A.Z., and Hudley, C. (1998). Exploring achievement values among ethnic and minority early adolescents. *Journal of Educational Psychology*, *90*, 606-620.

Grant, G. (1988). *The world we created at Hamilton High*. Cambridge, MA: Harvard University Press.

Grant, William T. Foundation. (1988). *The forgotten half: Pathways to success for America's youth and young families*. Washington, DC: Author.

Green, A., and Keys, S. (2001). Expanding the developmental school counseling paradigm: Meeting the needs of the 21st century student. *Professional School Counseling, 5*(2), 84-95.

Green, J. (2001). *High school graduation rates in the United States*. New York: Center for Civic Innovation at the Manhattan Institute.

Greenberger, E., and Steinberg, L. (1986). *When teenagers work: The psychological and social costs of teenage employment*. New York: Basic Books.

Greenleaf, C.L., and Schoenbach, R. (1999). *Close readings: A study of key issues in the use of literacy learning cases for the professional development of secondary teachers*. San Francisco: Strategic Literacy Initiative, WestEd.

Greenleaf, C.L., Schoenbach, R., Cziko, C., and Mueller, F.L. (2001). Apprenticing adolescent readers to academic literacy. *Harvard Educational Review*, *71*(1), 79-129.

Grissom, J.G., and Shepard, L.A. (1989). Repeating and dropping out of school. In L.A. Shepard and M.L. Smith (Eds.), *Flunking grades: Research and policies on retention* (pp. 34-63). London: Falmer.

Grossman, J.B. (1999). *Contemporary issues in mentoring*. Philadelphia: Public/Private Ventures.

Grossman, P., and Stodolsky, S. (1994). Considerations of content and the circumstances of secondary school teaching. In L. Darling-Hammond (Ed.), *Review of research in education volume 20* (pp. 179-221). Washington, DC: American Educational Research Association.

Grossman, P., and Stodolsky, S. (1995). Content as context: The role of school subjects in secondary school teaching. *Educational Researcher, 24*, 5-11.

Grosso de León, A. (2002). *The urban high schools' challenge: Ensuring literacy for every child*. New York: Carnegie Corporation of New York.

Grubb, W.N. (1995a). Coherence for all students: High schools with career clusters and majors. In W.N. Grubb (Ed.), *Education through occupations in American high schools: Approaches to integrating academic and vocational education, volume I* (pp. 97-113). New York: Teachers College Press.

Grubb, W.N. (1995b). "The cunning hand, the cultured mind": Sources of support for curriculum integration. In W.N. Grubb (Ed.), *Education through occupations in American high schools: Approaches to integrating academic and vocational education, volume I* (pp. 11-25). New York: Teachers College Press.

Grubb, W.N. (1996). *Working in the middle: Strengthening education and training for the mid-skilled labor force.* San Francisco: Jossey-Bass.

Grubb, W.N. (2002). *Who I am: The inadequacy of career information in the information age.* Paper prepared for the Organisation for Economic and Co-operation and Development review of policies for information, guidance, and counseling services. Commissioned jointly by the European Commission and the Organisation for Economic and Co-operation and Development.

Grubb, W.N., Lara, C., and Valdez, S. (2001). Counselor, coordinator, monitor, mom: The roles of counselors in the Puente Program. *Journal of Educational Policy, 16*, 572-587.

Grubb, W.N., Worthen, H., Byrd, B., Webb, E., Badway, N., Case, C., Goto, S., and Villeneuve, J.C. (1999). *Honored but invisible: An inside look at teaching in community colleges.* New York: Routledge.

Guiton, G., and Oakes, J. (1995). Opportunity-to-learn and conceptions of educational equality. *Educational Evaluation and Policy Analysis, 17*(3), 323-336.

Guo, G. (1998). The timing of the influences of cumulative poverty on children's cognitive ability and achievement. *Social Forces, 77*(1), 257-287.

Gustein, E. (in press). Teaching and learning mathematics for social justice in an urban, Latino school. Submitted to *Journal for Research in Mathematics Education.*

Gustein, E., Lipman, P., Hernandez, P., and de los Reyes, R. (1997). Culturally relevant mathematics teachers in Mexican-American context. *Journal for Research in Mathematics Education, 28*(6), 709-737.

Guthrie, J., and Wigfield, A. (2000). Engagement and motivation in reading. In M. Kamil, P. Mosenthal, P.D. Pearson, and R. Barr, *Handbook of reading research, volume III* (pp. 403-424). Mahwah, NJ: Lawrence Erlbaum.

Guthrie, J., Wigfield, A., and VonSecker, C. (2000). Effects of integrated instruction on motivation and strategy use in reading. *Journal of Educational Psychology, 92*, 331-341.

Guthrie, J.T., Schafer, W., Wang, Y.Y., and Afflerbach, P. (1995). Relationships of instruction to amount of reading: An exploration of social, cognitive and instructional connections. *Reading Research Quarterly, 30*(1), 8-25.

Gutiérrez, K., Baquedano-Lopez, P., and Tejada, C. (1999). Rethinking diversity: Hybridity and hybrid language practices in the third space. *Mind, Culture, and Activity, 6*(4), 286-303.

Gutiérrez, R. (1996). Practices, beliefs, and cultures of high school mathematics departments: Understanding their influences on student advancement. *Journal of Curriculum Studies, 28*, 495-530.

Gutiérrez, R. (1999). Advancing urban Latino youth in mathematics: Lessons from an effective high school mathematics department. *Urban Review, 31*(3), 263-281.

Gutiérrez, R. (2000a). Advancing African American urban youth in mathematics: Unpacking the success of one high school mathematics department. *American Journal of Education, 109*(1), 63-111.

Gutiérrez, R. (2000b). *Advancing urban Latina/o youth in mathematics: The power of teacher community.* Paper presented at the annual meeting of the National Council of Teachers of Mathematics.

Gutiérrez, R. (2002a). *Calculus for all: Collective teacher commitment and the practice of a new reform.* Paper presented at the Annual Meeting of the American Educational Research Association, April 1-5, New Orleans.

Gutiérrez, R. (2002b). Enabling the practice of mathematics teachers in context: Towards a new equity research agenda. *Mathematical Thinking and Learning, 4*(2/3), 145-187.

Gutiérrez, R. (2002c). Teacher community, biography, and math reform. In V. Lee (Ed.), *Reforming Chicago's high schools: Research perspectives on school and system level change.* Chicago: Consortium on Chicago School Reform.

Gutiérrez, R. (2002d). The complexity of language in teaching mathematics to Latinas/Latinos. *American Educational Research Journal, 39*(4), 1047-1088.

Gysbers, N.C. (2001). School counseling and counseling in the 21st century: Remember the past into the future. *Professional School Counseling, 5*(2), 96-105.

Hall, G.S. (1969). *Adolescence.* New York: Arno Books.

Haller, E.J., Monk, D.H., and Tien, L.T. (1993). Small schools and higher-order thinking skills. *Journal of Research in Rural Education, 9*(2), 66-73.

Hallinan, M.T., and Williams, R.A. (1990). Students' characteristics and the peer-influence process. *Sociology of Education, 63*, 122-132.

Hallinger, P., Bickman, L., and Davis, K. (1996). School context, principal leadership, and student reading achievement. *The Elementary School Journal, 96*, 527-549.

Hallinger, P., and Murphy, J. (1986). The social context of effective schools. *American Journal of Education, 94*, 328-355.

Halperin, S. (1998). *The forgotten half revisited: America's youth and young families, 1988-1998.* Washington, DC: American Youth Policy Forum.

Halpern-Felsher, B.L., Connell, J.P., Spencer, M.B., Aber, J.L., Duncan, G.J., Clifford, E., Crichlow, W.E., Usinger, P.A., Cole, S.P., Allen, L., and Seidman, E. (1997). Neighborhood and family factors predicting educational risk and attainment in African American and white children and adolescents. In J. Brooks-Gunn, G.J. Duncan, and J.L. Aber (Eds.), *Neighborhood poverty: Context and consequences for children, volume I* (pp. 146-173). New York: Russell Sage Foundation.

Hamilton, L., and Gill, B. (2001). *Edison schools 2000-2001: Annual report on school performance.* Santa Monica, CA: RAND.

Hamilton, M.A., and Hamilton, S.F. (1997). *Learning well at work: Choices for quality.* Washington, DC: National School-to-Work Office.

Haney, W.M. (2001). *Report on the case of New York Performance Standards Consortium v. Commissioner Mills et al.* Boston: Boston College, Lynch School of Education.

Hanushek, E.A. (1997). Assessing the effects of school resources on student performance: An update. *Educational Evaluation and Policy Analysis, 19*, 141-164.

Hardesty, P.H., and Dillard, J.M. (1994). The role of elementary school counselors compared with their middle and secondary school counterparts. *Elementary School Guidance and Counseling, 29*, 83-91.

Harter, S. (1992). The relationship between perceived competence, affect, and motivational orientation within the classroom: Process and patterns of change. In A. Boggiano and T. Pittman (Eds.), *Achievement and motivation: A social-developmental perspective* (pp. 77-114). New York: Cambridge University Press.

Hawkins, J., Catalano, R., Kosterman, R., Abbott, R., and Hill, K. (1999). Preventing adolescent health-risk behaviors by strengthening protection during childhood. *Archives of Pediatric Adolescent Medicine, 153*, 226-234.

Heckman, P.E. (1996). *The courage to change: Stories from successful school reform.* Thousand Oaks, CA: Corwin Press.

Heebner, A. (1995). The voice of students. In W.N. Grubb (Ed.), *Education through occupations in American high schools: Approaches to integrating academic and vocational education, volume I.* New York: Teachers College Press.

Hembree, R. (1988). Correlates, causes, effects, and treatment of test anxiety. *Review of Educational Research, 58*, 47-77.

Herr, E., and Cramer, S. (1992). *Career guidance and counseling through the life span: Systematic approaches, 4th edition.* New York: Harper Collins.

Hershey, A.M., Silverberg, M.K., Hamison, J., Hudis, P., and Jackson, R. (1998). *Expanding options for students: Report to Congress on the national evaluation of school-to-work implementation.* Princeton, NJ: Mathematica Policy Research.

Heymann, S.J., and Earle, A. (2000). Low-income parents: How do working conditions affect their opportunity to help school-age children at risk? *American Educational Research Journal, 37*(4), 833-848.

Hiebert, J., Gallimore, R., and Stigler, R. (2002). A knowledge base for the teaching profession: What would it look like and how can we get one? *Educational Researcher, 31*, 3-15.

Hill, K., Lui, C., and Hawkins, D. (2001). *Early precursors of gang membership: A study of Seattle youth.* Washington, DC: U.S. Department of Justice.

Hill, P.T., Campbell, C., and Harvey, J. (2000). *It takes a city: Getting serious about urban school reform.* Washington, DC: Brookings Institution.

Hill, P.T., Foster, G.E., and Gendler, T. (1990). *High schools with character.* Santa Monica: RAND.

Hilliard, A.G. (1991). Do we have the will to educate all children? *Educational Leadership, 49*(1), 31-36.

Hilliard, A.G. (1991-1992). Why we must pluralize the curriculum. *Educational Leadership, 29*, 12-14.

Hilliard, A.G. (1995). *The maroon within us: Selected essays on African American community socialization.* Baltimore: Black Classic Press.

Hillocks, G. (1999). *Ways of thinking, ways of teaching.* New York: Teachers College Press.

Hinshaw, S.P. (1992). Externalizing behavior problems and academic underachievement in childhood adolescence: Causal relationships and underlying mechanisms. *Psychological Bulletin, 111*, 127-155.

Hirsch, L. (1988). Language across the curriculum: A model for ESL students in content courses. In S. Benesch (Ed.), *Ending remediation: Linking ESL and content in higher education* (pp. 67-90). Washington, DC: Teachers of English to Speakers of Other Languages.

Hochschild, J. (in press). Can public schools promote the American dream for poor children? Submitted to *Journal of Social Issues, Special Volume on Social Class and Education.*

Hodkinson, P., Sparkes, A., and Hodkinson, H. (1996). *Triumphs and tears: Young people, markets, and the transition from school to work.* London: David Fulton.

Hollingshead, A.B. (1949). *Elmtown's youth.* New York: Wiley.

Honig, M., Kahne, J., and McLaughlin, M. (2001). School-community connections: Strengthening opportunities to learn and opportunities to teach. In V. Richardson (Ed.), *Handbook of research on teaching, 4th edition* (pp. 998-1028). Washington, DC: American Educational Research Association.

Hoover-Dempsey, K.V., Bassler, O.C., and Brissie, J.S. (1987) Parent involvement: Contributions of teacher efficacy, school socioeconomic status and other school characteristics. *American Educational Research Journal, 24*, 417-435.

Howell, J.C. (1998). *Youth gangs: An overview.* (Rep. No. 1-19). Washington, DC: U.S. Department of Justice.

Howell, J.C., and Lynch, J.P. (2000). *Youth gangs in schools.* (Rep. No. 1-7). Washington, DC: U.S. Department of Justice.

Howley, C. (2002). Small schools. In A. Molnar (Ed.), *School reform proposals: The research evidence.* (Rep. No. EPSL-0201-101-EPRU). Tempe: Arizona State University, Education Policy Research Unit.

Howley, C., and Bickel, R. (2000). *Results of four-state study: Smaller schools reduce harmful impact of poverty on student achievement.* Washington, DC: The Rural School and Community Trust.

Hoy, W.K., and Sabo, D.J. (1998). *Quality middle schools: Open and healthy.* Thousand Oaks, CA: Corwin Press.

Husman, J., and Lens, W. (1999). The role of the future in student motivation. *Educational Psychologist, 34*, 113-125.

Ide, J.K., Parkerson, J., Haertel, G.D., and Walberg, H.J. (1981). Peer group influence on educational outcomes: A quantitative synthesis. *Journal of Educational Psychology, 73*, 472-484.

Institute for Research and Reform in Education. (2000). *First things first: An introduction.* Philadelphia, PA: Author.

Institute for Research and Reform in Education. (2001). *First things first: A framework for successful school reform, 2nd edition.* A white paper prepared for the E.M. Kauffman Foundation, Kansas City, MO.

Institute for Research and Reform in Education. (2002). *Getting off the dime toward meaningful reform: First steps toward implementing first things first.* Philadelphia: Author.

Institute of Medicine. (1994). *Reducing risks for mental disorders: Frontiers for preventive intervention research.* P.J. Mrazek and R.J. Haggerty (Eds.). Committee on Prevention of Mental Disorders. Division of Biobehavioral Sciences and Mental Disorders. Washington, DC: National Academy Press.

Institute of Medicine. (1997). *Schools and health: Our nation's investment.* D. Allensworth, E. Lawson, L. Nicholson, and J. Wyche (Eds.). Committee on Comprehensive School Health Programs in Grades K-12. Division of Health Sciences Policy. Washington, DC: National Academy Press.

Irvine, J. (1990). *Black students and school failure.* New York: Praeger.

Iyengar, S., and Lepper, M. (1999). Rethinking the value of choice: A cultural perspective on intrinsic motivation. *Journal of Personality and Social Psychology, 76*, 349-366.

Jacob, B.A. (2001). Getting tough? The impact of high school graduation exams. *Educational Evaluation and Policy Analysis, 23*(2), 99-121.

Jacobs, J., Lanza, S., Osgood, D., Eccles, J., and Wigfield, A. (2002). Changes in children's self-competence and values: Gender and domain differences across grades one through twelve. *Child Development, 73*, 509-527.

Jencks, C., and Phillips, M. (Eds.). (1998). *The black-white test score gap.* Washington, DC: Brookings Institution.

Jerald, C.D. (2001). *Dispelling the myth: Preliminary findings from a nationwide analysis of high-performing schools.* Washington, DC: Education Trust.

Jessor, R., Turbin, M.S., and Costa, F.M. (1998). Protection in successful outcomes among disadvantaged adolescents. *Applied Developmental Science*, 2, 198-208.

Jimenez, R. (2000). Literacy and identity development of Latina/o students. *American Educational Research Journal, 37*(4), 971-1000.

Jimenez, R.T., Garcia, G.E., and Pearson, P.D. (1996). The reading strategies of Latina/o students who are successful English readers: Opportunities and obstacles. *Reading Research Quarterly, 31*(1), 90-112.

Jimerson, S. (1999). On the failure of failure: Examining the association of early grade retention and late adolescent education and employment outcomes. *Journal of School Psychology, 37*(3), 243-272.

Jimerson, S., Egeland, B., and Teo, A. (1999). A longitudinal study of achievement trajectories: Factors associated with change. *Journal of Educational Psychology, 91*, 116-126.

Johnson, D., and Johnson, R. (1985). Motivational process in cooperative, competitive, and individualistic learning situations. In C. Ames and R. Ames (Eds.), *Research motivation in education, volume II: The classroom milieu* (pp. 249-286). Orlando, FL: Academic Press.

Johnson, M.K., Crosnoe, R., and Elder, G., Jr. (2001). Students' attachment and academic engagement: The role of race and ethnicity. *Sociology of Education, 74*, 318-340.

Jordan, W., and Plank, S. (2000). Talent loss among poor students. In M.G. Sanders (Ed.), *Schooling students placed at risk* (pp. 83-108). Mahwah, NJ: Lawrence Erlbaum.

Jordan, W.J., and Nettles, S.M. (1999). *How students invest their time out of school: Effects on school engagement, perceptions of life changes, and achievement.* (Rep. No. ED428174). Baltimore: Center for Research on the Education of Students Placed-At-Risk.

Kahlenberg, R.D. (2001). *All together now: Creating middle-class schools through public school choice.* Washington, DC: Brookings Institution.

Kahne, J., Nagaoka, J., Brown, A., O'Brien, J., Quinn, T., and Thiede, K. (2001). Assessing after-school programs as contexts for youth development. *Youth and Society, 32*(4), 321-446.

Kahne, J., O'Brien, J., Brown, A., and Quinn, T. (2001). Leveraging social capital and school improvement: The case of a school network and a comprehensive community initiative in Chicago. *Educational Administration Quarterly, 37*, 429-461.

Kamil, M., Mosenthal, P., Pearson, P.D., Barr, R. (2000). *Handbook of reading research, volume 3.* Mahwah, NJ: Lawrence Erlbaum.

Kandel, D.B. (1978). Homophily, selection, and socialization in adolescent friendships. *American Journal of Sociology, 84*, 427-436.

Kandel, D.B. (1996). The parental and peer contexts of adolescent deviance: An algebra of interpersonal influences. *Journal of Drug Issues, 26*, 289-315.

Katz, R., Jackson, L., Reeves, K., and Benson, C. (1995). Urban career magnet high schools. In W.N. Grubb (Ed.), *Education through occupations in American high schools, volume I: Approaches to integrating academic and vocational education* (pp. 114-133). New York: Teachers College Press.

Kaufman, P., and Bradby, D. (1992). *Characteristics of at-risk students in NELS:88.* (Rep. No. NCES 92-042). Washington, DC: U.S. Department of Education.

Kaufman, P., Chen, X., Choy, S.P., Peter, K., Ruddy, S.A., Miller, A.K., Fleury, J.K., Chandler, K.A., Planty, M.G., and Rand, M.R. (2001). *Indicators of school crime and safety: 2001.* (NCES 2002-113/NCJ 190075). Washington, DC: U.S. Departments of Education and Justice.

Keesling, J.W., and Melargano, R.J. (1983) Parent participation in federal education programs: Findings from the federal government survey phase of the study of parental involvement. In R. Hasks and D. Adams (Eds.), *Parent education and public schools* (pp. 230-254). Norwood, NJ: Ablex.

Kemple, J. (1997). *Career academies—communities of support for students and teachers: Emerging findings from a ten-site evaluation.* New York: Manpower Demonstration Research Corporation.

Kemple, J. (2001). *Career academies: Impacts on students' initial transition to post-secondary education and employment.* New York: Manpower Demonstration Research Corporation.

Kemple, J., and Snipes, J. (2000). *Career academies: Impacts on student engagement and performance in high school.* New York: Manpower Demonstration Research Corporation.

Kendall, P.C., and Dobson, K.S. (1993). On the nature of cognition and its role in psychopathology. In K.S. Dobson and P.C. Kendall (Eds.), *Psychopathology and cognition* (pp. 3-17). San Diego: Academic Press.

Kessler, R.C., Foster, C.L., Saunders, W.B., and Stang, P.E. (1995). Social consequences of psychiatric disorders. *American Journal of Psychiatry*, *152*(7), 1026-1032.

Keys, S.G., and Bemak, F. (1997). School-family-community linked services: A school counseling role for changing times. *The School Counselor*, *44*, 225-263.

Khisty, L., and Viego, G. (1999). Challenging conventional wisdom: A case study. In L. Oritz-Franco, N.G. Hernandez, and Y. De La Cruz (Eds.), *Changing the faces of mathematics: Perspectives on Latinos* (pp. 71-80). Reston, VA: National Council of Teachers of Mathematics.

King, A. (1994). Meeting the educational needs of at-risk students: A cost analysis of three models. *Educational Evaluation and Policy Analysis*, *16*, 1-19.

Kirby, S.N., Berends, M., and Naftel, S. (2001). *Implementation in a longitudinal sample of new American schools: Four years into scale-up*. Santa Monica, CA: RAND.

Kisker, E.E., and Brown R.S. (1996). Do school-based health centers improve adolescents' access to health care, health status, and risk-taking behavior? *Journal of Adolescent Health, 18,* 335-343.

Knitzer, J., Steinberg, Z., and Fleisch, B. (1991). Schools, children's mental health, and the advocacy challenge. *Journal of Clinical Child Psychology*, *20*(1), 102-111.

Kohn, A. (1993). *Punished by rewards: The trouble with gold stars, incentive plans, A's, praise, and other bribes*. New York: Houghton Mifflin.

Kovacs, M. (1989). Affective disorders in children and adolescents. *American Psychologist*, *44*, 209-215.

Kozol, J. (1992). *Savage inequalities*. New York: Harper Collins.

Krei, M., and Rosenbaum, J. (2001). Career and college advice to the forgotten half: What do counselors and vocational teachers advise? *Teachers College Record*, *103*(5), 823-842.

Kuperminc, G.P., Leadbeater, B.J., and Blatt, S.J. (2001). School social climate and individual differences in vulnerability to psychopathology among middle school students. *Journal of School Psychology*, *39*(2), 141-150.

Ladson-Billings, G. (1994). *The dreamkeepers: Successful teachers of African American children*. San Francisco: Jossey-Bass.

Ladson-Billings, G. (1995). Making mathematics meaningful in multicultural contexts. In W. Secada, E. Fennema, and L. Adajian (Eds.), *New directions for equity in mathematics education* (pp. 126-145). New York: Cambridge University Press.

Ladson-Billings, G. (1997) It doesn't add up: African American students' mathematics achievement. *Journal for Research in Mathematics Education, 28*(6), 697-708.

Ladson-Billings, G. (2001) *Crossing over to Canaan: The journey of new teachers in diverse classrooms*. San Francisco: Jossey-Bass.

Lambert, N., and McCombs, B. (1998). *How students learn: Reforming schools through learner-centered education*. Washington, DC: American Psychological Association.

Lamborn, S.D., Brown, B.B., Mounts, N.S., and Steinberg, L. (1992). Putting school in perspective: The influence of family, peers, extracurricular participation and part time work on academic engagement. In F.M. Newmann (Ed.), *Student engagement and achievement in American high schools* (pp. 153-181). New York: Teachers College Press.

Langer, J.A. (2001). Beating the odds: Teaching middle and high school students to read and write well. *American Educational Research Journal*, *38*(4), 837-880.

Lareau, A. (1987). Social class differences in family-school relationships: The importance of cultural capital. *Sociology of Education*, *60*, 73-85.

Lareau, A. (1989). *Home advantage: Social class and parental intervention in elementary education*. New York: Falmer Press.

Larson, K.A., and Rumberger, R.W. (1995). ALAS: Achievement for Latinos through academic success. In H. Thornton (Ed.), *Staying in school: A technical report of three dropout prevention projects for middle school.* Minneapolis: University of Minnesota, Institute on Community Integration.

Lave, J., and Wenger, E. (1991). *Situated learning: Legitimate peripheral participation.* Cambridge, UK: Cambridge University Press.

Lee, C.D. (1993). *Signifying as a scaffold for literary interpretation: The pedagogical implications of an African American discourse genre.* Urbana, IL: National Council of Teachers of English.

Lee, C.D. (1995a). A culturally based cognitive apprenticeship: Teaching African American high school students' skills in literacy interpretation. *Reading Research Quarterly, 30*(4), 608-631.

Lee, C.D. (1995b). Signifying as a scaffold for literary interpretation. *Journal of Black Psychology, 21*(4), 357-381.

Lee, C.D. (1997). Bridging home and school literacies: A model of culturally responsive teaching. In J. Flood, S.B. Heath, and D. Lapp (Eds.), *A handbook for literacy educators: Research on teaching the communicative and visual arts* (pp. 330-341). New York: Macmillan.

Lee, C.D. (2000). Signifying in the zone of proximal development. In C.D. Lee and P. Smagorsky (Eds.), *Vygotskian perspectives on literacy research: Constructing meaning through collaborative inquiry* (pp. 191-225). New York: Cambridge University Press.

Lee, C.D. (2001). Is October Brown Chinese? A cultural modeling activity system for underachieving students. *American Educational Research Journal, 38*(1), 97-142.

Lee, S. (1994). *Family-school connections and students' education: Continuity and change of family involvement from the middle grades to High School.* Unpublished doctoral dissertation, Johns Hopkins University, Baltimore.

Lee, V., Bryk, A., and Smith, J. (1993). The organization of effective secondary schools. *Review of Research in Education, 19*, 171-268.

Lee, V., and Croninger, R. (1994). The relative importance of home and school in the development of literacy skills for middle-grade students. *American Journal of Education, 102*(3), 286-329.

Lee, V., and Smith, J. (1997) High school size: Which works best and for whom? *Educational and Policy Analysis, 19*(3), 205-227.

Lee, V.E. (2000). School size and the organization of secondary schools. In M.T. Hallan (Ed.), *Handbook of sociology of education* (pp. 327-344). New York: Kluwer Academic/Plenum.

Lee, V.E., and Burkam, D.T. (1992). Transferring high schools: An alternative to dropping out? *American Journal of Education, 100*, 420-453.

Lee, V.E., Croninger, R.G., and Smith, J.B. (1997) Coursetaking, equity, and mathematics learning: Testing the constrained curriculum hypothesis in U.S. secondary schools. *Educational Evaluation and Policy Analysis, 19*, 99-122.

Lee, V.E., Dedrick, R.F., and Smith, J.B. (1991). The effect of social organization of schools on teachers' efficacy and satisfaction. *Sociology of Education, 64*(3), 190-208.

Lee, V.E., and Ekstrom, R.B. (1987). Student access to guidance counseling in high school. *American Educational Research Journal, 24*, 287-309.

Lee, V.E., and Smith, J.B. (1995). Effects of high school restructuring and size on early gains in achievement and engagement for early secondary school students. *Sociology of Education, 68*(4), 241-270.

Lee, V.E., and Smith, J.B. (1999). Social support and achievement for young adolescents in Chicago: The role of school academic press. *American Educational Research Journal, 36*, 907-945.

Lee, V.E., and Smith, J.B. (2001). *Restructuring high schools for equity and excellence: What works. Sociology of education series.* New York: Teachers College Press.

Lee, V.E., Smith, J.B., and Croninger, R.G. (1995). *Another look at high school restructuring: More evidence that it improves student achievement and more insight into why.* Madison: University of Wisconsin.

Legters, N. (1999). *Small learning communities meet school-to-work: Whole school restructuring for urban comprehensive high schools.* (Rep. No. 31). Baltimore: Johns Hopkins University, Center for Research on the Education of Students Placed at Risk.

Legters, N. Balfanz, R., Jordan, W., and McPartland, J. (2002). *Comprehensive reform for urban high schools.* New York: Teachers College Press.

Legters, N., Balfanz, R., and McPartland, J. (2002). *Solutions for failing high schools: Converging visions and promising models.* Baltimore: Johns Hopkins University, Center for Social Organization of Schools.

Leitch, M.L., and Tangri, S.S. (1988). Barriers to home-school collaboration. *Educational Horizons, 66*, 70-74.

Leithwood, K., Begley, P., and Cousins, B. (1990). The nature, causes and consequences of principals' practices: An agenda for future research. *Journal of Educational Administration, 28*, 5-31.

Lemke, J. (1998). Multiplying meaning: Visual and verbal semiotics in scientific text. In J.R. Mart and R. Veel (Eds.), *Reading science: Critical and functional perspectives on discourse of science* (pp. 87-113). New York: Routledge.

Lepper, M., and Henderlong, J. (2000). Turning "play" into "work" and "work" into "play": 25 years of research on intrinsic versus extrinsic motivation. In C. Sansone and J. Harackiewicz (Eds.), *Intrinsic and extrinsic motivation: The search for optimal motivation and performance* (pp. 257-307). San Diego, CA: Academic Press.

Levine, D.U., and Sherk, J.K. (1990). *Effective implementation of a comprehension-improvement approach in secondary schools.* (Rep. No. ED 327 830). Kansas City: University of Missouri, Center for the Study of Metropolitan Problems in Education.

Lewis, A. (1996). *Building bridges: Eight case studies of schools and communities working together.* Chicago: Cross Cities Campaign for Urban School Reform.

Lieberman, A., and Miller, L. (Eds.). (2001). *Teachers caught in the action: Professional development that matters.* New York: Teachers College Press.

Lightfoot, S. (1973). Politics and reasoning: Through the eyes of teachers and children. Harvard *Educational Review, 43*(2), 197-244.

Linnenbrink, E., and Pintrich, P. (2000). Multiple pathways to learning and achievement: The role of goal orientation in fostering adaptive motivation, affect, and cognition. In C. Sansone and J. Harackiewicz (Eds.), *Intrinsic and extrinsic motivation: The search for optimal motivation and performance* (pp. 195-227). San Diego, CA: Academic Press.

Lippman, L., Burns, S., and McArthur, E. (1996). *Urban schools: The challenge of location and poverty.* (Rep. No. NCES 96-184). Washington, DC: U.S. Department of Education.

Little, J.W. (1993). Professional community in comprehensive high schools: The two worlds of academic and vocational teachers. In J.W. Little and M.W. McLaughlin (Eds.), *Teachers work: Individuals, colleagues, and contexts* (pp. 137-163). New York: Teachers College Press.

Locke, D. (1992). *Increasing multicultural understanding.* Newbury Park, CA: Sage.

Lotan, R.A. (1997). Principles of a principled curriculum. In E.G. Cohen and R.A. Lotan (Eds.), *Working for equity in heterogeneous classrooms: Sociological theory in practice* (pp. 105-116). New York: Teachers College Press.

Louis, K., and Marks, H. (1998). Does professional community affect the classroom? Teachers' work and student experiences in restructuring schools. *American Journal of Education, 106*, 532-575.

Louis, K., Marks, H., and Kruse, S. (1996). Teachers' professional communities in restructuring schools. *American Educational Research Journal, 33*, 757-798.

Louis, K.S., Jones, L.M., and Barajas, H. (2001). *Evaluation of the transforming school counseling initiative: Districts and schools as a context for transformed counseling roles.* Minneapolis: University of Minnesota, Center for Applied Research and Educational Improvement.

Lucas, S.R. (1999). *Tracking inequality: Stratification and mobility in American high schools.* New York: Teachers College Press.

Lucas, T., Henze, R., and Donato, R. (1990). Promoting the success of Latino language-minority students: An exploratory study of six high schools. *Harvard Educational Review, 60*(3), 315-340.

Ma, L. (1999). *Knowing and teaching elementary mathematics: Teacher's understanding of fundamental mathematics in China and the United States.* Mahwah, NJ: Lawrence Erlbaum.

MacIntyre, A. (1981). *After virtue.* South Bend, IN: University of Notre Dame Press.

MacIver, D., Stipek, D., and Daniels, D. (1991). Explaining within-semester changes in student effort in junior high school and senior high school courses. *Journal of Educational Psychology, 83*, 201-211.

MacMullen, M.M. (1996). *Taking stock of a school reform effort.* Providence, RI: Brown University.

Mahiri, J. (1998). *Shooting for excellence: African American and youth culture in new century schools.* New York and Urbana, IL: Teachers College Press and National Council of Teachers of English.

Marks, H., Doane, K., and Secada, W. (in press). Support for student achievement. In F. Newmann and Associates (Eds.), *Restructuring for student achievement: The impact of structure and culture in twenty-four schools.* San Francisco: Jossey-Bass.

Marks, H., Secada, W., and Doane, K. (1996). *Social support for achievement: Building intellectual culture in restructuring schools.* Washington, DC: U.S. Dept. of Education, Office of Educational Research and Improvement, Educational Resources Information Center.

Marks, H.M. (2000). Student engagement in instructional activity: Patterns in the elementary, middle, and high school years. *American Educational Research Journal, 37*(1), 153-184.

Marshall, J.D., Smagorinsky, P., and Smith, M. (1995). *The language of interpretation: Patterns of discourse in discussions of literature.* Urbana, IL: National Council of Teachers of English.

Martinez, M., and Bray, J. (2002). *All over the map: State policies to improve the high school.* Washington, DC: Institute for Educational Leadership.

Maxwell, N., and Rubin, V. (2000). *High school career academies: A pathway to educational reform in urban school districts.* Kalamazoo, MI: W.E. Upjohn Institute.

Mayer, S. (1991). How much does a high school's racial and socioeconomic mix affect graduation and teenage fertility rates? In C. Jencks and P. Peterson (Eds.), *The urban underclass* (pp. 321-341). Washington, DC: Brookings Institution.

McCombs, B.L. (1996). Alternative perspectives for motivation. In L. Baker, P. Afflerbach, and D. Reinking (Eds.), *Developing engaged readers in school and home communities* (pp. 67-87). Mahwah, NJ: Lawrence Erlbaum.

McCombs, B.L., and Quiat, M. (2000). *Results of pilot study to evaluate the Community for Learning Program: Publication series number 1.* Philadelphia: Temple University Center for Research in Human Development and Education.

McCord, M.T., Klein, J.D., Foy, J., and Fothergill, K. (1993). School-based clinic use and school performance. *Journal of Adolescent Health, 14*(2), 91-98.

McCoy, A.R., and Reynolds, A.J. (1999). Grade retention and school performance: An extended investigation. *Journal of School Psychology, 37*, 273-298.

McDermott, P.A., Mordell, M., and Stolzful, J.C. (2001). The organization of student performance in American schools: Discipline, motivation, verbal learning, and nonverbal learning. *Journal of Educational Psychology*, *93*(1), 65-76.

McDermott, R. (1987). Achieving school failure: An anthropological approach to illiteracy and social stratification. In G. Spindler (Ed.), *Education and cultural process, 2nd edition (*pp. 173-209). Prospect Heights, IL: Waveland Press.

McDill, E.J., Natriello, G., and Pallas, A.M. (1986). A population at risk: Potential consequences of tougher school standards for student dropouts. *American Journal of Education*, *94*, 135-181.

McDill, E.L., and Rigsby, L.C. (1973). *Structure and process in secondary schools: The academic impact of educational climates*. Baltimore: John Hopkins University Press.

McFarland, D.A. (2001). Student resistance: How the formal and informal organization of classrooms facilitate everyday forms of student defiance. *American Journal of Sociology, 107*(3), 612-678.

McLanahan, S. (1985). Family structure and the reproduction of poverty. *American Journal of Sociology, 90*(4), 873-901.

McLaughlin, D., and Drori, G. (2000). *School-level correlates of academic achievement student assessment scores in SASS public schools.* (Rep. No. ED441039). Washington, DC: U.S. Department of Education.

McLaughlin, M. (2000). *Community counts: How youth organizations matter for youth development.* Washington, DC: Public Education Network.

McLaughlin, M., and Talbert, J. (2001). *Professional communities and the work of high school teaching*. Chicago: University of Chicago Press.

McLaughlin, M.W. (1993). What matters most in teachers' workplace context? In J.W. Little and M.W. McLaughlin (Eds.), *Teachers' work: Individuals, colleagues, and contexts* (pp. 79-103). New York: Teachers College Press.

McLaughlin, M.W., and Talbert, J.E. (1993). *Contexts that matter for teaching and learning.* Stanford: Center for Research on the Context of Secondary School Teaching, Stanford University.

McMullan, B. (1994). Charters and restructuring. In M. Fine (Ed.), *Chartering school reform: Reflections on public high school reform* (pp. 63-77). New York: Teachers College Press.

McNeal, R.B. (1997a). Are students being pulled out of high school? The effect of adolescent employment on dropping out. *Sociology of Education*, *70*(206), 220.

McNeal, R.B. (1997b). High school dropouts: A closer examination of school effects. *Social Science Quarterly*, *78*, 209-222.

McNeely, C.A., Nonnemaker, J.M., and Blum, R.W. (2002). Promoting school connectedness: Evidence from the National Longitudinal Study of Adolescent Health. *Journal of School Health*, 72(4), 138-146.

McPartland, J., Balfanz, R., Joan, W., and Legters, N. (1998). Improving school climate and achievement in a troubled urban high school through the Talent Development Model. *Journal of Education for Students Placed at Risk*, *3*(4), 337-361.

McPherson, M., Smith-Lovin, L., and Cook, J.M. (2001). Birds of a feather: Homophily in social networks. *Annual Review of Sociology*, *27*, 415-444.

Mecartney, C., Styles, M., and Morrow, K. (1994). *Mentoring in the juvenile justice system: Findings from two pilot studies*. Philadelphia: Public/Private Ventures.

Meece, J. (1991). The classroom context and student's motivational goals. In M. Maehr and P. Pintrich (Eds.), *Advances in motivation and achievement, volume 7* (pp. 261-285). Greenwich, CT: JAI Press.

Mehan, H. (1979). *Learning lessons.* Cambridge, MA: Harvard University Press.

Mehan, H., Hubbard, L., and Villanueva, I. (1994). Forming academic identities: Accommodation without assimilation among involuntary minorities. *Anthropology of Education Quarterly, 25,* 91-117.

Meier, D. (1995). *The power of their ideas: Lessons for America from a small school in Harlem.* Boston: Beacon Press.

Meier, D. (1998). Changing the odds. In E. Clinchy (Ed.), *Creating new schools: How small schools are changing American education.* New York: Teachers College Press.

Meier, D. (2002). *In schools we trust: Creating communities of learning in an era of testing and standardization.* Boston: Beacon Press.

Melchior, A., (1997). *National evaluation of Learn and Serve America School and Community Based Programs: Interim report.* Waltham, MA: Brandeis University, Center for Human Resources.

Melnick, S.A., Shibles, M.R., Gable, R.K., and Grzymkowski, V. (1986). *A comparative study of the relationships between school district size and selected indicators of educational quality.* (Rep. No. ED305215). Hartford: Connecticut Association of School Administrators, Small/Rural Schools Committee.

MetLife. (1987). *The American teacher, 1987: Strengthening links between home and school.* New York: Louis Harris and Associates.

MetLife. (2001). *The MetLife Survey of the American teacher 2001: Key elements of quality schools.* New York: Author.

MetLife. (2002). *The MetLife Survey of the American teacher 2002.* New York: Author.

Mickelson, R. (1990). The attitude-achievement paradox among black adolescents. *Sociology of Education, 63,* 44-61.

Miserandino, M. (1996). Children who do well in school: Individual differences in perceived competence and autonomy in above-average children. *Journal of Educational Psychology, 88,* 203-214.

Mitchell, M. (1993). Situational interest: Its multifaceted structure in the secondary school mathematics classroom. *Journal of Educational Psychology, 85,* 424-436.

Mizell, L. (2002). Horace had it right: The stakes are still high for students of color. In T. Johnson, J.E. Boyden, and W.J. Pittz (Eds.), *Racial profiling and punishing in U.S. public schools: How zero tolerance policies and high stakes testing subvert academic excellence and racial equity* (pp. 27-38). Oakland, CA: Applied Research Center.

Moll, L., Estrada, E., Diaz, E., and Lopes, L.M. (1980). The organization of bilingual lessons: Implications for schooling. *The Quarterly Newsletter of the Laboratory of Comparative Human Cognition, 2*(3), 53-58.

Moll, L., and Greenberg, J.B. (1990). Creating zones of possibilities: Combining social contexts for instruction. In L. Moll (Ed.), *Vygotsky and education: Instructional implications and applications of sociohistorical psychology* (pp. 319-348). New York: Cambridge University Press.

Molnar, A. (2002). *Introduction and executive summary.* (Rep. No. EPSL-0201-101-EPRU). Tempe: Arizona State University, Education Policy Research Unit.

Moore, D., Bean, T., Birdyshaw, D., and Rycik, J. (1999). *Adolescent literacy: A position statement for the Commission on Adolescent Literacy of the International Reading Association.* Newark, DE: International Reading Association.

Moore, M.T., Strang, E.W., Schwartz, M., and Braddock, M. (1988). *Patterns in special education service delivery and cost.* Washington, DC: Decision Resource.

Morgan, S.L., and Sorensen, A.B. (1999). Parental networks, social closure, and mathematics learning: A test of Coleman's social capital explanation of school effects. *American Sociological Review, 64*, 661-681.

Morris, V.G., and Taylor, S.I. (1998). Alleviating barriers to family involvement in education: The role of teacher evaluation. *Teacher and Teacher Education, 14*(2), 219-231.

Morrow, K., and Styles, M. (1995). *Building relationships with youth in program settings: A study of Big Brothers/Big Sisters*. Philadelphia: Public/Private Ventures.

Moschkovich, J. (1999). Supporting the participation of English language learners in mathematical discussions. *For the Learning of Mathematics, 19*, 11-19.

Moses, R.P., and Cobb, C.E. (2001). *Radical equations: Mathematics literacy and civil rights*. Boston: Beacon Press.

Moses, R.P., Kamii, M., Swap, S.M., and Howard, J. (1989). The Algebra project: Organizing in the spirit of Ella. *Harvard Educational Review, 59*, 423-443.

Mullis, I.V.S., Jenkins, F., and Johnson, E.G. (1994). *Effective schools in mathematics: Perspectives from the NAEP 1992 Assessment.* (NCES Report No. 23-RR-01.) Washington, DC: U.S. Department of Education.

Murdock, T. (1999). The social context of risk: Status and motivational predictors of alienation in middle school. *Journal of Educational Psychology, 91*, 62-75.

Murnane, R.J., and Levy, F. (1996a). The first principle: Agree on the problem. In F. Murnane and R. Levy (Eds.), *Teaching the new basic skills: Principles of educating children to thrive in a changing economy*. New York: Free Press.

Murnane, R.J., and Levy, F. (1996b). *Teaching the new basic skills: Principles for educating children to thrive in a changing economy*. New York: Free Press.

Murnane, R.J., Willett, J., and Boudett, K.P. (1995). Do high school dropouts benefit from obtaining a GED? *Educational Evaluation and Policy Analysis, 17*(2), 133-148.

Murrell, P.C. (1999). Responsive teaching for African American male adolescents. In V.C. Polite and J.E. Davis (Eds.), *African American males in school and society: Practices and policies for effective education*. New York: Teachers College Press.

Nabors, L.A., Weist, M.D., Reynolds, M.W., Tashman, N.A., and Jackson, C.Y. (1999). Adolescent satisfaction with school-based mental health services. *Journal of Child and Family Studies, 8*(2), 229-236.

National Advisory Mental Health Council. (1990). *National plan for research on child adolescent mental disorders.* (Rep. No. NIMH 90-163). Rockville, MD: National Institute of Mental Health.

National Association of Secondary School Principals. (1996). *Breaking ranks: Changing and American Institution*. Reston, VA: Author.

National Association of Secondary School Principals. (2002). *What the research shows: Breaking ranks in education*. Reston, VA: Author.

National Center for Education Statistics. (1982). *High school and beyond 1980 sophomore cohort first follow-up: Data user's manual.* Washington, DC: U.S. Department of Education.

National Center for Education Statistics (1998a) *Common core of data: Overview of public elementary and secondary schools and districts, school year 1996-97*. Washington, DC: U.S. Department of Education.

National Center for Education Statistics. (1998b). *Pursuing excellence: A study of U.S. twelfth-grade mathematics and science achievement in international context.* (Rep. No. NCES 98-049). Washington, DC: U.S. Government Printing Office.

National Center for Education Statistics. (1999a). *Highlights from TIMMS: Overview and key findings across grade levels*. Washington, DC: U.S. Department of Education.

National Center for Education Statistics. (1999b) *National Assessment of Educational Progress* Available: http://www.nces.ed.gov/nationsreportcard/tables/Ltt1999/ [March 20, 2003].

National Center for Education Statistics. (1999c). *Teacher quality: A report on the preparation and qualifications of public school teachers.* Washington, DC: U.S. Department of Education.

National Center for Education Statistics. (2000a). *Digest of education statistics: 2000.* Washington, DC: U.S. Department of Education.

National Center for Education Statistics. (2000b). *Dropout rates in the United States: 1999.* Washington, DC: U.S. Government Printing Office.

National Center for Education Statistics. (2000c). *Teacher quality: A report on the qualifications of public school teachers.* (Rep. No. NCES 1999-080). Washington, DC: U.S. Department of Education.

National Center for Education Statistics. (2001a). *Nation's report card: Mathematics 2000.* (Rep. No. NCES 2001518). Washington, DC: U.S. Department of Education

National Center for Education Statistics. (2001b). *The condition of education.* (Rep. No. NCES 2001-072). Washington, DC: U.S. Department of Education.

National Center for Education Statistics. (2002). *The condition of education.* (Rep. No. NCES 2002-025). Washington, DC: U.S. Department of Education.

National Commission on Mathematics and Science Teaching for the 21st Century. (2000). *Before it's too late: A report to the nation.* Washington, DC: U.S. Department of Education. Available: http://www.ed.gov.americacounts/glenn/toc.html [August, 2002].

National Commission on Teaching and America's Future. (1996). *What matters most: Teaching for America's future.* New York: Author.

National Commission on Youth. (1980). *The transition of youth to adulthood: A bridge too far?* Boulder: Westview Press.

National Council of Teachers of Mathematics. (2000). *Principles and standards for teaching mathematics.* Reston, VA: Author.

National Panel on High School and Adolescent Education. (1976). *The education of adolescents.* Washington, DC: U.S. Department of Health, Education, and Welfare.

National Reading Panel. (2000). *Teaching children to read: An evidence based assessment of the scientific research literature and its implications for reading instruction.* (Rep. No. 00-4769). Washington, DC: U.S. Government Printing Office.

National Research Council. (1990). Social consequences of growing up in a poor neighborhood. In L.E. Lynn and M.G.H. McGeary (Eds.), Committee on National Urban Policy, Commission on Behavioral and Social Sciences and Education, *Inner-city poverty in the United States* (pp. 111-186). Washington, DC: National Academy Press

National Research Council. (1996). Signaling, incentives, and school organization in France, the Netherlands, Britain, and the United States. In E.A. Hanushek and D.W. Jorgenson (Eds.), Board on Science, Technology, and Economic Policy, *Improving America's schools: The role of incentives* (pp. 111-145). Washington, DC: National Academy Press.

National Research Council. (1999). How children learn. In J.D. Bransford, A.L. Brown, and R.R. Cocking (Eds.), Committee on Developments in the Science of Learning, Committee on Learning Research and Educational Practice, Commission on Behavioral and Social Sciences and Education, *How people learn: Brain, mind, experience, and school* (pp. 67-101). Washington, DC: National Academy Press.

National Research Council. (2000). *How people learn: Brain, mind, experience, and school, Expanded edition*. J.D. Bransford, A.L. Brown, and R.R. Cocking (Eds.), Committee on Developments in the Science of Learning, Committee on Learning Research and Educational Practice, Commission on Behavioral and Social Sciences and Education. Washington, DC: National Academy Press.

National Research Council. (2001). *Adding it up: Helping children learn mathematics*. Mathematics Learning Study Committee, J. Kilpatrick, J. Swafford, and B. Findell (Eds.), Center for Education, Division of Behavioral and Social Sciences and Education. Washington, DC: National Academy Press.

National Research Council. (2002a). *Achieving high educational standards for all.* Division of Behavioral and Social Sciences and Education, T. Ready, C. Edley, and C. Snow (Eds.). Washington, DC: National Academy Press.

National Research Council. (2002b). *Scientific research in education.* Committee on Scientific Principles for Education Research, R.J. Shavelson, and L. Towne (Eds.), Center for Education, Division of Behavioral and Social Sciences and Education. Washington, DC: National Academy Press.

National Research Council (2002c). Trends in the educational achievement of minority students since *Brown v. Board of Education.* In T. Ready, C. Edley, and C. Snow (Eds.), Division of Behavioral and Social Sciences and Education, *Achieving high educational standards for all: Conference summary.* Washington, DC: National Academy Press.

National Research Council. (2002d). Why racial integration and other policies since *Brown v. Board of Education* have only partially succeeded in narrowing the achievement gap. In T. Ready, C. Edley, and C. Snow (Eds.), Division of Behavioral and Social Sciences and Education, *Achieving high educational standards for all: Conference summary* (pp. 183-217). Washington, DC: National Academy Press.

National Research Council and Institute of Medicine. (2002). *Community programs to promote youth development.* Committee on Community Level Programs to Promote Youth Development. J.S. Eccles, and J. Gootman (Eds.), Board on Children, Youth, and Families, Division of Behavioral and Social Sciences and Education, Washington, DC: National Academy Press.

National Youth Employment Coalition. (1999). *Policy framework of the National Youth Employment Coalition. Policy and Legislation Committee.* Washington, DC: Author.

Neild, R.C., and Balfanz, R. (2001). *An extreme degree of difficulty: The educational demographics of the ninth grade in Philadelphia.* Baltimore: The Johns Hopkins University Center for Social Organization of Schools.

Nelson, F.H. (2000). *Trends in student achievement for Edison Schools, Inc.: The emerging track record.* Washington, DC: American Federation of Teachers.

New York City Board of Education, Division of Assessment and Accountability. (2001). *An examination of the relationship between higher standards and students dropping out.* New York: New York City Department of Education.

New York State Senate Democratic Task Force on Criminal Justice Reform. (2000). *Criminal justice reform: A time that's come.* Albany, NY: Author.

Newcomb, A.F., and Bagwell, C.L. (1995). Children's friendship relations: A meta-analytic review. *Psychological Bulletin, 117,* 306-347.

Newman, R., and Goldin, L. (1990). Children's reluctance to seek help with school work. *Journal of Educational Psychology, 82,* 92-100.

Newmann, F. (1992). *Student engagement and achievement in American secondary schools.* New York: Teachers College Press.

Newmann, F., Smith, B., Allensworth, E., and Bryk, A. (2001). Instructional program coherence: What it is and why it should guide school improvement policy. *Educational Evaluation and Policy Analysis, 23,* 297-321.

Newmann, F.M. (1992). Introduction. In F.M. Newmann (Ed.), *Student engagement and achievement in American secondary schools.* New York: Teachers College Press.

Newmann, F.M., and Oliver, D.W. (1967). Education and community. *Harvard Educational Review, 37,* 61-106.

Newmann, F.M., Wehlage, G., and Lamborn, S.D. (1992). The significance and sources of student engagement. In F.M. Newmann (Ed.), *Student engagement and achievement in American secondary schools* (pp. 11-39). New York: Teachers College Press.

Nicholls, J. (1983). Conception of ability and achievement motivation: A theory and its implications for education. In S. Paris, G. Olson, and H. Stevenson (Eds.), *Learning and motivation in the classroom* (pp. 211-237). Hillsdale, NJ: Lawrence Erlbaum.

Nieto, S. (1992). *Affirming diversity: The sociopolitical context of multicultural education.* New York: Longman.

Nieto, S. (2000). *Puerto Rican students in U.S. schools.* Mahwah, NJ: Lawrence Erlbaum.

Noddings, N. (1988). An ethic of caring and its implications for instructional arrangements. *American Journal of Education, 96*(2), 215-231.

Nolen-Hoeksema, S., Girgus, J.S., and Seligman, M.E.P. (1986). Learned helplessness in children: A longitudinal study of depression, achievement, and explanatory style. *Journal of Personality and Social Psychology, 51,* 435-442.

Nystrand, M. (1997). *Opening dialogue: Understanding the dynamics of language and learning in the English classroom.* New York: Teachers College Press.

Nystrand, M., and Gamoran, A. (1991). Student engagement: When recitation becomes conversation. In H.C. Waxman and H. Walberg (Eds.), *Effective teaching: Current research* (pp. 257-276). Berkeley, CA: McCutchan.

Nystrand, M., and Gamoran, A. (1992). Instructional discourse and student engagement. In D.H. Schunk and J. Meece (Eds.), *Student perceptions in the classroom* (pp. 149-179). Hillsdale: NJ: Lawrence Erlbaum.

Nystrand, M., and Gamoran, A. (1997). The big picture: The language of learning in dozens of English lessons. In M. Nystrand (Ed.), *Opening dialogue: Understanding the dynamics of language and learning in the English classroom.* New York: Teachers College Press.

O'Brien, D., Stewart, R., and Moje, E. B. (1995). Why content literacy is difficult to infuse into the secondary school: Complexities of curriculum, pedagogy, and school culture. *Reading Research Quarterly, 30,* 442-463.

O'Brien, S.F., and Bierman, K.L. (1988). Conceptions and perceived influence of peer groups: Interviews with preadolescents and adolescents. *Child Development, 59,* 1360-1365.

Oakes, J. (1985). *Keeping track: How schools structure inequality.* New Haven, CT: Yale University Press.

Oakes, J. (1990). *Multiplying inequalities: The effects of race, social class, and tracking on opportunities to learn math and science.* Santa Monica, CA: RAND.

Oakes, J., Gamoran, A., and Page, R. (1992). Curriculum differentiation: Opportunities, outcomes, and meanings. In P. Jackson (Ed.), *Handbook of research on curriculum* (pp. 570-608). New York: MacMillan.

Office for Civil Rights. (2000). *1997 elementary and secondary school civil rights compliance report.* Washington, DC: U.S. Department of Education.

Office of Technology Assessment. (1991). *Adolescent health.* Washington, DC: U.S. Government Printing Office.

Ogbu, J. (1992). Understanding cultural diversity and learning. *Educational Researcher, 21,* 5-14.

Ogbu, J. (1997). Understanding the school performance of urban blacks: Some essential background knowledge. In H. Walberg, R. Reyes, and R. Weissberg (Eds.), *Children and youth: Interdisciplinary perspectives.* Thousand Oaks, CA: Sage.

Ogbu, J.U. (1989). The individual in collective adaptation: A framework for focusing on academic underperformance and dropping out among involuntary minorities. In L. Weis, E. Farrar, and H.G. Petrie (Eds.), *Dropouts from school: Issues, dilemmas, and solutions* (pp. 181-204). Albany: State University of New York Press.

Oldfather, P., and Dahl, K. (1995). *Toward a social constructivist reconceptualization of intrinsic motivation for literacy of the International Reading Association*. Athens, GA: University of Georgia, National Reading Research Center.

Oldfather, P., and McLaughlin, H.J. (1993). Gaining and losing voice: A longitudinal study of students' continuing impulse to learn across elementary and middle level contexts. *Research in Middle Education, 17*(1), 1-25.

Oldfather, P., and Thomas, S. (1998). What does it mean when high school teachers participate in collaborative research with students on literacy motivations? *Teachers College Record, 99*, 647-691.

Olshavsky, J.E. (1976-1977). Reading as problem solving: An investigation of strategies. *Reading Research Quarterly, 12*(4), 654-674.

Orfield, G. (1999). Strengthening Title I: Designing a policy based on evidence. In G. Orfield (Ed.), *Hard work for good schools: Facts not fads in Title I Reform*. Cambridge, MA: Harvard University, Civil Rights Project.

Orfield, G. (2002). *Schools more separate: Consequences of a decade of resegregation*. Cambridge, MA: Harvard University, Civil Rights Project.

Orland, M.E. (1990). Demographics of disadvantage: Intensity of childhood poverty and its relationship to educational achievement. In J. Goodlad and P. Keating (Eds.), *Access to knowledge: An agenda for our nation's schools* (pp. 43-58). New York: College Entrance Examination Board.

Osborne, J. (1995). Academics, self-esteem, and race: A look at the underlying assumptions of the disidentification hypothesis. *Personality and Social Psychology Bulletin, 21*, 449-455.

Osborne, J. (1997). Race and academic disidentification. *Journal of Educational Psychology, 89*, 728-735.

Padilla, F. (1992). *The gang as an American enterprise*. New Brunswick, NJ: Rutgers University Press.

Pajares, F. (1996). Self-efficacy beliefs in academic settings. *Review of Educational Research, 66*, 543-578.

Panel on Youth of the President's Science Advisory Committee. (1974). *Youth: Transition to adulthood*. Chicago: University of Chicago Press.

Parker, J.G., and Asher, S.R. (1987). Peer relations and later personal adjustment: Are low-accepted children at risk? *Psychological Bulletin, 102*, 357-389.

Parker, J.G., Rubin, K., Price, J., DeRosier, M (1995). Peer relationships, child development, and adjustment: A developmental psychopathology perspective. In D. Cicchetti and D. Cohen (Eds.), *Developmental psychopathology, volume 2: Risk, disorder, and adaptation* (pp. 96-161). New York: Wiley.

Parrish, R., Hikido, C., and Fowler, W. (1998). *Inequalities in public school district revenues*. (Rep. No. NCES 98-210). Washington, DC: U.S. Department of Education.

Paulos, J.A. (1990). *Innumeracy*. New York: Vintage.

Paulos, J.A. (1995). *A mathematician reads the newspaper*. New York: Doubleday.

Pearson, G., Jennings, J., and Norcross, J. (1998). *A program of comprehensive school-based mental health services in a large urban public school district: The Dallas model*. Presented at the American Society for Adolescent Psychiatry's Annual Meeting, San Diego, CA

Pearson, P.D., and Dole, J. (1987). Explicit comprehension instruction: A review of research and a new conceptualization of instruction. *Elementary School Journal, 88*(2), 151-165.

Pearson, S.S. (2002). *Finding common ground: Service learning and education reform.* Washington, DC: American Youth Policy Forum.

Pedraza, R.A., Pauly, E., and Kopp, H. (1997). *Home-grown progress: The evolution of innovative school-to-work programs.* New York: Manpower Demonstration Research Corporation.

Perry, M., Teague, J., and Frey, S. (2002). *Expansion of out-of-school programs aims at improving student achievement.* Palo Alto: EdSource.

Phelan, P., Davidson, A., and Yu, H. (1998). *Adolescents' worlds: Negotiating family, peers, and school.* New York: Teachers College Press.

Philips, S. (1983). *The invisible culture: Communication in classroom and community on the Warm Springs Indian Reservation.* New York: Longman.

Phillips, M. (1997). What makes schools effective? A comparison of the relationships of communitarian climate and academic climate to mathematics achievement and attendance during middle school. *American Educational Research Journal, 34*(4), 633-662.

Phillips, M., Crouse, J., and Ralph, J. (1998). Does the black-white test score gap widen after children enter school? In C. Jencks, and M. Phillips (Eds.), *The black-white test score gap* (pp. 229-272). Washington, DC: Brookings Institution Press.

Pierson, L., and Connell, J. (1992). Effect of grade retention on self-system processes, school engagement, and academic performance. *Journal of Educational Psychology, 84*, 300-307.

Pillar, C. (1992). Separate realities: The creation of the technological underclass in America's public schools. *MacWorld*, September, 218-230.

Pintrich, P., and Schunk, D. (1996). *Motivation in education: Theory, research, and applications.* Englewood Cliffs, NJ: Merrill.

Pittman, T., Emery, J., and Boggiano, A. (1982). Intrinsic and extrinsic motivational orientations: Reward-induced changes in preference for complexity. *Journal of Personality and Social Psychology, 42*, 789-797.

Plank, S. (2001). *Career and technical education in the balance: An analysis of high school persistence, academic achievement, and post secondary destinations.* Minneapolis: National Research Center for Career and Technical Education.

Poe-Yamagata, E., and Jones, S. (2000). *And justice for some.* Washington, DC: Youth Law Center, Building Blocks for Youth Report.

Pope, D.C. (2000). *Caught in the grade trap: What students say about doing school.* (ERIC No. RIEFEB2001). New Orleans, LA: ERIC.

Powell, A., Farrar, E., and Cohen, D. (1985). *The shopping mall of high school.* Boston, MA: Houghton-Mifflin.

Pressley, M. (2000). What should comprehension instruction be the instruction of? In M.L. Kamil, P.B. Mosenthal, P.D. Pearson, and R. Barr (Eds.), *Handbook of reading research, volume III* (pp. 545-562). Mahwah, NJ: Lawrence Erlbaum.

Public Agenda. (1997). *Getting by: What American teenagers really think about their schools.* New York: Author.

Puma, M., Karweit, N., Price, C., Ricciuti, A., Thompson, W., and Vaden-Kiernan, M. (1997). *Prospects: Student outcomes final report.* Washington, DC: U.S. Department of Education.

Rabinowitz, P. (1987). *Before reading: Narrative conventions and the politics of interpretation.* Ithaca, NY: Cornell University Press.

RAND Mathematics Study Panel. (2002). *Mathematical proficiency for all students: Toward a strategic research and development program in mathematics education.* (Rep. No. MR-1643.0-OERI). Santa Monica, CA: Author.

Raywid, M.A. (1998). Small schools: A reform that works. *Educational Leadership, 55*, 34-39.

Reay, D., and Ball, S.J. (1997). "Spoilt for choice": The working classes and educational markets. *Oxford Review of Education, 23*(1), 89-101.

Rebell, M. (2002). Education adequacy, democracy and the courts. In T. Ready, C. Edley Jr., and C. Snow (Eds.), Division of Behavioral and Social Sciences and Education, *Achieving high education standards for all* (pp. 218-270). Washington, DC: National Academy Press.

Rich, D., Van Dien, J., and Maddox, B. (1979). Families as educators for their own children. In R. Brandt (Ed.), *Partners: Parents and schools* (pp. 26-40). Alexandria, VA: Association for Supervision and Curriculum Development.

Riehl, C. (1999). Labeling and letting go: An organizational analysis of how high school students are discharged as dropouts. In A.M. Pallas (Ed.), *Research in sociology of education and socialization* (pp. 231-268). New York: JAI Press.

Robinson-Lewis, G. (1991). *Summarative evaluation of the School-Within-A-School (SWAS) Program.* (Rep. No. ED346203). Kansas City, MO: Kansas City School District.

Rock, D.A., and Pollack, J.M. (1995). *Psychometric report for the NELS:88 base year through second follow-up.* (Rep. No. NCES 95-382). Washington, DC: U.S. Department of Education.

Roderick, M. (1994). Grade retention and school dropout: Investigating the association. *American Educational Research Journal, 31*(4), 729-759.

Roderick, M., and Camburn, E. (1999). Risk and recovery from course failure in the early years of high school. *American Educational Research Journal, 36*(2), 303-343.

Roderick, M., and Engel, M. (2001). The grasshopper and the ant: Motivational responses of low-achieving students to high-stakes testing. *Educational Evaluation and Policy Analysis, 23*(3), 197-227.

Roderick, M., Nagaoka, J., Bacon, J., and Easton, J.Q. (2000). *Update: Ending social promotion: Passing, retention, and achievement trends among promoted and retained students.* Chicago: Consortium on Chicago School Research.

Roehler, L., and Duffy, G. (1991). Teachers' instructional actions. In R. Barr, M. Kamil, P. Mosenthal, and P.D. Pearson (Eds.), *Handbook of reading research, volume II* (pp. 861-884). New York: Longman.

Roeser, R., Eccles, J., and Sameroff, A. (1998). Academic and emotional functioning in early adolescence. *Development and Psychology, 10*, 321-352.

Roeser, R.W., Eccles, J., and Strobel, K. (1998). Linking the study of schooling and mental health: Selected issues and empirical illustrations at the level of the individual. *Educational Psychologist, 33*(4), 153-176.

Roeser, R.W., and Eccles, J.S. (1998). Adolescents' perceptions of middle school: Relation to longitudinal changes in academic and psychological adjustment. *Journal of Research on Adolescence, 8*, 123-158.

Roeser, R.W., van der Wolf, K., and Strobel, K. (2001). On the relation between social-emotional and school functioning during early adolescence: Preliminary findings from Dutch and American samples. *Journal of School Psychology, 30*(2), 111-139.

Rogoff, B. (1990). *Apprenticeship in thinking: Cognitive development in social context.* New York: Oxford University Press.

Romaine, B., McKenna, M., and Robinson, R. (1996). Reading coursework requirements for middle and high school content area teachers: A U.S. survey. *Journal of Adolescent and Adult Literacy, 40,* 194-198.

Romo, H.D., and Falbo, T. (1996). *Latino high school graduation: Defying the odds.* Austin, TX: University of Texas Press.

Rosenbaum, J. (2001). *Beyond college for all: Career paths for the forgotten half.* New York: Sage.

Rosenfeld, L.B., Richman, J.M., and Bowen, G.L. (2000). Social support networks and school outcomes: The centrality of the teacher. *Child and Adolescent Social Work Journal, 17*(3), 205-225.

Roza, M., and Miles, K. (2002). *Moving toward equity in school funding within districts.* Providence, RI: Annenberg Institute for School Reform.

Rumberger, R.W. (1995). Dropping out of middle school: A multilevel analysis of students and schools. *American Educational Research Journal, 32,* 583-625.

Rumberger, R.W., and Larson, K.A. (1998). Student mobility and the increased risk of high school dropout. *American Journal of Education, 107,* 1-35.

Rumberger, R.W., and Palardy, G.J. (2001). *Does segregation matter? The impact of student composition on academic achievement in high school.* Paper presented at the annual meeting of the American Educational Research Association, Seattle, April 10-14.

Rumberger, R.W., and Palardy, G.J. (2002). *Raising test scores and lowering dropout rates: Can schools do both?* Paper presented at the annual meeting of the American Educational Research Association, New Orleans, April 1-5.

Rumberger, R.W., and Thomas, S.L. (2000). The distribution of dropout and turnover rates among urban and suburban high schools. *Sociology of Education, 73*(1), 39-67.

Rumberger, R.W., and Willms, J.D. (1992). The impact of racial and ethnic segregation on the achievement gap in California high schools. *Educational Evaluation and Policy Analysis, 14,* 377-396.

Rutter, M. (1985). Resilience in the face of adversity: Protective factors and resistance to psychiatric disorder. *British Journal of Psychiatry, 147,* 598-611.

Rutter, M., Maughan, B., Mortimore, P., Ouston, J., and Smith, A. (1979). *Fifteen thousand hours: Secondary schools and their effects on children.* Cambridge: Harvard University Press.

Ryan, A., and Pintrich, P. (1997). "Should I ask for help?" The role of motivation and attitudes in adolescents' help seeking in math class. *Journal of Educational Psychology, 89,* 329-341.

Ryan, R., Connell, J., and Grolnick, W. (1992). When achievement is not intrinsically motivated: A theory of internalization and self-regulation in school. In A. Boggiano and T. Pittman (Eds.), *Achievement and motivation: A social-developmental perspective* (pp. 167-188). Cambridge: Cambridge University Press.

Ryan, R., Connell, J., and Plant, R. (1990). Emotions in nondirected text learning. *Learning and Individual Differences, 2,* 1-17.

Ryan, R., and Deci, E. (2000a). Self-determination theory and the facilitation of intrinsic motivation, social development, and well-being. *American Psychologist, 55,* 68-78.

Ryan, R., and Deci, E. (2000b). When rewards compete with nature: The undermining of intrinsic motivation and self-regulation. In C. Sansone and J. Harachiewicz (Eds.), *Intrinsic and extrinsic motivation: The search for the optimal motivation and performance* (pp. 13-54). San Diego, CA: Academic Press.

Ryan, R., and La Guardia, J. (1999). Achievement motivation within a pressured society: Intrinsic and extrinsic motivations to learn and the politics of school reform. In T. Urdan (Ed.), *Advances in motivation and achievement, volume II* (pp. 45-85). Greenwich, CT: JAI Press.

Ryan, R.M., and La Guardia, J.G. (2000). What is being optimized over development? A self-determination theory perspective on basic psychological needs across the life span. In S. Qualls and N. Abeles, *Psychology and the aging revolution* (pp. 145-172). Washington, DC: APA Books.

Ryken, A.E. (2001). *Content, pedagogy, results: A thrice-told tale of integrating work-based and school-based learning.* Unpublished doctoral dissertation, School of Education, University of California, Berkeley.

Sanders, M.G. (1998). The effects of school, family, and community support on the academic achievement of African American adolescents. *Urban Education, 33*(3), 385-409.

Schellenberg, S. (1999). Concentration of poverty and the ongoing need for Title I. In G. Orfield and E.H. DeBray (Eds.), *Hard work for good schools: Fact not fads in Title I Reform.* Cambridge, MA: Harvard University, The Civil Rights Project.

Schneider, B., and Stevenson, D. (1999). *The ambitious generation: America's teenagers, motivated but directionless.* New Haven : Yale University Press.

Schoenbach, R., Greenleaf, C., Cziko, C., and Hurwitz, L. (1999). *Reading for understanding.* San Francisco: Jossey-Bass.

Schunk, D. (1995). Self-efficacy and education and instruction. In J. Maddux (Ed.), *Self-efficacy, adaption, and adjustment: Theory, research, and application* (pp. 281-303). New York: Plenum Press.

Schwartz, A. (1999). *School districts and spending in the schools.* (Rep. No. NCES 1999-334). Washington, DC: U.S. Department of Education.

Scott-Jones, D. (1987). Mother-as-teacher in the families of high-and-low income black first graders. *Journal of Negro Education, 56,* 21-34.

Sebring, P., Bryk, A.S., Roderick, M., Camburn, E., Luppescu, S., Thum, Y.M., Smith, B., and Kahne, J. (1996). *Charting reform in Chicago: The students speak.* Chicago: Consortium on Chicago School Research.

Secada, W.G. (1996). Urban students acquiring English and learning mathematics in the context of reform. *Urban Education, 30*(4), 422-448.

Sedlak, M.W., Wheeler, C.W., Pullin, D.C., and Cusick, P.A. (1986). *Selling students short: Classroom bargains and academic reform in the American high school.* New York: Teachers College Press.

Sheldon, K.M., and Biddle, B.J. (1998). Standards, accountability, and school reform: Perils and pitfalls. *Teachers College Record, 100,* 164-180.

Sheppard, L.A., and Smith, M.L. (1989). *Flunking grades: Research and policies on retention.* New York: Falmer Press.

Shirley, D. (1997). *Community organizing for urban school reform.* Austin, TX: University of Texas Press.

Shouse, R.D. (1996a). Academic press and sense of community: Conflict and congruence in American high schools. In A.M. Pallas (Ed.), *Research in sociology of education and socialization, volume II* (pp. 173-202). Greenwich, CT: JAI Press.

Shouse, R. (1996b). Academic press and sense of community: Conflict, congruence, and implications for student achievement. *Social Psychology of Education, 1,* 47-68.

Shouse, R.D. (1997). Academic press, sense of community, and student achievement. In J.S. Coleman, B. Schneider, S. Plank, K.S. Schiller, R. Shouse, and H. Wang, *Redesigning American education* (pp. 60-86). Boulder, CO: Westview Press.

Shujaa, M. (1994) *Too much schooling, too little education: A paradox of black life in white societies.* Trenton, NJ: Africa World Press.

Silver, E.A., and Lane, S. (1995). Can instructional reform in urban middle schools help students narrow the mathematics performance gap? Some evidence from the QUASAR project. *Research in Middle Level Education, 18*(2), 49-70.

Silver, E.A., Smith, M.S., and Nelson, B.S. (1995). The QUASAR project: Equity concerns meet mathematics education reform in the middle school. In W.G. Secada, E. Fennema, and E. Adajian (Eds.), *New directions for equity in mathematics education* (pp. 9-56). Cambridge: Cambridge University Press.

Siskin, L.S. (1994). *Realms of knowledge: Academic departments in secondary schools.* London: Falmer Press.

Sizemore, B. (1985). Pitfalls and promises of effective schools research. *Journal of Negro Education, 54,* 269-288.

Sizemore, B. (1995). *Ten routines for high achievement.* Chicago: DePaul University, School Achievement Structure.

Sizer, T. (1984). *Horace's compromise: The dilemma of the American high school.* Boston: Houghton-Mifflin.

Skiba, R., and Peterson, R. (1999). The dark side of zero tolerance: Can punishment lead to safe schools? *Phi Delta Kappan, 80,* 372-376, 381-382.

Skiba, R.J., Peterson, R.L., and Williams, T. (1997). Office referrals and suspension: Disciplinary intervention in middle schools. *Education and Treatment of Children, 20*(3), 295-315.

Skinner, E., and Belmont, M. (1993). Motivation in the classroom: Reciprocal effects of teacher behavior and student engagement across the school year. *Journal of Educational Psychology, 85,* 571-581.

Skinner, E., Wellborn, J., and Connell, J. (1990). What it takes to do well in school and whether I've got it: The role of perceived control in children's engagement and school achievement. *Journal of Educational Psychology, 82,* 22-32.

Skinner, E., Zimmer-Gembeck, M., and Connell, J. (1998). Individual differences and the development of perceived control. *Monographs of the Society in Child Development, 63*(2-3), 1-220.

Skinner, R., and Chapman, C. (1999). *Service learning and community service in K-12 public schools.* Washington, DC: U.S. Department of Education.

Smerdon, B. (1999). Engagement and achievement: Differences between African American and white high school students. *Sociology of Education and Socialization, 12,* 103-134.

Smith, M., and Hillocks, G. (1988). Sensible sequencing: Developing knowledge about literature text by text. *English Journal*, October, 44-49.

Snow, C. (2002). *Reading for understanding: Toward an R and D program in reading comprehension.* Arlington, VA: RAND.

Snow, M., and Brinton, D. (1988). The adjunct model of language instruction: An ideal EAP framework. In S. Benesch (Ed.), *Ending remediation: Linking ESL and content in higher education* (pp. 33-52). Washington, DC: Teachers of English to Speakers of Other Languages.

Somerton, W.H., Smith, M.P., Finnell, R., and Fuller, T.W. (1994). *The MESA way: A success story of nurturing minorities for math/science careers.* San Francisco: Caddo Gap Press.

Spencer, M. (1999) Social and cultural influences on school adjustment: The application of an identity-focused cultural ecological perspective. *Educational Psychologist, 34*(1), 43-57.

Spencer, M.B. (1991). Identity, minority development of. In R.M. Lerner, A.C. Peterson, and J. Brooks-Gunn (Eds.), *Encyclopedia of adolescence* (pp. 525-528). New York: Garland.

Spencer, M.B. (1995). Old issues and new theorizing about African-American youth: A phenomenological variant of ecological systems theory. In R.L. Taylor (Ed.), *Black youth: Perspectives on their status in the United States* (pp. 37-70). Westport, CT: Praeger.

Spencer, M.B., Cross, W.E., Harpalani, V., and Goss, T.N. (in press). Historical and developmental perspectives on Black academic achievement: Debunking the "acting white" myth and posing new directions for research. In C.C. Yeakey (Ed.), *Surmounting all odds: Education, opportunity, and society in the new millennium.* Greenwich, CT: Information Age.

Spencer, M.B., Dupree, D., and Hartmann, T. (1997). A phenomenological variant of ecological systems theory (PVEST): A self-organization perspective in context. *Development and Psychopathology, 9*(4), 817-833.

Spencer, M.B., and Harpalani, V. (2001). African American adolescents, research on. In R.M. Lerner and J.V. Lerner (Eds.), *Today's teenager: Adolescents in America* (pp. 30-32). Denver, CO: ABC-CLIO.

Spencer, M.B., Noll, E., Stoltzfus, J., and Harpalani, V. (2001). Identity and school adjustment: Revisiting the "acting white" assumption. *Educational Psychologist, 36*(1), 21-30.

Stake, R.E. (1995). The invalidity of standardized testing for measuring mathematics achievement. In T.A. Romberg (Ed.), *Reform in school mathematics and authentic assessment* (pp. 173-235). Albany: State University of New York Press.

Stasz, C., and Kaganoff, T. (1998). Work-based learning: Student perspectives on quality and links to school. *Educational Evaluation and Policy Analysis, 20*(1), 31-46.

Steele, C. (1992, April). Race and the schooling of black Americans. *Atlantic Monthly, 269*(4), 67-78.

Steele, C., and Aronson, J. (1995). Stereotype threat and the intellectual test performance of African Americans. *Journal of Personality and Social Psychology, 69*, 797-811.

Steele, C., and Aronson, J. (1998). Stereotype threat and the test performance of academically successful African Americans. In C. Jencks and M. Phillips (Eds.), *The black-white test score gap* (pp. 401-427). Washington, DC: Brookings Institution Press.

Steele, C.M. (1999). Thin ice. *Atlantic Monthly, 284*(2), 44-53.

Stein, M.K., Silver, E.A., and Smith, M.S. (1998). Mathematics reform and teacher development: A community of practice perspective. In J.G. Greeno and S.V. Goldman (Eds.), *Thinking practices in mathematics and science learning* (pp. 17-52). Mahwah, NJ: Lawrence Erlbaum.

Steinberg, L. (1997). Why school reform has failed. *Vassar Quarterly (Spring)*, 8-13.

Steinberg, L., Brown, B., and Dornbusch, S. (1996). *Beyond the classroom: Why school reform has failed and what parents need to do.* New York: Simon and Schuster.

Steinberg, L., Darling, N.E., Fletcher, A.C., in collaboration with Brown, B.B., and Dornbusch, S.M. (1995). Authoritative parenting and adolescent adjustment: An ecological journey. In P. Moen, G.H. Elder Jr., and K. Luscher (Eds.), *Examining lives in context: Perspectives on the ecology of human development* (pp. 426-466). Washington, DC: American Psychological Association.

Steinberg, L., Lamborn, S.D., Dornbusch, S.M., and Darling, N. (1992). Impact of parenting practices on adolescent achievement: Authoritative parenting, school involvement, and encouragement to succeed. *Child Development, 63*, 1266-1281.

Stern, D. (1989). How students used to work. In D. Stern and D. Eichorn (Eds.), *Adolescence and work: Influences of social structure, labor markets, and culture.* Hillsdale, NJ: Lawrence Erlbaum.

Stern, D. (1999). Improving pathways in the United States from high school to college and career. In *Preparing youth for the 21st century: The transition from education to the labour market.* Paris: Organisation for Economic Co-operation and Development.

Stern, D., Dayton, C., Paik, I., Weisberg, A., and Evans, J. (1988). Combining academic and vocational courses in an integrated program to reduce high school dropout rates: Second-year results from replications of the California Peninsula Academies. *Educational Evaluation and Policy Analysis, 10*, 161-170.

Stern, D., Dayton, C., and Raby, M. (2001). *Career academies: Building blocks for reconstructing American high schools.* Berkeley: University of California, Career Academy Support Network, School of Education.

Stern, D., Raby, M., and Dayton, C. (1992). *Career academies: Partnerships for reconstructing American high schools.* San Francisco: Jossey-Bass.

Stevenson, D.L., and Baker, D.P. (1987). The family-school relation and the child's school performance. *Child Development, 58*, 1348-1357.

Stevenson, H., and Stigler, J. (1992). *The learning gap.* New York: Summit Books.

Stigler, J., and Hiebert, J. (1999). *The teaching gap: Best ideas from the world's teachers for improving education in the classroom.* New York: Free Press.

Stipek, D. (2002). *Motivation to learn: Integrating theory and practice 4th edition.* Boston: Allyn and Bacon.

Stipek, D., and MacIver, D. (1989). Developmental change in children's assessment of intellectual competence. *Child Development, 60,* 521-538.

Stodolsky, S., and Grossman, P.L. (2000). Changing students, changing teaching. *Teachers College Record, 102*(1), 125-172.

Stringfield, S., Millsap, M.A., Herman, R.Y.N., Brigham, N., Nesselrodt, P., Schaffer, E., Karweit, N., Levin, M., Stevens, R., with Gamse, B., Puma, M., Rosenblum, S., Beaumont, J., Randall, B., and Smith, L. (1997). *Urban and suburban/rural special strategies for educating disadvantaged children.* Washington, DC: U.S. Department of Education.

Sue, D.W., and Sue, D. (1990). *Counseling the culturally different.* New York: Wiley.

Sui-Chu, E.H., and Willms, J.D. (1996). Effects of parental involvement on eighth-grade achievement. *Sociology of Education, 69,* 126-141.

Supovitz, J.A., and Poglinco, S.M. (2001). *Instructional leadership in a standards-based reform.* Philadelphia: Consortium for Policy Research in Education.

Swanson, C.B., and Schneider, B. (1999). Students on the move: Residential and educational mobility in America's schools. *Sociology of Education, 72,* 54-67.

Talbert, J. (1995). Boundaries of teachers' professional communities in U.S. high schools: Power and precariousness of the subject department. In L.S. Siskin and J.W. Little (Eds.), *The subjects in question* (pp. 68-94). New York: Teachers College Press.

Talbert, J., and Ennis, M. (1990). *Teacher tracking: Exacerbating inequalities in the high school.* Stanford, CA. Center for Research on the Context of Secondary School Teaching.

Talbert, J. and McLaughlin, M.W. (1994). Teacher professionalism in local school contexts, *American Journal of Education, 102*(2), 123-153.

Tang, S., and Hall, V. (1995). The over justification effect: A meta-analysis. *Applied Cognitive Psychology, 9,* 365-404.

Tate, W.F. (1995). Returning to the root: A culturally relevant approach to mathematics pedagogy. *Theory into Practice, 34,* 166-173.

Taylor, R., Casten, R., Flickinger, S., Roberts, D., and Fulmore, C. (1994). Explaining the school performance of African American adolescents. *Journal of Research on Adolescence, 4,* 21-44.

Tharp, R., and Gallimore, R. (1988). *Rousing minds to life: Teaching, learning, and schooling in social context.* New York: Cambridge University Press.

The Advancement Project and the Civil Rights Project. (2000). *Opportunities suspended: The devastating consequences of zero tolerance and school discipline.* Report from a National Summit on Zero Tolerance, June, Washington, DC.

The Kaiser Family Foundation. (1999) *Kids and media at the new millennium: A comprehensive national analysis of children's media use.* Available: http://www.kff.org/content/1999/1535/ChartPack.pdf [March, 2003].

Tierney, J., Grossman, J.B., and Resch, N. (2000). *Making a difference: An impact study of Big Brothers, Big Sisters.* Philadelphia: Public/Private Ventures.

Timpane, M., Abramowitz, S., Bobrow, S.B., and Pascal, A. (1976). *Youth policy in transition.* (Rep. No. R-2006-HEW). Santa Monica, CA: RAND.

Tinto, V. (1993). *Leaving college: Rethinking the causes and cures for student attrition, 2nd edition.* Chicago: University of Chicago Press.

Tocci, C.M., and Englehard, G. (1991). Achievement, parental support and gender differences in attitudes toward mathematics. *Journal of Educational Research, 84*(5), 280-286.

Treisman, U. (1990). A study of the mathematics performance of black students at the University of California, Berkeley. In H.B. Keynes, N.D. Fisher, and P.D. Wagreich (Eds.), *Mathematicians and education reform,* Proceedings of the July 6-8, 1988 Workshop, Issues in Mathematics Education, Conference Board of Mathematical Sciences (pp. 33-56). Providence, RI: American Mathematical Society, Mathematical Association of America.

Trusty, J. (1996). Counseling for dropout prevention: Applications from multicultural counseling. *Journal of Multicultural Counseling and Development, 24*(2), 105-117.

Tschannen-Moran, M., Hoy, A.W., and Hoy, W.K. (1998). Teacher efficacy: Its meaning and measure. *Review of Educational Research, 68,* 202-248.

Tsuzuki, M. (1995). Senior projects: Flexible opportunities for integration. In W.N. Grubb (Ed.), *Education through occupations in American high schools, volume I: Approaches to integrating academic and vocational education.* New York: Teachers College Press.

Turner, J., Thorpe, P., and Meyer, D. (1998). Students' reports of motivation and negative affect: A theoretical and empirical analysis. *Journal of Educational Psychology, 90,* 758-771.

Twenge, J.M., Catanese, K.R., and Baumeister, R.F. (2002). Social exclusion causes self-defeating behavior. *Journal of Personality and Social Psychology, 83*(3), 606-615.

Urquiola, M., Stern, D., Horn, I., Dornsife, B., Chi, B., Williams, L., Merritt, D., Hughes, K., Bailey, T. (1997). *School to work, college, and career: A review of policy, practice, and results* 1993-97. (MDS-1144). Berkeley: University of California, National Center for Research in Vocational Education.

U.S. Department of Education. (2000). *Promising results, continuing challenges: The final report of the National Assessment of Title I.* Washington, DC: Author.

U.S. Department of Education. (2002). *No child left behind.* Washington, D.C: Author. Available: http://www.nochildleftbehind.gov. [August 16, 2002].

U.S. General Accounting Office. (1993). *School linked human services: A comprehensive strategy for aiding students at risk of school failure.* Report to the Chairman, Committee on Labor and Human Resources. Washington, DC: Department of Health and Human Services.

Valdes, G. (1996). *Con respecto. Building the distances between culturally diverse families and schools.* New York: Teachers College Press.

Valdes, G. (2001). *Learning and not learning English: Latino students in American schools.* New York: Teachers College Press.

Valenzuela, A. (1999). *Subtractive schooling: U.S.-Mexican youth and the politics of caring.* Albany: State University of New York Press.

Verhoeven, L., and Snow, C. (2001). *Literacy and motivation: Reading engagement in individuals and groups.* Mahwah, NJ: Lawrence Erlbaum.

Villeneuve, J.C., and Grubb, W.N. (1996). *Indigenous school-to-work programs: Lessons from Cincinnati's co-op education.* Berkeley, CA: National Center for Research in Vocational Education.

Vygotsky, L. (1981). The genesis of higher mental functions. In J. Wertsch (Ed.), *The concept of activity in Soviet psychology.* Armonk, NY: Sharpe.

Wagner, M., and Shaver, D. (1989). *Educational programs and achievements of secondary education students: Findings from the National Longitudinal Transition Study.* Palo Alto, CA: Social Research Institute.

Walberg, H.J. (1989). District size and student learning. *Education and Urban Society, 21*(2), 154-163.

Walberg, H.J. (1992). On local control: Is bigger better? In J. Nathan and K. Febey (Eds.) *Source book on school and district size, cost, and quality* (pp. 118-134). Minneapolis: Minnesota University, Hubert H. Humphrey Institute of Public Affairs and Oak Brook, IL: North Central Regional Educational Laboratory.

Walberg, H.J., and Fowler, W. (1987). Expenditure and size efficiencies of public school districts. *Educational Researcher, 16*(7), 5-13.

Waller, W. (1932). *The sociology of teaching*. New York: Wiley.

Wang, M., Haertel, G., and Walberg, H. (1997). *What we know about coordinated school-linked services: Publication series no. 1*. Philadelphia: Mid-Atlantic Lab for Student Success, National Research Center on Education in the Inner Cities.

Wasley, P., Fine, M., Gladden, M., Holland, N., King, S., Mosak, E., and Powell, L. (2000). *Small schools, great strides: A study of new small schools in Chicago*. New York: Bank Streets College.

Wehlage, G., Rutter, R., Smith, G., Lesko, N., and Fernandez, R. (1989). *Reducing the risk: Schools as communities of support*. New York: The Falmer Press.

Wehlage, G., Smith, G., and Lipman, P. (1992). Restructuring urban schools: The New Futures Experience. *American Educational Research Journal, 29*, 51-93.

Wehlage, G.C., and Rutter, R.A., (1986) Dropping out: How much do schools contribute to the problem? *Teachers College Record, 87*(3), 374-392.

Weiler, D., LaGoy, A., Crane, E., and Rovner, A. (1998). *An evaluation of K-12 service learning in California*. Sacramento: California Department of Education, Youth Education Partnerships Office.

Weist, M.D. (1997). Expanded school mental health services: A national movement in progress. In T.H. Ollendick and R.J. Prinz (Eds.), *Advances in clinical child psychology, volume 19* (pp. 319-352). New York: Plenum Press.

Weist, M.D., Paskewitz, D.A., Warner, B.S., and Flaherty, L.T. (1996). Treatment outcome of school-based mental health services for urban teenagers. *Community Mental Health Journal, 32*, 149-157.

Wenger, E. (1998). *Communities of practice: Learning, meaning, and identity*. Cambridge, MA: Cambridge University Press.

Wenglinsky, H. (1998). *Does it compute: The relationship between education technology and student achievement in mathematics*. Princeton, NJ: Educational Testing Service, Policy Information Center.

Wentzel, K. (1997). Student motivation in middle school: The role of perceived pedagogical caring. *Journal of Educational Psychology, 89*, 411-419.

Wentzel, K. (2002). Are effective teachers like good parents? Teaching styles and student adjustment in early adolescence. *Child Development, 73*, 287-301.

Wenzel, S.A., Smylie, M.A., Sebring, P.B., Allensworth, E., Gutiérrez, T., Hallman, S., Luppescu, S., and Miller, S.R. (2001). *Development of Chicago Annenberg schools: 1996-1999*. Chicago: Consortium on Chicago School Research.

West, M.M., and Baumann, V. (2002). *Student achievement in mathematics: Arkansas sites of the Southern initiative of the algebra project*. An evaluation report submitted on behalf of the Program Evaluation and Research group at Lesley University.

Whiston, S.C., and Sexton, T.L. (1998). A review of school counseling outcome research: Implications for practice. *Journal of Counseling and Development, 76*, 412-426.

White, J., and Wehlage, G. (1995). Community collaborations: If it is such a good idea, why is it so hard to do? *Education Evaluation and Policy Analysis, 17*, 23-38.

Wiatrowski, M., Hansell, S., Massey, C., and Wilson, D. (1982). Curriculum tracking and delinquency. *American Sociological Review, 47*, 151-160.

Wiest, D.J., Wong, E.H., Cervantes, J.M., Craik, L., and Kreil, D.A. (2001). Intrinsic motivation among regular, special, and alternative education high school students. *Adolescence, 36*(141), 111-126.

Wigfield, A., and Harold, R. (1992). Teacher benefits and children's achievement self-perceptions: A developmental perspective. In D. Schunk and J. Meece (Eds.), *Student perceptions in the classroom* (pp. 95-121). Hillsdale, NJ: Lawrence Erlbaum.

Wilson, B.L., and Rossman G.B. (1993). *Mandating academic excellence: High school responses to state curriculum reform.* New York: Teachers College.

Wimberly, G. (2002). *School relationships foster success for African American students: ACT policy report.* Iowa City, IA: ACT.

Wineburg, S. (1991). Historical problem solving: A study of the cognitive processes used in the evaluation of documentary and pictorial evidence. *Journal of Educational Psychology, 83*(1), 73-87.

Wineburg, S.S., and Wilson, S.M. (1991). Subject matter knowledge in the teaching of history. In J.E. Brophy (Ed.), *Advances in research on teaching.* Greenwich, CT: JAI press.

Wirth-Bond, S., Coyne, A., and Adams, M. (1991). A school counseling program that reduces dropout rate. *The School Counselor, 39,* 131-137.

Wong, E.H., Wiest, D.J., and Cusick, L.B. (2002). Perceptions of autonomy support, parent attachment, competence, and self-worth as predictors of motivational orientation and academic achievement: An examination of sixth and ninth-grade regular education students. *Adolescence, 37*(146), 255-266.

Yonezawa, S., Wells, A., and Serna, I. (2002). Choosing Tracks: "Freedom of choice" in detracking schools. *American Educational Research Journal, 39,* 37-67.

Yowell, C. (1999). The role of the future in meeting the challenge of Latino school dropouts. *Educational Foundations, 13,* 5-28.

Zahner, G.E., Pawelkiewicz, W., DeFrancesco, J.J., and Adnopoz, J. (1992). Children's mental health service needs and utilization patterns in an urban community: An epidemiological assessment. *Journal of the American Academy of Child and Adolescent Psychiatry, 31*(5), 951-960.

Zevenbergen, R. (2000). "Cracking the code" of mathematics classrooms: School success as a function of linguistic, social, and cultural background. In J. Boaler (Ed.), *Multiple perspectives on mathematics teaching and learning.* Westport, CT: Ablex.

Biographical Sketches of Committee Members

Deborah Stipek *(Chair)* is the dean of the School of Education at Stanford University. Stipek is a professor of education and her research and scholarship focus on early childhood education, the effects of instruction and classroom climate on student motivation, and issues related to child, family, and educational policy. Stipek earned a doctorate in developmental psychology from Yale University in 1977 and a bachelor's degree in psychology from the University of Washington in 1972. Before coming to Stanford in 2000 she directed UCLA's laboratory elementary school, and the Urban Education Studies Center. Stipek also served on the National Academy of Sciences Board on Children, Youth, and Families. Recent books include: *Constructive and Destructive Behavior: Implications for Family, School, and Society* (with A. Bohart, 2001); (with K. Seal, 2001); *Motivation to Learn: Integrating Theory and Practice* (4th edition, 2002).

Carol Ames is a professor of educational psychology and dean of the College of Education at Michigan State University. She is interested in the development of social and academic motivation in children. Her research focuses on the effects of classroom structure, competition, and teaching practices on children's motivation to learn, and on school and family relationships and specific strategies for increasing parental involvement in children's learning. Dr. Ames' areas of expertise include disadvantaged children and youth; motivation; motivation and learning in family/community/schools; motivation and social development; and parent involvement in family/community/schools.

Thomas J. Berndt is professor and head of the Department of Psychological Sciences at Purdue University. Before coming to Purdue, Berndt was on the faculty of both the University of Oklahoma and Yale University. His primary research interests are in friendships and peer influence in childhood and adolescence, but he has also published research on achievement motivation, self-esteem, social cognition, school adjustment, and other topics. He previously served as the associate editor of the journal *Developmental Psychology* and as a consultant for the National Research Council and the National Institute of Health. He received his Ph.D. in Child Psychology from the University of Minnesota.

Emily Cole served as the principal of Jefferson Davis High School in the Houston Independent School District from 1988 until the summer of 2001. During her tenure, with the help of several collaboratives, a reform movement named PROJECT G.R.A.D. (Graduation Really Achieves Dreams) was initiated. This innovative program included all the schools in a K-12 setting to work together toward the graduation of its students. The success of this reform program is seen in the 48 percent increase in students' graduation rates and a 74 percent increase in awarding of college scholarships. At the national level, she received invitations to address the White House convening on Hispanic Children and Youth and to join a select committee on the U.S. Department Forum on English Language Learner/Native American/Dropout and selected to participate in Aspen Institute on High School Reform. At the state level, she was appointed to two educational committees on school reform initiatives. She received her formal education from Southwest Texas State University and the University of Houston, with added training at Principal's Center at Harvard University, Brown University, and the Ford Foundation's National Center for Urban Partnerships. She is currently teaching in the Urban Education Center at the University of Houston.

James Comer is the Maurice Falk Professor of Child Psychiatry at the Yale University School of Medicine's Child Study Center and has been a Yale medical faculty member since 1968. He has concentrated his career on promoting a focus on child development as a way of improving schools. Dr. Comer founded the Yale Child Study Center School Development Program in 1968, which promotes the collaboration of parents, educators, and community to improve social, emotional, and academic outcomes for children that, in turn, help them achieve greater school success. Dr. Comer has authored a number of books and has been awarded a number of awards and honorary degrees. James Comer is a member of the Institute of Medicine.

James Connell is a former special education teacher and associate professor at the University of Rochester and is currently the president of the Institute for Research and Reform in Education, based in Philadelphia. His work in youth development and education spans 25 years—he has written numerous basic and applied research articles and helped design and support youth development and education projects across the country. Dr. Connell started IRRE with Louisa Pierson at the University of Rochester in 1989. He created First Things First—a research-based framework for district-wide school reform—in 1996. He has authored a White Paper commissioned by the Ewing Marion Kauffman Foundation on the reform framework and a recent report for the Department of Education, *Getting Off the Dime: First Steps Toward Implementing First Things First.* He is co-project director of Scaling Up First Things First—the national project sponsored by the Department of Education that Riverview Gardens, MO, Shaw and Greenville, MS, and Houston, TX, have joined (along with Kansas City, KS). For the past 2 years, he has been working directly with all of the participating schools and districts involved in this project. Jim received his Ph.D. in developmental psychology from the University of Denver.

Michelle Fine is a professor in the Social/Personality Psychology Program at The Graduate Center, City University of New York. Dr. Fine previously taught for 12 years at the University of Pennsylvania. Her research focuses on small urban high schools, and more recently, on access to higher education within prisons. Her recent books include *Construction Sites: Community Spaces for Urban Youth* (with L. Weis, 2000); *The Unknown City* (with L. Weis, 1990); *Becoming Gentlemen* (with L. Guinier and J. Balin, 1997); and *Charting Urban School Reform: Reflections on Public High Schools in the Midst of Change* (1994). She has been awarded the Janet Helms Distinguished Scholar Award (1994) and a Spencer Foundation National Mentoring Award (1998).

Ruth T. Gross is professor emerita of pediatrics at Stanford University. At Stanford, where she was director of general pediatrics, she established a training program in adolescent medicine and directed the general pediatrics academic development training program. She was active in several research activities and was the national study director of the multisite clinical trial, the Infant Health and Development Program. In 1979, she was elected to the Institute of Medicine and is a member of numerous academic societies. She has served as a member of the IOM council as well as a member of the Mental Health and Behavior Board, the Board on Health Promotion and Disease Prevention, and the Board on Children, Youth, and Families. She has an M.D. from Columbia University College of Physicians and Surgeons.

W. Norton Grubb is a professor and the David Gardner Chair in Higher Education at the School of Education, the University of California, Berkeley. He received his doctorate in economics from Harvard University. He has published extensively on a variety of topics in the economics of education, public finance, education policy, community colleges and "second chance" programs, and social policy for children and youth. He is also the faculty coordinator of the Principal Leadership Institute, a program to prepare urban school principals in the Bay Area. He is currently working on a book about the development and consequences of occupational roles for schools and colleges, *The Vocational Roles of American Schooling: Believers, Dissenters, and the Education Gospel.* He is the author most recently of *Honored But Invisible: An Inside Look at Teaching in Community Colleges* (Routledge, 1999); *Learning to Work: The Case for Re-integrating Education and Job Training* (Russell Sage Foundation, 1996); *Working in the Middle: Strengthening the Education and Training of the Middle-Skilled Labor Force* (Jossey-Bass, 1996); and *Education for Occupations in American High Schools* (Teachers College Press, 1995), a two-volume edited work on the integration of academic and occupational education.

Rochelle Gutierrez is assistant professor in the Department of Curriculum and Instruction, College of Education and in Latina/Latino Studies, College of Liberal Arts and Sciences at the University of Illinois at Urbana-Champaign. She currently serves as an invited member on OERI-RAND's National Study Panel for Mathematics. She has been a summer fellow at the Center for Advanced Study in the Behavioral Sciences at Stanford University, a dissertation fellow with the Spencer Foundation, a postdoctoral fellow with the National Academy of Edcuation/Spencer Foundation, and a faculty fellow in the Bureau of Educational Research at the University of Illinois. Her research interests center on issues of equity for marginalized students, especially those living in the inner city. She is specifically concerned with the sociocultural and organizational factors that play out in the teaching of mathematics to Latina/Latino and African American students. She received her bachelor's degree in Human Biology from Stanford University, and her master's and Ph.D. in curriculum and instruction from the University of Chicago.

Carol Lee is associate professor of education in the Learning Sciences program at Northwestern University's School of Education and Social Policy. Dr. Lee's research addresses sociocultural foundations of literacy; literacy expertise within specific ethnic speech communities and their implications for learning and teaching processes; and cultural models for knowledge representations in literacy related-tasks. She received her Ph.D. from the University of Chicago. She has been a recipient of a Spencer Research Mentor Award. Her research has been funded by the Spencer Foundation, the McDonnell Foundation's Cognitive Studies in Educational Practice, the National Science Foundation, and the National Council of Teachers of English. She is a past president of the National Conference on Research on Language and Literacy (NCRLL) and is a fellow of NCRLL. She has also been awarded a fellowship at the Center for Advanced Study in the Behavioral Sciences at Stanford University. Dr. Lee has worked in the field of education since 1966, as a classroom teacher, a founder of two independent schools, and a school principal in addition to her university based research. She is the author of *Signifying as a Scaffold for Literary Interpretation: The Pedagogical Implications of an African American Discourse Genre* (National Council of Teachers of English) and co-editor of *Vygotskian Perspectives on Literacy Research* (Cambridge University Press).

Edward L. McDill is professor emeritus of sociology at the Johns Hopkins University and principal research scientist at the Center for Social Organization of Schools (CSOS). He is founding director (1966-1969) and co-director (1976-1993) of CSOS. He also served as chair for the Department of Sociology, Johns Hopkins University, from 1970 through 1985. For the past 35 years, Dr. McDill's primary research interests have been in the sociology of education, with a focus on how the formal and informal organizational properties of schools influence the cognitive and affective development of students. In the past 15 years he has concentrated much of his research on the effects of the current American educational reform movement on the academic and personal development of disadvantaged students. His primary publication in this area is (with G. Natriello and A.M. Pallas) *Schooling Disadvantaged Students: Racing Against Catastrophe*, Teachers College Press, 1990.

Russell Rumberger is professor of education at the University of California, Santa Barbara, and was appointed director of the University of California's Linguistic Minority Research Institute methods. Rumberger's interest in decreasing high school drop-out rates has led him to examine such issues as student mobility and school effectiveness. He has published widely on education and work; the education of disadvantaged students, particularly school drop-outs; and education policy. His research on education policy has focused on school performance, school segregation, and most recently, student mobility.

Carmen Varela Russo is chief executive officer of the Baltimore City Public School System. Her career in urban education spans 3 decades during which she has held positions as teacher, principal, director, and superintendent in New York and Florida. She most recently served as associate superintendent in Broward County Public Schools in Fort Lauderdale, Florida, where she was in charge of technology, strategic planning, and school accountability.

Lisbeth B. Schorr is lecturer in social medicine at Harvard University, and director of the Project on Effective Interventions at Harvard University. She heads the Project's Pathways Mapping Initiative and co-chairs the Aspen Institute's Roundtable on Comprehensive Community Initiatives for Children and Families. Ms. Schorr has woven many strands of experience with social policy, community building, education, and human service programs together to become a national authority on "what works" to improve the future of disadvantaged children and their families and neighborhoods. She is a member of the Brookings Children's Roundtable and the National Selection Committee of the Ford Foundation/Kennedy School Awards for Innovations in American Government. Lisbeth Schorr is the author of *Within Our Reach: Breaking the Cycle of Disadvantage* (1988), and *Common Purpose: Strengthening Families and Neighborhoods to Rebuild America* (1997). She is a member of the Institute of Medicine.

Index

Q

R

S

V

W

Y

Z